Praise for *Our Problem, ...*

"*Our Problem, Our Path* lays the groundwork for engaging in compelling and critically important conversations, and for reimagining what is possible when discussing how we think and feel about race. This book will challenge and energize anyone who reads it and takes the journey to widen their path; it is visionary, practical, courageous, and invitational."

Peggy Brookins, president and CEO
National Board for Professional Teaching Standards

"With compassion and humility, Michael and Bartoli offer a practical handbook for White antiracist awareness and practice. Filled with relatable examples and nuanced explanations, this is a step-by-step guide for responding to the obstacles—both internal and external—of unlearning our White socialization and challenging systemic racism. *Our Problem, Our Path* is a must-read for starting and maintaining the life-long process of White antiracist practice."

Robin DiAngelo, author
White Fragility and *Nice Racism*

"It is rare to find a book that places White people at the center of understanding their Whiteness. *Our Problem, Our Path* is exactly what it says: a path for White social justice activists to take if they honestly want to understand the impact of their Whiteness on themselves, on society, and on systems. This will not be an easy read, but it is a must-read. Take the path and start creating #GoodTrouble."

Eddie Moore Jr., founder
The White Privilege Conference

"This is the book. This is it. A lot of antiracism work needs to happen within, before it can be effective. That within-work is not only your 'inner' work but also the within-race work that White people need to have with their family, friends, colleagues, and neighbors. As a Black woman and racial-equity scholar, I make this suggestion often, but it is usually met with a combination of resistance and terror. For most White people, racial conversations are unfamiliar terrain and risk exposing loved ones and respected colleagues as racially inept or downright racist. *Our Problem, Our Path* takes on the essential tasks of White people understanding their own racial stress response *and* engaging other White people in frank, kind, and practical terms. It is both a starting point and an endgame.

"You can have honest race conversations without being mean or snarky. Discomfort and guilt are not the endgame of *Our Problem, Our Path*. To the contrary, racialized stress is part of the path to racial competency. The true goals of *Our Problem, Our Path* are to grow racial competency, build an antiracist society, eliminate racial hierarchies, and remedy the harms that occur as a result. This book provides clear examples and solution-focused strategies to move beyond antiracist performance to effective action. *Our Problem, Our Path* is not just another book club selection for nice White people. This book is made for learning, growth, and doing the right thing (consistently). *Our Problem, Our Path* has the 'get right and gather your people' work that Black, Indigenous, and other People of Color have been yearning to see from our allies.

"*Our Problem, Our Path* meets White people where they are on their racial journey, without making Black, Indigenous and other People of Color's humanity fodder for debate. As such, *Our Problem, Our Path* recognizes how White people have been socialized to understand race and racism while demonstrating how they can do better in socializing their own children and make a difference in their own communities."

Keisha Bentley-Edwards
Associate professor of general internal medicine and associate director of research/director of the Health Equity Working Group
Samuel DuBois Cook Center on Social Equity at Duke University

"If you're a White person looking for a guide to transition you away from racial complacency and towards an antiracist practice, this is it. *Our Problem, Our Path* starts with something rarely articulated: What does the path look like and where might it lead us? This story-rich jewel promises to gather up White people and equip us with strategies that build the awareness, knowledge, and skill we need to find and support one another on the path to liberation for all."

Debby Irving, author
Waking Up White and *Finding Myself in the Story of Race*

"This book serves as a master class and recipe for what is practically needed to talk about and address racism in the world along with the mental and emotional steps needed to accomplish genuine change one person, one family, one neighborhood, and one community at a time. As a member of the global majority, as an African American, and as a cisgender man with a clinical psychology doctorate degree, I found that reading this book provided me with much-needed and timely hope that someone understands us and that we have at least two allies on the inside. We have at least two superheroes mightily using their superpowers of empathy to educate, challenge, and awaken those willing to listen. Readers are provided well-outlined steps to break down hate and fight for a just and equitable world for us and for all our children."

Tim Barksdale, senior executive director of
Clinical Services, Merakey IDD Services

"Our Problem, Our Path: Collective Antiracism for White People is a roadmap to intercept Whiteness and define key practices necessary to embody antiracist leadership. As a Black woman leading efforts toward systematizing equity, I sought out the expertise of 'Ms. Ali.' She humbly supports and unpacks various complexities and intersections one encounters when walking the path toward transformation. Although her work is framed for a White audience, through her discourse and facilitation I have witnessed People of Color and Indigenous folk grapple with the manifestations of their own internalized oppression. Dr. Michael's work exemplifies that the study of self is one of the greatest tools in addressing racism."

Myla Pope, director
Office of Equity, Saint Paul Public Schools, Saint Paul, Minnesota

"The hard work to ensure a more racially just American society cannot live solely in the work of Black, Brown, and Indigenous people alone. Whether in neighborhoods, classrooms, school systems, or car rides home, White America is either undermining racial justice or undermining racism. To be able to understand where one is on the continuum of cultural proficiency takes honesty, humility, and courage. Racial justice can never be fully realized without self-reflection, intellectual rigor, and truth. But, unfortunately, too often, too many White people are more than comfortable ignoring how race, class, power, and privilege intersect to create unbalanced systems, experiences, and outcomes along racial lines.

"Our Problem, Our Path, by Dr. Ali Michael and Dr. Eleonora Bartoli, raises a clarion call and charts a path for White people to not only reflect on their mindsets but also to probe their own experiences to better understand their own potential for harboring and nurturing racial biases and, just as importantly, how they arrived, consciously or unconsciously, at the conclusions they have about race and People and Communities of Color. Was racism taught at school, learned from social media, derived from an experience, or reinforced at mealtime with family and friends?

"Many claim to be antiracist but too often gleefully swim in the most shallow of waters ignoring the depth of work it takes to actually be antiracist. Teachers must understand that one can slide from cultural proficiency and antiracism to being culturally destructive and racist from child to child or minute by minute. Deconstructing one's mindsets and assumptions based on race takes sincerity and vigilance. It demands an understanding of history and how one's personal journey is influenced by it. This book challenges us to move well beyond woke language to authentic action.

"As Malcolm X said, I tell sincere white people, 'Work in conjunction with us. . . . Let sincere white individuals find all other white people they can who feel as they do . . . to work to convert other white people who are thinking and acting so racist. . . . In our mutual sincerity we might be able to show a road to the salvation of America's very soul.'

"*Our Problem, Our Path: Collective Antiracism for White People* is a powerful road map that helps to light a path of action to create a society that is more consistently educationally and racially just. We all deserve nothing less."

Sharif El-Mekki, CEO
Center for Black Educator Development

"Michael and Bartoli have written the book I've been waiting for, one for all the White people who know racism is wrong, who want to do the right thing, and who want their children to live in a better world. Writing with clarity and from deep experience, the authors explain what antiracism means and how to do it without adopting the hectoring tone that can turn people away from this essential work. While James Baldwin correctly identified racism as a White people's problem, Michael and Bartoli manage to frame it as a positive life mission that will benefit us all in the end.

"Above all, *Our Problem, Our Path* offers the wise guidance, with generous helpings of empathy and compassion, that White people need if we are to talk with one another about (and eventually eradicate) the invisible caste system in which we all live."

Maureen Costello, executive director
Center for Antiracist Education, STAND for Children

Our Problem, Our Path

To all the children's children's children's children's children's children's children

Our Problem, Our Path

Collective Antiracism for
White People

Ali Michael
Eleonora Bartoli

FOR INFORMATION:

Corwin

A SAGE Company

2455 Teller Road

Thousand Oaks, California 91320

(800) 233-9936

www.corwin.com

SAGE Publications Ltd.

1 Oliver's Yard

55 City Road

London, EC1Y 1SP

United Kingdom

SAGE Publications India Pvt. Ltd.

Unit No 323-333, Third Floor, F-Block

International Trade Tower Nehru Place

New Delhi – 110 019

India

SAGE Publications Asia-Pacific Pte. Ltd.

18 Cross Street #10-10/11/12

China Square Central

Singapore 048423

President: Mike Soules

Vice President and Editorial Director: Monica Eckman

Program Director and Publisher: Dan Alpert

Senior Content Development Editor: Lucas Schleicher

Content Development Editor: Mia Rodriguez

Editorial Assistant: Natalie Delpino

Project Editor: Amy Schroller

Copy Editor: Laureen Gleason

Typesetter: Hurix Digital

Proofreader: Talia Greenberg

Cover Designer: Candice Harman

Marketing Manager: Melissa Duclos

Library of Congress Cataloging-in-Publication Data

Names: Michael, Ali, author. | Bartoli, Eleonora, author.

Title: Our problem, our path : collective antiracism for white people / Ali Michael, Eleonora Bartoli.

Description: Thousand Oaks, California : Corwin, [2023] | Includes bibliographical references and index.

Identifiers: LCCN 2022011258 | ISBN 9781071851326 (paperback) | ISBN 9781071851333 (epub) | ISBN 9781071851340 (epub) | ISBN 9781071851357(ebook)

Subjects: LCSH: Anti-racism. | Racism. | Whites—Race identity. | Whites—Attitudes.

Classification: LCC 1563 .M53 2023 | DDC 305.8/00973—dc23/eng/20220309

LC record available at https://lccn.loc.gov/2022011258

This book is printed on acid-free paper.

MIX
Paper from responsible sources
FSC® C103567

23 24 25 26 27 10 9 8 7 6 5 4 3 2 1

Contents

Part 3: Who Will We Be as the Racial Hierarchy Falls?

Publisher's Acknowledgments

Corwin gratefully acknowledges the contributions of the following reviewers:

Nancy Foote
Teacher
Sossaman Middle School/Higley USD
Gilbert, Arizona

Jennifer French
Elementary School Principal
Clark County School District
Las Vegas, Nevada

Shawn White
Teacher
Weston McEwen High School
Milton Freewater, Oregon

About the Authors

Ali Michael, Ph.D., is the co-director and co-founder of the Race Institute for K–12 Educators; she works with schools and organizations across the United States to help make research on race, Whiteness, and education more accessible and relevant to educators. Ali is the author of *Raising Race Questions: Whiteness and Inquiry in Education*, winner of the 2017 Society of Professors of Education Outstanding Book Award. As a member of a multiracial editorial team, she has co-edited *The Guide for White Women Who Teach Black Boys, Teaching Beautiful Brilliant Black Girls,* and *Everyday White People Confront Racial and Social Injustice: 15 Stories.* With her colleague Toni Graves Williamson, Ali adapted Robin DiAngelo's *White Fragility* for a young adult audience. Ali sits on the editorial board of the journal *Whiteness and Education.* Her article "What White Children Need to Know About Race," co-authored with Dr. Eleonora Bartoli in *Independent Schools Magazine*, won the Association and Media Publishing Gold Award for Best Feature Article in 2014. When she is not writing, speaking, or training, Ali is striving to be an antiracist co-parent to two amazing kids. Her writing and speeches are available at **alimichael.org**.

Photo by Anthony
Rugnetta, Philadelphia

Eleonora Bartoli, Ph.D., is a consultant and licensed psychologist specializing in trauma, resilience-building, and multicultural/social justice counseling. In all her work, she integrates an understanding of neuroscience, focusing on how it informs symptom development as well as healing and resilience-building strategies. Eleonora earned her Ph.D. in Psychology: Human Development/Mental Health Research from the University of Chicago. After receiving her clinical license, she opened a small independent practice that she has held since. After 15 years in academia (12 of those as the director of the Master's in Counseling program at Arcadia University), she became a full-time consultant. Her mission is to share the tools of counseling and psychology in support of social justice work.

Throughout her career, Eleonora has held leadership positions in professional organizations at the state and national levels. She has also presented at numerous conferences and is the author of a number of publications focused on multicultural counseling competence, White racial socialization, and the integration of social justice principles in evidence-based counseling practices (see her website, **dreleonorabartoli.com**, for details). Eleonora has received academic awards, including the Lindback Foundation Award for Distinguished Teaching and the Provost Award for Outstanding Advising and Mentoring. The Gillem-Bartoli Alumni Award for Contributions to Social Justice was established to honor the contributions of Eleonora and her colleague, Dr. Angela Gillem, in their roles as activist-scholars within academia.

PART 1
BEGINNINGS

Prologue

· ·

By Ali Michael

"Do you want to start a White affinity group?"

T hese were the first words Eleonora ever said directly to me. We were sitting in an overheated classroom on a cold February day at Teachers College in New York, having just finished a workshop on how White people can talk with other White people about race and racism in an intentionally White, explicitly antiracist group.[1] I didn't know Eleonora, but I had admired her boldness and conviction in how she talked about race throughout the workshop—I had never before seen a White person be so forthright and vulnerable in public. Apparently, she had noticed me, too. Inspired, I said, "Yes."

At the time, Eleonora was a psychologist-in-training. I was studying for my M.A. in anthropology and education. I lived in a two-bedroom apartment in New York's Washington Heights with my partner and my sister, both of whom were engaged in their own antiracism learning. We formed a group—Eleonora, my partner, my sister, my sister's partner, and me. Every other month, Eleonora would travel from Philadelphia to New York and sleep on our couch, and the five of us would read books about racism and discuss them.

Whenever Eleonora visited, a 24-hour marathon of race conversation would commence. We'd begin preparing food and talk in the kitchen—five people in a two-person kitchen. We'd move to the living room, carrying dishes while we talked, for more intentional book conversation and self-facilitated discussion. After dinner, we'd take a walk while we continued processing, only to return for more conversations over hot tea and wine late into the night. When we read books with activities, we would do the activities together. When we revisited moments in which we had perpetuated racism or witnessed racism, we'd use the space to brainstorm and role-play how we could have responded more proactively and effectively. We came to love one another, and we loved the learning space we created. We could speak from the heart and head. We could get vulnerable. We would correct one another—not in a competitive way but in the spirit of mutual accountability, knowing we all had the same goal of taking the next step on our antiracist paths. *Not* correcting one another would have been a violation of the commitment we made to one another as allies.

This space gave Eleonora and me—as well as the other group members—the opportunity to begin learning what it looks like for White people to invite one another to an antiracist path and to help one another keep moving. Our ability to learn arose from the powerful combination of company, camaraderie, accountability, challenge, friendship, and love. It gave us the opportunity to ask all the questions we needed to ask—questions we were unable to ask elsewhere because we felt that we already should have known the answers. It helped us become more systematic in our own learning and gave us a structure in which we were accountable for the learning we set for ourselves.

That space served as the headwaters of a relationship that has now been flowing through our lives for two decades. Since then, we have grown as individuals, as allies and accountability partners to each other, and as colleagues. We have continued to talk—on long walks, over Zoom, in meetings, at birthday parties, and in somewhat larger kitchens. We have also gained insight from our different professional backgrounds and have come to see how a fusion of our distinct subject areas has propelled us forward as White people striving to fully participate in building a more racially just world.

This book is our attempt to share our learning with others, to convey not just the knowledge but also the love that has been so fundamental to fueling our commitment to engage in a consistent antiracist practice. This practice is not restricted to our professional lives. We certainly engage in it as we do our work and teach our students, but we also apply it as we raise our children, make friends, decide where to live, connect with neighbors, choose schools for our children, ride public transit, choose which routes to drive through Philadelphia (a city we both now call home), stay politically active, walk, live, and breathe.

In these pages, we hope to infuse the spirit of our original group and our continued engagement in learning with each other, so that you have what you need to form accountable, challenging, loving, supportive, honest, antiracist relationships with the White people in your life. To have just, equitable, and loving relationships with People of Color and Native people, White people have work to do. And we need one another to do it well.

Note

1. This idea was presented in a workshop at the Winter Roundtable at Teachers College, Columbia University, by Elizabeth Denevi, one of the first scholars we encountered who was promoting the use of White "affinity" spaces, or White antiracist learning groups for the purpose of helping White people build racial competency.

About This Book

....

By Ali Michael and Eleonora Bartoli

Whom This Book Is For

This book is for White people who identify as antiracist but who don't
know how to engage—or who struggle to engage—other White people
(their children, partners, neighbors, friends, students, colleagues, other
White people in their voting district) in a way that builds momentum
for positive social change. While it's important to look outward when
engaged in social change, it is also essential to look inward. To this end,
our book encourages readers to recognize that each of us is our own
most effective tool in the struggle for racial justice—that we need to
learn to care for, sharpen, and calibrate ourselves to be instruments
for change.

This book is written by White people and addresses White people
directly. When we refer to White people and use the term *we*, this is to
indicate that we count ourselves as White—and that anything we say
about White people applies to us as well. This does not mean that People of Color and Native people cannot or should not read this book.
Janet Helms's seminal book on White identity is subtitled *A Guide to
Being a White Person or Understanding the White Persons in Your
Life*. Books *about* White people can be helpful to People of Color and
Native people who seek to understand the work that White people need
to engage in to challenge the racial hierarchy and their place in it. But
let's say you are one of a few People of Color on your school faculty. The
135 White teachers on your faculty are reading this book as part of a
professional development program or book group. Maybe you're glad
they are reading it, but at the moment you do not want to spend more
time understanding White people—not because you don't think it's
important but because it's just not what you need right now. Perhaps
your goal is to understand how to navigate racial stress, practice self-
care, learn about the experiences of other groups of People of Color,
or challenge racism in your sphere of influence. If that is the case, we
encourage your school to provide options that are more focused on you
and your own learning needs.[1]

Why is it important that White people engage deeply in antiracist work
now? In this historical moment, the United States is divided by politics
and racism. A good portion of the country, including a large number of

White people (as evidenced by the protests following the police killing of George Floyd in 2020), recognizes the possibility and the need for building a healthy multiracial society. But another sizeable, predominantly White chunk of the population believes that we can still have—indeed, should have—a nation in which White people continue to hold the majority of power and access to resources. While none of us has direct control over the myriad systemic and historical factors that have created this divide, we do have control over our own actions, as well as how we talk with other White people about racism.

They say that in social movements, 20 percent of the people are already willing to get on board, 20 percent will never be on board, and 60 percent could be on board if given the right combination of knowledge and support. This book is not about reaching the most overtly racist White people. It's about sustaining and buttressing the 20 percent who are already engaged or are willing to engage. And it's about building momentum among the 60 percent who could be actively antiracist if given the opportunity and support. If you count yourself among the 20 percent who are committed to antiracism no matter what, this book is designed to help you think about yourself and the ways in which you share and model antiracism so that you can be highly effective in your conversations and can bring more people along with you. It will help you recognize how you talk to yourself when you are stuck, find the support you need, and get unstuck so that you can keep moving forward. It will also help you create, run, and participate in White antiracist discussion groups. If you count yourself among the middle 60 percent, this book will clarify why antiracism is good for you. It will help you get on an antiracist path and learn how to talk with other White people about it—and in so doing help shift society toward a healthy multiracial whole.

What This Book Aims to Do

Our goal is to catalyze millions of White people to act for racial justice in their own lives. But this book is not a guide to designing a million-person march, or a "how-to" on mass action. The mass movement we envision is one in which millions of White people seek to engage in an ongoing, daily, lifelong, antiracist practice exactly where they are. First and foremost, this means locating and uprooting the racism that lives inside us. It involves millions of White people engaged in the antiracist action of self-reflection focused on undoing the internalized dominance that comes from living in the top tiers of a centuries-old racial caste system (Wilkerson, 2020). It involves millions of White people engaging in deep, empathetic relationships with People of Color and Native people that help us connect with the feelings, experiences, and realities of those who are positioned differently from us in the racial hierarchy. It is this empathetic connection that can bridge our often separate worlds. It involves White people seeing clearly, advocating for, and then passing antiracist policies in their townships, schools, businesses, streets, and communities. It involves White people unabashedly intervening with the racism of other White people in a way that *calls them in* to an antiracist path. It involves picking ourselves up and dusting ourselves off when we have made a mistake or acted out of bias and can't stop shaming ourselves. It involves White people supporting one another to keep traveling along this path, day in and day out, for the rest of our lives and for generations to come.

Why This Book Matters

The system of racism in the United States today was created over the course of 500 years through billions of micro-moments, macro-policies, interpersonal interactions, historical myths, bogus science, stereotypical ideas, second glances, bad jokes, legalized violence, the banging of gavels, automatic thoughts, and unconsidered words and deeds—all of it uninformed and deeply intentional. As Isabel Wilkerson (2020) notes in her seminal work *Caste: The Origins of Our Discontents*, slavery was legal in the United States longer than it has been illegal. Those timelines will not be balanced chronologically until the year 2111.

Trauma expert Resmaa Menakem (2021) says that completely ridding our society of racism will take the work of eight generations: "If enough white bodies commit to this foundational practice—and stay committed, year after year and generation after generation—perhaps in nine generations (or eight, or ten) our descendants will be born into an embodied antiracist culture" (para. 35). The idea that it will take eight generations to root racism out of our bodies and institutions does not mean that it's inevitable that we will succeed. It does not mean that we can simply let history take its course. It means that if we work *collectively* as hard and as consciously and as persistently as we can during our lifetimes to root out racism, and if we teach our children to do the same, perhaps our children's children's children's children's children's children's children will live in a more loving, respectful, inclusive world. And in the meantime, the work we do today can shift our communities and society as a whole in the right direction—toward a "more perfect union"—and make a significant difference in the lives of People of Color, Native people, and White people.

Does this sound like a lot? It is. This is why White people need one another. We need to travel an antiracist path together, to help one another recover and keep going when we tire or fall, to remind one another of the critical importance of racial justice to our humanity and our collective future, and to help one another withstand and heal the shame of looking at our history and seeing how its assumptions and biases still live in us.

We are aware of the pitfalls of this work—especially how, too often, White people can push less racially conscious White people off an antiracist path by trying to validate their own standing as antiracist people. Sometimes, in what is sarcastically called the "Woke Olympics," White people compete with one another to prove to themselves and others that they are the *most antiracist*, that they are one of "the good ones." We address this issue in the book as well. The goal should never be to alienate other people from a liberation movement that needs more of us. And we hope it's obvious that it's not enough to have a handful of super-sharp, antiracist White people doing their thing. We literally need millions of White people to journey an antiracist path in all the different corners of our world. This book will help White people who are trying to travel an antiracist path work on themselves—their skills, knowledge, and mindset—as well as with other White people.

How Can Two White Women Write a Book About Racism?

This is a great question—one we would be asking if we picked up this book. We would know very little about racism without the People of Color and Native people who taught us through friendships, work relationships, books, movies, podcasts, workshops, and role-modeling. For White people, racism—unless overt and violent—is often very hard to see. Our Colleagues of Color and Native colleagues have helped us see how, for all intents and purposes, we live in different worlds, even when we share the very same space or role. Being a Black woman professor is a wholly different experience from being a White woman professor, whether one teaches about race or math. Being a Vietnamese American teacher and parent is a wholly different experience from being a White teacher and parent, even if both individuals live in the same neighborhood or work in the same school. People respond to and interact with us differently based on our racial backgrounds in ways that create radically different experiences of the same environment. And while our experiences as White people are widely portrayed in the mainstream, the experiences of People of Color and Native people are often invisible to—and therefore easily ignored by—that same mainstream, which includes us.

In our personal and professional relationships, we often work with People of Color and Native people who spend their days—like us—trying to help people understand and unlearn patterns and assumptions shaped by racism. We often collaborate strategically, knowing that White people are going to hear things differently when/if it comes from a White person. For example, one of us (Ali) has a Black colleague who asks Ali to step in when a White person says something racist, so that she can step back and take a breath. However, when People of Color and Native people question how they can respond to racism, Ali's colleague usually steps forward, knowing that her experiential knowledge of their question will help address the concern in ways Ali cannot.

In every collaboration, it's clear that there are things that White people cannot say about race or racism because we haven't experienced racism viscerally and from an early age in the way that People of Color and Native people have. But it's also clear that there are things we need to say and do as White people because we are on the same antiracist journey as other White people. We can teach through modeling in a way our Peers of Color and Native peers cannot. We do know viscerally the stages of questioning, doubt, confusion, and fear that so many of our White peers and colleagues experience.

As you read this book, know that we are deeply rooted in relationships with People of Color and Native people who have asked and encouraged us to share our knowledge and strategies with other White people. You will find many of their names in the acknowledgments: People of Color and Native people who have taught us, mentored us, shaped our learning, and read drafts of this book. This doesn't mean that there won't be People of Color and Native people who disagree with what is written here; one of the truths about living in a complex society is that every question has myriad responses. While we cannot be accountable to all People of Color and Native people in our work, all our work on racism must be deeply accountable to close Colleagues of Color and Native colleagues who work toward similar ends.

While many White people know that they cannot travel an antiracist path without learning from or being in relationship with People of Color and Native people, too often we think we can do so *without* other White people. There is a lot of learning, unlearning, and feeling that White people need to do *in order to* build deep, authentic relationships with People of Color and Native people. It's critical that White people support one another in doing that. When you hear someone say, "White people need to *do their own work* before they can help end racism," that is the work we seek to help readers do here, in community with one another.

A Short Glossary of Essential Terms

Many terms used in discussions of race are imperfect and evolving. Thirty years from now, we might shudder that we ever used certain terms in print. This is because racial categories are social constructions that change with time. But if we wait until we have the perfect terminology, we won't have the conversation. We hope that the terms used in this book will enable us to have an honest and straightforward discussion and will make it possible to talk about this elusive topic with minimal confusion. That said, we encourage you to use the terms that are accepted and affirming within your own context. And we invite feedback on the choices that we have made here, some of which we will now explain further.

Antiracism

Antiracism is a term that has gained prominence over the past few years, particularly with the popularity of Ibram X. Kendi's (2020c) book *How to Be an Antiracist*. When we use the term, we think of anti-racism as a *stance*, a way of engaging with the world with full aware-ness that we live in a society heavily shaped by race and racism. While we assume that most White people do not wake up intending to be rac-ist or to be unaware of the racial realities of People of Color and Native people, we also assume that most White people (including us) have internalized racist ideologies. We also assume that most of us witness racism as we go about our days. Antiracism is a stance and a practice that prepares a person to recognize and intervene with racism within themselves, outside of themselves, in their sphere of influence, and in the systems embedded in their lives. We don't think of antiracism as a stance against a person who says something racist; rather, we see it as a stance that prepares us to recognize the ways in which our soci-ety primes us and others for racist ideas, explanations, actions, and outcomes. The practice allows us to intervene when we ourselves or someone else says or does something racist in a way that helps reveal the systemic roots of the comment or action, and that challenges those roots—not just the singular comment or action.

Allies

We use the term *ally* with an awareness that there are many great, newer, harder-hitting terms such as *co-conspirator* and *accomplice* that challenge and refine the role of ally. We do this partly because we don't want to get caught up in the ever-accelerating demand to use the most trendy language as proof of our relevance. It's possible that by the time this book is published, there will be an even better term for ally-ship or co-conspiratorship than we have now. We also want to model writing and talking and acting against racism with the knowledge that our actions matter more than the title of our aspirations. Whether we strive to be allies, co-conspirators, or accomplices, what matters most is how we enact those identities, not what we call them. We certainly don't want to willfully use offensive or outdated language. But there will always be new terminology we don't know or aren't used to. We write with the awareness that our contributions will be imperfect and with the belief that those imperfections should not render anyone's contribution to antiracism irrelevant or even less needed. We want to show up imperfectly with all we have to offer—and we invite you to do the same. In fact, that's the only way any of us can show up on this path.

That said, we think of allies (and all variations on the term) not as "helpers" to People of Color and Native people but as antiracist actors, accomplices, and teammates in the collective work to dismantle racism for the benefit of all. And we think of allyship not as a performative badge of honor that makes us "the good ones" but rather as a genuine commitment to taking an antiracist stance in all areas of our lives.

Critical to this understanding is White people's realization that we are working not only in support of People of Color and Native people but also in support of other White people on the antiracist path. The practice of antiracism can be exhausting to anyone who undertakes it. Even though White people are often buffered from some of the most challenging aspects of the journey, it is not easy. We often experience loneliness, burnout, resentment, and abandonment on our antiracist paths. And yet the most important part of the journey is that we keep going. Throughout this book, we encourage White people who are trying to be antiracist to be allies to other White people, so that we all stay involved and continue to invite more White people onto a sustainable path toward racial justice.

Racism, Systematic Racism, and White Supremacy

A recent letter to the editor in *Teaching Tolerance* magazine (now *Learning for Justice*) said that after 50 years of fighting against active white supremacists in white sheets, the author resented the discussions of white supremacy as if it's everywhere. This reaction doesn't surprise us. It's the same response some people have when we talk about systemic racism, particularly if people are used to thinking about racism as an overt and intentional act of hatred. It can seem like hyperbole to say that we live in a white supremacist society or that white supremacy shapes our reality.

In our language throughout this book, we want to support readers in thinking about all the big and small ways in which U.S. society has historically put White people first in terms of power, governing, standards of beauty, narratives, books, products, education, work, opportunities, medical care, criminal justice, and so on. People who were not classified as White were used as labor and property to generate wealth for those who were White. Native people—because they were not White and not Christian, and because they resided on the land colonists wanted—were seen as less human and undeserving of civil or human rights. They were systematically killed, displaced, and denied access to the land they had tended for millennia. Is there a comfortable shorthand for referring to this history and its continued presence and impact on our social, political, and economic structures?

In this text, we alternate between using terms such as *racism*, *systemic racism*, and *white supremacy* because we want to be clear that we're talking about an ideology, a way of organizing society that leads with an assumption about the primacy of Whiteness. Another way to refer to this system is as a *racial caste system* that consistently puts White people at the top. Historian Isabel Wilkerson (2020) describes the term this way:

> There developed a caste system, based upon what people looked like, an internalized ranking, unspoken, unnamed, unacknowledged by everyday citizens even as they go about their lives adhering to it and acting upon it subconsciously to this day. . . . And though it may move in and out of consciousness, though it may flare and reassert itself in times of upheaval and recede in times of relative calm, it is an ever-present through line in the country's operation. (p. 23)

If the term *white supremacy* makes you uncomfortable, replace it in your mind with *systemic racism* or *racial caste system* and keep reading. Don't let terminology be the thing that blocks your learning.

The term *white supremacy* differs from the term *White Nationalism* in substantial ways, even though the two are sometimes used interchangeably. We understand White Nationalism as a movement aimed at creating a White-only nation in which People of Color, Native people, and Jews would be removed. White Nationalists believe that Whiteness is biological and needs to be protected from the efforts of Jews to use People of Color and Native people to achieve global domination and annihilate the White race. While White Nationalism and white supremacist thinking are mutually reinforcing, White Nationalism is fundamentally based on a wildly unrealistic notion of power and of who actually controls our society. In this book, we are talking about the more pervasive and insidious impact of white supremacy, a race-based caste system that places White people at the top, with Black and Native people at the bottom, and with other groups of People of Color (including Asian Americans, Latinx people, and multiracial people) somewhere in between. The progression from superior to inferior runs through race in white supremacy in a way that is different from White Nationalism. This can be particularly confusing to European-descended Jews who are targeted by White Nationalism but who in many ways are treated as White within white supremacy. We address this conundrum further in Chapter 6, where we review the racial history of the United States. If you struggle with this very question, you might choose to make Chapter 6 your first chapter.

People of Color and Native People

We use the terms *People of Color* and *Native people*. We consciously do not use the term *BIPOC* (*Black, Indigenous, People of Color*). BIPOC has become common parlance in some organizations and has been disregarded as confusing by others.[2] While we welcome the evolution of new and potentially more affirming terms, we generally oppose abbreviating terms for groups of people, because we find it diminishing. We do not use the term *POC*, for example; instead, we always write out *People of Color*. But there is no good way to do this with exact consistency. We want to acknowledge that Black people are differently racialized and impacted by anti-Black racism and the racial caste system than any other group in the United States. We want to acknowledge that People of Color (Black people, Asian American people, Latinx people, and multiracial people) are differently racialized from Native people or Indigenous people in the United States, whose indigeneity is both an ethnic and a political designation. While Native people do experience racism, they also experience the impact of Settler Colonialism.

Because we are talking primarily about race and racism in this book, we generally use the term *People of Color*. And because we are often referring to the impact of white supremacist ideology and history, which affects Native people, too, we often refer to *People of Color and Native people*.[3] We include Native people in our framing as a way of recognizing how they are impacted by white supremacy, without assuming that their experience of oppression is only about racism. In fact, we do further harm to members of Native nations when we assume that their identity as Native people is a racial designation rather than recognize them as members of sovereign political entities. At the same time, the individual-level impact of white supremacy on Native people in schools or workplaces operates a lot like racism. We would be remiss if the work we do as White people in unlearning racism and white supremacy did not include thoughtful reference to Native people in addition to People of Color. As you likely can already tell, this framing is awkward at times. But it hopefully reminds us and the reader that Native people are not purely figures of the past and that they should be visible in all examinations of white supremacy. Even the practice of adding *and Native people* to our framing of People of Color has expanded our own thinking about how white supremacy impacts different groups, mitigating for us some of the invisibility of Native people that is so prevalent in U.S. society.

To Capitalize or Not to Capitalize?

We capitalize the terms *Asian American, Black, Indigenous, Latinx, Native, People of Color*, and *White*. We do so because these terms are racial and sociopolitical categories that have been socially constructed and should not be confused with literal colors, such as white, black, or brown. However, we choose not to capitalize the term *white* in *white supremacy*, because it is not a proper noun and because we want to avoid validating the very grandiosity that fuels its oppressive ideology.

Book Structure

The book is divided into three parts:

Part 1—Beginnings—comprises the prologue, this About the Book section, and two introductory sections—one from each of us—in which we share our stories of coming to understand Whiteness in our own lives and work. Our purpose in telling these stories is twofold: we want to share how we have come to learn what we know, but we also want to be transparent about how unflattering and how powerful our separate journeys have been. We have found it very useful to hear from other White people how they have come to choose this path, and we hope that hearing about our journeys will support you on your own.

Part 2—Seeing Ourselves Clearly in the Here and Now—includes the first six chapters. Collectively, it is designed to provide a clearer sense of what it means to be White in this historical moment, how one comes to be White, how knowledge about racism and Whiteness can affect us, how White socialization impacts our effectiveness in working against racism, and what kind of socialization could help White people (and White children in particular) develop racial competence early on. It includes six chapters, all of which end with a section from Eleonora that will help you understand how to mobilize and activate your body to overcome some of the physiological resistance that gets us stuck when we try to engage in antiracist learning and action.

Chapter 1: Racism Is a White Person's Problem

This opening chapter asks the book's *central* question: "What does antiracism have to do with White people?" In various ways, over the course of his writing career, James Baldwin (among others) made it clear that racism is a White person's problem. If that's the case, what can White people do about it? Here Ali shares her experience of how antiracism is in the interest of White people.

Internal Work: Antiracism in a Human Body

Eleonora helps us begin to recognize what goes on for White people internally when we challenge a system that was set up to keep us safe. She introduces tools for engaging our bodies' consent—for getting our bodies to be in sync with our minds and hearts—which is key to speaking and acting for racial justice.

Chapter 2: Myths of White Supremacy

Ali explores the myths of white supremacy that keep racism in place. Recognizing these myths helps us assess their direct impact on our lives and how they keep us separate, both from People of Color and Native people and from other White people. This information intrinsically offers avenues for beginning to widen the antiracist path so that more White people can join it, keep moving along it, and help others do the same.

Internal Work: To Act, You Must Pause

Eleonora demonstrates the critical nature of pausing while taking robust antiracist action, in a way that is both thoughtful and effective. This is especially important for counteracting the purposeful forces that aim at keeping us reactive and complicit.

Chapter 3: What White People Learn About Race

By design, Whiteness is supposed to be invisible. So it's essential to understand how White people have come to be who we are today and understand what we learned as children about race and racism. Here, Ali explores key questions: How did we learn to be White? How is it that we can live in a multiracial society yet remain so unfamiliar with the realities of People of Color and Native people? How did so many of us grow up so ill-equipped to challenge racism? This chapter will help you recognize patterns of unhealthy racial socialization so that you can begin to unlearn them. It will help parents identify unhealthy messages they may be passing on to their children as well.

Internal Work: Antidotes to White Supremacist Priming

While the socialization we experienced as children runs deep inside us, childhood is not the only time when we are socialized about race. We take in messages about race from our society on a daily basis. In this section, Eleonora offers strategies for recognizing and countering how we are primed to think and act in ways that uphold the racial hierarchy.

Chapter 4: Now We Know What Not to Say . . . What *Do* We Say?

This chapter describes what healthy White racial socialization could look like. Ali asks this question: If we, as White adults, want to be healthy, contributing members of our multiracial society, what knowledge, skills, and self-awareness do we need? And as teachers, parents, and guardians, what knowledge and skills do we need to teach our White children so that they develop racial competence?

Internal Work: Empathy Is Our Superpower

This section reinforces the idea that antiracism is good for White people—that when we override our knee-jerk fears instilled by the myths of white supremacy, we tap into our deep psychological capacity for community and connection. Eleonora describes how we can use empathy for learning and as a compass for action. She reminds us that, as humans, we are already powerfully wired for empathy in ways that are foundational to building a healthy multiracial community.

Chapter 5: Can White Antiracist People Feel Proud of Being White?

The chapter answers the million-dollar question about Whiteness: Is it okay to be White? What does it mean to be a *White* person trying to be antiracist? Can White people feel proud of themselves for being White? Using the framework of White racial identity development, Ali explains the different stages White people go through as they learn about racism, the many complex feelings and questions that come up, and, ultimately, our answers to these questions.

Internal Work: Don't Get Stuck in Stereotype Threat

Eleonora introduces the concept of stereotype threat in this section, to help White people understand what is happening to their sense of self when they move through the stages of White racial identity development. Embracing our White identities— and our responsibility for racism—can be hard because of the stereotype threat that people might see us as intrinsically racist. This section gives you strategies for grounding yourself in your values and intentions, so that stereotype threat doesn't derail you from your antiracist goals.

Chapter 6: Who Is White . . . and Why?

Here, Ali offers some historical context in bite-sized chunks. Through this brief history, she helps explain how we got here—how White people became *White*. She also explores the complexity of the question of *who is White*, as well as why it matters that we grapple with this question. It is a reminder that no individual exists outside of the historical trajectory of the moment in which they live.

Internal Work: But It's Not Fair!

In this section, Eleonora offers exercises for dealing with the inevitable feeling that comes with righting historical wrongs—the sense that because it requires giving up a privileged position we thought we were entitled to, it is necessarily unfair. We can know cognitively that something is fair while resisting it physiologically. So we need tools to make doing the right thing actually feel right.

Part 3—Who Will We Be as the Racial Hierarchy Falls?—explores the question of who we want to be as individuals and who we want to be collectively as antiracist White people. It examines the question of what we want Whiteness to mean and how we model that for others. It also offers guidance on how we can take effective action for racial justice in our personal spheres of influence.

Chapter 7: Taking Feedback and Using It Wisely

This chapter is about taking feedback and accepting it as a gift. Ali helps us understand that if we are going to collectively unlearn white supremacy, we need to hear challenging feedback from one another—from People of Color and Native people and from other White people. This is how we begin to know what we don't know. And by extension, learning how to give feedback effectively requires that we appreciate and work with how tender and vulnerable others need to be to take in our feedback.

Internal Work: On Moral Injury and Racial Competence

If we are indeed programmed for empathetic connection with other human beings, and if we truly can override our priming for racism, why do we still experience so much fear when it comes to taking antiracist action—or even just talking about race? In this section, Eleonora introduces the concept of moral injury, which can stop White people from recognizing and intervening in the racial hierarchy. She shows how to respond to the psychological threat posed by moral injury in a way that builds our racial competence and capacity to intervene.

Chapter 8: Talking to Other White People About Race

This chapter addresses the challenge of talking with other White people about race and intervening when they say or do something racist. Here, Ali shares strategies for finding ways to talk with White people that don't shame them but rather help them learn—and keep us all moving forward on an antiracist path.

Internal Work: Healing Is Essential to Antiracist Practice

In this section, Eleonora emphasizes the incredible importance of having places to do your own healing. The goal is to do your own healing, so that you don't confuse the pain and anxiety of challenging racism with preexisting hurts and fears that already hold you back. When we heal ourselves, we inevitably create new ways of being that prepare us for antiracist action.

Chapter 9: Creating and Sustaining White Antiracist Learning Spaces

Here Ali introduces the concept of antiracist learning spaces, a common tool for helping White people do the skill-building they need to engage in so that they can be more effective allies, colleagues, and friends to People of Color and Native people. These spaces may be all-White, like Eleonora's and Ali's were, or they might be multiracial. Throughout Ali's life, such groups have been spaces where her deepest and most profound learning has taken place. In this chapter, she introduces the rationale behind such groups, as well as strategies for starting one in your own neighborhood, workplace, school, or friend group.

Internal Work: To Prepare for Antiracist Action, You Must Train for Courage

In this section, Eleonora helps us prepare our bodies for taking action through training for courage. At this point in the book, it will be clear that while some of the fear you experience along your antiracist path is temporary, disrupting white supremacy is an intrinsically dangerous—and therefore legitimately scary—proposition. Our bodies will not let us take action unless we train them to sustain and confront the fear that arises when we dare to challenge systems that we have been taught to trust.

Chapter 10: Taking Action

The goal of this book is to encourage and support White people in taking action. Here, we offer ways to take action that will be meaningful within your own life. We include some brief stories about how we have taken action in our lives, which we hope will inspire, support, and accompany you as you find your way along the path.

As you can see, the book alternates between our first-person perspectives, except for this About the Book section and the last chapter, on taking action. While there is much that we share, our expertise and experiences are distinct, and we want you to get both.

Wayfinding

You now have a sense of the intention behind the order of words in this book. We have structured it this way because we have certain beliefs about the importance of balancing outer work with inner work, balancing knowledge about the world with awareness about oneself, balancing taking feedback with giving feedback, balancing our vision of where we're going with knowledge of where we've been.

But you know yourself the best. You know what you know and—if you're lucky—you know what you don't know. We encourage you to read this book in the order that helps you continue to engage with it, starting with what resonates the most first.

No matter what order you read the chapters in, please make sure you do not gloss over the Internal Work sections. These are short, digestible perspectives that include a lifetime of resources for managing racial stress and moving from theory to action. Treat them as exercises you might do on a daily basis, like lifting weights or eating sustaining foods. Without food or exercise, our bodies would wither. Without ways to recognize and manage internal racial stress, we will continuously get stuck in the muck of confusion and hesitation. Combining the inner work with the outer work is like adding yeast to flour; it's how we rise to the challenge of deconstructing white supremacy and building something new and wholesome for ourselves and our society.

Authors' Acknowledgments

Joint Acknowledgments

To Corwin, for taking on this book project and for having so much faith in us as writers and thinkers—thank you to Dan, Megan, Mia, Lucas, Melissa, Laureen, and Natalie for your commitment to publishing high-quality books that support and challenge readers to think deeply about race. Thank you to Corwin's reviewers, whose feedback made this such a better book.

To our colleagues who have read parts of the book in different iterations—thank you for giving us feedback, support, ideas, corrections, and additions: Myla Pope, Judy Osborne, Toni Graves Williamson, Peggy Brookins, Wendy Thompson, Mary Conger, Debby Irving, Casper Calderola, Shelly Tochluk, Erica Fortune, and Keren Sofer.

To our incredible editor, Michael Brosnan, thank you for editing with integrity, brilliance, and a push toward brevity. We always feel more confident in our work after it has passed under your pen.

To Rabbi Yael Levy, thank you for holding our hearts and inspiring us with your wisdom. Thank you for reminding us—week in and week out—of the importance of practice, the truth of interconnection, and the need for each of us to show up whole, with *chutzpah* and humility.

To all the people, named and anonymous within the text, who lent their wisdom, knowledge, and stories to help readers learn—thank you.

Ali's Acknowledgments

To my co-director at the Race Institute and co-author, Toni Graves Williamson, thank you for your teamwork, collaboration, leadership, inspiration, vulnerability, trust, and friendship.

To our team at the Race Institute for K–12 Educators—Jeri, Jacqueline, Sarah, Deidre, and Christine—which holds space for educators' long-term and personal development. This is truly work that requires more than a two-hour workshop, and you commit long days to supporting the deep antiracist development of educators. Thank you.

To my graduate-school mentors, Drs. Howard Stevenson, Shaun Harper, Lesley Bartlett, Kathy Schultz, and Susan Lytle—thank you for creating space in the academy for me. Thank you for supporting me, loving me, and challenging me. Thank you for prioritizing work that impacts students and teachers in classrooms, especially around racial equity and Whiteness.

To my graduate-school colleagues in Students Confronting Racism and White Privilege and on Dr. Stevenson's *Can We Talk?* research team, I am so grateful for all I learned through our research, our conversations, our friendships, and our ongoing journeys as parents and educators.

To my mentors at Training for Change and White People Confronting Racism: Lorraine Marino, Antje Mattheus, Sarah Halley, Molly McClure, Erika Thorne, Nico Amador, and Daniel Hunter—so much of what you taught me lives in these pages.

To my editorial teammates, Drs. Eddie Moore Jr., Marguerite Penick, Bola Delano Oriaran, Shemariah Arki, and Orinthia Swindell—working with you over the past decade has helped me learn so much about race, activism, publishing, editing, writing, teamwork, and friendship in multiracial groups.

To all the teachers I've worked with in workshops and coaching sessions who have helped me develop and practice this material, supporting me and challenging me all the way.

To my team of White women who support me in the loneliness of this work and challenge me with your very excellence, commitment, and deep embodiment of antiracism—thank you.

To my second families, the Virchez-Azuara family in Toluca, the Ortiz-Caballero family in Lima, the Massacesi family in Rome, the Berthelet-Goulpeau family in Paris—thank you for helping my family and me learn how to navigate so many kinds of difference to build a foundation of love that stretches across oceans and lifetimes. I'm so grateful to know you and to be a part of an international family with you.

To the Sgwentu family in Hout Bay, who adopted me as your own when I was only 20 and have shared this journey with me every day of every year since then. I'm so grateful to know you, to learn from you, and to grow with you. It is my deep love for you that feeds my contempt for any system that would treat people differently based on race or would refuse to examine current responsibility for historical policies that did so. Thank you for navigating the quagmire of this history with me in love and for sharing your stories of the past so that we might face it together, in our own countries, from our own bodies.

To Jacqueline Berry, who holds it all together—I could not do what I do without you.

To Judy Osborne, who has worked to convince me of my worth since the first day we met—thank you for your vision, your brilliance, your support, and your trust in me. You make it possible for me to spend part of every week writing. I cannot think of a more powerful gift.

To Mary Conger, my partner in the art and practice of seed germination, who knows what it is to sit and wait, to nurture and care, to keep each other company while things grow—thank you for picking up the phone.

Thank you to Mary, Frances, Jim, Erica, and Rory, our children, and all the Ramberg cousins, who teach me, learn with me, and create beautiful moments full of good books and good food every time we are together.

Thank you to Carolyn, Aaron, Bob, Heidi, Lindsay, Jason, and all the niblings, who are part of who I am, who bring fun and adventure into my life, who willingly explore our early years together with a new and antiracist lens, and who show me what it looks like to live antiracism in a context different from my own. You inspire me and keep me laughing.

Thank you in particular to my parents, who have always said that I can share any stories from our lives together, if that sharing will help people learn. This is an incredible gift to me and to readers. I hope that the learning people take away warrants the vulnerability you have accepted in doing this. I hope that I hold myself to the high standard as a parent and as a human being that you hold yourselves to in granting me this generous permission.

Thank you to my children and my partner, Michael, who have kept me company and kept me laughing throughout the long pandemic during which this book was written. You are hilarious, brilliant, thoughtful, truthful, patient, caring, loving, and fun. I am so grateful we get to move through life together.

Thank you, finally, to my beloved Eleonora, who has walked with me on an antiracist path through so many terrains these 20 years—parenting, teaching, research, building community, and maintaining our health. I am so grateful for your good counsel, your affirmation, your support, your generosity, your cooking, and your willingness to embark on this project with me.

Eleonora's Acknowledgments

I often say that I am the least self-made person in the world. And that's because I am who I am thanks to all the people who have believed in me, supported me, paved the way for me, and opened doors for me. I wish I had a better memory for names and people! But my heart doesn't forget. My explicit memory may not be so great, but my body has learned, and I hope my whole life is a song of gratitude to them all. To start, so many of my teachers saw something in me I didn't and helped me cultivate my love of learning, including my first elementary school teacher, who encouraged my ambition; my philosophy teacher in high school, who ignited my passion for thinking deeply; and my college adviser, Dr. Joseph Cunningham, without whose compassionate and selfless mentoring I would have never even considered graduate school.

To my dear friend and colleague Dr. Aarti Pyati, with whom I have spent countless hours over decades sharing deeply about the intersection of counseling and social justice. To my dear friend and colleague Dr. Angela Gillem, who mentored me and worked alongside me for most of my academic career and who is the truest definition of a co-conspirator. To my once supervisors, now good friends, who opened doors within and outside of me that propelled me straight onto this path: Dr. Cyndy Boyd, Dr. Allan Goldberg, and Dr. Marilia Marien. To my first mentors on this path, Sarah Halley and Molly McClure. And to all the guides I have never met, but whose writing has seeped into every fiber of my being, their legacy a timeless, transformative power for so many of us.

Thank you to my daughter, Sofia Bartoli-Wright, whose fierce authenticity and sense of justice, mixed with a hardy dose of lightness and humor, are already creating a new world. To my partner, Chris Wright, whose unconditional love and support have allowed for so much growth and healing. And to my Italian elders: my biggest fan always, my mother, Chiara Piccolomini, who has read every single sentence I have ever written; to my late father, Cesare Bartoli, who sincerely believed in my intellectual capacities, in spite of his time, and who financially supported my studies; and to my maternal grandmother, Nicoletta Freschi, who taught me the strength and power of morals.

There are not enough words to thank my clients and my students, whose willingness to enter in relationship and grow through vulnerability has taught me more than all the books I have read combined. And yes, last but not least, *my* beloved Ali Michael, my friend, colleague, co-conspirator, and sister, in whose love and passion and brilliance I have grown, rested, cried, fumbled, and rejoiced.

For every person I have mentioned here, there are countless whom I have taught with, hiked with, been in endless committees with, raised my daughter with, taken workshops with, and eaten with, and whose openness to struggle, to engage, and to remain in relationship has created my ability to see and live everything you are reading in this book. I hope you, the reader, find as much magic and love in and through this work as we have.

Notes

1. We recommend *Ratchetdemic: Reimagining Academic Success* by Christopher Emdin; *Minor Feelings: An Asian American Reckoning* by Cathy Park Hong; *Centering Possibility in Black Education* by Chezare A. Warren; *Emergent Strategy: Shaping Change, Changing Worlds* by adrienne maree brown; *The Seven Necessary Sins for Women and Girls* by Mona Eltahawy; *Everything You Wanted to Know About Indians but Were Afraid to Ask* by Anton Treuer; *Black Fatigue: How Racism Erodes the Mind, Body, and Spirit* by Mary-Frances Winters; *Crying in H Mart: A Memoir* by Michelle Zauner; and *Begin Again: James Baldwin's America and Its Urgent Lessons for Our Own* by Eddie S. Glaude Jr.

2. For more on this persistent question, see https://www.nytimes.com/2021/11/01/us/terminology-language-politics.html.

3. We struggled with whether to use the term *Native* or *Indigenous*. With Native colleagues and friends, we came to the decision to use *Native* because we are talking about people who are Native to the United States, rather than *Indigenous people*, which includes a broader group of people from around the globe. Both *Native* and *Indigenous* are acceptable terms, according to the Native Governance Center's (2021) *How to Talk About Native Nations: A Guide* (https://nativegov.org/resources/how-to-talk-about-native-nations). But this set of guidelines discourages the use of *Indian* or *American Indian* by non-Native people. We encourage people to use this guide when determining their own use of language to refer to Native people. And whenever possible, we encourage people to use an individual's Native nation affiliation when describing a particular individual's background, rather than a more generalized term like *Native*.

Ali's Journey

. . . .

Finding a Trailhead to an Antiracist Path

I grew up in a predominantly White suburb of Pittsburgh. In my family and community, race rarely came up as a topic of conversation. It's not like we had a rule against talking about race. It was just not done. Perhaps in the vein of "If you don't have something nice to say about someone, don't say anything at all," our default mode was to keep quiet because the rare comments we did hear tended to be amplifications of the national narrative that painted People of Color and Native people as deficient. The result is that I grew up feeling hesitant to talk about race and embarrassed when I did. I wasn't embarrassed because I had been openly instructed not to talk about race; I registered it as a shameful topic simply because *it was systematically not spoken about.*

If you had asked me at that time if I grew up in a segregated community, I would have said no. There were several Families of Color in our professional-class suburb of Pittsburgh, and we all went to school and work together. Back then, I was unable to zoom out and see that, in reality, my community was, in fact, 99.8 percent White. We lived 10 miles away from predominantly Black communities in the city, yet we never mixed. If that's not segregation, I'm not sure what is.

If you had asked me back then if we were antiracist, I would have said yes. We were against racism. But we thought of racism as overt acts of violence, men in white hoods, Jim Crow laws, racial slurs, and hatefulness. We didn't hate anyone. We thought racism was wrong, but we thought about racism as individual meanness or violence. We didn't know about and didn't think about systemic racism—about all the social and public policies that went into creating a community that was almost 100 percent White just 10 miles from a community that was almost 100 percent Black. We lived in the North. We thought of racists as people who lived in the South. We were middle-class, and our parents were college-educated. We thought of racists as poor and uneducated White people. As far as we could tell, racism had nothing to do with us.

If you had asked me back then what I thought about being White, I would have said, "I'm colorblind.[1] It's rude to notice difference." In my family and community, we didn't consciously think of ourselves as "White" or as coming from an all-White community. The homogeneity of our suburb was invisible to us. Our Whiteness was unspoken.

In truth, I didn't actually know that we didn't talk about race or see that there was anything to talk about until I went to college. I attended a historically and predominantly White liberal arts college in New England. The campus was crowded with kids from day and boarding prep schools. The few Black students in attendance had to travel an hour to get their hair done in a nearby city because there were no Black hairdressers near or on campus. Nevertheless, it was there where I was first asked to talk about race and see that I'm White. I'm sure the irony of learning about race while attending an elite institution escaped nobody, but it was my grandfather who said it first: "We send you to this fancy liberal arts school and suddenly *you're* calling everybody racist!?"

When I first took part in race conversations, I did so because it was an academic requirement. It's not that I was uninterested; I had heard great things about the professor, and I was curious and excited about the material. I saw in those conversations a profound connection to the values of community and fairness I had been raised with. But I still saw the topic of race as something that wasn't about me. In spite of my interest, I probably wouldn't have signed up for a course on African American literature had it not been required.

In class, at first, I choked on my words. I would stumble in my speech, trying to evade certain words. I would leave silent, audible ellipses when it came time to say "White," "Black," "Asian," "Latinx," or "Native." My mind would race anxiously. *Is it "Black" or "African American"? Am I cool enough to use the word "Black"? Is it "Asian American" or "Asian"? Is it "Latinx" or "Hispanic? Is it "Indigenous," "Native American," or "American Indian"? I've heard some people use the term "American Indian," but they were American Indian. What is respectful? What is racist? Maybe I should just keep my mouth shut. . . .*

Because I wasn't sure what to say or how to say it, I listened. I listened to Peers of Color talk about racism in their own lives. I felt empathy and sadness as I heard their stories. I assumed my role was to nod and listen, to witness. And then one day a classmate turned to me and said, "What about you, Ali? What is your racial story?"

I drew a blank. I could not fathom that I had a racial story. I'm White! Do White people have a racial story? We weren't racist, as far as I could tell. My parents didn't use racial slurs. What else could constitute a racial story for White people? How could I have a racial story?

It wasn't until many years later—in a White antiracist learning space— that I heard another White person talk about silence and omission *as a racial message*. The fact that I grew up in a colorblind community *was* a racial message. Recognizing that colorblindness, colormuteness, silence, and an implicit belief that race had *nothing to do with us* was a racial message. This changed everything for me. It was like acquiring an invisible-ink pen. As I rubbed the pen over the pages of my life, where I had once seen only the absence of color, images suddenly popped from the page, and I could recognize forms in the Whiteness; I could see racialized messages, a racial story, a life shaped by race. Contrary to my belief that being White was meaningless, akin to nothingness, I began to see that being White was integral to how my life had unfolded.

I didn't actually realize how deeply I had been socialized to be color-blind until I came home from college and tried to talk about this with my parents. They were uncomfortable with the conversation. They didn't buy my systemic analysis. They said they tried to be colorblind, to treat everybody the same. They were open to what I was learning, but they were not convinced by my argument. In fact, they seemed to think I was racist for noticing race. And for my part, I lacked the skills or background knowledge to convince them otherwise.

One day in May, after I had returned home from college for the summer, my dad and I had a disagreement. I don't even remember now what the disagreement was about. He thought I was being impractical; I thought he was being unfair. I didn't know how to respond. I believe what came out was something along the lines of "That's just racist!"

When my dad is angry or disappointed, he gets very quiet. The rest of us—my siblings and I—are left wondering what we did or said to render this quiet, introverted man even more subdued. I attribute my strong inner compass today to this dynamic. He never yelled, never lectured, rarely explained what I did wrong. He would withdraw. And I would be left to discern for myself which lines I crossed and how far. In this case, I knew what I had done. For years after, he did not engage with me when the topic of the conversation was race. I don't believe this was intentional. I think it's just how he manages conflict. He considered me a disrespectful adversary. And because of that, he withdrew.

For a long time, I felt that I had a foot in two different worlds—one where I understood how much racism had shaped my life, where I was trying to get to know more People of Color and Native people, where I was trying to unlearn my habits, language, and expectations that had been shaped by White people and White cultural norms. The other was a world where I could enjoy my time with my parents and the friends I'd grown up with, talk about other stuff, and not be so hyper-focused on race. I wanted to keep a foot on both paths, but I sometimes felt that if I did, I would split in two. My family had always been one of the most important parts of my life; I couldn't walk a path that they were not on. At the same time, I couldn't unknow what I had learned about racism and the ways in which it had shaped my life. I couldn't enjoy my time with friends and family if we weren't willing to address racism.

One day, well after college, I was driving somewhere with my father, and I said to him, "I know I haven't always been great at talking about race with you. The truth is that there's a lot I don't know and I don't understand. But I want to be able to talk about it with you because it's important to me—and you're important to me. I can't explain everything or even justify all my own ideas and beliefs. But I just want to offer that if you ever have questions, I would listen to them. And then maybe we could think through the answers—or possible explanations—together."

This was the beginning of a new relationship for my dad and me, one in which we began to walk an antiracist path together. Even though I was further along on my journey than he was on his, that didn't mean we couldn't walk together. I knew more about racism than he did, but he knew more about sports, economics, fiscal policy, and history than I did. So as we walked, he brought things into the conversation that were relevant and critical to my journey—information I did not know I was missing. I knew a lot about antiracism, but I only really knew how to listen to people who knew more than I did. I didn't know how to talk to White people who disagreed with me or had different assumptions or who knew less than I did about race. He taught me that. He challenged me to defend my ideas, and he questioned me. But he never engaged with me from a desire to defeat me, to twist my logic in his favor, or to impart an ideology. He challenged me and allowed himself to be challenged. He sought mutual understanding. He listened to me and expected me to listen to him.

More than any other person, my dad has taught me how to talk *with* White people about race. He has helped me learn—through the experience of helping him learn—what works and what doesn't work to help White people shift their belief systems, their actions, and their hearts. This gave me the opportunity to experience what a change of heart can feel like from the outside and how to meet this shift in another person with my own humility and an utter absence of gloating or competition, so that I can support the other person's journey without seeing their progress as a reflection on me. The reward for continuing to engage with my dad on the subject of race has been that, as an adult, I am surrounded by White people who are working hard to recognize and intervene in racism: my parents, my siblings, our partners. The channels of communication between us are open. Now, when my dad is confused or has questions about race, he calls me, and we talk them through. My parents now grandparent my children with an antiracist lens. Every conversation, every tear, every frustration has been worth it.

I share this story in detail because I believe this is White people's work: to talk with one another in a way that helps people step onto—and stay on—an antiracist path. Too often, White people take up the decision to be "antiracist," and then look around for the nearest "racist" from whom they can differentiate themselves. I once did this, too. Initially, in calling my dad's ideas "racist," I got to perform the role of the "antiracist" because I was *anti*-him. He was a convenient foil. But this is the short view. And ironically, it is an orientation shaped by white supremacy, which teaches us to value competition and individualism over mutual support and interdependence.

In time, I learned that my original reaction to my dad was predictable. It's part of a pattern of how White people coming into racial consciousness interact with other White people. Essentially, I had just found out that I benefited from a racist system. I had learned that I am fragile. But I didn't know what to do with that information. Because I knew it made me feel bad and guilty, I figured that's what I was supposed to do with other White people—make them feel bad and guilty, too.

I would come to better understand that if I truly wanted to effect societal change, I needed to shift away from trying to differentiate myself from the White person standing next to me. Trying to make myself look good compared to them *fails* as an antiracism tactic in multiple ways. First, it shames them and makes them feel disillusioned with the "woke" person who seems concerned only with making *them* into the racist. Second, it deludes me into thinking I'm somehow different from them in qualitative ways and therefore not invested in a racist system, when I so clearly am, particularly with regard to how much I benefit from that system and have been socialized to uphold that system. Third, it means I am fighting the wrong thing—focusing on an individual rather than the system that has shaped and continues to shape us both. Each of these failures is a failure of strategy. It would take me more time to learn to engage *with* people so that more White people stay on an antiracist path and work for change.

Managing Anxiety

Today, I spend my time leading public conversations about race. And no matter how many race conversations I've been a part of, I always feel some anxiety. I'm anxious that people will question my value, my knowledge, and my background. I worry that I might not be radical enough or that I'm too damaged as a White person with biases and insecurities to lead effectively. I also have self-doubt as a White person who wants very badly to make change but feels cautious about staying in my own lane. I'm very clear that there are things I can never know about racism because I don't experience them directly. At the same time, I don't want to stay silent about racism simply because there are certain things I can't understand. In fact, my identity as a White person is the reason I feel I must speak up.

A big part of what makes it possible to keep showing up—in spite of my doubts—is that I have a lifetime of experience managing anxiety. When I was in fifth grade, I would lie in bed, tormented by whether I should leave the light on in my closet. If I did, it might explode and cause a fire. If I didn't, I would be sleeping in the dark, which seemed possibly more threatening than fire. At the time when this anxiety started to spin out of control, my grandmother was visiting. She recognized what was happening and diagnosed my panic attack. It was familiar to her because she had them regularly. I happen to be quite similar to my grandmother in personality and body type, so it followed that the anxiety that plagued her throughout her life might also plague me. My parents took me to a therapist, and thus began a lifetime of learning strategies for managing the anxiety that has always been a part of who I am.

I still have anxiety today. When the pandemic first began in March 2020, I was just finding my feet again after being diagnosed with multiple sclerosis (MS) less than two years before. I was immunocompromised due to my MS meds and unsure what any of this would mean for me. I remember waking up several nights, unable to breathe, convinced I had the coronavirus, and only after deep breathing and meditation using an app on my phone—one night for three hours—was I able to convince myself that my inability to breathe was panic-induced, not viral.

The anxiety I experience in my work comes just before the start of workshops or presentations. I worry that I don't know enough, that I'm not sufficiently up-to-date on current events, and that I'm not sufficiently tapped into the experiences of People of Color and Native people to talk about racism and white supremacy. But every time I get anxious, I have strategies for grounding myself. I tell myself that I don't know everything; I can't know everything. I tell myself that I'm there to teach—but also to listen and to facilitate the conversation to help people hear one another. I reassure myself that I'm there to make mistakes and learn from those mistakes. In fact, I'm there to model what it looks like to be a White person and a teacher who makes mistakes and takes feedback—and continues to move forward. I don't need to know everything. I just need to be honest about what I don't know and forthright about what I do. I need to show up and be a part of the conversation with all my gifts and imperfections—and make it possible for others to do the same. I share this because I know I'm not alone in my anxiety around racial stress. Throughout the book, Eleonora and I will both share strategies for managing the anxiety that threatens to derail our personal power. These strategies work to relieve anxiety *and* keep us engaged in the conversation.

360-Degree View on Race

You already know that I spent the first 18 years of my life knowing very little about race. By the time I arrived in my doctoral program, I had been on my own journey of learning how to live an antiracist life for seven years. In college, I had taken at least one class per semester on racism, African American literature, African history, colonialism, or racism in education. I had spent more than two years living in South Africa and writing the biography of Black feminist activist Nomzwakazi Gertrude Sgwentu. After college, I had spent a year on a Watson Fellowship studying local NGOs (nongovernmental organizations) in Senegal, Bangladesh, India, and Ghana. And I had been teaching—substitute teaching at Wilkinsburg Middle School in Pittsburgh; teaching Spanish at the Oregon Episcopal School in Portland, Oregon; teaching math at the East Harlem School at Exodus House in Harlem; and teaching GED equivalency to adults at La Guardia Community College in Queens.

Through all these experiences, I knew race mattered. In particular, I knew racism explained the incredible differences in opportunities that students from all my different teaching experiences faced. But I still had no idea what I was supposed to do about it, or how/if I was supposed to talk about it with students. I was teaching in the context of a white supremacist society . . . but was I supposed to talk about that with my seventh-grade math students? I didn't understand my Black students' humor or references . . . but how was that possible when I had studied so much?

I took these questions to my Ph.D. program, where I would leave one class on the psychology of race focused on my breath, locating my feelings, considering what it means to be White—as I had been taught to do in that class. I'd arrive next in a class on the anthropology of race, and the teacher would challenge me: "But are you really White? Is anybody actually Black? If race is a social construction, these categories aren't actually real." After going back and forth between classes for a few weeks, virtually unable to reconcile the notion of race that we talked about in one class with the notion of race presented in the other, I went to visit my anthropology professor. "I don't understand how both classes can be about race but can feel so different," I said. "I feel like I need to watch you in conversation with the other professor so that I can figure out where your arguments overlap and where they conflict." My professor laughed. She said that even if she were to debate my psychology professor, we'd probably see that they ultimately agree on much, if not everything. It is the academic silos that give the impression of a disconnect.

Ultimately, I came to love the fact that these two disparate disciplines can coexist within the field of education. In education, we cannot talk effectively about race without talking about the history, the sociology, or the socially constructed nature of race. This is crucial to knowing how we got to be where we are; how false the lived categories of race actually are; how white supremacy was built through social, political, and legal means; and then, in turn, how it has been taught to us subtly through media, geography, religion, language, and school. But we can't actually change things as parents, teachers, administrators, counselors, professionals, and policy makers if we can't identify how race and racism operate on the individual level, in our communication with students, in the eye contact we make or do not make with one particular colleague, or in the pit that forms in our stomachs when a student asks a certain type of racialized question. While it is immensely useful to understand racism conceptually, it is *operationalized* through these micro-moments, through this endless series of actions we perform at the individual and group levels. Understanding these micro-moments is the work of psychologists and counselors.

Eleonora and I bring to this book a 360-degree disciplinary lens on race, antiracism, and Whiteness. We want readers to break down the siloed approach to antiracism. No single lens can explain enough about how racism is operationalized, so it can't provide full guidance on how to disrupt it. Counseling and psychology have much to offer education, but most of the psychology classes aren't open to preservice teachers, even when those departments are housed in the same schools of education. Education has much practical application to lend to counseling, but again, it does not penetrate the cellular walls that divide departments. We want anthropology and sociology's emphasis on the social construction of race to impact how we think about race in counseling and education. We want a historical lens that tells us how we landed here in the first place to be part of all of it. And we want counseling and psychology to connect the dots between history and our daily lived experience, so that we all can understand what's happening in our bodies when race is lived and not just studied.

When we look at our work, we see how all these elements come together for us *all the time*. Each discipline doesn't just add something "extra" to the ways in which we operationalize antiracism in our lives. These multiple bodies of knowledge actually converge in, and shine light on, every decision we make. This book offers an integration of what we have learned and utilized over the years to shape our own antiracism practice and is reflective of the questions and "stuck" places where many White allies frequently find themselves—just as we have. It offers a map and a language to go from theory to action, from discernment to disruption. It decodes how we have learned to see the racialized world around us, to reengage when our own human bodies get tangled into confusion and paralysis, and to implement concrete tools for antiracist decision-making and action.

The next section introduces you to my colleague, Eleonora, whose perspective on race and approach to antiracism are both different from mine and wholly aligned with mine. We hope that reading both of our stories will help you see broad possibilities for yourself in terms of where you will start on the path, how you will travel it, and how you will choose to make a change in your spheres of influence.

Note

1. When my parents used this term, *colorblindness* was widely used in our society as a way of saying, "I don't see race." We use the terms *colorblind* (Bonilla-Silva, 2022) and *colormute* (Pollock, 2005) throughout the book to describe attitudes of pretending not to see race, trying not to see race, intentionally not talking about race, or acting as if racial difference and racial inequality do not exist. We have great respect for the theorists who have helped coin and define these race-specific terms and for how they allow us to describe phenomena and attitudes like the one that was playing out in my family at that time. We also want to acknowledge that these terms play on the words *blind* and *mute* in a way that devalues disability. We hope that as we continue to engage in this conversation about race as a society, we will begin to have no need for these particular terms. And until then, we hope to find new terminology to describe these longstanding problems.

Eleonora's Journey

A New Country, a New Mirror

I've been a licensed psychologist for more than 15 years. At no point in my five years of graduate school and three years of supervised training was I taught to apply counseling and psychology principles to social justice work. While my graduate program at the University of Chicago focused on the intersection of culture and mental health, it was devoid of any conversation about power and oppression. In fact, it wasn't until my final internship before graduation (in the early 2000s) that I was exposed to *multi*cultural concepts that addressed how systems and power impact people's lives and experiences. I will never forget watching the now-iconic documentary *The Color of Fear* by activist, educator, and filmmaker Lee Mun Wah. *The Color of Fear* records a group of racially diverse men meeting over a weekend to discuss racism. I was transfixed by one of the characters, David, a White man, who struggled for most of the documentary to grasp his own privilege and collusion with racism. While I could tell that he was meant to be the foil, the one who didn't "get it" (to the exasperation of the other group members), I related to him. I had all the same questions he had and few, if any, of the answers. What I learned in watching that documentary explained much about my own observations of life in the United States, as well as my own life experiences.

I grew up in 1970s Italy as a cisgender woman in a loving but rather conservative family, where sexism was espoused and unquestioned. My family's attitudes toward women were echoed by the Italian culture of the time, so I internalized both the subtle and the overt misogyny I encountered as "truth." When I was nine years old, we moved from Rome to a small town near Venice, for financial reasons and to be closer to family. It was at that time when I became aware of the ethnic tensions between the North and South of Italy, with discrimination flowing from the former to the latter. The subtle Roman inflection in my speech easily marked me as a non-Northerner and engendered social ostracism. However, the social rejections I experienced were mitigated by the class privilege I held because of my extended family's status in the town. To complicate things further, while my class rank held much clout outside of my family, it did much less so within it, as my mother had violated familial, religious, and gender norms, first by marrying outside of "rank" and then by divorcing. While I embodied both dominant and marginalized identities that had tangible consequences, I did not have language or contextual knowledge to understand how my experiences were shaped by or connected to these identities, or how they influenced how I viewed myself and others.

At the age of 19, I was afforded the chance to come to the United States to experience the U.S. university system. What began as a one-year commitment, aimed primarily at learning English and living abroad, opened doors beyond my wildest imagination. I relished the ability to study multiple subjects—something that was not possible within the Italian university system. I discovered the world of graduate school. Attending college had already been a dim expectation for me as a woman; I had not been aware that educational opportunities past college even existed. I unexpectedly found much fulfillment in intellectual pursuits, which surprised me after a lifetime of being told that my intelligence was naturally lacking because of my gender. And I was astounded to find that I had professional prospects within academia, especially given that I had no social capital in that world, which would have been essential had I sought an academic career in Italy.

While I was learning English and acculturating into the U.S. academic system, I was also being indoctrinated into U.S. norms and the racial caste system (Wilkerson, 2020). Prior to arriving in the United States, my imagination was full of images of the American Dream; I thought of the "new world" as a place where individual freedom reigned (in contrast to the centuries-old restrictive traditions of the "old world") and where opportunities to become anything one might desire were boundless. It wasn't long before those beliefs were sorely challenged. While no one around me would admit that there were rules of engagement, I kept bumping into what felt like invisible walls, which quickly curbed ways of being that did not fit what was, in fact, "expected" and deemed "proper" according to U.S. standards. I wasn't shy about asking questions and had a lifetime of training for identifying safe ways to navigate my world, so I learned quickly: emotions were not welcomed; presenting as "doing great" at all times meant you were "normal"; one-upping other students in the classroom meant you were smart; asking anyone how much money they earned was intrusive; as a woman in the United States, I was supposed to dislike and be bad at math; and so on.

Past the hurdles of learning English, wrapping my head around the U.S. educational system, and trying to function within U.S. cultural norms, I began noticing racial disparities and tensions, all while unconsciously absorbing racial stereotypes. Again, being willing to ask questions, it became apparent to me that race was a very sore subject, which was either vehemently avoided or consistently brought up with negative connotations. In other words, it was never a simple descriptive or positive factor. Early in my clinical training, I worked in an adolescent inpatient psychiatric unit, where, as part of my training, I joined a seasoned Black psychiatric nurse in co-leading a therapy group. The group members were all Black youth, except for one White teen. I remember struggling to follow the conversations filled with idioms, while trying to discern how to be helpful by watching the experienced nurse. In one of the group meetings, the conversation became animated, and suddenly the nurse reprimanded the youth while pointing at me as a White person, a symbol of what they had to contend with outside of the hospital. I did not understand the context in which the comment arose or the content of the comment itself. My language difficulties could explain some of that but not all of it. I don't know what the youth made of the comment, but as a White person (in a position of relative authority), at best, I looked like a deer in the headlights, and at worst, I showed utter incompetence when it came to matters clearly central to the youth's well-being. This is one of my clearest memories of learning that being White was problematic and that as a White person I was not expected to belong in race conversations—or to be able to contribute to them. I had not been trained to do so, nor did I have the skills I needed.

Around the same time, I had asked my White male supervisor about the hierarchy among the mental health staff that very obviously coincided with race: all the psychologists and psychiatrists were White, while all the lower-ranking staff and the vast majority of the patients were People of Color and Native people. It was such a visible, patent fact that I had simply become curious about its potential significance. Without missing a beat, my supervisor replied that my observation was, in and of itself, a sign that I was racist, because why else would I have noticed? Having already been the target of overt sexism by this same supervisor, I didn't give much credence to his answer, per se, but I still learned from the interaction that race was clearly a taboo subject.

In addition to these moments when I was taught about my place as a White person, I have a flurry of memories where in retrospect I can see that I invalidated experiences of racism conveyed by my fellow Students of Color. In my eagerness to understand what I was missing, I revealed my biases and ignorance, quickly frustrating whomever I was speaking with. While I cringe at these past microaggressions, I also grieve the message I kept receiving: as a White person, I wasn't expected to learn or understand much when it came to race. I had undoubtedly failed to understand many other aspects of U.S. culture, but I can't think of any that engendered as much pushback as race. Being White was obviously significant, just as I had learned early in life that being a woman was significant. Specifically, the significance was a sign that there was something *wrong* with these identities, albeit in different ways. I can only dream about what a difference it would have made to have had White allies to learn from during my early years in the United States.

In the absence of that, watching *The Color of Fear* was nothing short of revolutionary. It openly spelled out and answered many of the "inappropriate" questions I had been asking. Through David, I could witness the same resistance I had encountered throughout my life when I had attempted to challenge sexist notions. I noticed that this same resistance now lived within me when I felt challenged to see myself as a White person (rather than as Italian or as a woman). While racism and sexism cannot be necessarily equated or compared, my own experiences of being silenced, gaslighted, physically unsafe, or otherwise marginalized allowed me to relate viscerally to the dialogue I witnessed in the documentary. These new lenses felt so deeply meaningful and useful in understanding my personal and professional worlds that from that point forward, multiculturalism became the primary focus of my career.

Building an Antiracist Path

After completing my clinical training and becoming licensed as a psychologist, I opened a small private practice while pursuing an academic career. I worked in academia for 15 years, including 12 years as the director of a graduate program that trained master's-level counselors. In addition to pursuing research on White racial socialization and multicultural counseling competence, my position as director of the program enabled me to do systemic work. Over the years, our leadership team hired a diverse faculty wholly committed to infusing social justice principles into both the program's curriculum and the administrative structure, much to everyone's benefit. Every decision we made within the program tried to counteract the ways in which racial injustice manifested within the program and in the field, with the aim of creating opportunities for healing and transformation within and outside of the curriculum.

While as a faculty and staff we worked collaboratively, we were strategic about who was going to be the face of each initiative. For example, as the program director, I used my position to take the lead in educating students about the prejudice faced by Faculty of Color. I introduced newly hired Faculty of Color into our program in intentional ways, in an attempt to reduce the bias they would face. I also advocated for the program to be staffed by a majority of Faculty of Color, making sure they taught a variety of clinical—not exclusively multicultural—content, while we hired White faculty with the competency to deliver portions of our multicultural curriculum.

The development of our formal multicultural curriculum was a massive collaborative undertaking, which took a decade to design and fully implement. It included self-awareness labs where students could learn about their sociopolitical identities and support one another in seeing how these played out in real time while in the program. We invited speakers who expanded students' knowledge of specific populations (e.g., Arab Americans, trans people, undocumented immigrants) and issues (e.g., visible and invisible disabilities) that they may not have been exposed to previously but would be critical to their clinical effectiveness.

Each year we added topics or shaped the conversations to address the prevailing sociopolitical narratives of the moment, explicitly tying our professional ethics to current social justice issues. We integrated a study of U.S. multicultural history in several classes, thus educating students and faculty about the social context that created the injustices we witnessed around us. We emphasized understanding the cultural context from which counseling theories and techniques emerged, as well as how best to tailor them to each individual client given their unique identities. We envisioned and created an orientation that invited students and faculty to use the concepts of growth mindset and stereotype threat, so that students—especially those from marginalized groups—had resources for combating the predictable and unfairly onerous impact of marginalization on their educational attainment. Students were closely mentored by faculty, and they were also invited to participate in the shaping of their educational experiences via mutual feedback loops. Our intention was to teach students how to become agents of social change in the very process of learning how to advocate for themselves within our program. All the while, we instituted a self-care curriculum that acknowledged the challenging histories that many of us bring to the counseling profession, as well as the toll that clinical and social justice work can take on top of that. Not all strategies were successful or reached their full potential; however, taken together, they created a widespread sense of community and allyship, and our program became well known for graduating multiculturally competent counselors.

The journey to envisioning and implementing these strategies was neither linear nor smooth. At each step, I could lead the operationalization of our social justice agenda only to the extent that I was aware of the ways in which white supremacy operated around me and through me. For those of us who are White, this is not an easy feat. We navigate a world that is not invested in having us see the ways in which we collude with or promote white supremacy; the status quo requires our participation and ignorance, and the norms, policies, and procedures of our institutions all but ensure that we remain complicit. What made all the difference for me was having the opportunity to develop authentic and loving relationships with Colleagues of Color—through whose experiences I could see a reality that I was otherwise not privy to—as well as friendships and allyships with other White people—with whom I could process what it means to be White in the United States, as well as the numerous blunders I made along the way. I was also fortunate to develop my template for collaborating with other White people through the antiracist learning group described by Ali in the prologue. In both of those sets of relationships, two skills were key: my ability to stay in relationship and my capacity to emotionally regulate. No real learning would have been possible without both of these skills.

Trauma-Informed Antiracism

Seven years into my director position, I took a sabbatical, during which I retrained as a trauma specialist. Treating trauma now integrates neuroscience and mindfulness-based principles, in addition to the traditional behavior and cognitive behavior strategies. After returning from my sabbatical, I took on the coordination of our program's trauma concentration, through which I emphasized the contextual (versus simply individual) forces that produce trauma and consequently our responsibility as clinicians to assess the impact of, and respond to, social power imbalances. So there I was, a licensed psychologist specializing in trauma and social justice, steeped in multicultural research. But I still kept coming to my work mostly from an intellectual, scholarly standpoint. In other words, my strategies relied on the knowledge I learned from books, research, and my relationships with allies in antiracist circles. This knowledge was immensely helpful and effective in enlarging antiracist spaces and antiracist practices within the institutions and individuals I was working with. But such enlarging still operated mostly within the confines of what was permissible by white supremacy. I was missing a fundamental understanding of how white supremacy infiltrates our physiology. In other words, I was missing the role of our human bodies.

Growing in our awareness of the dynamics of power and oppression is most often a drop-by-drop process. Yet occasionally we are gifted with insights that propel us exponentially forward. In fall 2019, I attended a weekend workshop by writer, activist, and ordained Zen priest Reverend angel Kyodo williams, co-author of *Radical Dharma: Talking Race, Love, and Liberation*. Attending Reverend angel's workshop was one of those moments. Early in the workshop, she stated, "If you are not talking about the body, you are not talking about race."[1] Despite the fact that I had been reading, writing, and teaching about multiculturalism for almost 20 years, that statement gave me pause. I could not quite tell what she meant. Reverend angel repeated the statement twice and then asked us to consider what we thought had to happen to a White woman's body in the 18th century as she walked through an open market to shop for her family. What feelings did she have to suppress in order to nonchalantly witness the brutal selling and parceling out of Black enslaved families, all while holding the hand of her own child? What part of her own humanity did she have to disengage from in those moments to deny the humanity of Black people? While this might feel like a shocking image, anti-Black terrorism is what we have been witnessing in various forms daily for decades—not to mention the past few years. What must happen to our White bodies to make terrorism against Black people tolerable to us?[2]

And there it was, in plain sight: the realization that, indeed, if we don't talk about the body, we are not talking about race. If we are not talking about the body, we are not talking about antiracist action. This insight became the thread that tied together my knowledge of trauma and social justice in ways I had not been able to do before. Our bodies are designed for survival first and to thrive only after that. As White people, we are taught that survival means upholding the current system. Our safety is directly proportional to the extent to which we do so. Without understanding what is happening to us *physiologically* when we encounter injustice, our bodies will stand in our way of doing anything about it. Because so many White people have been *trained* to be numb to the pain of People of Color and Native people and to be complicit with racism, we have to untrain and retrain in order to be antiracist. Without *training* our bodies to reenlist our innate capacity for presence, perspective-taking, and empathy first and foremost, it's unlikely that any antiracist knowledge or intention will yield concrete actions. Empathy, as we'll see, is a force that allows us to resonate so deeply with the terror and pain we witness that it all but propels us to act. This is where our bodies matter very much.

By the time I was learning from Reverend angel, I had already left academia with the intent of sharing the tools of counseling and psychology in the service of social justice. But this newfound perspective brought into focus the extent to which counseling and psychology have the power to transform antiracist practice from an aspiration into a concrete and persistent path. Conversely, it made me realize how unlikely we are to take antiracist action—in spite of all our aspirations—when we don't incorporate an understanding of the body.

To be sure, knowing how our bodies are designed to protect us from real and imagined dangers, learning to discern their messages, and enlisting their support as we attempt to operationalize racial justice may not be all we need to create a just world. But our ability to work with our physiology is nothing short of essential for our antiracist effectiveness. When we don't consider our bodies, it is almost inevitable that our good intentions will remain mostly just that: aspirations—to everyone's frustration and consternation.

Throughout this book, I offer tools and practices that you can employ to work with your physiology so that you can take action toward social justice while connecting and collaborating with People of Color and Native people and with other White people. If some of this feels confusingly theoretical, don't worry. Getting unstuck doesn't rely on a sophisticated understanding of biology or complicated practices. The principles and practices I offer will make intuitive sense and are fully within your grasp. I hope they support your work as much as they have supported and continue to support mine.

Notes

1. It wasn't until summer 2020 that I came across and read *My Grandmother's Hands* by Resmaa Menakem (2017). As a trauma and multicultural specialist, he details in profound ways the connection between our historical legacies of violence, our physiological responses in the presence of People of Color and Native people, and how these in turn inform and support our racist social structures.

2. What I describe in this paragraph is my recollection of what I took from Reverend angel's workshop, and I take responsibility for any misinterpretations or misapplications.

PART 2

SEEING OURSELVES CLEARLY IN THE HERE AND NOW

CHAPTER #1

Racism Is a White Person's Problem

The moment we choose to love we begin to move against domination, against oppression. The moment we choose to love we begin to move towards freedom, to act in ways that liberate ourselves and others.

—bell hooks (2006, p. 298)

When I first started learning about racism, I thought the goal of every race conversation was to make me feel bad. Not me, specifically, but White people in general. I came away from race conversations feeling guilty about being White, uncertain about myself, and out of touch with the proficiency and skill with which I faced most other aspects of my life. Because of this, I assumed that feeling guilty was my task. *It's a hard job, but somebody has to do it . . . finally something tangible I can do for racial justice.* And beyond that, I thought that if I could make other White people feel guilty—my friends, my students, my father (especially my father)—I could compound my already significant contribution. I set out to make all the White people I knew do penance for our racial inheritance.

Honestly, these thoughts didn't come through me consciously, as I've laid them out here. But because I felt raw and unresolved about my own White identity and privilege, I reached out to other White people from a place of woundedness, yearning for validation, ready to defend. Every conversation was a setup for one of us to win and one of us to lose. Even in multiracial conversations, I could join only from a place of sin and sorrow—with no room for liberation.

In this mindset, I experienced race conversations as a dead end—a cul-de-sac. We all traveled together down the dead-end street of race talk, made a few loops around the cul-de-sac of shame and guilt (for me), anger and sadness (for others), frustration and anxiety (for others), and then traveled out the same way we entered. We felt bad together. And inexplicably, that was how I believed we would end racism.

What I know now is that the road does not dead-end at all. It meets a roundabout, not a cul-de-sac. The roundabout is a place where we pause, reflect, and take a few turns around the circle before we decide what happens next. We talk about the racial dynamics that have played out so far on our journey. We look again at where we came from and where we are going. And while we can see where we came from as we round the circle, we don't return to that place as we would from a dead end. We choose a path forward together. Race conversations do produce feelings of guilt, shame, anger, sadness, frustration, and anxiety in many people—not just me, and not just White people. But when any particular race conversation comes to a close, we are changed by the humanity we have shared with one another. We are changed by our deeper understanding of how the systems within which we live have affected us on personal, group, familial, and ancestral levels. And because we are changed, we cannot go back the way we came. The only way out is onward, toward the next roundabout. When we brave this conversation, when we face this history, we put ourselves on a road—a path—that leads us closer to racial justice.

Racism Is Not a Person of Color's Problem

James Baldwin (1924–1987) is widely renowned for his novels, essays, and plays, as well as his unflinching willingness to look at racism and ask others to do the same. Among his numerous insights into race in the United States, he often implored people to see that racism is not a Person of Color's or Native person's problem, as it is so often framed. Racism is a White person's problem, he said in so many words, and it won't change until White people see that and do something about it.

This makes sense from a practical perspective. Assuming that People of Color and Native people could end racism without White people would be like suggesting that women could end sexism without men. How could that be? To what extent is it women who maintain the patriarchy? It would be like insisting that trans people could end transphobia without cisgender people, that Muslims should put a stop to Islamophobia without non-Muslims, or that Jews could stop anti-Semitism without non-Jews. No, racism is not going to change unless White people see it as our problem, too.

But the issue is that when a person is part of a mainstream group, it can be hard to even recognize the oppression that affects other groups, much less intervene in it. Most non-Muslims, for example, have no idea what Islamophobia looks like in the United States beyond the most overt graffiti, slurs, or violence. Islamophobia also includes not having non-pork options at company-sponsored dinners or not having a clean, safe place to pray five times a day. It means having your name mispronounced or your choice to fast during Ramadan questioned. When you are not part of a group, it can be hard to see the marginalization and oppression that members of that group must deal with.

White people cannot even see racism without People of Color and Native people sharing their realities with us and challenging our White-centric lenses. Yet this sharing comes at a price. And People of Color and Native people should not have to pay this price, precisely because racism itself already exacts a high toll. Racism almost killed James Baldwin. His life was threatened not just by the brutality of police violence or the substandard health care provided to most Black Americans in his lifetime but also by the everyday indignities of racism. Baldwin said that living in a racist society meant that on a daily basis, he waffled between restraining himself from killing White people and trying not to kill himself (Glaude, 2020). It took all his energy to avoid doing either.

White people cannot begin to make a dent in racism if learning about it comes at the expense of the lives of People of Color and Native people. We must realize the preexisting cost of living with racism before we demand that they tell us about it in a way that we can take in—and therefore incur even more of a price. We cannot expect People of Color and Native people to talk more gently to White people, patiently explain the historical background, turn the other cheek when White people mess up and say the wrong thing in a way that hurts them, or hold our hands while we walk this path. This is not because they can't or won't do these things—indeed, many People of Color and Native people in my own life have talked gently to me, explained aspects of history I didn't know, forgiven my mistakes, and held my hand. No doubt many more are doing the same for White people all over the United States right now. But Baldwin's story teaches us that how People of Color and Native people choose to respond to racism is largely a choice in which their own survival hangs in the balance. What they need to say or do in any given moment is determined by self-preservation, avoiding trauma, and supporting people they love. While it may be that a Person of Color or a Native person will decide to respond to a White person in ways that help that White person learn, White people cannot let our willingness to confront racism hinge on the gentleness or amiableness with which People of Color and Native people share their pain and experiences. It is not something I should expect or demand as a White person.

Yet it is something I need. I need this kind of gentleness, patience, and forgiveness to take my own next steps and to move through the inevitable shame-storms that I experience as I look at this history. I need encouragement and support to believe that my individual-level actions and interventions can help shift the system. I need someone to help me maintain the humility and audacity required to keep meeting my Colleagues of Color and Native colleagues eye to eye, even as I learn the outrageous injustice of what they have to face in the United States, in a system I benefit from. I need someone to travel this path with me, help me understand, and keep me rooted when I want to run away.

This is where White people come in. Our work is to keep moving along an antiracist path and to support other White people in doing the same. This means that we will support one another so robustly that we can handle the truth of systemic racism and colonialism without being crushed with guilt or hopelessness. We will create many varied points of entry to an antiracist path and encourage other White people to take them, with opportunities for companionship and belonging throughout. This turn comes as a surprise to many White people. Too often, the way White people attend to one another's racism is with a self-righteous fury proportionate to the size of the system, rather than the size of the one comment we are addressing. Sometimes the fury is so consuming that it leaves us speechless—or capable only of talking behind one another's backs. In lieu of intervention, we cut off the relationship. Or we shame one another. The result is that people give up before they even have a chance to begin.

This is driven home for me by various accounts written by parents of teenagers who became seduced by white supremacist movements (Anonymous, 2019; Kamenetz, 2018). Why would teenagers be attracted to such movements? Throughout the stories, one common theme prevails (McLaren, 2017). The teens were lonely and isolated. White supremacist movements were places that offered belonging and respect, where young people were treated like rational adults. These stories haunt me because white supremacists are reaching out to young White people with the promise of belonging—to recruit them into a hate movement. Meanwhile, I consider the work of building an antiracist world to be part of a love movement. But many White people don't want to be a part of this love movement because the bar for entry seems so high. It makes them feel bad. They often don't know the right words, don't know the accurate history, or unwittingly offend. One woman said to me, "I didn't know we could be nice to each other *and* be antiracist!" Again, this is not to say that there is not a lot we need to learn and do as White people. But if we don't support one another—especially as we begin this learning—and if we don't create opportunities for belonging and respect within our learning processes, White people will opt out.

Some people might call this bending to white fragility. On some level, I suppose it is. But our argument in this book is that white fragility (DiAngelo, 2018) is not an indictment or a verdict rendered as a result of bad behavior that can be corrected with the right intention—or the right punishment. As Robin DiAngelo explains, white fragility is a condition caused by our common socialization as White people in a racial caste structure (Wilkerson, 2020); it is a condition that most White people embody, given the sociohistorical context that we occupy. Supporting other White people by steadying them on an antiracist path—and being supported in turn—is not a capitulation to oppressive Whiteness; it is a strategic way forward toward racial justice.

Too often, when White people are trying to be antiracist, we focus on how we look, trying to demonstrate to the people around us that we are not racist. Our antiracism becomes performative, a way of earning credit or projecting a particular self-image, none of which has anything to do with ending racism. This phenomenon is not new and not unique to the United States. Steve Biko (1978/2002), a Black Nationalist from South Africa who was executed by the Apartheid government for his resistance to Apartheid, wrote, "Instead of involving themselves in an all-out attempt to stamp out racism from their white society, liberals waste a lot of time trying to prove to as many blacks as they can find that they are liberal" (p. 23).

This performative antiracism is a problem. Not only does it *not* advance racial justice; it also puts another form of pressure on People of Color and Native people, who then need to recognize or contend with our performance, once again centering Whiteness. It also has a polarizing effect, often driving White people in the political center further away because antiracist culture appears caustic and superficial. What if we stopped trying to look antiracist and instead started trying to *engage* in the practice of antiracism for the purpose of fundamentally changing our society? To do so means not basing our self-image on who sees our activism but quietly, steadily, and strategically engaging in antiracism, regardless of how much recognition we get. It means reaching out to support and challenge White people who hold basic assumptions that contribute to a racist worldview—but not in a way that makes them more defensive and resistant. This means challenging racist assumptions one on one after the big public discussion. It means engaging with them over time, not just in one heated moment. It means learning from them and giving them a chance to learn from you, rather than entering into an interpersonal battle.

Furthermore, what if White people worked against racism, not only because it's the right thing to do, and not only for the sake of a just society, but because racism is damaging White people, too? As Eddie S. Glaude Jr. (2020) writes:

> In *No Name*, when Baldwin recalls his first visit to the South, he says that he "felt as though [he] had wandered into hell." He wasn't talking about the hellish lives lived by black southerners under Jim Crow, but rather how the racial dynamics of the region had hollowed out white southerners. The lies and violence had so distorted and overtaken the private lives of white people in the region that their lived lives felt empty. (p. 48)

Baldwin was no more optimistic about White liberals than he was about slaveholding Southerners. Similar to Steve Biko, he said, "I'm a little bit hard-bitten about white liberals. I don't trust people who think as liberals. . . . I don't want anybody working with me because they are doing something for me" (Glaude, 2020, p. 97). He wanted White people to see what he saw in the South: how racism was actively destroying White people, just as much as it destroyed Black people.

His comments echo in the words of historian Ibram X. Kendi, who was asked this question: "If you could design the ideal White ally, what traits would that person possess?" Kendi (2020a) responded, "I would want that White person to understand that it is in their interest to build an antiracist society . . . that it is in the interest of people of all racial backgrounds to create a more just, more equitable society." In other words, racism is a White person's problem—not just because People of Color and Native people can't change it alone . . . but because racism hurts White people, too.

How Does Racism Hurt White People?

How exactly does racism hurt White people? Racism certainly does not hurt White people to the same degree or in the same ways that it hurts People of Color and Native people. It also does benefit White people a great deal spiritually, materially, politically, socially, professionally, and so on. Yet to be effective antiracist allies, as Kendi said, White people need to be able to answer this question. While individual White people might answer this question differently, I will share some of my own answers as an example of what this might look like.

At the end of the nineteenth century, W. E. B. Du Bois (1899/1995) wrote, "[Racial] discrimination is morally wrong, politically dangerous, industrially wasteful, and socially silly. It is the duty of whites to stop it, and to do so primarily for their own sakes." Du Bois was referring to all that the United States lost as a country because the opportunities to work, to learn, to practice medicine, to create policy, and to wield power were reserved exclusively for White men for so long. Look at Charles Drew, creator of the blood transfusion, who attended medical school as an African American when very few non-White students were accepted and faced a deeply segregated medical system. He ultimately resigned as the director of the first Red Cross Blood Bank because the Red Cross insisted on segregating Black blood from White blood (National Museum of African American History and Culture, 2017; NewYork-Presbyterian, n.d.). So many lives were saved throughout World War II and beyond because of Dr. Drew's pioneering work. How many other Black people, Native people, Asian people, and Latinx people might have contributed such innovation but were denied access to education—and thus denied the opportunity to contribute to science, philosophy, business, medicine, law, policy, education, art, and history?

For so long, rather than draw from the vast talent and possibility of our diverse population, we have artificially limited who could be educated, who could contribute, and who could shape our society. Anti-racism widens these possibilities in ways that often feel threatening to White people, who believe the spaces once reserved for them in elite institutions should continue to belong to them. But in fact, this kind of inclusive expansion and diversification benefits everyone because our entire society is improved by it.

Racism Is a Mechanism for Control

In *The Sum of Us: What Racism Costs Everyone and How We Can Prosper Together*, policy expert Heather McGhee (2021) writes about how easily manipulated we (the U.S. public) are when we are invested in racism. Most White voters, she says, vote with their race interest rather than their class interest. By dredging up old racial stereotypes about Black people abusing government resources, self-serving politicians garner votes in spite of the fact that they promote policies that benefit only the very wealthiest in our society. Time and again, White people who depend on government programs for survival have voted in favor of a reduction in those programs out of a belief those same policies will unfairly help or coddle Black people.

McGhee depicts municipalities all over the United States that built state-of-the-art swimming pools in the 1920s and 1930s, when there was no air conditioning and few other ways to stay cool. But when those municipalities realized in the 1950s that they would have to allow Black swimmers to use the pools, many of them closed the pools or paved them over to avoid having them become racially integrated. People with financial means built their own swimming pools or created private clubs. But many White people forwent the luxury of summer swimming altogether, because of their unwillingness to swim with Black people.

McGhee shows how the housing crisis in 2008 was also facilitated by racism. Federal policies that allowed for subprime mortgage lending caused a stock market crash, robbing millions of families of all racial backgrounds of their retirement savings and even their homes. When the fiscally irresponsible policies that led to the crash were created, politicians and bank executives justified them by drawing on well-worn stereotypes of Black and Latinx people as careless homeowners. The racist stereotypes justified the reckless policies. The policies, in turn, ended up hurting many working- and middle-class people—including White homeowners. The policy makers and the bankers, on the other hand, were largely unscathed. Stereotypes of People of Color and

Native people as fiscally irresponsible and government-dependent perpetuate a national economic policy that does not benefit most people in the United States. This is how racism works against us—and why antiracism benefits White people, too.

Antiracism makes us harder to manipulate. It helps us see our society with a more balanced lens. It helps us interpret and address societal problems with more accuracy—and therefore more success. On the other hand, racism itself is a tool of control, with tangible material downfalls for most White people. And that's before even considering—as Eleonora will help us see in the Internal Work section following this chapter—how it keeps us afraid, angry, and distressed. Racism keeps White people unwell in ways that are both psychologically and physiologically detrimental to us.

Losing Friends

I can recognize how racism and antiracism have affected me personally in many ways. For example, in college, I took a winter study course in which we studied how the civil rights movement was taught to the public. To do this, our class traveled around the South, visiting museums and historically important sites. There were only five students in the group—three White and two Black—and we became quite close. When we returned to campus for the spring semester, my Black classmate invited me to hang out in his common room. All-gender socializing was a very normal thing to do—in fact, I lived with two White men in a suite across campus, and I was very used to hanging out in common rooms with men. But what I didn't realize was that I was mostly accustomed to hanging out with White students. When I arrived at my friend's common room, he was there with three other Black junior classmen. And as I came into the room, I panicked. I don't think I'd ever been in a room with four Black men before. Racist tropes were unconsciously playing in my mind, triggering fear, anxiety, and insecurity. Regardless of how much I had just learned on the civil rights trip, I didn't know how to calm down. My body was having a defensive reaction in response to something that was not threatening and not in fact dangerous. For all practical purposes, it was a delusional, unhelpful, and unhealthy reaction—one that racism had conjured up in a very real way inside of me. In this case, sadly, I left. And I lost touch with that friend.

When I think about antiracism, I think about how I have garnered the tools to distinguish real threats from fabricated threats. I think about the friendships I might still have if my discomfort had not been so activated by racial difference. I think about the fact that our ability to detect safety becomes warped by racism. Alternatively, my antiracist practice has made it possible for me to build robust, honest, loving relationships with People of Color and Native people whose lives, worldviews, and perspectives have expanded my own. I shudder to think of my life without some of the relationships that have sustained me over the past 20 years—relationships that could exist only because of my ongoing efforts to unlearn my early racial socialization. And in truth, it was within the context of those relationships—with support and love from those friends and colleagues—that so much of my unlearning transpired.

Racism Renders Us Less Competent

Racism hurts White people because it convinces us that we are fundamentally incapable of building healthy multiracial community with People of Color and Native people. I once spent an entire eight-hour day training the predominantly White faculty of a small independent school that served about 50 percent Black students and 50 percent White students. The school invited me because they wanted to be more effective in serving their Black students by understanding their own Whiteness. At the end of the training, the White principal essentially threw up his hands. "This was really great," he said, "we learned so much. But let's face it. When it's all said and done, Black kids aren't going to trust me. And why should they?"

I agree with the principal on several points. Black students may have an implicit distrust of White administrators when they first come into the school. They have every right to. Black students need Black teachers and administrators in their lives. White educators need to support the hiring and retention of more Faculty of Color and Native faculty. All of that is true. But his belief that he could not muster the necessary competence to become the administrator who quelled that distrust meant that he was giving up on relationships with Black students. He was abdicating the responsibility to build mentoring relationships with Black students.

When I first started learning about racism, I felt very much like this principal. When it came to race conversations, I believed White people would always be wrong, and People of Color and Native people would always be right. I also thought that People of Color and Native people were basically born with the ability to talk about race, while White people were born with an intrinsic deficiency. In reality, nobody is born with the ability to talk about race or the knowledge needed to navigate racially stressful situations. People of Color and Native people aren't all skilled at talking about race. When they are, it's because they have practiced. It's because they deal with racism on a regular basis, they talk about it, and they strategize about it. Because People of Color and Native people need to navigate racial stress to survive, they often have well-honed skills for doing so.

Not all White people are unskilled at talking about race or navigating racial stress. But by and large, White people have less practice than People of Color and Native people do. We're not bad at it because we're White. We're bad at it because most of us don't have to do it to survive. We lack the skills because we lack the practice.

Dr. Howard Stevenson was the first person I heard talk about racial competence as a set of skills that anyone can learn. As he says, our capacity to navigate racial stress is a reflection of our competence, not character (Stevenson, 2014). In other words, not knowing how to respond or what to do in a racially complex scenario doesn't make us bad people; it just makes us unskilled. The corollary to this is also true: we can be very good people, but that does not mean we know how to navigate racially stressful situations. Good intentions are valuable but not sufficient for building racial competence. For that we need skills and practice.

In this book, we define *racial competence* as the knowledge, skills, and self-awareness that enable a person to recognize and intervene in racism, both inside themselves and outside themselves (see Figure 1.1).[1] Racial competence is liberating and exciting. It allows us to move through the world with more confidence, less fear, and more receptors for building connections with People of Color and Native people. And as Stevenson (2014) says, it is something that anybody can develop with practice.

We See What We Believe

On a weekend trip to New York City during grad school, I stopped briefly to get some coffee. I remember walking out of a busy rest stop in New Jersey behind an older White woman. As she approached the exit door, four teenage boys who were Black were entering from the other side. I looked up to see them smiling and joking. But I saw them get serious as they glimpsed the older woman in front of me, who had stopped in her tracks and appeared to be frozen in fear. This whole

Figure 1.1   Definition of Racial Competence

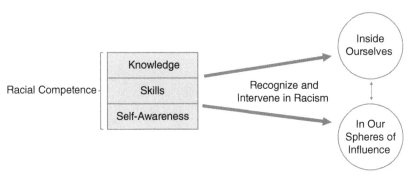

exchange happened in an instant, but I knew what she had perceived when she saw them, because it was a perception I might have had in the same scenario at a different point in my life. And it was clear from their reaction that they knew what she perceived as well. In the moment, I moved ahead of her and held the door, ushering her out, hoping that the young men could then go on their way without a second thought. In myself, I noticed a complete lack of fear or confusion; I knew in my gut that those young men were not a threat. I also knew that years before I may have seen them as such. The racial competence I had gained in the interim was like a new pair of glasses that clarified things that had previously been blurry and inaccurate. I was grateful for this greater capacity to see people clearly, knowing that a White woman's faulty fear is a very real threat to Black men (and, in this case, boys).

As Eleonora will explain further in the Internal Work section on priming (following Chapter 3), we don't actually believe what we see; we see what we believe. Our view of the world we live in—and our ability to enjoy its richness—is severely distorted by the racist views we inherit. It reminds me of my dad's reaction to reading *The Guide for White Women Who Teach Black Boys*. When he finished the book, he said, "I will never look at a Black man the same way again." Recognizing and intervening in the racism that has taken root inside ourselves changes our lenses, so that we see the world differently. The human community and our sense of belonging within it open up to us in a whole new way.

Racism Robs Us of a Certain Joy

Finally, joy! Joy may be the number-one motivating factor for engaging in antiracism. I have found that talking about race and racism—and being honest about how we get treated differently by society—makes it possible to take relationships to a whole new level. It is similar to how couples counseling helps my partner and me maintain a relationship that is mutually satisfying while helping each of us grow into the people we want to be. Counseling is not usually easy or fun, but it helps us build a family and a life that is deeply gratifying and full of joy. Antiracism helps me see people clearly and wholly because we have processed together how our racial backgrounds affect our relationships with and our reactions to one another. I experience joy with People of Color and Native people and with other White people along this path. We will talk more about joy in the final chapter.

Reimagining What Could Be

As a White person practicing antiracism, I have long been guided by James Baldwin's words, which he shared in so many different ways throughout his life: *Racism is not a problem only for People of Color and Native people. It's a White person's problem. It's not going to change unless White people do something about it.* In summer 2020, I picked up Eddie Glaude Jr.'s biography of Baldwin and began to reacquaint myself with him in a way I never had before. To my surprise, while it is true that Baldwin said what I had understood him to say about racism being a White person's problem, he did not say it in the way I remembered.

After Baldwin moved to Paris to escape racism in the United States, he answered a question about what it felt like not to have to constantly think about how White people perceived him. Baldwin said, "I didn't have to walk around with one half of my brain trying to please Mr. Charlie and the other half trying to kill him. Fuck Mr. Charlie! It's his problem. It's not my problem" (Glaude, 2020, p. 34).

"Fuck Mr. Charlie! It's his problem. It's not my problem." That's what Baldwin actually said. *Fuck White people. Racism is their problem, not mine.* It's essentially the same statement I remembered, but in vastly different words. It's almost certain that Baldwin made other statements at different points in his life similar to the one I recalled. But it's also possible that I somehow heard these words and recast them into a less dismissive, more inviting account.

Either way, Baldwin's insight had already changed my life. It upended my childhood understanding of racism as a problem only for People of Color and Native people and clarified for me the need to play my part in ending it. It was like a calling, an invitation, a passing of the baton. It was a door opening to a place where I formerly felt I didn't belong, rendering obsolete questions such as "What right do I have to go into that class with so many Students of Color and Native students?" "What do I have to say against racism?" "What right do White people have to speak up about racism or, for that matter, to write a book about racism?" and "What do I even know?" For me, Baldwin's insight became a benediction: *Stop doubting yourself. Do something. Who are you* not *to take responsibility for this? This is your problem. This is about you.*

My hope is that by engaging White people in an antiracist practice, we can help the United States finally live up to its democratic principles in a way that enables people of all racial backgrounds to live in safety, to care for their families, to manifest their unique talents, and to thrive as professionals and individuals. In particular, I hope that when White people engage in this work, People of Color and Native people can stop wasting energy on trying to communicate a message of injustice in precisely the right way so that White people will hear it. And then, because of the time and energy White people put into supporting one another, we will hear all the words spoken by People of Color and Native people as an invitation, no matter how it is conveyed.

Note

1. Our definition builds on Sue and Sue's (2019) definition of *cultural competency* and the scope of White antiracist work laid out by Mattheus and Marino (2011).

INTERNAL WORK

Antiracism in a Human Body

My heart races, yet again, as I'm about to utter the word *Black* in a large faculty meeting. As I feel my blood pressure rise, I begin to forget what I was going to say, and my own exasperated inner voice screams at me: *Why is this so damn hard? What's wrong with me?* The colorblindness that has been ingrained in me insists that I should stay quiet, and I feel my mouth stutter, caught between what I know intellectually to be right and the feeling that saying *Black* out loud is wrong. To get beyond this moment, I employ my compassionate inner voice and reassure myself: *It's okay. . . . It's okay. . . .* And with that reassurance, I'm back, present in the meeting and refocused on my comments.

While I couldn't bypass that first reaction, I have trained myself to recognize it and come back from it fairly quickly, much of the time. This practiced internal skill allows me to lean into, engage in, learn from, and act when faced with uncomfortable topics or interactions, even ones as simple as overcoming the taboos arising from color-blind socialization. These skills allow me to get myself unstuck over and over again as I attempt to operationalize my antiracist knowledge and intentions.

This is the essential rationale behind the Internal Work sections of this book: it's impossible to take antiracist action to any extent without enlisting our body's consent—regardless of how knowledgeable or well-intentioned we might be. And when I say "action," I don't simply mean attending protests, organizing, voting, or speaking up. We are biological beings, and as such, anything we intend to do must enlist our physiology; this includes thinking, listening, empathizing, and staying in relationship. And most of us White people find it indeed challenging to talk with other White people about race, hear about the racism experienced by People of Color and Native people, and even just think about how race shapes our lives—not to mention act in antiracist ways.

Because we are socialized within white supremacy, most of us grow up believing that speaking about race is impolite, even shameful.

So when we are asked to engage in conversation on race and racism—say, in school, the workplace, or the community—we promptly feel under threat. Given this anxiety on the one hand and our lack of knowledge and skills on the other, we can fear the topic in all its forms. Simply uttering the word *race* or using a term such as *Latinx* can be anxiety-provoking. And this physiological response only deepens as the curtains are pulled back on white supremacy and we come to understand that the racism experienced by People of Color and Native people is in fact true. Early in these conversations, many of us can start feeling bad simply for being White, as if we carry some kind of indelible original sin. When someone points out our microaggressions, we all too often internally shame ourselves, deeming ourselves hopelessly racist, or we desperately try to prove ourselves otherwise. In short, engagement with the topic of race is intense. The body perceives it as a threat to such a high degree that, more often than not, it activates the areas of our brains designed to protect us. It encourages us to shut down and step away. This is why no amount of antiracist intellectual understanding alone will lead us to antiracist action. We need our bodies to stop preventing us from listening and learning—and, by extension, from acting. When we don't train to meet these challenges, we manifest "fragile" behaviors (DiAngelo, 2018), and we do so in very predictable ways, to the exasperation of our peers and allies—and often even to our own dismay.

The good news is that in spite of what our bodies have been taught, sound waves produced by words reaching our ears are not actually physically dangerous. No race-related word has intrinsic harming power. No truth spoken by a Person of Color, a Native Person, or a White ally is physically harmful to us; in fact, such truths are incredibly useful gifts along an antiracist path. We perceive race-related words or truths about racism spoken aloud as a threat only because we are trained to do so. And our bodies are great students, especially when it comes to our safety.

While our culture and educational systems teach us to privilege the part of our nervous systems responsible for higher-order thinking, which is where our antiracist knowledge and planning reside, that capacity is not always primary, nor do we have unconditional access to it. As it turns out, fear unhinges it quite effectively and without our volition: when our bodies detect danger, we go into survival mode, which in turn overrides our attempts to notice race, think about race, speak about racism, or follow through with our antiracist intentions. So, indeed, it can feel *that damn hard* to align our antiracist words and actions with our antiracist plans. Our bodies are, quite literally, blocking us. And if you have picked up this book, you are most likely all too aware of that very fact. Just think back to any recent unresolved racially charged event when you felt anger, frustration, anxiety, or shame. You probably felt your blood pressure rise, your heart rate quicken, and your mind speed up and get foggy. Your body detected danger and, without your conscious consent, initiated what is called a *stress response*.

Our Survival Mechanism: The Stress Response

Our bodies are evolutionarily, biologically, and genetically designed first and foremost to survive. We come into the world profoundly underdeveloped (more so than any other species) and take a very long time to reach full development (more than 20 years, when it comes to our brains). While our need for care to survive is most apparent during our earlier years, our likelihood of surviving outside of community at any point during our lifetimes is slim to none. To demonstrate this intrinsic interdependence, simply take stock of how many people you have relied on by the time you eat breakfast in the morning, including the people who ensure that you have running water, that your electricity works, that there was milk stocked at the store, and that it was brought to the store from the farm so that you could pour it on your cereal (to paraphrase Martin Luther King Jr., 1963/2010). Think about what it would mean not to rely on that broad network of human beings, not to mention animals and nature.

Our intrinsic vulnerability and interdependence have profound implications for our biology, and the ways in which we maximize our chances of survival are encoded all over our nervous systems. Some of our neural survival mechanisms are reflexive and completely out of our control (e.g., blinking when an object approaches our eyes). Others depend on judgment calls, which still happen very quickly and often bypass our higher-order thinking centers. Think again about a recent tense conversation about race—chances are that you were already flushed and ready to react by the time you even registered what might have triggered you, and once you were triggered, I bet you felt all but clear-headed.

While we might not be able to control our reflexes, we can absolutely modulate our response to perceived danger. This Internal Work is about understanding what happens in our bodies when we engage in any antiracist practice—when we push back on the white supremacy myths that Ali will describe in Chapter 2. To be sure, our stress response is a supremely powerful, deeply hardwired neural strategy. Simply knowing about it is not enough to change its grip on us. But if we train to work with it, it does not have to prevail, either. The Internal Work sections in this book will help you do just that.

What exactly is the stress response, and how is it involved in our deep discomfort about race? It is the same neural mechanism designed to protect us from imminent danger. It became encoded into our genes a very long time ago, and it's present throughout most of nature. While this part of our nervous systems can be quite effective at allowing us to survive moments of acute danger (e.g., when we step onto the curb while a car is fast approaching), it's a rather blunt instrument: it reacts to all threats in the same exact way. Our stress response does not distinguish between real or imagined threats to our physical integrity, social status, or emotional well-being. Inconveniently, all these threats feel equally deadly and are responded to as such. Evolutionarily, this makes sense. Because communal support was essential to our physical survival, our bodies evolved to experience threats to our standing within the community as lethal, in the same way a saber-toothed tiger posed a lethal threat. However, the social and environmental contexts in which we live today are quite different from the milieu in which our genes evolved. Therefore, our neurological bias for overestimating what might constitute imminent danger can cause serious problems at a time when imminent threats from the natural world are not what we contend with most in our daily lives.

How Do Our Bodies Respond to Perceived Danger?

I am going to outline next exactly what happens when our nervous systems perceive danger. Before I do that, I want to specify that here I am not talking about the perceived danger generated by our bodies because White people are often taught to be afraid of People of Color and Native people—to see Black men as dangerous and to see Brown Muslim people as terrorists. Although our stress response is activated in these instances as well, this is not what causes most of our angst on an antiracist path. In fact, these might be some of the easiest and most obvious fears to recognize as unfounded. Here, I am pointing to the perceived danger our bodies detect in merely talking about race, in taking a risk of getting something "wrong" and unwittingly offending a Person of Color or Native person, or in being excluded from a respectable social circle. In other words, People of Color and Native people are not the threat that triggers our nervous systems in ways that impair us from acting in antiracist ways. It is challenging racism in other White people or in our institutions that scares us and limits us. It is the intensity of our guilt or shame that we find profoundly threatening. It is the fear of losing community and belonging that makes us retreat and stay silent. These pitfalls plague us the most while being the least visible to us.

What exactly happens, then, in our nervous systems when we detect danger in any form, real or imagined? In response to threats, our stress responses initiate a cascade of events, implicating a number of hormones, which compel us to enact one of three strategies. Which strategy we enact depends on our nervous systems' assessment of our ability to confront the threat:

1. If our nervous systems think we can overcome the danger, they propel us to *fight*. This strategy can manifest as physical or verbal aggression but also as intense thinking or ruminating and overplanning. It can look like blaming the victim, complaining about the timing and form of the feedback we receive, or replaying over and over what we should/could/would have said or done. It is most often associated with feelings of anger and frustration.

2. If our nervous systems think we can outrun the danger, they propel us toward *flight*. This strategy can manifest as physical avoidance or emotional/psychological withdrawal. It can look dramatic, like changing careers, quitting a committee, or physically leaving a conversation; it can also be more subtle, like disengaging emotionally or verbally or letting the urge to give up prevail. It is most often associated with feelings of fear and anxiety.

3. If our nervous systems think that there is no chance for either overcoming or escaping the danger, they make us *freeze*. This strategy is meant to lessen the psychological and physiological pain of succumbing to the threat. Personally, I know I'm freezing when my mind goes blank. On the outside, we might look like a deer in the headlights or appear to be checked out. On the inside, we feel stuck, even utterly exhausted, all the energy draining from our bodies. We could go as far as feeling outside of ourselves or no longer in contact with what's happening around us. The freeze response is most often associated with feelings of shame and helplessness.

The more we feel unsafe, the more our nervous systems deploy these fight, flight, or freeze strategies. The more these strategies are deployed, the less access we have to the parts of our brains that allow us to think, learn, and empathize. In other words, in moments of perceived danger, our physiology is designed to concentrate all its energy on reestablishing safety and minimizing pain. Those moments are not the time to look around, get some perspective, befriend the enemy, or recall stored information. As you think back on a recent unresolved racially charged event in your life, you might begin to identify how these specific strategies manifested specifically for you.

As helpful as this mechanism is to survive a real, imminent threat to our physical integrity, it causes problems for the routine day-to-day interactions in which there is no real, tangible threat but toward which we initiate an all-out, out-of-proportion defensive response. Further, our stress response is actually toxic to us in the long term. Short bursts of a fight, flight, or freeze response stress our physiology just enough to strengthen it, like a good workout. But when these responses become too frequent, they are poisonous and have serious health consequences—just like our muscles are meant to be used but not overtrained. Chronic use of our stress response is not only detrimental to our health (e.g., by fostering heart disease, impairing our immune system, dysregulating cell repair, increasing inflammation, impairing learning and memory) but also highly problematic when it comes to race conversations. To the extent that these conversations feel scary, this mechanism will make it difficult to remain in relationship, use our antiracist knowledge, or notice all that is said to us or that is taking place around us. All these capacities are physiologically diminished. So you are not wrong—white supremacist training has made it *that damn hard* to practice antiracism in all its forms. But contrary to other species, we have a choice: we can follow the path of least resistance and remain reactive to what scares us, or we can train for courage and keep access to all our capacities, even when our bodies detect danger.

It is crucial to our antiracist effectiveness to realize that this is the biological context within which we receive messages about race. As Ali will describe in laying out five of the myths of white supremacy in Chapter 2, we are overtly trained to fear conversations about race by one part of our society—and then harshly judged by another part as intrinsically defective (read: racist) if we don't enter such conversations smoothly and with full competence. Even if others don't berate us for failing to do so, we berate ourselves. To make things worse, we are taught to suppress our emotions, which means that we often don't even know when we are having a fight, flight, or freeze response. And we are certainly not taught emotional-regulation skills that would help us manage our stress response.

In sum, very little in our cultural and social contexts prepares us to handle tensions around race in nonreactive ways. In fact, it would be more accurate to say that we are actively trained to be reactive. But we can't build racial competence on our reactivity. In fact, racial competence depends on our ability to recognize our reactivity and moderate it.

Strengthening Your Antiracist Practice

Notice Your Stress Response: Graduated Exposure

Graduated exposure is a great way to build your ability to notice when you are in a flight, fight, or freeze state and the particular forms these states take in your life under different circumstances. To start, list a few racially charged events that are distressing for you. You should list a mix of both mildly and intensely distressing events. For me, a mildly distressing racially charged event would involve becoming aware that I'm taking too much space as a White person in a conversation or realizing that I did not see how another White person's behavior was racist before a Person of Color or Native person pointed it out to me. I feel a lot more distress when I am told I have acted in racist ways. I still cringe thinking back to having mistaken a Neighbor of Color for someone else and remembering the expression on his face when I called him by the wrong name. We might even experience distress after speaking up against racism or while planning an event that challenges our institution to think differently, as we begin to imagine the potential for backlash.

Here are the steps to practice exposure:

Step 1: Identify five to ten racially charged events that are clearly distressing for you, thinking back to racially tense experiences you've participated in or witnessed in the past few months.

Step 2: Rate each experience from 0 (not distressing at all) to 10 (most distressing). Your distress scale should reflect your level of distress in general, not just as it pertains to racial tensions, so a rating of 0 reflects times when you were completely relaxed, and a rating of 10 indicates times when you were the most distressed you have ever felt, in any situation. In counseling, we call these Subjective Units of Distress.

Step 3: After you assign a Subjective Unit of Distress to each event, select any one event with a rating of 5 to 7 as your initial focus for exposure, and commit to working on it for few minutes each day—perhaps while you are commuting to work, doing the dishes, or brushing your teeth.

(Continued)

(Continued)

Working on an event means

- *thinking* about it for a few seconds;
- *noticing* when your body begins to initiate a fight, flight, or freeze reaction;
- *watching* the physiological sensations that begin to emerge, again for a few seconds;
- and then spending as much time as needed re-grounding your body, by taking some deep breaths or mindfully tracking physical sensations (I offer a few additional practices in the Internal Work section following Chapter 2).

Once you feel relaxed again—whether it takes a few seconds or a couple of minutes—*repeat the process* a few times: go back to thinking about that same event again, notice and watch your fight, flight, or freeze reaction, and then re-ground yourself.

Step 4: Once you become relatively quick at re-grounding yourself, select an event that has a higher Subjective Unit of Distress, perhaps around 8, and repeat the same exact procedure for this new target. But don't rush the process! No one's watching; no one's keeping tabs on how quickly you move through the list of events you have created. Only you can know when each event you have selected to work on still offers good practice—or when it has become too easy and is not offering you a challenging enough opportunity to practice pausing and re-grounding. The point is to train the muscle of re-grounding, and moving too quickly—but not thoroughly—up the ladder will not actually build your skills.

As you work through each of the scenarios you have selected, you will become quite proficient at handling not only the specific instance you've practiced and trained for, but also most instances that provoke a similar level of distress. In other words, the re-grounding muscles you develop in one context will automatically generalize to others with similar emotional undertones. So don't worry about working with all the events that you rated as a 5, for example, or that feel very similar. Keep challenging yourself to move up the scale or through different kinds of situations.

CHAPTER 2

Myths of White Supremacy

I now know that hopelessness is the enemy of justice. Hope allows us to push forward, even when the truth is distorted by the people in power. It allows us to stand when they tell us to sit down, and to speak when they say be quiet.

—Bryan Stevenson (as cited in Cretton, 2019)

So how do we travel an antiracist path in a way that moves the needle on racism and gets other White people to do so as well?

One answer involves recognizing how white supremacy still lives in us—in our society, our assumptions, our relationships, our bodies, and even our antiracism efforts. In the following section, I will share five myths of white supremacy that affect how White people talk to other White people about racism.

The mythological pillars of white supremacy are many. The lies and stories on which we have built our society are too numerous to count. But five myths in particular underlie the logic that guides White people in our relationships with one another, particularly with regard to how we talk (or don't talk) about race. These myths—and the ways in which we continue to act as if they are true—are part of why this love movement for racial justice feels unwelcoming and inaccessible to so many.

The myths:

Myth 1: It's rude to talk about race; we should all be colorblind.

Myth 2: We can and should be perfect—or at least appear perfect.

Myth 3: We need to "win" by competing with one another.

Myth 4: It's better to think, rather than feel, about racism.

Myth 5: Race is real and biological; racial differences are immutable.

Myth 1: It's Rude to Talk About Race; We Should All Be Colorblind

As I wrote in my introduction, I was raised to be colorblind. As far as I knew back then, my colorblindness was a phenomenon of social comfort. We didn't talk about race in my family because it was awkward, and we didn't know what to say.

Today, I can see other explanations, all of which help explain our collective studious avoidance of the topic. Educational researchers would say that my family didn't talk about race because we lacked the background knowledge and skills—the racial literacy—to do so (Sealy-Ruiz, 2021; Stevenson, 2014). Sociologists would say we didn't talk about race because we were all White people, and we didn't realize that "race" was about us, too (Lewis, 2004). Philosophers like Charles Mills (1999) would say we didn't talk about race because we were invested in the racial contract, which traded our silence and complicity for the material gains of a system that put White people first in line for resources and opportunities and made us think we deserved them the most. Writers like James Baldwin and Toni Morrison would say we didn't talk about race because we thought racism wasn't our problem. Psychologists like Beverly Daniel Tatum and historians like Ibram X. Kendi would say we didn't talk about race because we thought of ourselves as non-racist, and we thought that was enough. From a parenting perspective, perhaps we didn't talk about race because of how my parents had been socialized to be colorblind (Bonilla-Silva, 2022) and colormute (Pollock, 2005). From a group dynamics perspective, we didn't talk about race because our Whiteness was invisible to us (Sue, 2004b).

From a political perspective, we didn't talk about race because when I was growing up in the 1980s, politicians like President Ronald Reagan overtly framed Black activists as "racists" for talking about race. He did so while methodically resisting and undoing policies meant to address historical racial inequities. Reagan promoted the message that it's racist to talk about race while restoring and re-creating the structures necessary for the maintenance of the racial caste system. The same message is prominent in conservative politics today.

My colorblindness, and that of my family, was part of our family and community culture, and it seemed relatively innocuous at the time. But I can see now all the different incentives and messages that played into our sense that colorblindness was the right way to be White. I can see how the national narrative that said *people who talk about race are the racists* distracted much of White society from thinking critically about race. I can see how I unconsciously absorbed the nightly images of Black violence, drug use, and economic dependency that saturated the media without questioning. I can see now that I wasn't afraid of traveling to Black communities simply because I had unexamined stereotypes. I was afraid because I had been socialized into playing the role that politicians, the media, and our society at large had written for me—a White girl in the suburbs who would be safer if she stayed away from Black people. The poverty, vulnerability, and violence that Black people experienced at the hands of a hostile state during that time meant that many Black youth were cornered into similarly playing the role written for them.

For all the historical, psychological, sociological, social, political, and educational reasons why my family didn't talk about race, the impact was that we didn't and couldn't talk about racism. We came to see all racial talk as racist talk. I still encounter this misunderstanding today when I mention the racial background of a person, and a teenager will say in response, "Why do you need to name their race? Isn't that racist?" It is common in our society to conflate "racial" talk with "racist" talk. The distinction between racial and racist talk comes from anthropologists Michael Omi and Howard Winant and will be covered in greater detail in Chapter 4. It is a framework that can help us begin to grow away from colorblindness, which demands that we cease and desist from all "racial" talk, lest we be seen as racist.

For White people trying to walk an antiracist path, a first step is to understand that part of our fear and discomfort with talking about race is coming from the way we were raised. I was taught in my community that talking about race is rude, just as surely as I was taught to say thank you to the waitress at Friendly's. And talking about race still often makes my heart beat faster and face go red, just as it would if I tried to go to a restaurant and be rude to the waitstaff. It's hard to go against our home training.

A teacher once followed me into a taxi after a six-hour workshop I had delivered at her school because she had so many questions, "You seem so comfortable talking about race. I always feel so bad after I do it. When will that change?" I had to admit to her that I commonly feel bad after I talk about race. Even then, I was about to board a train back to Philadelphia, and no doubt I would spend time on the commute lingering on what I said that was wrong, or how I screwed up. Part of this is my desire to have integrity in my work. But part of it is the way that I search for an explanation of why I feel so bad after I have done a public presentation on race. And ultimately, it's not because I did something wrong—it's because I did something I was taught not to do. The *feeling bad* comes from acting in ways I was raised to believe were wrong.

Unlearning colorblindness, or what some people would call *learning color consciousness* (Appiah & Gutmann, 1998), means learning to recognize those unconscious physiological reactions and finding a place to put them so that they don't overwhelm you into being silent. It requires that you find spaces for talking about race, not just for the sake of talking but so that you have an opportunity to actively practice and unlearn the habits and ways of being that are integrated into who you are. In Chapter 9, I will share more about forming White antiracist learning spaces that exist for the explicit purpose of giving White people space to practice, learn, and grow with regard to color consciousness and developing racial competencies.

Myth 2: We Can and Should Be Perfect—or at Least Appear Perfect

Be perfect.[1] Appear perfect. It's a White cultural norm and a middle-class norm, but where does it come from? It seems to be particular to people who see following the rules as in their best interest. As Betsy Leondar-Wright (2005) says in her book *Class Matters*, it's a particular feature of middle-class culture to believe that following the rules will help you succeed. Leondar-Wright says that people outside of the middle class (people who are very poor or very rich) tend to eschew the rules. For the very poor, it's because the rules don't work for them. For the very rich, it's because there's no sense that rules must apply. In a capitalist society, if you have some money, and you have some access to credit, following the rules does seem to be a fairly certain path for advancement. For people who are White and middle-class, there's a sense that if we do everything right, things will go well for us. Or we believe that if things are going well for us, it's because we do things right. Many people's experience of meritocracy suggests that if things don't go well for you, it's because you did something wrong—not because the system failed you. For People of Color, Native people, poor folks, folks with disabilities, and trans and queer folks, this system is more evidently broken—or, rather, it was not set up for you to succeed to begin with. Marginalized people within this system learn early that even if they do everything right, the system may still fail them. For middle-class White people, particularly cisgender, able-bodied, straight White people, it might seem like a pretty good system. So those of us who are White and middle class set about crossing all our *t*'s and dotting all our *i*'s so that we can get the most out of it.

Deluded by the sense that perfectionism will help us get ahead, middle-class White people tend to bring this demand for perfection into our relationships with People of Color and Native people, as well as into our efforts to be antiracist. I suspect that is part of the reason this demand for perfection pervades antiracist culture and communities. Even as we are trying to be allies to People of Color and Native people, we place on them a demand that they be perfect and blame the failures of antiracism on their imperfections. But we also carry this myth of white supremacy into our own antiracism efforts, trying to be perfect and expecting other White people to be perfect as well. It's why so many don't want to speak up in conversations, for fear we'll use the wrong word or say something offensive. It's why so many people don't speak up against racism in public or even behind closed doors. We don't want to do it unless we can do it perfectly.

But it's not just our tendency toward the appearance of perfectionism at work here. It's also a genuine desire not to be hurtful to People of Color and Native people, or not to cause even more damage. The problem with this desire is that the alternative to speaking up—and possibly saying the wrong thing—is silence. Silence is not neutral when speaking up is what is called for. I can remember working with Eleonora and our small antiracist group as we role-played possible interventions to a racist encounter one of us witnessed on the subway in New York. Someone tried speaking directly to the "aggressor" in the role-play, and then we ruminated on the possibility of someone getting hurt by using that strategy. Someone tried talking directly to the "victim" to help them find a way out of the situation, but then we cautioned the possibility of overstepping our bounds or blowing things out of proportion. We wondered if any of these solutions would actually make a difference, or if we were simply falling into the trap of wanting to be some kind of White superhero. We could see the pitfall of every potential action. Then Eleonora pointed out that there was a problem with silence and inaction as well. She said, "Maybe when we're in situations like that, we should just plan to do the wrong thing—like Nike, only the antiracist version." Since we can always come up with reasons not to take action—and if not taking action is wrong, too—what if we just take action and then learn from those mistakes? From then on, our motto became *Do the Wrong Thing*.

What is the antidote to this desire for perfection? A colleague and mentor of mine, Sarah Halley, says that mistake-making in antiracism needs to be more like mistake-making in figure skating: it's going to happen if we want to get good. Figure skaters can't perform a triple axel the first time they try. They probably fall hundreds of times before they actually do it. It's not solely their skating ability that helps them become great; it's also their ability to fall and recover. It's their willingness to mess up and try again, to learn from their mistakes, all as a part of the process of developing competencies. This is hard to do because the task is dire; People of Color and Native people need White people to be racially competent yesterday. And yet we can't just be good at something that we haven't practiced. If White people want to become effective antiracists, we need to learn how to fall and recover. If we could recover quickly and easily from the corrections and feedback that we receive on all the ways in which our language and actions are still not quite antiracist, think how quickly we could all move forward.

It's our inability to receive feedback that makes others (People of Color, Native people, *and* White people) hesitant to give it, knowing that if they do so, they have to put it in a way we will hear it, then make us feel better about ourselves when we are hurting, and possibly risk having us retaliate or withdraw from the relationship. White people end up not getting the feedback we need to become better antiracists because we have such a strong belief that we can and should be perfect (or at least look perfect). Maybe not accidentally, the very thing that prevents us from getting feedback and learning comes from a white supremacist framework. Being able to be imperfect, to *do the wrong thing* and reevaluate afterward, to take feedback and make change, to fall and recover—all these measures are critical to disrupting white supremacy's rules around perfectionism and moving the needle on racism.

I have worked with several White people, one of whom has shared his story in this book, who willingly showed up imperfectly. They took risks, they opened themselves up to feedback, and they made racial equity a priority in their professional practice. When they received public feedback on their imperfections, they stayed open to it, worked to learn more, sought to make amends, and did not run away from the feedback. But in some cases, their places of work, unable to tolerate the discomfort of imperfection and the messiness of racial stress, actively worked against community healing by taking a legal stance, dictating that they avoid interpersonal repair, and telling them to say nothing while publicly distancing the institution from them. Treated as irremediably tarnished by their errors, they became persona non grata in their own communities.

I write this because our desire for perfection is not just an individual flaw; it's a collective problem that stands in the way of growth. Again, People of Color and Native people need White people to stop acting through biased lenses altogether. That should always be the immediate intention and goal. At the same time, that is not always possible. But when White people are willing to learn from their mistakes, make repairs, and be transformed by the experience, we become even more the people that antiracism asks us to be.

Throughout this book, we will address how White people can support other White people through difficult but inevitable learning moments for the good of racial equity. And we will also address how we can deal with the discomfort of falling and recovering for ourselves. For as much as we want to help other White people walk an antiracist path, the primary thing we have control over is ourselves. We need to hold ourselves accountable and develop the skills to accept the accountability that others offer us.

Myth 3: We Need to "Win" by Competing With One Another

Another aspect of white supremacist culture that shows up in how White people interact with one another is competition—the idea that there's enough room for only one White person to be antiracist. I still remember a moment in graduate school when, in our White antiracist learning space meeting, my friend Sue suddenly sat up straight and said, "I just realized something! It's not about me being the best antiracist White person in the room. It's about ending racism! It's not about me at all." The rest of us looked at her, stunned, and then laughed. She was one of the most humble, self-reflective, thoughtful, and supportive members of our group. The realization that even she had felt a need to compete was revealing, and it shone a light on a tendency we each had felt.

In that moment, she named the predictable and toxic dynamic in which White people compete against one another to be more antiracist, thereby making the air of antiracist group dynamics less friendly, less desirable, and less welcoming. A White person actually blocks other White people from joining an antiracist path when their impulse is to earn praise for being the one who shines—the one who "gets it." Even when we can rein in this impulse, too many White people are quicker to see racism in other White people than in themselves. We are quicker to ask, "But we're the choir; how do change those other, more racist White people?" Stopping this competitive mindset allows us to look at ourselves, how racism lives in us, what else we can do to change, and how we might practice antiracism with a vigor and vulnerability that will encourage and support other White people to take part in the process. When millions of White people are drawn to an antiracist path and begin to use their personal locus of control to dismantle the racial hierarchy in the systems within which they work, systemic racism begins to crumble. That is why every one of us is needed. That is why the winner of *The Best White Person* award is irrelevant.

The competitive mindset also plays into the white-savior dynamic, which so many of us learned as children. I can still remember watching Michele Pfeiffer's character in the movie *Dangerous Minds* roll into a school full of Children of Color and turn it around with her wit and charm. I wanted to be Michele Pfeiffer as Ms. Johnson. I wanted to be a teacher who saved Children of Color, just like her. I learned early in college to be critical of my inner white-savior desires, but if I'm telling the truth, it probably still connects to why I do what I do today. But as I learn to see and name that tendency toward Ms. Johnson-ism, or white saviorism, I can continuously bring myself back to my reasons for practicing antiracism that are not about looking bad-ass in a leather jacket or saving all the Black and Brown kids. It's about doing my part to help create a just, equitable, antiracist world; enlisting other White people in the effort; and trying to get out of the way of Black and Brown people so that they can live and shine as they were born to do.

It is in White antiracist learning spaces that we learn how to be allies with other White people, rather than just friends. Friends are people we get together with, talk to, laugh with, and care about. Allies are the same. But allies also share our antiracist goals. Allies hold us and themselves accountable to a larger intention of walking an antiracist path.

I still remember taking a walk with a White colleague in graduate school and telling her that I had unwittingly called a Black student by another Black student's name. I was embarrassed, annoyed, and angry that I had done this. I knew it was a hurtful microaggression, and I needed to talk through it. This friend said to me, "Oh, Ali. You're not racist. You're the least racist person I know. You don't need to worry about that." In my head, I realized that this friend was not yet an ally. That's not to label her or make her wrong. But in that moment, I needed an ally who could hold me in loving accountability rather than dismiss my concerns. Learning to identify my allies helps me discern whom to call when I need to be held accountable.

Eleonora and our antiracist learning group became my allies. When I told them about the same microaggression, they said things like, "Ouch. I hate it when that happens. I've done that before. It hurts when that happens. Tell us more about it. What was going on at the time? What are your relationships like with those two students? What did you do? What do you wish you'd done?" They gave me space to process, to explore, to better understand the bias that led to that moment, and to help me consider how to prevent the same thing from happening in the future. They helped me look at my bias squarely without hiding it or sweeping it under the rug.

When White people are my allies, they provide the scaffolding that helps me grow beyond my current possibilities. When I was leading a workshop recently, a participant reached out privately and lovingly to tell me how much she was learning but also to offer me feedback on using the term *blind spot*, which she understood—from disability rights advocates—to be an ableist term. Initially I bristled at her feedback, but she had written with such generosity that I was able to write her back to tell her honestly that I had bristled, explaining that I think of a blind spot as something that all people experience when we're driving. She wrote back that she agreed, yet she had heard multiple people from the disability rights community say it was offensive. In this back and forth, I was able to sort through some of my own resistance, get more information from her, process my thinking, and ultimately decide that

I should reconsider my language. (I now try to use the term *oversight*.) If she had simply corrected me or shamed me, or if she had brought it up publicly, I may not have been able to process it in the same way. I think of her as an ally because she allowed me to sit with my discomfort, voice it, process it, and then integrate something new into my thinking. Her gift was staying in relationship with me through it all.

Being an ally to White people is never about cutting others down for their shortcomings. It's about holding them accountable to their antiracist and social justice intentions—and doing so in a way that helps them stretch in the direction in which they hope to grow.

Myth 4: It's Better to Think, Rather Than Feel, About Racism

Janet Helms (2020), a Black psychologist who studies White racial identity development, says that for White people to be effective antiracists, we need to grow beyond a stage called *pseudo-independence*, in which White people tend to *think* about racism, rather than *feel* about it.

We need to grow beyond this stage to be antiracist, yet I find myself stuck in it time and time again. It is one of my growing edges—a place where I need to keep putting time and energy. From the inside, I find it hard to know the difference between thinking and feeling, but every once in a while, it becomes glaring. I can still remember sitting in a research meeting with Eleonora and receiving a text. At the time, we were working with the same school, and a teacher from that school had included both of us on a group text. The text was a picture from that morning's Halloween parade. One of the teachers marching in the parade had worn a noose around his neck. When the picture showed up on my phone, I said, "Oh no. What an idiot." Eleonora, on the other hand, said, "I feel like I've been punched in the gut." In the heat of that moment, it occurred to me that Eleonora was in her feelings, while I was not. I was only able to see that this was an unthinking action and to predict that people were going to be hurt and angry—but I did not feel hurt and angry myself.

I contrast this moment with another conversation I had with a parent of my daughter's friend, who said she had heard that one of the adults working with the older children in our community organization was creepy. "Creepy, how?" I asked. She said, "Creepy, as in with girls." In that moment, I could feel my blood turn to ice. I felt the cold spread through my body, and almost simultaneously, I could hear my thoughts turn to planning an escape: "We need to move. We need to sell our house. We need to quit that organization. My child will not work with a creepy adult."

When I reflect on these two moments, I can see how the second moment, which included a potential threat to my own child, created a physiological reaction in me that moved me to action. We didn't end up leaving, but I did investigate the claims, which turned out to be connected to a former coach who didn't work at the organization anymore. But what stayed with me was the fact that I had felt my blood run cold in a way that it hadn't really since college, when I sat through a graphic presentation on how to stay safe from rape. How many times had I heard stories from People of Color and Native people about the trauma that they have experienced in schools, and never once had my blood run cold in that same way? I don't say that to judge my initial numbness; judgment only makes this harder. Yet recognizing my reaction helps me understand my action or inaction with regard to other aspects of racism. If I really felt the terror of racism in my body, as a physiological reaction, the urgency and immediacy of doing something about it would be real to me in an entirely new way. If I cannot *feel* about racism, I cannot engage in deep, empathetic responsive action.

This tendency of White people to think our way into understanding racism—to intellectualize it or see it as theoretical—has many roots. Like many other White people, I learned about racism through theory. As I described in the introduction, I first learned about racism in an African American literature class. And while my Black classmates shared some of their own experiences with racism, most of the class was focused on the words and experiences of authors, many from another era, such as James Baldwin, Richard Wright, Toni Morrison, Jamaica Kincaid, and Audre Lorde. When I hear people criticize White people for being so theoretical about racism, I often wonder, "How else could we possibly be?" It's a necessary critique, but it seems as if it should be less of a criticism and more of a statement of fact: White people are theoretical about racism, in part because they first learn about it as theory. Very few White people experience racism directly, overtly, and viscerally in the way that People of Color and Native people experience it. We live in a deeply segregated society in which most of our relationships are with people of racial backgrounds similar to our own. With the exception of White people who are in intimate relationships with People of Color or Native people through partnerships, marriages, stepparents, children, and friendships, very few White people even get exposed to the rawness of lived racism. Very few White people even know what it's like to be disrespected by a police officer, an experience that is common and well known among most People of Color and Native people. Beyond that, when we do get to hear how People of Color and Native people are affected by racism, we are primed to conjure explanations that make the victim the "other" or "at fault," which means that we don't get proximal in ways that would actually make us empathize.

If we can't feel, we don't have much chance of taking action. So what steps can we take to feel more about race? The first is simply recognizing when we are being led by thoughts rather than by feelings. We can *track* our reactions internally. *Tracking* is a group-dynamics term that means *noticing without judgment*. We can notice that we are thinking about race rather than feeling about it. Then we can push ourselves to feel about it by asking ourselves and one another, "What if that were me or a loved one?"

Sometimes I notice myself start to feel something as I read a troubling headline in the newspaper, and then I numb the feeling by continuing to scroll on to other, often equally horrifying, headlines. People have created a term for this: *doomscrolling*. It's bad for our health for so many reasons, but it's particularly effective at numbing us from any individual story. When I'm reading the paper, I try to stop after one story—to write down the names of the people in the story, to find a few reports on that particular story. I do this particularly when Black people are victimized by police violence. But I also do it with COVID stories or with healthcare policies—racialized and emotional things that we often numb ourselves to. In this way, I can become emotionally invested in a person's story, rather than just vaguely aware of the general reality.

Eleonora's work throughout this book will introduce you to other exercises that will support a shift from exclusively *thinking* about racism to *feeling* about it, too. It is the feeling that ultimately generates both motivation and direction for action.

Myth 5: Race Is Real and Biological; Racial Differences Are Immutable

The final myth that gets in the way of antiracism—whether it's White people or People of Color and Native people practicing it—is the idea that race is real and biological and that racial differences are immutable. This is a problem of paradigm. It's a paradox. We can't recognize and intervene with racism if we can't talk about race. Yet race is not real, nor is it biological. Historically, it has been based on biological features, such as skin color and hair texture (albeit in subjective and inconsistent ways), but it's fundamentally a made-up category.

This is a confusing idea, but we have to name and expose this myth if we are going to build an antiracist society. Foundational to white supremacist thinking is the idea that race is real, genetic, and biological. White supremacy holds that White people are biologically and intellectually superior to People of Color and Native people. It holds that Black people are biologically inferior to White people but somehow genetically wired to be athletes or manual laborers. Scientists and anthropologists have debunked this hierarchy. Researchers have demonstrated that we are usually more genetically similar to people who are technically categorized as other "races" than we are to others in our own racial group (Mukhopadhyay et al., 2013). There is no biological justification for the notion of race (Goodman et al., 2003). The paradox is that we have to use the notion of race to undergird antiracist thinking and action, even though antiracist action ultimately requires that we abolish said categories. James Baldwin wrote, "We find ourselves bound, first without, then within, by the nature of categorizations" (as cited in Glaude, 2020, p. 92). How did Baldwin navigate this paradox, given that he was a scholar and narrator of the impact of race and racism? Baldwin's biographer writes, "Black identity politics, for Baldwin, was only a means to an end. They could never be an end in itself because a certain acceptance of blackness sprung the trap, imprisoning us in the very categories we needed to escape" (Glaude, 2020, p. 92).

The creation of "race" involved putting people into boxes based on skin color, then assigning value, rights, access to resources, and opportunity based on those boxes. People in the "Black" box were not only denied rights; they were denied humanity. They were deemed enslavable; they and their children could not own even themselves. Those in the "White" box were given political rights, humanity, access to jobs, access to their White progeny, education, and mobility, to name a few.

One way to see the absurdity of race is to look at two states in the Jim Crow South. In one state, a person had to be one fourth Black to be considered Black. In the neighboring state, a person had to be one sixteenth Black to be considered Black. What this meant is that a person could literally cross state lines and turn from being considered Black to being considered White. And in that designation, established by the state, lay the legally enforced rights and mandates of the person's place in the racial caste system. If they were White, that meant they had access to an entirely different array of jobs, schools, stores, safety, protection from police, public office, jury duty, voting, and so on.

Because of the socially constructed nature of race, Black writer and public intellectual Ta-Nehisi Coates, author of *Between the World and Me* and *The Water Dancer*, does not write about *White Americans* but rather *those Americans who believe that they are White* (Coates, 2015, p. 6). I have always struggled with this framing, not because it is untrue, but because I actually think most White people don't even consciously identify with being White or see themselves as part of a racial group called "White." I think part of bringing White people into an antiracist consciousness requires that we first learn that we are White, that we've been framed as such by social and legal structures that confer advantages on us because of that framing, and that we have a responsibility to challenge racism because of it. Then we have to remember that we're not actually White; we're just human beings stuck in a society that insists on putting people into racial boxes. At this time in history and geography, we are in the White box.

The fact that those racial boxes are constructed and based on false-hoods does not mean that we can ignore them. Many social construc-tions in our society affect us, even though they are actual fictions. Take Santa Claus, for example. It does not matter whether you believe in him—or even whether you like him—you cannot raise a child in the United States without answering questions about Santa. He may be a social construction, a story that you tell, but that does not mean he goes away if you don't want to perpetuate the myth or if you don't cel-ebrate Christmas. Capitalism is also a social construction. It's not an economic framework found in nature. We made it up. We regulate it (sometimes); we set the rules; we decide what happens when you break them. But just because it's a social construction doesn't mean that a person can choose to opt out of it. Similarly, the social construction of race and racism have been well integrated into our society—and into our bodies. Ignoring them will not make them go way.

Moving Away From the Myths

We start moving away from these myths by facing the realities:

Reality 1: We cannot challenge racism if we are colorblind. Talking about race is not racist.

Reality 2: We will make mistakes, and we need to learn to fall and recover quickly so that we can learn from them and keep going.

Reality 3: We are interconnected and interdependent. We can go further together than we can alone. Placing value on teamwork, cooperation, and community is antithetical to white supremacy.

Reality 4: When we acknowledge our feelings—as well as our minds—and when we connect deeply and empathetically with People of Color and Native people, how to take action becomes clear.

Reality 5: Race is a social construction. We are often more alike across racial differences than we are like others in our racial group.

When we find ourselves—or one another—unwittingly embracing any of these myths, sometimes our reaction can be further shame or exclusion: "How dare you bring white supremacist myths or styles into this antiracist space?! We're trying to be antiracist, and you are poisoning our efforts. How can we end racism when you can't let that stuff go?" The problem with this reaction is this: white supremacy is the language we speak. It's the *only* language we speak. Accidentally using a word or phrase in that language is inevitable. The project we are engaged in is not to learn a new language but to *create* a new language that has never been spoken before. When we find ourselves using the language of white supremacy, or operating out of these myths, we need to put aside the shock, anger, and judgment and just notice it. If we have been successful at helping other White people climb onto an antiracist path, a small noticing—and an offer to help brainstorm alternative ways to move forward—should be sufficient for helping White people move beyond it. Shaming one another out of a sense of competition or a belief that we should be perfect means that we are continuing to uphold white supremacy by playing into its mythology.

Note

1. The dynamic of perfectionism as an aspect of white supremacy has been explored by researcher Tema Okun (2020) in her highly circulated piece "White Supremacy Culture."

INTERNAL WORK

To Act, You Must Pause

. . . .

In some senses, all antiracist action starts with a pause. There's no need for the pause, of course, if you haven't started yet. That would be like practicing patience when no one bothers you. You must practice pausing while engaging in antiracist activities and conversations, so that you can open yourself up to learning from—and building on—each of those experiences.

Pausing does not mean inaction, nor bypassing, nor giving up. Think of Thich Nhat Hanh, the Vietnamese Buddhist monk and peace activist who nominated Dr. Martin Luther King Jr. for the Nobel Peace Prize. Throughout his life, he was able to harness tremendous power, insight, and courage for causes he believed in. He was exiled and risked his life multiple times for speaking truth to power. By today's measure of activism, in which we have come to value speed and boisterous displays of competence as a sign of commitment, he would come up wanting. If you look at any video of him speaking, walking, or otherwise engaging with audiences, you will see the intensely slow and deliberate fashion in which he paused between words and actions long enough to bring his full presence to them. Sometimes the pauses are so long that they are uncomfortable to watch, even for me, a therapist who has been trained to hold space for silence. But by bringing his full presence, Thich Nhat Hanh made it possible to challenge the systems of oppression that surrounded him. Slowing down in the moment actually allows for maximum learning and impact.

How do we pause while engaging in antiracist action? The trickiest part is knowing when it's time to pause, because it requires us first to notice when our systems begin to rev up a defensive (fight, flight, or freeze) response. This is a conceptually easy proposition but a very challenging one in practice. Here is where most of us get tripped up. Remember that you will feel compelled to believe the "danger" signals that your body alerts you to, and you will absolutely want to follow them. The gravitational pull toward fight, flight, or freeze is tremendous. So how can we work with that? In my own practice, I have found it useful to rely on three habits.

Habit 1: The first habit is grounded in the assumption that no matter how many times I engage in conversations about race or act in antiracist ways, I will still continue to experience the surge of fight, flight, or freeze energy, even in minor interactions. So I am always on the lookout for such surges to occur.

Habit 2: The second habit involves telling myself[1] that a flight, fight, or freeze response is useful only in truly dire and life-threatening situations—for example, when I need my adrenaline to help me quickly and instinctively jump back on the curb when a car is fast approaching. At all other times, I am better off overriding that response so that I can enlist my full thinking and empathizing capacities. By assuming that a full-out fight, flight, or freeze response is not necessary, I rebalance the overpowering gravitational pull toward reactivity and defensiveness.

Taken together, these first two habits make it a lot more likely for me to notice when my body is initiating an unnecessary fight, flight, or freeze reaction that needs to be paused, instead of followed.

Habit 3: The third habit entails identifying on an ongoing basis the defensive styles my nervous system tends to utilize, as well as exactly what behaviors I tend to manifest when I experience each style. While each of us employs all three fight, flight, or freeze strategies in different circumstances, we tend to gravitate toward one of them more than the others at various times in our lives and in given contexts. Earlier in my racial identity development,[2] I had a strong preference for the fighting response, to prove to myself and others that I was a "good" person and a "worthy antiracist ally." To this day, I still feel a considerable pull to flight, especially when my heartfelt antiracist efforts are rebuked or criticized. My flight behaviors are often accompanied by a private muttering of "I give up!" or "You do it, then, if you think you can do better!" As I have accrued more practice and experience with antiracist conversations and actions, I have been able to mitigate both of these styles, so I now tend to freeze when I get stirred up.

My freeze reaction is not subtle. I am very rarely out of words, but in these moments, I become speechless. I first noticed this reaction a few years back in situations when I was teaching, especially at times when I felt the room suddenly "go cold" without knowing what had just happened or how to address it. More recently, I have drawn a blank multiple times when some of the People of Color and Native people in my life have shared their

pain and outrage at the *macro*aggressions they have increasingly experienced during the Trump presidency and its aftermath, and all the more
during the pandemic. As a therapist, theoretically I know how to sit with
and listen to pain. Even then, by virtue of knowing myself to be complicit
with white supremacy (as a White person) and of feeling helpless to prevent it, I freeze—and as I freeze, I also begin to panic because I know that
I'm freezing! Both reactions are powerful and immediate. But knowing that
about myself is tremendously helpful. As soon as I notice what's happening, I can begin to coach myself, reminding myself to take a few breaths,
slow down, and listen more attentively and with my full heart. I may be
more or less effective interpersonally in any one of those moments, but I
always learn from them: to listen better, to witness with more presence, to
recognize more opportunities to disrupt white supremacy by hearing how
People of Color and Native people experience it, to better offer support,
and to know when to appropriately share my own process.

No matter the form it takes, it is harder than it might sound to slow
down in these ways. Whether it's the grief and helplessness I feel in
realizing I don't have the power to end white supremacy and its horrific
impact by myself or all at once, or the guilt and shame at having been
less than perfect in an interaction, my body's impulse to retreat into
safety is strong. And that's exactly what motivates me to intentionally
train for these moments.

How Can I Train so That I'm Ready to Pause?

You'll have plenty of opportunities to practice noticing your fight, flight,
or freeze reactions in the moment. The *graduated exposure* exercise
described in the Internal Work section for Chapter 1 gives you a structured way to hone this skill. It might be helpful to keep in mind that
the particular forms your flight, fight, or freeze reactions take in your
life can differ greatly depending on the circumstance. For example, after
two decades of working with students and training fellow clinicians, I
have become quite comfortable speaking about uncomfortable topics in
virtually any setting where I am the presenter. But recently I attended
an antiracist weekend workshop as a participant, and it didn't take long
to realize how "out of shape" I was at sitting with the discomfort of not
being the teacher. While I always enjoy having the opportunity to be
a student and learn from other professionals, I found myself becoming deeply distressed when a White man's fight strategy manifested

as pedantic "mansplaining" at the presenter, and again when a White woman embodied her flight strategy as helplessness. My distress rating on a 10-point scale was easily an 8 or 9 for each instance! I was immediately flooded with anger at the two participants. I felt an acute urge to protect the presenter (a Person of Color) in true white-savior style and prove myself as ignorant to everybody there. In the midst of my internal sense of urgency, I lost all perspective about the presenter's expertise, agency, and resilience. I didn't consider the fact that both participants were investing time and energy in attending an antiracism workshop, were fully engaged in the conversation, and had great potential for learning. In the moment, I didn't recollect the numerous and even recent times when I had exhibited the same reactions as these participants did in both overt and subtle ways, and I didn't stop to consider what stereotypical White behaviors I was exhibiting through my own reactivity. In reality, I had a lot to learn from these two participants and everyone else's engagement with the conversation. But my fight reaction was overpowering and pulled me completely out of my ability to think and empathize—and therefore learn—in that moment, let alone remain in connection with White people I could have potentially supported.

Sometimes we realize that we are in fight, flight, or freeze mode but can't get out of it nonetheless. I was definitely overwhelmed by my fight reaction during the workshop. However, I had trained enough in grounding practices to at least pause, watch myself become intensely reactive, and do nothing. If nothing else, I didn't make things worse. After the workshop ended, surprised by how off-balance I had felt, I made a point to work with those incidents by doing the graduated exposure technique described in the Internal Work section for Chapter 1. Now, I will share a few grounding practices that will keep you steady when you realize that your nervous system is overrun by a fight, flight, or freeze response.

Strengthening Your Antiracist Practice

Ease the Grip of the Stress Response: Grounding Practices

These three practices will help you strengthen your capacity to release your nervous system's defensive grip. The beauty of these grounding practices is that they are quick, simple, free, available to you at any moment, and no one knows you are accessing them. I suggest you pick one of these practices each day and try it a few times, for one to two minutes at a time. None of these practices is better than the others; it's just a matter of preference. Once you have tried all three, decide which one you will continue to practice and make your own. Again, these are muscles you train outside of crisis moments, so that you can more easily access them to re-ground yourself when you need it.

Practice 1: Body Scan

Take one to two minutes to slowly mentally scan your body, from the top of your head to the tip of your toes: head, neck, shoulders, arms, torso, pelvis, thighs, calves, feet. Simply notice what each part feels like. You don't have to change anything about it at all. Simply notice whatever sensations might be there, bringing an attitude of curiosity and care to each part. Tell yourself that you have nothing else to do and nowhere else to be for those one to two minutes, but notice how your body feels.

Practice 2: Engaging Your Parasympathetic Response

Try two or three of the following (whichever you prefer) for about 20 to 30 seconds each:

- Focus right in front of you, then allow your peripheral vision to take over, by focusing on what you can see on your sides while still looking forward.

- Go to a window or outside, and look up at the sky, the top of trees, or far away at the horizon.

- Place your attention on your body as a whole, while sitting upright or standing tall in a relaxed fashion.

- Picture in your mind's eye your favorite nature scene (real or imagined), and let your mind rest on it.

You will know that your parasympathetic system (responsible for feeling calm and grounded) is kicking in when you feel your mouth watering, a yawn coming up, or a deeper breath emerging spontaneously.

Practice 3: Belly Breathing

Put one hand on your belly, and notice how your hand moves as your belly expands with air. Inhale and exhale slowly but

(Continued)

(Continued)

easefully (anywhere from three to six seconds for the inhale, making the exhale one to two seconds longer than the inhale). Try to breathe mostly with your belly. Repeat for one to two minutes.

Remember that sometimes the difference between acting in service of liberation and remaining complicit with oppressive forces will be determined by our ability to take a single, well-trained, intentionally placed breath.

Notes

1. I say that I *tell myself* this, rather than I *believe* this, because I can't be certain that this is true in all cases for all people.

2. Ali will describe a model of White racial identity in Chapter 5.

What White People Learn About Race

....

CHAPTER 3

By refusing to pass on the trauma we inherited, we help heal the world.

—Resmaa Menakem (2017, p. 83)

How did we learn how to be White? How did we grow up in a multiracial society and remain so unfamiliar with the realities faced by People of Color and Native people? How did so many of us grow up ill-equipped to challenge racism? This chapter will help readers recognize their socialization so that they can begin to undo it. It will also help parents recognize unhealthy messages they may be giving to their own children.

To start, I will share common messages that White youth tend to receive at home about race and racism. These are messages we collected in a small qualitative study[1] of White families. While this study was local (suburban Philadelphia) and time bound (2010–2012), the conversations that emerged have helped us see commonalities in what White people learn about race. In the years since, as we've met with other White families across the United States, we have found the same themes coming up time and again. Everywhere we go, these themes resonate with White people, both in terms of what they are teaching their own children *and* what they themselves learned as children.

Common Themes
Being White Is Meaningless

When we asked White teenagers how they identified racially, most struggled with this question. Some said they identified with being Italian or Irish or Jewish more than they identified with being White. Being Irish meant something; being White was akin to nothing. Some said they weren't White; they were just "normal." Many parents also said that it wasn't Whiteness they identified with but all the other parts of their identity—architect, Christian, athlete, and so forth. Overwhelmingly, the fact of their Whiteness was meaningless to the youth and their families.

Be Colorblind; Never Think in Racial Terms

The idea of colorblindness came up in almost every interview. The theme was so prevalent that one of the academic papers we wrote on this research was titled "Training for Colorblindness." Colorblindness was one of the few concepts that White parents adhered to as an overt strategy for socializing their children around race. Essentially, they taught their children to judge people by their character and by their actions, rather than by the color of their skin. Notably, they did so because they thought it was the right and fair thing to do, what they were *supposed* to do. In the meantime, by focusing on colorblindness, they taught their children not to talk about race and not to develop competencies for navigating a multiracial society.

Focus on Values

Families of White youth emphasized that they did not judge people based on skin color but rather focused on values. They went on to mention their own values, including the value of hard work. They also named values that align closely with White cultural norms, such as individualism and competition. Some of these families justified the fact that they weren't friends with Families of Color—or that they didn't live in more racially diverse neighborhoods—because they simply did not share the same values as People of Color. It was not clear how they knew what values they shared or didn't share, because they didn't know the People of Color they were referring to. In some cases, the interviewees seemed to be extrapolating the values of Black people or Latinx people as a group based on one person they had interacted with at work or on the basis of racial stereotypes.

Don't Be an Overt Racist

Parents emphasized to their children that they should not be racist. But their conception of racism was very narrow. They were talking only about individual-level racism, such as using racial slurs or excluding somebody based on race. They were clear that they did not want their children to be hurtful or to offend. One mother, quite concerned, said to her son in the middle of the interview, "I just have to know. Are you . . . racist?" Her son, matching her intensity, responded, "No, Mom, no!" Both took a breath and looked visibly relieved.

Racism Is in the Past

Students in our study felt that racism is a phenomenon of the past and that our society naturally and spontaneously gets more equitable over time. They felt that racism lessens, not because anyone is doing something about it, but because there is a natural evolution toward more fairness. These teens came of age during the presidency of Barack Obama, and they felt that his presidency was evidence that there is no more racism. This has obviously changed, after four years with Donald Trump as president and much more overt and visible racist actions showcased in the media. But it underscores the potential complacency that youth—and many adults—feel when we have visible markers of racial progress.

Assimilation-Based Integration Is Best

Many parents felt that skin color was not an issue in and of itself. They were fine with their children being in friendships with Children of Color—but only if those children conformed to standards that the White families had adopted. In other words, they could be in community together as long as People of Color were largely assimilated into White middle-class cultural and linguistic styles. They told us that it's not Black people who scare them—it's Black teens who wear their pants hanging low and who live in certain areas. They were quick to add that they would be afraid of White kids who exhibited the same movements and actions.

For Young Children, Multicultural Literature; for Teens, Youth-Led Socialization

Many of the parents we talked to were intentional about reading multi-cultural literature to their children when they were young. As their children got older, however, the parents tended to have less control over what the children read or watched. We heard from multiple families that they believed that, with teens, they were supposed to talk about race only when their child brought it up.

Just Do It (Integration), and Don't Talk About It (Race)

Finally, there were a couple of parents in our study who sent their children to "racially integrated" schools and figured that their children would get what they needed essentially through osmosis. By being members of a "racially integrated" community, the parents assumed their children would know how to be a part of and contribute to that community without needing particular skills or knowledge—and without confronting the biases and stereotypes they had absorbed from the media-rich environment around them.

The Problem With These Predominant Themes

Ultimately, the parents in our study wanted to raise their children in a world where race didn't matter. They knew—and they told us in their parent-only interviews—that race did matter. But they didn't think it should. Subsequently, they acted around their children as if race didn't matter. The message that their children seemed to get from this socialization is that race *actually* doesn't matter. This was a huge disconnect. The parents knew race mattered but didn't want it to. By acting like it didn't, they conveyed the message that, in fact, race does not matter.

The White youth in our study were part of families who were willing to let researchers come to their homes with video cameras to talk about race for three hours. These tended to be White people who believed that racism was wrong. The parents often walked us to the door after the interviews and asked, "Did we get it right? What *are* we supposed to teach our kids about race? We didn't realize there *was* something we should teach our kids about being White. What is it?" We left them on their front stoops, promising to send them the article when we finished the research, acutely aware of their desperate desire to *get it right*. There are other White families who would not consent to such an interview. But so many White families we have talked to over the past decade are eager to know how to raise antiracist White children but totally unsure how to go about it.

I will now revisit each of these themes and explore how these methods of racial socialization interfere with the essential work of being consciously antiracist. These messages, in other words, prevent us from developing racial competence or the skills we need for navigating racial stress.

Being White Isn't Meaningless

The "meaninglessness" of Whiteness that so many youth expressed is echoed in the research of Dr. Derald Wing Sue (2004a), who interviewed White people about being White in his study "What Is White?" In the study, a 42-year-old businessman told Sue, "Frankly, I don't know what you're talking about! . . . I'm Italian, not White." A 34-year-old White female stockbroker told him, "I don't know; I've never thought about it." A 65-year-old White male construction worker said, "That is a stupid question." From his research, Sue determined that a large percentage of White people (1) find the question perplexing, (2) would rather not think about their Whiteness, and (3) are uncomfortable or react negatively to being labeled as White.

Because being White is a mainstream racial identity, it makes sense that it doesn't resonate with many White people. People who are heterosexual rarely consider their sexual orientation very deeply because it is a mainstream identity—widely affirmed, expected, and reinforced by the majority of society. Yet part of being an antiracist White person requires an acknowledgment that we live in a society that racializes all its members. White people are racialized, too. The teen who said he was just "normal" was unfortunately quite accurate about how Whiteness gets framed in our society. He wasn't wrong that Whiteness is often seen as a norm against which People of Color and Native people are found wanting. Yet for him to develop an antiracist practice or identity, he needs to see Whiteness as a thing and recognize that the framing of Whiteness as an unnamed "normal" is part of the problem.

Being Colorblind Perpetuates Racism

The end result of youth being socialized to be colorblind is that they can't talk clearly about race. When it came to the topic of race, the youth in our study struggled to know what to say and how to say it. As they ingested ideas about race and racial groups from the society around them, they had nobody to talk with about it, no one to help them process their thinking. When asked why his AP English class was all-White, for example, one youth struggled to find a non-racist explanation for racial disparity. "I don't know," he said, "maybe the other kids aren't as interested in academics." Without a parent or teacher helping him consider systemic explanations for racial disparity, he arrived at a hypothesis that blames the individual students affected by systemic and historical racism.

The irony of the notion of colorblindness is that children are bombarded by racist explanations for the racial inequality they see around them. Because they have no space for disconfirming these explanations and are encouraged to keep quiet, they can only absorb and internalize the mainstream narratives of racism. In the Internal Work section following this chapter, Eleonora describes the psychological impact of these narratives, which unconsciously prime us to then collect even more information that confirms our biases, in a self-reinforcing circle.

Colorblindness is a strategy that is often employed by people who are very well intentioned. They don't want race to have such an outsized impact on our society, and they certainly don't want to contribute to the problem. As a result, they hope that by pretending not to see race, things will change. The mindset is one of simply being kind to everyone.

But there are more than a few problems with colorblindness, including the following:

1. Race does not just make a person a target of racism; it often plays a role in shaping people's identity, community, and family. If you are colorblind, you can't honor and understand how a person's racial background is part of who they are.

2. Our society racializes everybody. So while bias is part of the human experience, racial bias is part of the experience in

the United States. If we are being colorblind, we can't see or acknowledge the racial bias in ourselves and others—and thus can't change it. This means, ironically, that our bias will actually have more control, not less, in our relationships, interactions, and decisions. Despite our best intentions, aiming to be non-racist (instead of antiracist) simply excuses White people from doing anything about racism and lets white supremacy stand uninterrupted.

3. We can't fight racism if we don't acknowledge race. Colorblindness silences racial talk and makes it impossible to develop an antiracist practice or lens.

4. At the national level, colorblindness in the U.S. Congress or the U.S. Supreme Court makes it impossible to rectify centuries of race-based discriminatory policies. Legislation involving race is seen as racist if it does not adhere to the rules of colorblindness. Cases get thrown out because the Supreme Court justices don't want to treat groups differently based on skin color, when that is precisely what needs to happen to redress historical disparities.

Focusing Only on Values Misses the Point

Values in the United States are heavily racialized. Many people of all racial backgrounds believe that if you work hard, you get ahead. This is called *meritocracy*. As a corollary, many White people believe that if you are not getting ahead, it must be because you are not working hard. In fact, many People of Color and Native people work hard throughout their lives and do not get as far ahead as they would if they were White. This is due to several factors created by systemic oppression, including access to job networks, access to educational opportunities that come with access to resourced social networks, ability to get mortgages, ability to buy homes in communities where the homes will accrue in value, access to capital, the benefit of the doubt from law enforcement, and callbacks from job interviews. If we look at a Family of Color or a Native family and assume that they don't share the value of hard work because they don't have material success similar to a comparable White family, we would be wrong. In reality, because of racism, what each of us gets as a result of our hard work is rarely proportionate to our efforts.

Another heavily racialized value is that of individualism—the idea that the individual is the unit of primary value, rather than the family or the community, which is more common in Native communities and many Communities of Color. This value of individualism is connected to the value of competition, which suggests that the whole society is better off when we compete with one another and the "best" person wins. For the most part, our schools are set up in this way, as are many of our workplaces. Students and employees are encouraged to compete against—rather than uplift—one another.

To illustrate what collectivism and mutuality could look like in schools, my colleague who is Native[2] shares a story from one of her White student teachers. My colleague had taken a group of student teachers to observe a classroom in a reservation school. The children were all Native, and the head teacher was White. The teacher gave the students a math problem and asked them to raise their hands when they got the answer. The first child got the answer immediately, so quickly that the student teacher sitting near him assumed it must be wrong. Having completed the problem, the child stopped working and sat there, not raising his hand. The second child got the answer soon after. He too did not raise his hand. The first two boys noticed the third child struggling with the problem, so they leaned in to help him. When all three of them had the answer, they turned back to the student teacher and raised their hands.

My colleague uses this example to show how the value of competition in White culture is not the only way to motivate people, to run schools, or even to run a society. But it is so embedded in our cultural values that many of us don't even see it. We don't see how valuing competition might harm us or our children. We don't see how we judge and marginalize those who value the collective over the individual. We don't see what else is possible in terms of our own values. Sometimes we don't even recognize our values as things that we choose. And we don't see how a difference in values is not a deficit.

Ironically, from an evolutionary perspective, competition is not actually how we have come to thrive as a species—cooperation is (Christakis, 2019; Hare & Woods, 2020). Pure individualism is actually impossible for human beings. Overemphasizing individualism simply ends up hiding the ways in which we are globally interconnected and interdependent. It is the invisibility of our interdependence that makes it possible for people to believe they've made it on their own and that others should "pull themselves up by the bootstraps," too. Not acknowledging how deeply interconnected we are ends up being just another way of blaming individuals for their own predicaments, rather than pointing to systemic oppression as a root cause. It's a very effective smoke-and-mirrors strategy.

By Equating Racism With Individual Bad Behavior, We Overlook the Bigger Challenges

When we say, "Don't be racist," we are telling children (and other White people) what *not* to do. Most teachers and child development specialists will tell you that if you want a child to learn, instead of telling them what they shouldn't do, tell them what they *should* do. Only saying "Don't be racist," without any kind of positive guidance for being antiracist, leads to paranoia and denial as people try very hard not to be caught out as racist. It also encourages people not to risk behavior or make an attempt to say something antiracist, for fear that could be interpreted as racist. The focus on "Don't be racist" is particularly maddening in the context of the socialization we receive, in which we are implicitly taught racist narratives through our media, segregated in ways that make it difficult to have real relationships with one another across racial groups, and shamed for talking about race in any context. We are, in short, primed for racism while being told not to be racist.

Ibram X. Kendi (2020c) has said that denial is the heartbeat of racism in the United States. We persist and insist that we are not racist because we have been told, "Don't be racist." But denial doesn't move the needle. "Confession," Kendi offers, "is the heartbeat of antiracism." Learning how much we breathe the air of racism will help us learn to recognize the ways in which we inhale racist messaging, even without our consent. What if, instead of telling children not to be racist, we told them (and one another), "Learn to recognize racism inside yourself or around you," or "Practice an antiracist skill"?

Racism Is Not Just in the Past; It's Fully in Our Present-Day World, Too

Kendi (2020c) suggests that antiracist thinking requires challenging the notion that racism will inevitably diminish with time, while considering racism and antiracism as parallel trajectories that have always been at play in the history of the United States. Sometimes one is more visible than the other, but both are at work at all times. When we don't maintain this awareness, we are more susceptible to the mythology that we are a post-racial society. This is why the young people we interviewed thought racism was over when Barack Obama was elected president. It is why so many White people were shocked by the overt and visible racism that emerged during and after the 2016 election. We can't always see both paths, but they have both been there for 500 years.

When we feel despair at the state of the country, we have to remember that both paths are still there. To the extent that we have diminished racism in the United States, it's because of the people walking an antiracist path. Even when racism appears to be winning, we have to remember that it would be doing even more damage if the antiracist trajectory were not running through the present moment. That is why it is so valuable to see antiracism as an ongoing practice. We need to keep going, even when it looks like we cannot win. Winning might not be something that ever looks possible, but our efforts nevertheless contribute to the mitigation of racism in ways that matter deeply.

Assimilation-Based Integration Reaffirms Racial Bias

This is an idea that I internalized in my own childhood—the idea that Black communities are unsafe, and therefore it is only logical to fear and avoid them. Fear of Black communities and of Black people runs deep in our society, making it possible to find myriad justifications for such a rationalization. The desire to demonstrate non-racism by being in community with Black people and other People of Color and Native people who are assimilated to White ways of being is widespread. But while such contact could promote antiracism, it simultaneously reaffirms racist biases and racial exceptionalism when the only difference we actually welcome is a difference of pigmentation.

Part of being antiracist means working to accept and appreciate not just skin-color differences but differences in cultural styles, linguistic styles, clothing styles, names, relationships to time, and more. While racial groups are not monolithic cultural groups unto themselves, there are cultural styles that align with big segments of given racial groups because those groups often formed, grew, and developed in segregated communities, where ways of talking and acting developed locally. Scholars have researched the origins of Black Vernacular English (Baker-Bell, 2016),[3] for example, and have demonstrated that it is a grammatically consistent language with roots in the dialects of English to which enslaved people were exposed (Alim & Smitherman, 2012). The reason why it is denigrated today as "unprofessional" or "thuggish" is not because there is anything inherently wrong with it as a language but because Blackness itself is so widely denigrated in U.S. society (Baker-Bell, 2016). Working to appreciate diverse racial, cultural, and linguistic styles without judgment is part of being antiracist.

Youth-Led Socialization Overfocuses on Problems and Conflict

Apparently, there is some common wisdom that says we shouldn't bring up hard topics with teens; we should wait for them to bring them up. When we do this with regard to race, it means that we primarily talk about race during times of conflict. Teens told us that they didn't talk much about race with their parents, except when they would bring it up because something happened at school—someone used a racial slur, or there was a fight—or because they saw a race-related story on the news. What this means is that when youth *did* talk to their parents about race, they were doing two hard things at the same time: (1) talking about race and (2) processing conflict. Because they didn't talk about race on a regular basis, doing so was hard, and it was made more so by the conflation of race with problems. They had no skill or practice for just talking about race when tensions were low and there was no friction.

This particular phenomenon happens frequently in schools and other places of work. People do not talk about race on a regular basis because we are taught that silence about race reflects the values of politeness and respect. So when race comes up during times of strife, White people experience more discord, more tension, and more confusion than they might if they were well practiced in—and were told that they had permission for—talking about race. Racial talk is therefore experienced as problematic and associated with conflict, rather than illuminating or even just routine.

Pushing for "Integration" Without Also Talking About Race Doesn't Get Us Close to Integration

I put "integration" in quotes to honor the notion that true integration is not possible in such a racially segregated society. What our interviewees called "integration" anthropologist Ruth Frankenberg (1993), author of *White Women, Race Matters*, would call "quasi-integration," because even in schools that technically have people of different racial groups attending them, it's almost impossible to have true integration within the larger context of systemic racism. What Frankenberg wrote in 1993 still applies today:

> I qualify "integration" in this way because it seems to me that true integration would require a broader antiracist social context than existed in the United States [at the time in question]. It might involve, for example, that no area of physical space be marked by racial hierarchy and that racist ideas be entirely absent—a situation that is impossible in the United States as it is presently constituted. (p. 62)

Similarly, most schools in the United States are merely "quasi-integrated" (Frankenberg, 1993), not only because of the larger social context in which they exist but also because multiple mechanisms are often at work within schools that keep the student and family populations racially segregated. These include overt school-based practices such as academic tracking, as well as more subtle practices such as hiring few Teachers of Color and Native teachers or not affirming Black identity in the curriculum and beyond.

Additionally, White children who have not had exposure to students of racial backgrounds that are different from their own might ask objectifying questions or cast insults, not realizing the ways in which they have been socialized into stereotypical ideas of other groups. When White students lack racial competency in this way, they create trauma for Students of Color and Native students, which can lead to self-segregation. Students bring social norms from their own families and communities to school. If their families socialize only with people of similar racial backgrounds, they will likely unconsciously do the same. Children are navigating unconscious bias and untruths they may not even know they have while, at the same time, trying hard to avoid being racist. Unfortunately, sometimes this means that they default to not interacting with Peers of Color or Native peers, so as not to make a mistake. Ultimately, if we do not build racial competence, attending a "racially integrated" school or living in a "racially integrated" neighborhood or working in a "racially integrated" office is no guarantee that people will possess the skills they need to help make that multiracial community a healthy one.

Conclusion

For any White adult in our society who was raised with this type of socialization, you can begin to see how maddening it is. From a young age, we are implicitly and explicitly taught racist narratives. We are kept from having *real* relationships with one another across racial groups by a false distinction of "values," as well as residential segregation that is caused by public policy decisions. We are told it is racist to talk about race—and therefore have few opportunities to learn about racism or practice recognizing it. We are not taught what *to* do, but only what *not* to do. No wonder White people are confused.

In the next chapter, we will examine what healthy White racial socialization can look like, for both children and adults. What do White people need to learn to contribute to a world in which race truly does not matter—not because we're ignoring it or wishing it away but because we have confronted and dismantled racism in our society and in ourselves?

Notes

1. The research shared here comes from a research project that Eleonora and I conducted in collaboration with Dr. Howard Stevenson, Dr. Keisha Bentley-Edwards, and two colleagues who at the time were our graduate assistants, Rachel Shor and Shannon McClain (Bartoli et al., 2016). The study involved interviews with White families about how they racially socialize their children. For more detail on the study, see our article in the journal *Whiteness and Education*: https://doi.org/10.1080/23793406.2016.1260634.

    Here is some of the backstory to this project: In graduate school, I had the incredible opportunity to work with racial socialization scholar Dr. Howard Stevenson. Stevenson studies Black racial socialization and how families can socialize Black children so that they are prepared to navigate the racial stressors they encounter in school. At one point, he turned to me and said, "I have an idea for how you could connect our research to your interest in White people. Black students would have less racial stress in schools if their White peers showed up with racial socialization that prepared them to be antiracist. What do we know about White racial socialization? What can you find out?"

This invitation launched me into a multiyear study with Eleonora. At the time, I was newly pregnant with my first child, while Eleonora's daughter was three years old. We were both deeply invested in knowing how to talk about race with White kids because we wanted to know what to say to our own. We read lots of books in search of answers to this question, but they often suggested lifestyle changes that we had already made, such as "live in a racially diverse neighborhood" or "read books by Authors of Color." Very few said exactly what we should say and do with our children at different ages. None of them mentioned Whiteness. Both of us were highly critical of how we had been socialized around race, but we didn't really know what we *should* be saying and doing.

2. I don't share her Native nation affiliation to protect her identity.

3. Black English is also sometimes called African American Vernacular English.

INTERNAL WORK

Antidotes to White Supremacist Priming

Can We Truly Unlearn Racism?

Those of us who are White come to our antiracist paths with a great deal of practice in the ways of white supremacy. The good news is that we are never done learning. We endlessly receive new information and integrate it with the old. This takes no effort; it's just what the nervous system does. Even white supremacy doesn't indoctrinate us into racist beliefs and values only once. If that were the case, we would forget it, or new information would quickly disconfirm it. White supremacist logic permeates many aspects of our culture; its messages are reinforced daily at both the individual and structural levels. However well-meaning they may be on the surface, our norms, values, and laws, by and large, have the uncanny effect of supporting racist thinking and practices. So we are learning and relearning this framework every day.

This is why it didn't take long for me to learn all about it, albeit implicitly, when I immigrated to the United States as a young adult. I didn't have to attend a course on how to be racist, and I didn't enroll in special continuing education workshops to reinforce my racial biases. I simply had to try to function within U.S. society. The better I functioned as a White person, the safer and more effective I felt, and the more complicit I became with racist beliefs and practices. Simultaneously, I moved away from some Italian norms simply because they were not useful or were not rewarded in this new cultural context. For example, answering truthfully when asked "How are you?" was off-putting to my peers in the United States. I grew up answering this question truthfully as a way of connecting and normalizing the variability of human experience from day to day. But in the United States, answering in this way violates norms around personal boundaries and privacy, as it might raise questions about one's worthiness because of the belief in meritocracy. Getting to the point where I could give people the answer they wanted required a personal collision with some of the values I wanted to retain. It took me several years to smoothly reply, "Great, thank you! And how are you?" without then expecting a truthful answer in return. But in the end, that is what I learned to do.

So the question is not whether we can learn or unlearn information, change habits, or transform cultural practices. The question, rather, is one of identifying both the learning we are exposed to on a daily basis and the learning we want to purposefully expose ourselves to, even if it's not readily available. In the context of antiracism, at a minimum, we must learn to detect white supremacist teachings and practice ways to inoculate ourselves against them—given that we are bound to be continuously exposed to them.

While we may not be able to fully disentangle certain neural pathways and therefore altogether eliminate certain habits, we have an unlimited capacity for shaping and adding to our wiring. This means that we can lessen the strength of old habits and create new ones. The more we rehearse these new habits and skills, the more they literally become us (neurologically). When it comes to antiracism, however, embodying these new habits and skills requires serious practice and a concerted effort, given that we are training to become antiracist while remaining embedded in—and thus constantly re-socialized into—racist ways of thinking.

How to Counteract White Supremacist Priming

As counterintuitive as it might seem, we don't actually believe what we see. Rather, we *see what we believe*. This means that because racist narratives pervade the ways in which we think, they make us susceptible to only seeing data that confirm such narratives (aka *confirmation bias*). And most of this happens outside of our awareness.

Every time I think about the concept of priming, I think of a childhood riddle I learned growing up in Italy, which goes something like this:

1. Take a moment to consider: What is the color of this page?

2. Take another moment to consider: What do babies drink?

3. Now, repeat the word *silk* a few times out loud.

4. Finally, quickly answer this question: What do cows drink?

If you said "milk," it's not because you don't know that cows drink water; it's because your mind was primed to say "milk" by a series of overlapping associations. Our minds are primed all the time by the sensory information that surrounds us, by everything we are exposed to, consciously and unconsciously. This is why white supremacy doesn't have to provide specialized training to prime us for seeing data that confirm beliefs grounded in it. We do that instinctively and unconsciously simply by living in a racialized society.

To further illustrate this concept, I will share my own experience with counteracting priming as it relates to my heteronormative biases. I was raised in a heteronormative and heterosexist context. I didn't consciously question my biases until graduate school, where I developed close relationships with gay peers, worked closely with gay faculty, participated in research projects supporting the mental health of LGBTQ+ communities, and was trained to affirm clients' sexual orientations. At some point along the way, I became aware of my own bisexuality. Through all these experiences, it became clear to me that human beings embody a variety of sexual orientations, all of which are healthy and normative expressions of human relationships.

However, I was still embedded in cultures on both sides of the ocean deeply steeped in heteronormative and heterosexist beliefs; thus, I was constantly primed for them. Despite my conscious beliefs affirming the LGBTQ+ community, I still instinctively assumed that the people I met were in heterosexual relationships and found myself surprised when I learned someone was dating a person of the same sex. Knowledge and acceptance were apparently not enough to counteract my internalization of heteronormative messages. So I decided to actively train myself to assume that everyone I met was part of the LGBTQ+ community, until it became instinctive for me to genuinely not know the sexual orientation of anyone I had just met. Notice that I didn't end up assuming that everyone I met was part of the LGBTQ+ community; making a habit to assume this simply compensated for the recurrent heteronormative narratives I was exposed to and rebalanced my biased vision. (I will share more about exactly how I trained myself in the exercise at the end of this section.)

I repeated the same self-training after I moved to a neighborhood where families were more diverse than I had previously been exposed to (in terms of race, culture, religion, gender identity, sexual orientation, etc.). Once again, I actively trained myself to assume that anyone could be related to anyone else, regardless of their phenotypical appearance, until I found myself genuinely *un*surprised at any number of family compositions and relationships.

In the past few years, I have come to realize how powerful gender-binary norms still are in my own mind. So I am now in the process of training myself not to assume gender identity. I still notice my implicit biases emerge, especially when I hear a first name that has a culturally gendered connotation (e.g., Cyndi, who uses they/them pronouns). My mind is so trained to assume the gender implied by the name Cyndi that I run the risk of misgendering the person, even when I know perfectly well that they identify as nonbinary. This is similar to the task of reading the name of a color when it's printed on a background that is a different color (e.g., *red* on a green background). The cognitive challenge of bypassing the automatic assumption associated with a cue is called the Stroop effect. It's not that we can't overcome the challenge; we are just slower at it and make more mistakes at first. In this kind of task, accurate perception requires both concentration and practice, until new habits are formed.

So I keep practicing thinking of everyone as nonbinary. This is creating new associations, which at some point will become strong enough to inoculate me against constant exposure to gender-binary thinking. I can still feel the exhilaration of the first time my gut instinctively paused and wondered about someone's pronouns before assuming them! I have a long way to go, but I no longer feel quite like Sisyphus—the boulder is not rolling all the way down the hill anymore.

We must work in similar ways with our racist thinking. Identifying our biases and learning about how racism is infused into our cultural norms, values, and practices is an essential first step. But knowledge is not sufficient to eliminate our biases, which will continue to operate, albeit unconsciously, and corrupt both our intentions and our actions. For us to see real change in how we understand and engage with the world around us, we have to actively practice new narratives. For example, it doesn't matter if you consciously believe that the average Black person is just as smart as the average White person. You are receiving constant messages to the contrary—by seeing mostly White people in positions of power in the news; by being taught throughout most of primary and secondary school to reflect on and appreciate literature written primarily by White authors; and by watching movies portraying White people as heroes and People of Color and Native people as the villains, people who need to be saved, or secondary characters. Your gut is readily processing all of this input and then using it to absorb confirmatory information. So you have to actively strengthen new associations between Blackness and intelligence. You must practice new ways of thinking until it becomes genuinely distasteful to look at any portrayal of People of Color and Native people that doesn't honor their full humanity and complexity.

In sum, tangible shifts in our vision and actions will happen only if we build new instinctive associations among concepts, visual representations, emotions, and behaviors. Intellectual understanding or mere knowledge of biases won't lead to concrete changes. In the following exercise, I will describe the same steps I used to retrain my "eyes" around sexual orientation and gender, applied to racial bias.

Strengthening Your Antiracist Practice

Inoculation to White Supremacist Priming: Rehearse the Opposite Narrative

Because we see what we believe, to overcome our biases, we must inoculate ourselves against the constant priming of white supremacist narratives. In this Internal Work section, I have described ways in which I have intentionally rehearsed beliefs that countered what I was taught. You can use this same practice any time you realize you have been carrying a racial bias about a specific group of people (e.g., Black men are violent). As soon as you gain that insight, create a statement describing the opposite of the biased belief (e.g., Black men are gentle and caring), then rehearse it in your mind—both in real time, as you encounter people within that group, and in your imagination, as you think about individuals within that group.

You will know you have made significant progress in inoculating yourself against that bias when you find yourself instinctively and automatically making new associations in real time (e.g., you see a Black man and you instinctively feel warmth, instead of fear, toward him, and you feel instinctively surprised when you hear someone making a biased assertion to the contrary).

CHAPTER #4

Now We Know What Not to Say . . . What *Do* We Say?

I am a settler, but indigenous resurgence is my interest. It will make me a better human being and a worse settler.

—Lorenzo Veracini (2017)

Now that we know what so many White youth are learning (or not learning) about race, as well as what so many White adults have grown up to believe about race, we turn to what healthy antiracist White racial socialization could look like. This is some of the foundational knowledge that will help us unlearn the colorblind socialization upholding a racial hierarchy. These are the building blocks for antiracist socialization that we need at every age.

Establish Your Goals and Intentions for Talking With White Children and Adults About Race and Racism

As we consider what White people *should* be learning, we need to ask ourselves, "To what end?" What kind of White children do we want to raise? What is *your* end goal when you consider what you want White children to learn? And if you don't have children (or don't teach them), what kind of White person do you want to be and encourage other White people to become? What made you pick up this book?

What if we framed White antiracist learning around something more affirming and aspirational than simply *not being offensive*? I don't want White children to be silent about racism. When they hear about racism, I don't want them to say, "It's not me. Racism has nothing to do with me." But I also don't want them to be paranoid and skittish about making mistakes, causing them to avoid People of Color and Native people and stay silent for fear of doing the wrong thing. When I think about antiracist learning for myself and for my own kids, I want to raise kids who will be contributing members to a healthy multiracial community. I want to raise emotionally strong and resilient White people who can confront racism *with* People of Color and Native people, rather than feel, even in their antiracist resistance, like they are tiptoeing around People of Color and Native people or fighting racism out of some kind of white saviorism. I want kids who can be friends and allies to their Peers of Color and Native peers—kids who can be racially competent in their schools, their communities, and, eventually, their places of work. I want kids who have a strong positive racial identity, as I will describe in more detail in Chapter 5. I want to raise and nurture White people who do not ignore the multiracial, multicultural nature of U.S. society and who feel compelled to work to ensure that all people have the right to live and work and go to school with their full humanity intact.

Where Do We Start?

A parent once said to me, "A few months ago, we had a family member die. And when he died, I knew I had to talk with my child about it. I didn't know what to say, but I did have some instinct to begin the conversation and guide me from there. I talked about my own beliefs about death, and I asked my son what he thought. I held him while he cried. I didn't rush him. I wasn't sure I was doing the right thing, but I had a sense of direction. When it comes to talking about race, I have no instinct. Zero. I have no idea how to even start. What are the guideposts for beginning this conversation?"

There are probably a hundred different places where you can start, but in terms of laying a foundation and creating the conditions for a healthy "instinct" with regard to talking about race and racism, I would begin with the following: skin color, social construction, and systems. These three foundational concepts have to stay in the back of our minds as we talk about race, even if they are not always the direct topic of conversation.

Skin Color

Melanin is what gives us different skin colors. Melanin is real and biological. How much melanin we have is related to how much melanin our biological parents have, but it's not always a direct reflection of theirs, just as hair color is connected to our biological parents' genes but can vary considerably. Melanin tells a story about where a person's biological ancestors came from. People whose ancestors were from Africa or South Asia needed more melanin to protect them from the sun. If a person's ancestors were from Europe or Northern Asia, they needed less melanin so that they could absorb more vitamin D from the little sun they were exposed to. Our skin color tells a story about where we come from, but it doesn't tell us who we are. We all have melanin, in different amounts. The amount we have doesn't make us better or worse than anybody else; it's simply part of what makes us who we are.

The meaning people superimpose on that melanin, however, is what gives us race.

Social Construction

Melanin often determines race, but "race" is not a biological reality. It is a social construct. There is only one biological species of humans. But in the United States and elsewhere, we have divided people socially by their melanin levels. Those in power have ascribed rights, meaning, and even value to these melanin-based social categories, which were created centuries ago and have continued to evolve ever since.

Being "Black" or "White" in the United States has nothing to do with being literally black or white. To state the obvious, many White people are actually more peachy or pink. In some cases, they have darker skin than people who are considered People of Color or Native people. The racial categories were created by the nation's founders and early leaders—predominantly White, Anglo-Saxon Protestants—with the intention of dividing people in ways that favored those in power. Throughout history and to this day, the laws, rules, and cultural practices of the dominant White group have sustained inequities and injustices based on these divisions. Civil rights–era legislation may have ended legal segregation and repression, but policies and practices in many areas of life in the United States continue to undermine the ability of Black people, Native people, and other People of Color to thrive.

To be clear, there is no inherent connection between biology and race. Scientists say that there is actually more biological variation within racial groups than between them (Angier, 2000; Chou, 2017; Sue & Sue, 2019). No racial group is intellectually or athletically superior to any other group. Part of why race has so much power today, as noted, is that the United States has used race as a tool for separating people for hundreds of years, for the benefit of some at the expense of others. Race determined where given groups could live, where they could go to school, what they could study, who they could marry, whether they could be a citizen and own land, what kind of job they could have, whether they could join a union, and so on. This is why understanding history—some of which is laid out in Chapter 6—is so important for anyone who wants to be antiracist. Antiracism does not make sense if we don't understand how racist policies and laws have shaped the history of the United States and how history shapes our current racial landscape.

The opposite of social construction is the notion of *biological determinism*—the idea that race is biological, that certain racial groups actually are superior or inferior to other groups, and that one's race really does determine one's intelligence or ability. This belief that race is biological is foundational to white supremacist (actual, self-identified white supremacists') thinking. White supremacists believe—or act as if they believe—that the "races" should be separate and that the White race should be protected from infiltration or dilution caused by mixing with other racial groups. This is what many of the founding fathers of the United States believed, which is how race and racism became codified in U.S. law. The notions of "hypodescent"[1] and the "one-drop rule" emerged from White Americans who enslaved people from African nations and increased their holdings by raping enslaved women and then enslaving their children. Even "one drop of Black blood"[2] would render a child Black, with all the social and legal consequences embedded therein. Whether that child was Black or White was not about their melanin or about their biology; it was about how those categories were defined by people with power (White people) in a way that reinforced and replicated their power. Preserving Whiteness meant maintaining a socially constructed category of eliteness that could give and take away power as it benefited the people within that category.

Social constructionists understand that there is no such thing as "preserving a race," because race is entirely made up. And once we clearly see how it's fabricated, we can also better understand that the White racial socialization described in Chapter 3 is not random but key to maintaining this false notion of White superiority.

If you are talking with a child, it could suffice to say, "Skin color is real, but race is a made-up idea. It matters today because racism still impacts people's lives. But we are not actually different from one another biologically. Intelligence, strength, and athleticism are evenly distributed across groups. No group is better or worse."

Systems

Systems and institutions (laws, stores, banks, schools, prisons, health care, etc.) participated in establishing and maintaining the racial caste system that was created by the government and reinforced with social norms. Banks had race-based rules about who could get loans, which persist in practice today. Stores had race-based rules about who could enter through the front door and who had to enter through the back door, the order in which customers would be served, and how much deference or respect they would be accorded when served. Schools in the United States have been racially segregated longer than not, and while legal school segregation ended almost 70 years ago, schools still are largely segregated by race, both across schools and within schools (Rothstein, 2019).

Almost 70 percent of Black children, for example, attend schools with a high concentration of Students of Color (Garcia, 2020). But beyond that, even within racially integrated schools, students are often segregated by academic tracks (Sparks, 2020). If you are explaining this to a child, it's enough to say that every institution in our society had rules that reinforced the false idea that White people were better than people who were not White. Those systems kept us separate and gave us different things—and they continue to reproduce inequality today.

With kids, it's important to plant this seed of understanding that these systems were designed to divide us. Too often, kids are divided against one another, even in antiracism. In their small world of the individual classroom, students perform battles to try to one up one another rather than seeing the system as the common enemy. They need to see how it benefits all of them to work together to change the systems that hurt all of us. They may have different roles to play in doing so, but all of them are needed.

If Race Is Not Real, Why Can't We Be Colorblind and Just Ignore It?

The instinct to move back into colorblindness will be strong for White children and adults alike. It can feel like talking about race creates unnecessary ruptures. This is the case especially when we learn about how much harm the construct of race has caused. The hope is that if we ignore race, it will lose its power. This idea is so instinctive to many of us who were trained for colorblindness[3] that we are confused by the idea that colorblindness itself could be harmful. Why shouldn't we revert to colorblindness?

First, we can't intervene in racism if we don't talk about race. If society were already racially equitable, colorblindness wouldn't even come up, because like eye color is today, skin color would just be part of who we are, and there would be no need to train ourselves not to see it. But given our history and how racially unjust our society is today, we have to talk about race and racism so that we can confront it and undo it.

Second, colorblindness makes it impossible to understand how race is a part of people's identities, communities, and experiences because it has had profound meaning for so long. With every person we meet, we can safely assume that race and racism have affected their life. If we are being colorblind, we ignore this essential aspect of a person's identity.

Finally, colorblindness renders us unable to recognize bias. Bias is a natural, normal human phenomenon (Ross, 2020). And in a racialized society like the United States, racial bias is a common part of daily life

(Banaji & Greenwald, 2016; Ross, 2020). Being common doesn't mean it's right; it simply means that it's very unlikely that any member of our society does not have racial bias. Our job is not to pretend we don't have bias; instead, we need to see it and stay conscious of our bias so that it doesn't shape our decisions and judgments—and so that we may accurately view the full richness of each human being we encounter. A colorblind approach renders us incapable of doing anything about our own bias or about racism.

The opposite of colorblindness is *color consciousness* (Appiah & Gutmann, 1998). Color consciousness enables us to recognize how race affects people's identities, allows us to recognize racism so that we can do something about it, and makes it possible for us to discuss and address bias.

Distinguish Between Racial Talk and Racist Talk

Because so many people have been actively socialized to be colorblind, we have a general mainstream perception that it is racist to talk about race.[4] One mother told me after a talk, "I feel like I can't say anything to my son. He's 15 years old, and he doesn't listen to me to begin with. But also, anytime I bring up race—even just to describe someone's skin color—he says, 'That's racist, Mom. We shouldn't be talking about that.'"

This makes it nearly impossible to discuss race in a way that would help us learn about it or develop antiracist ideas. This is where we need to differentiate between *racial* talk and *racist* talk (Omi & Winant, 2015). *Racial talk* enables us to discuss race—how it is part of our histories, communities, and identities. It enables us to identify and work against racism and undermine racial hierarchies. Racial talk makes antiracism possible. *Racist talk*, on the other hand, perpetuates racial hierarchies. Racist talk stereotypes or demeans. Racist talk reinforces racism.

Ibram X. Kendi (2020c) takes this differentiation one step further by delineating *racist* talk and *antiracist* talk. Racist talk, according to Kendi, blames individuals for group-level disparities. Antiracist talk places the blame for group-level disparities with the policies and systems that created those groups and treated them differently.

Children and teens will probably feel comfortable talking with you and asking you questions about race to the extent that you engage in antiracist talk. But their observations and questions can also be a starting point for you to practice racial talk with them. When they ask a question about racial disparity, such as "Why do so many Black people live in this part of the city?" you have a strategy for feeling your way through.

- First, breathe. Acknowledge their comment or question: "I appreciate you noticing that. It can be hard to talk about race, and I'm glad you are willing to. Hmm. What are you thinking? What do you make of that?"

- Second, listen. Give them a chance to say more about why they brought up this question, what they heard at school, what they saw on a YouTube commentary, and so forth. That will give you a lot of information about why this question is coming up now and what their starting premise is.

- Third, differentiate the explanation that relies on individual behavior from the explanation that looks at group-level treatment by systems and policies. For example: "It's easy to fall into a trap here of thinking that people choose to live near people who are like them or that Black people just like the city. And while that might be true for many individuals, if people could choose freely where they live with no restrictions, our city would look much more racially mixed. Some of the predominantly Black neighborhoods around our city are the only places Black people were allowed to live in for a long time. A lot of the suburban communities would not allow Black people to buy homes in them, and many banks wouldn't give mortgages to people moving from Black areas of the city. I've heard stories of Black people going to visit friends in predominantly White communities and being intimidated by the police. My friend Grace's son, who's Black, was stopped by police in his own predominantly White community because a neighbor thought he looked suspicious. There are so many different forces at work that affect our city, which is really very segregated racially."

Most people don't require such a long answer, but as you engage, keep reaching for the systemic explanations rather than the individual ones. Remember that nobody is biologically programmed by race to be good with money, a responsible homeowner, or a hard worker. As you consider the question, keep asking yourself, "What is the explanation for how this group has been treated by systems and institutions that might yield this racial disparity?"

Sociologists have studied racial *gaps* in society—gaps that quantify the impact of centuries of racially oppressive policies in the United States. It's helpful to know some of them as you begin to develop your own systemic lenses. For example, the death gap, a term coined by David Ansell (2017), shows how residents of a low-income, Black urban community like Strawberry Mansion in Philadelphia can have a life expectancy of 68, while residents of a predominantly White part of the city called Society

Hill can have a life expectancy of 88 (Tanenbaum, 2016). That is a death gap of 20 years, which is low compared to many U.S. cities. The wealth gap, which has been widely reported over the past decade, demonstrates that White residents of most U.S. cities have up to 10 times the net worth of Black residents (McIntosh et al., 2020). This is true in Philadelphia, Chicago, Boston, and other cities across the United States.

As another example of a gap, early in the COVID-19 pandemic, before vaccines were available, Black, Latinx, and Native Americans were infected with COVID-19 at rates four to five times the rate of White and Asian Americans. Native people were hospitalized at five times the rate of White Americans. Black Americans died at twice the rate of White Americans. Meanwhile, in the first two months of the vaccine rollout, White Americans were vaccinated at two to three times the rate of Black Americans (Centers for Disease Control and Prevention, 2020).

How do we explain racial gaps?

- Look to the systemic and historical explanations, as Kendi (2020c) suggests.

- Be wary of any explanations that suggest that Black, Latinx, and Native people are inherently inferior to White and Asian American people. This includes explanations that suggest they are irresponsible, lazy, or unintelligent, or that they choose to be less successful.

- Avoid generalizations you might make about a whole group based on the behavior of one individual or a subset of that group. White people tend to do this for People of Color and Native people but not for other White people.

- Finally, as Kendi (2020a) says, remind children (and yourself) that just because a White person might *have* more, it doesn't mean they *are* more. Just because a Black person might *have* less, it does not mean that they *are* less. This is an antiracist challenge to a deeply held belief embedded in capitalism—one that says our worth is determined by how much we have.

Read articles on your own and with children that help make sense of these disparities. Black, Latinx, and Native people were affected by COVID-19 at higher rates than White people because they tend to have worse healthcare options than White Americans; tend to have higher rates of asthma and diabetes, which are connected to environmental racism and food access; tend to live in homes with more people, which means that transmission rates are higher; tend to rely more on public transportation; and tend to have work that is considered essential and not as accessible via online platforms.

These are systemic explanations. Explanations that suggest that Black, Latinx, and Native people were being irresponsible or unwilling to wear masks don't add up. While there may have been one group of kids you saw without masks at the mall or one Black man who runs a shop and didn't wear a mask when you visited, don't assume that you can know about an entire group based on the actions of a few people. We don't usually make generalizations about White people like that, because we don't tend to see White people as representatives of their group.

With Young Children
It's Never Too Late, and Never Too Soon

I often hear people with adult children say, "I never talked with my kids about race. Unfortunately, they are grown up now, and I wish I had. We still don't talk about it. But I do have grandchildren I can talk to. When is it the right time to start talking with children about race?"

With these particular parents and grandparents, I encourage them to begin to open the conversation with their children. It's never too late to start the conversation and engage in long-term, ongoing inquiry about how race and racism affect their collective family lives.

It's also never too soon. I advise people to begin talking to their children about race when they are babies. The baby won't necessarily understand what is being said, but it's more for the parent than it is for the baby. The parent can take that opportunity to practice, to begin saying words that might make sense to a small child, and to overcome their own colorblindness. I highly encourage people to read Ibram X. Kendi's (2020b) *Antiracist Baby* to their children. Again, the child won't necessarily understand it, but it is helpful for the parent to read Kendi's advice and take it in. Each of his nine suggestions is an incredibly valuable part of an antiracist parenting journey for any age. The very first point he makes addresses colorblindness and the social construction of race:

> *Antiracist Baby learns all the colors,*
>
> *Not because race is true.*
>
> *If you claim to be color-blind,*
>
> *You deny what's right in front of you.*

Many people believe that young children are naturally colorblind, or that they won't see race if we don't teach them to. But consider the ways in which children as young as two or three already have deep knowledge about how gender gets expressed in society and often work to convey their own gender identity in clear and unambiguous terms. Three-year-olds can tell you about boy colors and girl colors—and they can monitor one another's behavior accordingly. If they are given support and instruction to challenge these norms, they can also tell you that boys can wear pink and girls can wear blue or that Michael's trans father gave birth to him. They are capable of learning that gender is a spectrum or that it's okay to break gender norms—but without the invitation to think outside the gender binary, they absorb it as truth from a young age. We know from research studies that children notice skin color and race from infancy (Sullivan et al., 2021).

If a five-year-old tells you that they are colorblind, it's because they learned that colorblindness is preferred by adults, not because they don't ever notice skin-color differences or absorb both racial and racist ideas from the society around them. If a child is old enough to say racially offensive things to a Friend or Classmate of Color, they are old enough to begin to learn about race and antiracism.

Give Them Words if They Don't Have Them

Kids (and many adults) don't always know the words to use in conversations about race. Sometimes they use words that are offensive, are old-fashioned, or have negative connotations. Sometimes—even at four years old—they might try to avoid describing someone racially because somewhere along the way they learned that noticing race was rude. Give them the words if they don't have them. Help them think about their friends, neighbors, and peers in ways that describe them accurately. Whenever possible, be specific about someone's cultural or ethnic background. You could, for instance, describe a neighbor as Black but also talk about their identity as Bahamian or Jamaican or African American. You could describe someone as Native but also get specific about the tribal nations they identify with. When people are multiracial or mixed, you could mention that and describe what you know of their background. All of us are more than our racial identity.

All of this feels uncomfortable, however, if you don't also describe White people as White. When you are describing a White person, try to mention their being White, along with any other social identifiers. This will feel awkward at first, but over time it will feel easier, and you will find subtle ways to make it part of the conversation.

You can even talk with children about light or dark skin. Remember that underneath this conversation is the knowledge—which you can also mention from time to time—that melanin is what gives us different skin colors and that how much melanin a person has does not make them better or worse than anyone else. Different shades of skin are part of what makes us unique and special.

Having these conversations when children are young helps us practice racial talk in a way that sets us up for greater capacity to dialogue with them when the racial talk becomes more complex and multifaceted. My colleague Deidre Ashton talks about teaching kids the basic words for racial talk as being similar to using the correct words for body anatomy. When, as small children, kids learn to feel comfortable talking about the different parts of their bodies with accurate language, it makes things clearer and less awkward when it comes time to talk with them about puberty and sex. When we are able to talk with young children about race, racial identity, and racial difference by using specific and accurate terminology, we set ourselves up for clear communication and for color *consciousness* as children age.

Acknowledge That We Are All Different and That Difference Is Good

Through my own colorblind socialization, I learned that racial difference was something we shouldn't talk about because it was embarrassing for someone to be different, especially racially. Other differences—such as differences in nationality or in sports played—have not been corrupted in the same way. When unlearning our own colorblindness, we need to repeat to ourselves and to children that our differences are important and that they make us who we are. When talking with children, emphasize the power and beauty of differences. Help them figure out what makes them unique, and help them appreciate the things that make their friends and classmates unique as well.

When You Don't Know the Answer, Wonder With Them

If you don't know the answer, you can always say, "Good question. Let's find out together!" No matter where you are in your own learning process, it's not about being *comfortable* during such exchanges; it's about sharing in the child's (or person's) curiosity and eagerness to make sense of the world around them.

We don't have to have the answers, but unlearning colorblindness means that we don't evade the questions. When we don't know what to say, we can dive in and ponder together or find the answers together. With children, even if you do know the answer, or you've done some background reading to figure it out, it's still a good tactic to think and wonder with them as if you don't know and then help construct the answer together.

Preempt Misconceptions

It's pretty common for children to have erroneous beliefs about skin color, like the idea that brown skin color washes off or that Asian American people are actually foreigners. They don't necessarily escape these misconceptions just because their parents know that such beliefs are not true. They might pick them up from the internet and TV shows or from other kids at school. But kids aren't the only ones who hold misconceptions; many non-Asian adults have made the mistake of assuming the foreignness of an Asian American person.

Adults can actively debunk these assumptions—and do so even before they come up. You can say, "Did you know that some people believe that skin color can rub off or be added on, like with paint? But that's not true! Skin color comes from something we're born with, called melanin." For teachers in preschool and kindergarten, this is the kind of lesson you might do with kids early in the school year, particularly if you notice that students are coming into school with such misconceptions. It does not hurt to correct this misconception with every age group, and it is critical knowledge for anyone who is going to contribute to a healthy multiracial community.

My colleague Sarah Lee Fung is a Korean American first-grade teacher who does precisely this type of preemptive lesson with regard to hair. She noticed that every year she had to mediate conflict that originated when a non-Black student touched a Black student's hair. While the Black student didn't always express offense, the teacher would interrupt this behavior, knowing that it represented the beginning of a lifelong assault on the Black child's dignity. She developed a lesson about hair, differences in hair, and the importance of not touching one another's hair. When one of the students observes another child touching someone's hair without permission, they can be heard saying, "Wait! Do you have consent?"

The invasiveness and presumption required to reach out and touch someone's body without consent comes—unconsciously—from a racial caste system that says White people have and deserve more bodily boundaries than Black people. So while the assertion of power is not always intended when a White person touches a Black person's hair, it activates (and is facilitated by) tropes loaded with meaning and—for the person who is violated—feeling. Unlearning this presumption and fascination at a young age can help dismantle the unconscious assumptions that make such momentary interactions so momentous. The same goes for other widely held misconceptions about race.

Affirm Blackness and Brownness

There are ways in which we can affirm Blackness and Brownness without even talking about race. When my children were young, I observed multiple times when we denigrated the colors black or brown without intending to. My children would mix all their paints together, and I would say, "Oh, no, no, don't do that! You are going to make *brown*," as if brown were the worst thing that could possibly happen to their paints. Now when my kids mix all their colors, I say, "Ooh, look. That's going to make brown. I love that color. What would you call that particular shade of brown?" When kids ask me what my favorite color is, I always say that it's black. I don't make it about race—I tell them I love black because I love to read, and if there were no black in the world, there would be no words on the pages of my books. This is an example of how we can subtly counteract the negative priming of implicit anti-Black narratives.

How to Respond When a Child Asks Embarrassing Questions in Public

Thandeka (1999), theologian and author of *Learning to Be White*, writes about how White people develop shame in talking about race because we are shushed at a young age. We ask questions—often in public, because that's when our curiosity about difference is piqued—and then our parents or caregivers, worried about embarrassing someone (including themselves), shush us, saying, "It's rude to talk about race."

My kids used to ask questions about race that felt wrong. "How does her hair do that?" one of them asked in reference to a Black woman passing us in Target. In spite of all the awkwardness this has caused over the years, I always try to respond first by affirming the question: "I'm so glad you asked that! Even lots of adults don't feel comfortable talking about race and racial difference, so it's great that you feel comfortable asking questions about it."

I also knew that my response might be heard by the person the question was about. I said, "Isn't her hair amazing? She can do some cool things with her hair because she's Black. My hair doesn't do what her hair can do because I'm White and my hair is not as curly. Black hair and White hair are often pretty different. It's cool that our hair is different—it creates so many possibilities." Again, these are not the "right" answers, but they're not wrong, either. I'm certain we could find better ways to respond if we practice and strategize together. But the important thing is to engage the question, not shame the child (or adult) for asking, and to affirm differences rather than suggest that difference is bad.

Practice

When a person has witnessed a racist incident, you can invite them to brainstorm and role-play ways they could respond if it happens again. Say your fifth grader comes home from school having seen one child taunt another by using a racial slur. How do you respond? First, you can praise your child for recognizing the problem and bringing it up to you. Ask them how it made them feel and what they did. You can let them know you don't necessarily know the right answer, but you're happy to brainstorm possible responses. You might empathize, saying, "I would be overwhelmed if I saw that happen. I think I might freeze." Help them think about different options they have in that moment. Having options is what helps people feel less helpless and panicked in the moment of witnessing harm. Some options include talking to the teacher, approaching the victim to get them out of the situation, or saying to the offender, "Stop," or "You are being mean," or "I always thought you were kind—I can't believe you would say such a thing." After brainstorming responses, you can say, "Okay, I'll be Person A who says the racial slur. You be you, and tell me what you want me to hear." Role-play the incident a few times until the child feels like they have some agency and options for future incidents.

With Older Children
Engage in Critical Media Analysis

Analyzing media is one of the most important skills we can give to children as we help them become antiracist. This is because they consume media on a daily basis, usually in greater doses than they consume our sage wisdom. They will also consume media for their entire lives. And while we don't want to ruin their viewing pleasure, we do want them to think critically about the messages they are taking in as they watch.

Some of the media elements to focus on—and coach children to see—are common stereotypes about different racial groups. In so many cartoons, for instance, the Latinx character is accompanied by swanky, romantic Latin music, and they are often more romantically inclined than the other characters. The Asian American characters are often science-, math-, or computer-oriented. Or the Asian American characters might also be portrayed as sneaky or dishonest. Longstanding Black stereotypes include characters who are less intelligent or more violent than the other characters or who are interested only in sports. Black characters whose cultural or linguistic styles are used as a source of humor are more subtle but still troubling—and still very present. Think of the character Donkey in the movie *Shrek*. His use of Black Vernacular is part of what makes him funny. This trend is so prevalent in mainstream movies that White people seem practically trained to laugh when we hear Black Vernacular.[5] When my Black colleague says something in Black Vernacular in our presentations, I often hear the audience chuckle, even when he's saying something serious. A similar phenomenon happens with stereotypical portrayals of gay characters. Their cultural or linguistic styles often become the source of humor, rather than the character's vehicle for delivering humor.

White characters are often the protagonist. Look at how so many shows exist in an all-White, all-heterosexual, all-able-bodied, all-cisgender world. Question when Whiteness is the unnamed norm or the only salient racial background shown in a program. Are the White characters and their reunification with other White people central to the emotional catharsis of the movie? Conversely, are the Characters of Color and Native characters disposable? Are they the first to die? Do they have names or speaking parts?[6] Are they complex or one-dimensional? Are the People of Color and Native people presented in a single story, whether it's a story of oppression or athletics? Asking these kinds of questions helps children think about what to watch, as well as the kinds of questions that can be asked once they choose to watch a show or movie. Encourage them to look for movies and shows where Characters of Color and Native characters are presented in whole and complex ways.

When we start a conversation about media with harsh critique, children can often feel judged and resentful. A child is much more likely to care what you think if you care what they think. Given that, do not approach conversations about race and racism as if there is only one right answer—the one you provide. Process and explore ideas with children. Listen to the things that don't make sense to them. Allow them to ask questions, and share your own questions with them. Don't fall into the trap of feeling like you have to know everything. In fact, when you model imperfection, when you talk about what you don't know and what you wonder about, you model what it looks like to engage in antiracist learning with a growth mindset. Don't shame a child for what they think or what they like. If they happen to like a TV show that you are critical of (say, *Barbie*, to choose an example that is a little too close to my particular home), find out what they like about it, watch some of it with them, and then ask questions to help them think about it critically.[7]

Emphasize That Racism Affects All of Us, so Antiracist Action Is for Everyone

Sometimes it can feel like racism is a problem that belongs to People of Color and Native people, so White people have no business talking or thinking about it. It is true that racism does not affect White people in the same way that it affects People of Color and Native people. And there is a lot I cannot know about racism because I have not experienced daily life as a Person of Color or Native person in a society so heavily shaped by white supremacy and racism. But racism dehumanizes everybody. So White people can and should be offended by racism, just as men can and should be offended by sexism—not as a way of performing allyship, but because sexism hurts men, too. We should feel a responsibility to say that we will not participate in or uphold a system that treats people differently based on race.

I remember interviewing a 17-year-old White girl who told me the story of when she confronted White classmates who were using the n-word. "What do you care?" they asked her. "You're White."

She responded, "Yeah, I'm White. And that word dehumanizes people. I'm not okay with dehumanizing people. Please don't use that word." She didn't have to say that it might offend a Person of Color or that she had a Black friend who would be hurt, speaking up on behalf of someone who wasn't there. She clearly and directly told her classmates that the word offends her—as a White person—and asked them again not to use it.

When schools and organizations observe Black History Month, it can feel like a month in which we support and honor Black people *for the sake of Black people*. But Black history is not just for Black people. Black history *is* U.S. history; it's world history. The world as we know it would not exist without Black history. The United States was not only built by the labor of Black people; time and again, Black people challenged the United States to live up to its stated ideals. Black History Month is a time for us to honor and celebrate the achievements of Black Americans, which have benefited the entire nation. Non-Black people should feel called each year to celebrate Black History Month and Black holidays, such as Juneteenth. Both are celebrations of freedom and Black Americans' accomplishments. White people are not centered in those celebrations, which can make it feel as if I don't belong there. But in fact, it frees me up from the false dichotomy that says being White means I can't love Black people or that I can't celebrate what Black people have done for the country. Pro-Black does not mean anti-White. When I show up as a White person at a Juneteenth event, it's because I see a celebration of liberation as a celebration of progress—of coming closer to the values that the United States as a country has said it wants to live by. This can be liberating. The more I see this, the more intrinsically I want to celebrate Black history and feel gratitude for it in my bones.

Remember That It's Not What We Say as Much as the Relationship That Counts

This chapter is not about parenting. It's about talking with White children—and White people—about race. How you parent a child or interact interpersonally with others is up to you. While you may notice that much of the socialization I have been describing involves talking, helping a child learn racial competence requires that you be in relationship with the child, just as helping another White person learn racial competence requires that you be in relationship with that person.

Whether you're talking with a White child or a White friend, helping other White people learn about racism requires patience and support. Unlearning mainstream narratives and learning to be critical of the often invisible racial caste system takes a lot of cognitive and emotional work. Don't shame people for what they believe; the fact that they have learned and continue to learn racist thinking means that they are good students of the world around them, which also means they have the skills to continue learning more accurate information. Help them learn the facts and ideas that will enable them to see another truth. Don't fight with them, as fighting can make them dig their heels in, raise their defenses, and generally approach the topic in a guarded and wary way (aka ignite their fight, flight, or freeze response and inhibit their empathy).

All people—but especially adolescents—need to feel like there's a give-and-take dynamic to the conversation to stay open to listening. Probably the best thing I've done to help my contentious preteen hear my point of view is say, "You're right." Youth are not always going to be right, but acknowledge it when they are. Listening to them and learning more about why they think what they think can be an effective way to expand our own understanding while also keeping the lines of communication open. Find ways to affirm some aspect of their knowledge and ideas. Invite the child or friend to explore and question collaboratively with you. Model imperfection by naming the open questions you still have yourself and letting them know when you don't know something. This is a great strategy, not just with children but with adults as well. Leading with curiosity is key to learning about another person's beliefs, as well as the fears and concerns that might lie underneath their beliefs. Because their fears and concerns determine their sense of safety, helping them feel understood will increase the chance that they will empathize with and learn from you as well.

Sometimes I get into a rut of needing to be the authority or the one who knows. When my daughter corrects my pronunciation of an author's name or corrects my choice of race-related words, I feel an internal resistance that says, "I'm supposed to be teaching you." But that runs contrary to the idea that we are on a journey together and that she will teach me in myriad ways throughout her life, especially given her particular vantage point as a youth. When she corrects me, I have to override my urge to say, "Do you have to be so snarky when you say that?" and instead model what it looks like to take feedback. I'll say,

"Thank you for correcting me. I didn't know how to pronounce her name. Every time you do that, it's one more person she doesn't have to listen to mispronouncing her name."

At All Ages

Offer Both Windows and Mirrors

One of the reasons many White people get so easily flustered when race and racism come up is that White people—unlike any other racial group—are able to live in a world that we perceive to be pretty much all-White. We grow up with books, movies, dolls, TV shows, LEGO sets, and comics that portray White people, often in all-White worlds. Educators call these *mirrors*. White people tend to have a lot of mirrors of people who look like them racially, but usually they have very few examples of White people who can model what it looks like to be White and antiracist. White people also do not have many *windows* into the lives of people who are racially different from them.

All children need both windows and mirrors, but Children of Color and Native children tend to have all too many windows into the lives of White people, with few mirrors reflecting back to them complex and multidimensional images[8] of people who are racially or culturally like them. White people almost exclusively have mirrors. Purposely giving a White child more windows by buying them baby dolls of different skin colors, introducing them to books and movies with Protagonists of Color or Native protagonists, and generally interrupting the unconscious Whiteness of their world can support them in engaging across racial groups and disrupting the assumptions of the racial caste structure as they get older.

Be Consistent and Persistent

According to researchers who study it, racial socialization is what parents do in a "consistent, persistent, and enduring manner" (Boykin & Toms, 1985, as cited in Hughes & Chen, 1999, p. 471). In other words, if we regularly do not talk with kids about race, we are actively socializing them to not talk about race—to not recognize racism. If we talk with kids about it on a regular basis—even if we don't always know exactly what to say—we are more likely to be engaging in racially conscious, antiracist parenting.

The idea that racial socialization should be "consistent and persistent" often intimidates people because it suggests that we need to talk about race and racism both within and outside of the home 100 percent more than we have been. While that is true, I actually find it reassuring. When I try to talk with my kids and they don't quite understand me, or I feel like I didn't quite convey my intended meaning, or they ask a question and I don't know what to say, I always know that there will be another chance to revisit the conversation again soon.

Provide Opportunities for Action

Helping children take action can be a valuable way to turn their concern and frustration into hope. Without action, antiracist concern can turn into despair. Participating in multiracial marches can be incredibly powerful and liberating for me as I try to stave off my own despair. For my own children, it has been overwhelming, loud, and tiring. That means that I still go to marches, but I don't usually bring them with me. They prefer to show their support by chalking the driveway or role-playing responses to class discussions in school. Helping children take action means meeting them where they are and helping them channel their knowledge and power to do something good right where they are, with who they are. There is no one right way.

While I don't think that marching in the streets is necessarily a bad action to take with kids, I see it as a rather narrow take on what we need to do to raise antiracist kids who become antiracist grownups. It's great for kids to advocate for racial justice, and it sometimes makes sense to march with them. But in and of itself, marching is not the solution and not the best way to educate children to be antiracist. It's the equivalent of feeling that we've done our work simply by saying that racism is wrong—as if racism is a clear, well-defined enemy that we merely have to disavow to defeat.

There are times when marching can be very powerful, but we have to make sure we do more with children to develop a daily antiracist practice. And when we do march, we must make sure we are not doing it in a performative way that assuages our guilt without increasing understanding or making change.

Curb Entitlement

A big part of unlearning White superiority is acknowledging and acting with the belief that your life is not inherently more valuable than another person's life because you're White. While this belief is rarely conscious, it is often operationalized in the way we live our lives. For children, part of what this means is that their concerns and desires will not always be addressed immediately. They should not feel entitled to have whatever they want whenever they want it. When I cannot or will not give my child what they want, I have to remind myself that it's good for them not to have all their desires satisfied at all times. Another way to think about this is that a child is part of a family and a community. Sometimes the needs of the family or the community are going to take precedence over the desires of the individual child. That is how they learn to live in and cultivate community. The child should be invited to see the needs of the family and community and to contribute to them as well. This is a key practice for unlearning the distorted messages embedded in the ideology of individualism.

Avoid Accusations of Privilege

A parent in one of my sessions once told me, "I sometimes get so angry at my child for this very thing. He won't do his chores, and he acts all entitled when I try to enforce our rules. I tell him that he's acting out of his White privilege, but it doesn't seem to help."

Telling a child—or any person—that they are privileged is not going to help them act less entitled. It is almost like name calling. It will shame them, make them feel resentful of the term, and does not provide a clear course of action for how to change the situation. A child may be privileged racially (if they are White) and economically (if they are middle- or upper-class). But that is not to their fault or credit. If they are behaving in an entitled manner, consider ways to curb that entitlement. Say no the next time they ask for something, and then affirm their ability to tolerate the denial. Give them more responsibility for running the household, and praise them when they follow through. Think about the structures in your family life that make them act entitled or privileged, and consider how to expect more from them, as well as how you would like them to treat you. Remember that while it's hard not to give a child everything they want, it makes them a nicer person and more capable of being in reciprocal relationships. Those relationships will be much more deeply meaningful in a child's life than the plastic *tchotchke* that you buy them in the grocery store or the immediate gratification they feel when they skip out on their chores.[9] Finally, model this restraint of your own sense of entitlement as you move about the world. Consider what you feel you *deserve*, and then consider whether that is something everyone *deserves*.

Develop Relationships With People of Color and Native People

A Black parent once told me, "You know, our daughter sometimes doesn't get invited to the class parties. And this is really hurtful. So I would say you should include all the kids in the class if you're going to have a party. But then our daughter was invited to a party, and the mom posted the pictures of my daughter all over Facebook, as if to say, 'Look—our child has a Black friend.'"

This statement speaks for itself. And it presents two calls to action. The first is not to exclude People of Color and Native people. The second is not to objectify People of Color and Native people. Don't invite People of Color or Native people to your party or befriend a Person of Color or Native person to show how hip or antiracist you are. Be mindful of the ways in which People of Color and Native people often get tokenized by White people or by their schools, and be particularly cautious about advertising their pictures publicly or otherwise violating their privacy. But do engage in relationship. Do reach out and have the families of your child's Friends of Color or Native friends over for a meal. Do give extra care and attention to those relationships, which can sometimes be harder to form because there can be inexperience and doubt on both sides. Do encourage your child's cross-racial friendships. Do cultivate your own cross-racial friendships with intention and care. Do support your children's interracial relationships as they get older and start dating.

Return to the Goal

I was doing a workshop for the faculty of a community college in California, and I was riding into town on a Lyft from the airport. My Lyft driver—a 20-something Mexican American man—asked me what I was doing there. I told him in vague terms about the workshop, and he wanted to hear more. It turned out that he attended the same college I was going to work with. He said, "Here's the thing. Something racist did happen here. But now the administration is holding all these anti-racism events, and people are just getting *weird*. I was waiting tables, and a White woman smacked her husband for asking me where I was from. She said, 'That's a microaggression—you're not supposed to ask that.' White kids at school no longer talk to us because they're afraid they're going to get our names wrong and offend us. Please tell them that we want people to stop doing racist things, but we also want people to just stop being weird. Can you tell them that?"[10]

When we think about talking with kids about race, many parents and teachers seem to believe that the goal is to give them enough know-how so that they will understand how to be politically correct. It's commendable that we don't want them to be offensive or hurtful, but we also need to recognize that we can—and should—give them much more. When kids learn only what *not* to say or do and don't have the skills to engage in meaningful relationships with People of Color and Native people, we shouldn't be surprised that they end up feeling paranoid and acting weird.

We want them to engage in relationships without getting *weird*. And this means they need to understand that there is no way to engage in relationships without messing up sometimes. How do we support both a desire to engage and a willingness to mess up? First, we model this ourselves. Second, we support them unconditionally as a partner on this path.

Notes

1. *Hypodescent* technically means the automatic assignment of children of a mixed union between different socioeconomic or ethnic groups to the group with the lower status, regardless of proportion of ancestry in different groups (Kottak, 2002).

2. This graphic metaphor for reproduction has no basis in science; mixing blood does not actually happen when people reproduce.

3. As described in Chapter 3.

4. In her book *The Purpose of Power*, Alicia Garza (2020) explains how the racial rhetoric of the 1980s and 1990s was shaped by a conservative president, Ronald Reagan, who evoked and stoked stereotypes of Black people to explain racial inequality while actively promoting an ideology of colorblindness so that people couldn't talk about it. By blaming Black activists for being "racists" because they talked about Blackness and Whiteness, Reagan was able to claim the ideological middle and suggest that anyone who talks about race is racist. This belief in colorblindness that I grew up with did not come out of nowhere; it existed for explicit political purposes. And while people who promote colorblindness don't always do so for political purposes, it is important to recognize that when they adopt this stance, conservative agendas benefit.

5. Black Vernacular is sometimes called African American Vernacular English or Black Language (Baker-Bell, 2016).

6. Much of my knowledge about media analysis comes from Dr. Frederick Gooding Jr.'s work with the Minority Reporter and the book *You Mean, There's RACE in My Movie?* (Gooding, 2017).

7. For parents looking to improve their conversations with their children, I highly recommend the book *How to Talk So Kids Will Listen and Listen So Kids Will Talk* by Adele Faber and Elaine Mazlish (2012). This is not a book about race, but it gives a general orientation to talking with kids that will support any conversation you want to have.

8. Thank you to Alethea White for explaining this concept in a way that helped me see it more comprehensively.

9. In full disclosure, I don't always make my kids do their chores, and I often give in to them when we are at the store. All the pitfalls of parenting find me regularly. I share this not because it's something any parent could do 100 percent of the time but because these thoughts help me hold the line when my children challenge it.

10. Some people might think of this story as evidence that we shouldn't teach so much about antiracism. If we stop thinking about race and racism so much, perhaps nobody will start acting weird? But I disagree. If White people start acting weird when we learn about our own racism, that's another nervous system response, perhaps a more awkward iteration of freezing. We need to get better at learning about our own racism and working to change it, not get so weird. That said—again—it's better to be real than to try to be perfect. If you find yourself getting weird, name it . . . and keep going.

INTERNAL WORK

Empathy Is Our Superpower

· ·

When we talk about racial socialization for antiracism, we are really talking about racial *re*-socialization. In other words, we must learn new ways of seeing and relating to People of Color and Native people. Pausing and re-grounding ourselves facilitates this process by initiating a U-turn away from the reactivity and defensiveness that come up as we encounter new information about racism. It also turns us toward reengagement, reopening our hearts to People of Color and Native people so that deep learning can happen. Our hearts matter because it's physiologically impossible to learn about racism without empathizing with people impacted by it. Unlike other species, we have a choice between reactivity (including the defensiveness rooted in white supremacist priming) and authentic, genuine connection.

And this choice rests, fundamentally, on one key ability: the courage to empathize. So in this Internal Work section, we will look at how to cultivate empathy so that we can connect to the pain of racism in ways that are helpful.

Empathy as a Compass for Antiracist Action

Human beings cannot survive outside of community. As you know by now, our stress responses keep us temporarily alive by protecting us from imminent danger, but they do not facilitate our long-term survival—neither individually nor as a species. Antiracism, at least in part, calls to us because divisions, distrust, and animosity feel bad and are bad for us (and I mean this physiologically, not only psychologically). Just learning to decrease our reactivity (i.e., simply not being scared or not being in a fight, flight, or freeze state) is not enough to make us thrive long-term, because homeostatic states don't build community in and of themselves. So our physiology is also designed to seek and maintain ties to one another; both our physical health and our emotional well-being depend on our success in doing so. Chronic reactivity leads to physical and societal illness. Genuine, loving connections lead to well-being and collective liberation.

Empathy for Learning

When our physiology is not restricted by our stress responses, our natural propensity toward *learning* and *empathizing* (i.e., emotionally connecting with others) reemerges. Both capacities appear very early in our development, as they are key to our ability to adapt and make the most of our environments. Learning and empathizing are not distinct or disconnected from one another. Empathy is an essential learning tool. How else do we figure out what is going on with others so that we can connect and build community with them? This means that we cannot learn about racism or implement antiracist intentions effectively without simultaneously practicing empathy.

Empathy for Action

Empathy plays another critical role in propelling us to operationalize our antiracist aspirations. When we empathize, our bodies reproduce what the person in front of us is feeling. It's as if we breathe another person's state of being. Emotions are quite literally contagious. Because of this, we are generally pretty accurate in perceiving another person's joys and sorrows, and this is not simply a cognitive process; it is an embodied one. What's more, the neural pathways involved in detecting others' emotions reach our empathy and motor centers simultaneously. This means that when we deeply empathize with another human being, we can't help but want to actively care for them because we feel the pinch of their condition within ourselves. In short, empathy and compassionate action are physiologically linked. Since empathy means feeling what others feel, responding to others' joy will deepen our own joy. Relieving someone else's pain will also relieve the distress we feel in the process of empathizing with them. In fact, I suspect that most of us who have moved onto an antiracist path have felt compelled to do so because at some point we have resonated deeply with the deleterious impact of injustice on real people, to the point that it began to require effort *not* to do something about it.

This brings us right back to the fourth myth of white supremacy that Ali discussed in Chapter 2 ("It's better to think, rather than feel, about racism"). As we enter antiracist conversations, disconnecting from our feelings would make antiracism exclusively an intellectual journey, but it's essential that we feel deeply what racism actually does to the people it targets—and to White people. If we can sustain that level of empathy, it offers us a compass for action.

White people on an antiracist path usually want to know how to dismantle white supremacy. However, we can get so stirred up by the enormity of the task or by a desire not to see ourselves as complicit that we tend to immediately go in reactive fight mode. One of the ways in which our fight behaviors manifest is in compulsively searching for answers outside of ourselves, believing that only others hold the key to the puzzle. This is most often a fight response because when the distress of truly seeing racism overwhelms us, we panic and reactively reach for quick solutions. Getting others to give us the seemingly "right" answer might temporarily soothe our distress—but only until the next time we notice racism or are unclear about the next step. Relying exclusively on others to tell us what to do means that our power and effectiveness to address racism are considerably stunted. Often, this fight dynamic manifests in us turning to People of Color and Native people and asking, "What should I *do*? What do *you* want me to do?"

It's one thing to seek consultations, form coalitions, follow the leadership of People of Color and Native people, and join forces. It's another thing to use this fight impulse as a way to escape our own discomfort of reckoning with the injustice we see and abdicate our own locus of control for taking action. When that happens, we inevitably miss our ever-present internal source of answers, which comes from deeply empathizing with the impact of racism on People of Color and Native people.

As we train to sustain our ability to empathize without becoming overwhelmed by it, our bodies begin to know how to respond to it. Connecting to the pain of racism experienced by People of Color and Native people gives us precious insight into a reality we don't have direct access to. It's not by chance that our socialization actively works to cut us off from the pain experienced by People of Color and Native people. For example, studies have shown that White medical students believe that Black patients experience less pain, are used to pain, are able to handle pain better, have fewer nerve receptors, or are otherwise tougher than White patients—all of which results in lower levels of medical support offered to Black patients, with lethal consequences. White people must buy into these false beliefs to remain complacent with white supremacy, or we would not be able to witness the atrocities committed against Black people and do nothing about it.

So we must continuously work to reengage and cultivate our empathy—to rehumanize ourselves. And this process of leaning in and empathizing gives us both the knowledge and the gut sense of how to intervene appropriately and most effectively to dismantle racism. As with any practice, the more we give ourselves to this cycle of empathizing, learning, and responding, the more wisdom and effectiveness we accrue.

Empathy as Fuel for Antiracist Action

What exactly do we mean when we talk about empathy? It's helpful to distinguish between three kinds of empathy (Zaki, 2019):

- *Cognitive empathy:* understanding what others feel

- *Emotional empathy:* "feeling with," or actually experiencing what another person feels

- *Empathic concern:* a desire to relieve another person's distress

When it comes to racism, White people tend to be most comfortable with, and often stop at, cognitive empathy—an intellectual, detached understanding of racism, which shields us from feeling shame, guilt, or despair. We are actively socialized out of emotional empathy, with strong emotions being considered childish and a sign of weakness. And divisive narratives dehumanize "the other," steering us away from empathic concern. However, all three types of empathy, working in tandem, are useful and needed in directing our antiracist actions.

Knowledge about racism—leading to cognitive empathy—makes it easier to detect how racism manifests in our communities and does damage. Through emotional empathy, we resonate with the experiences of People of Color and Native people and begin to taste some of the actual pain caused by racism. This direct experience of the pain caused by racism then opens the door to empathic concern—the desire to actually relieve that pain. Empathic concern involves feeling genuine care for the people we are emotionally empathizing with, and the combination of this genuine care and emotional empathy gives us clarity regarding the action we should take to stop the harm.

In sum, the more you learn about racism, the more you see it happening, the more you resonate with those who are hurt, and the more you care and feel compelled to do something about it. Strengthening all three kinds of empathy will help us walk an antiracist path.

How to Strengthen Your Empathic Capacities

Reading Ali's chapters in this book provides you with superb workouts for growing your cognitive empathy. Through these readings, you learn about racism, its impact, and how to recognize it in your communities. The exposure and grounding techniques described in the Internal Work sections for Chapter 1 and Chapter 2 will strengthen your ability to sustain emotional empathy, so that you can remain open to learning without shutting down. And practices such as the Loving-Kindness Meditation (described at the end of this section) can strengthen your ability to engage your empathic concern, which in turn will propel you to act in ways that challenge injustice. Let's take a closer look at the inner workings of emotional empathy and empathic concern.

Emotional Empathy: How to Keep Yourself on Top of the Hill

Emotional empathy, again, is *feeling with*, or actually feeling what another person feels. It is physiologically activating. While deeply resonating with the pain that racism inflicts on People of Color and Native people can open us up to act in compassionate ways, it can also overwhelm us, thus making us act impulsively, retreat into defensive behaviors, and potentially burn out.

While cognitive empathy teaches us to detect racism, if we let that understanding of racism sink in without the ability to sustain emotional empathy, we'll attempt to shut back down. We might then flight into merely collecting antiracist knowledge and keeping our work just at an intellectual level. Or we might end up debilitated by our own pain (a freeze reaction). Or we might add insult to injury by going into fight mode and invalidate People of Color and Native people or ask them to do all the work for us.

Not long ago, the child of a close friend of mine received a bullying social media message from a peer. I was enraged. The energy of my emotions immediately propelled me into fight mode. I considered calling the school, calling the peer's parents, and processing the incident openly with other friends. I was definitely *feeling with* my friend and her child; I wanted to take care of my pain as much as their pain. But while my impulse to intervene was understandable, it wasn't actually the best course of action. My friend wanted her daughter to have the space to process the experience and decide for herself what she wanted to do about it. Thankfully, while I felt a strong urge to intervene, I also understood that it wasn't my place to do so if not asked. I was able to modulate my emotional empathy, take a step back, remain in dialogue with my friend, and let her and her daughter chart their own course while being there for support—which was what they asked.

I wasn't quite as emotionally nimble as I witnessed the pain and horror of the murder of George Floyd. *Feeling with* George Floyd and his family became debilitating for me. I resonated so intensely that it took me out of my center and froze me for weeks. My inability (due to the pandemic) to regulate my emotional empathy by grieving effectively and in community[1] brought me closer to burnout than to actions springing from empathic concern. My effectiveness in responding to the tragedy was greatly diminished.

If you have taken an Introduction to Psychology course, you might have learned about the Yerkes–Dodson law.[2] It describes the relationship between levels of arousal and performance. Visually, it looks like a gradual hill, representing how well one might perform under stress—low at the bottom of the hill, high at the top of the hill. If arousal is too low, we are sluggish (the bottom of the hill on one side). If the arousal is too high, we are paralyzed by anxiety (the bottom of the hill on the other side). But with a moderate amount of arousal, we perform optimally (the top of the hill). Early in my clinical training, one of my supervisors encouraged me to hit that optimal performance by keeping "one foot in and one foot out" as I learned to listen deeply to clients. Regulating our emotional empathy to remain on top of the hill is critical to our antiracist effectiveness.

Again, the capacity to keep one foot in and one foot out of others' emotional experiences rests on practices such as the exposure and grounding techniques described in the Internal Work sections for Chapter 1 and Chapter 2, respectively. By using these practices over time, I've learned quick ways to upregulate or downregulate my emotional responses. At the end of this section, I offer additional suggestions for how you can do that as well. Whatever your own unique ways to emotionally regulate may be, the aim is to keep yourself at the top of the hill while you let yourself emotionally empathize. Once you can do that, you can learn what you need to know through your emotional empathy and then let it fuel your empathic concern, which is all about action.

Empathic Concern: The Best Fuel for Antiracist Action

Empathic concern is the desire to relieve someone else's distress. My ability to deeply feel *with* my friend's daughter (emotional empathy) and my sincere love for her propelled me to want to actively intervene on her behalf (empathic concern)—which turned out to mean listening rather than marching into someone's office with a list of demands. In other words, when emotional empathy meets genuine caring, acting becomes irresistible. If I had experienced what happened to my friend's daughter only intellectually, or if I didn't genuinely care about her, I would not have felt viscerally compelled to act. Empathic concern is *feeling with* coupled with a sense of tenderness toward the people with whom we are emotionally empathizing. But how do we tend to and strengthen this essential kind of empathy?

Many cultural traditions offer techniques to expand our capacity to deeply care for others, and no one method is necessarily better than another. Here, I describe one such technique called Loving-Kindness Meditation. It actually took me quite a while to seriously consider it. Despite being a psychologist and believing in the scientifically proven healing power of empathy and connections, I tend to be a pragmatic, action-oriented person. Culturally, as an Italian, I was raised to be comfortable with emotions, not for emotions' sake but rather as an authentic, open expression of a person's beliefs and experiences. In other words, while I am comfortable with and deeply value emotions as vehicles for honest communication, I'm not particularly touchy-feely. So while I had read all about the power of Loving-Kindness Meditation, I shied away from actually practicing it until a few years ago.

At the time, I was one of the leaders of a project advocating for counseling psychology students, which made me the target of professional animosity. As much as I wanted to defend myself, it was clear that our organization's success would depend on not answering in kind. Rather than respond with self-righteousness or defensiveness, we needed to ground our actions in empathy and respect for one another. Having pretty much maximized my ability to access my empathic concern for the other side through doing exposure and grounding exercises, engaging in my own counseling, and practicing mindfulness, I decided to take a look again at Loving-Kindness Meditation. While it's a simple practice born from Buddhist philosophy, on its surface it can sound a bit Pollyannish. What ultimately convinced me to give it a try was the extensive research done on it in neuroscience circles.[3]

Loving-Kindness Meditation is the practice of silently wishing yourself and others well, by means of uttering phrases such as "may you be happy," "may you be healthy," or "may you be safe." The entire practice entails five steps, although you can practice them separately and in any order. Traditionally, the practice begins with sending good wishes to yourself, then directing them toward a loved one, then a neutral person, then a difficult person, and finally all living beings. It all seemed simple enough.

Because this practice was new to me, I decided to jumpstart it by attending a weekend workshop offered by Sharon Salzberg, who is well known for her teachings on this. In the workshop, she addressed the concern that many of us in the audience voiced about not feeling much empathy or love at all while repeating the good wishes. We were physically engaging the practice, but empathy was not magically sprouting within us. Salzberg addressed our question by reframing the concept of love as an action, not a feeling—as a verb, not a noun. She specified that the success of the practice does not rest in its ability to rouse loving feelings in the short term or during the practice itself. Rather, the aim is to expand one's empathetic muscles. Still quite skeptical, but at least curious, I identified four sentences I could get behind (around health, happiness, peace, and living with ease) and decided to begin practicing just the first step. So I started sending good wishes to myself a few minutes a day, thinking I could use some self-compassion: "May I be healthy.... May I be happy. ... May I be peaceful.... May I live with ease...."

I don't think I consciously noticed much change along the way, but one day I was in my kitchen, and I dropped something that made a big mess. I expected to feel intensely annoyed with myself and tell myself off. Instead, I felt myself leaning into my own annoyance silently, saying, "Aww," just as I might do if I were to soothe a child. I was quite stunned by my own reaction, and half-jokingly I asked myself, "Who *is* that?!" The practice seemed to have slow-cooked me into a much more tender, caring, and self-compassionate person. As I continued to strengthen my ability to lean into my difficult feelings with a degree of self-compassion, I realized how much more I could feel genuine compassion toward others—whether colleagues, students, clients, or family members. To be sure, I remained fully human with my fight, flight, or freeze impulses completely intact and my eyes wide open to the evils of the world. But I didn't feel as threatened by others' negative feelings and therefore didn't shut down as often. Conversely, I felt considerably better able to access and act on my emotional empathy.

Shortly after the incident in the kitchen, I decided to venture into the step of the practice that I dreaded the most: sending good wishes to a difficult person. I was careful to identify someone I found irritating but not overly triggering. For a few weeks, I split my practice between sending good wishes to myself and then to the difficult person. The contrast between the two practices was striking. As I switched between sending myself good wishes to sending good wishes to the difficult person, my mind went from fairly settled to wildly distractable, the warmth in my heart replaced by a pit in my stomach. While I sent myself plenty of good wishes, I could hardly concentrate long enough to repeat the same wishes more than a few times for my difficult person: "May you be healthy. . . . May you be happy. . . . May you be peaceful. . . . May you live with ease. . . ."

After a few weeks of what I thought was a complete failure of a practice, I decided to try it in the very moments when I felt my anxiety or anger rise at work. The advocacy for master's programs in counseling psychology that had become so contentious was an ideal practice ground. Once again, it proved a most powerful tool. Wishing the difficult person well in moments of conflict allowed me not to feel overpowered by the people involved, to see them as human, to appreciate their struggles and vulnerabilities, and then to respond honestly but kindly. To be sure, the difficult person of the moment did not change their behavior, nor did they facilitate the internal shift for me. Rather, my increased capacity for empathic concern toward them lowered my defensiveness, allowed me to learn from the conflict itself, and fueled my ability to stay in a relationally productive space where I could respond with clarity and integrity. One of my proudest professional accomplishments that year was when two prominent leaders opposing my professional advocacy went from publicly belittling me to openly thanking me after a particularly tense moment when I had an opening to lash back at them but didn't. For the

first time in several years, however briefly, we were openly and genuinely in relationship with one another. Since that time, I have used the
Loving-Kindness Meditation toward a difficult person quite regularly
in moments of tension. It's my go-to anchor to bring myself back into a
relational space, with potential for transformation on both sides.

As you can see, I've been slow-going in implementing all the steps of
this practice, despite how helpful it has been. In fact, I started practicing the last step (sending wishes to all living beings) only several years
after beginning the practice. What prompted me this time was feeling
myself sinking again emotionally as the video of Daunte Wright's tragic
death appeared on social media during Derek Chauvin's trial for the
murder of George Floyd. I found myself caught between hatred for the
police officers and intense sorrow for the victims and their families. I
also felt a sense of hopelessness at watching Chauvin be held appropriately responsible for his actions but without a clear, open acknowledgment of the racist, patriarchal system that created him.

While a part of me rejoiced at seeing justice served in such a historically
significant way, another part of me felt hopeless in witnessing a system that sees the only solution to racism as the putting away of human
beings who learn the rules of racism so well that they lose their humanity in the process. How many people do we need to put away, and how
fast, to eradicate racism in the United States, not to mention the world?
What would it mean to hold someone unequivocally accountable while
recognizing that they are doing exactly what the system asked of them?
What would it mean to hold individuals accountable while also wondering how Chauvin's behavior and his seeming complete lack of regret
have been able to exist in his role as a public servant for that long?
What do we continue to tolerate and avert our eyes from what Chauvin's verdict will not solve? I was on the brink of despair, and I realized
that the way forward for me in that moment was to try to expand my
heart to everyone involved. Because if I couldn't, there would be no way
for me to imagine a different future for our world other than an endless
string of murders and trials.

I developed a list of wishes I felt I could genuinely send everyone, from
people I love dearly, to people I'm grieving with, to people I really,
really don't love at all. I decided that I could wish everyone, no matter
what, the following: belonging, compassion, connectedness, grace,
health, joy, justice, life, love, peace, and truth. I thought that if people
felt these things, they wouldn't be just healthy and happy; they also
would not harm others. As I felt moments of hopelessness and despair
rise within me in that political moment, I imagined sending those
wishes to everyone involved. Doing that was nothing short of essential
to my ability to remain present with the pain of injustice without
sinking once again into hopelessness and paralysis, as I did after the

murder of George Floyd. It was so helpful in keeping me moving forward that it has quickly become my go-to medicine in intense moments of collective reckoning around injustice that require me to keep both my eyes and my heart open.

In my personal and professional lives, the more I practice approaching situations from an expanded empathic capacity, the more my efforts are both effective and sustainable. Guilt and shame can certainly provide moments of learning about and reckoning with our racist inheritance.[4] But as Ali shared in Chapter 1, guilt and shame by themselves are very poor fuel for antiracism. Empathy and compassion for oneself and others not only provide infinitely more plentiful and renewable energy but also create the emotional and psychological climate that gives us the vision, clarity, and courage we need on our antiracist path.

Empathy and Strong Boundaries Go Hand in Hand

Whenever I speak about empathy, I am always questioned about the appropriateness of using empathy when we interact with people with whom we strongly disagree. I'm always asked: How can it be good to empathize with those who harm us? Isn't that bad for us? Doesn't that give them a pass and allow them to continue harming others? Haven't we been too nice for too long with people and structures that take advantage of us in return?

The answer to these questions is both yes and no. The determining factor is whether we can empathize with clear boundaries. While empathy in and of itself it not dangerous, it can indeed become dangerous when we don't extend it within the protective confines of appropriate boundaries.

A few years back, I came across a concept popularized by Tibetan Buddhist teacher Chögyam Trungpa Rinpoche: idiot compassion. Setting aside for a moment my dislike for the term *idiot*,[5] idiot compassion refers to putting no boundaries between us and those who harm us. As Buddhist nun and author Pema Chödrön argues, a lack of boundaries is an indication of neither empathy nor compassion; it's closer to enabling (W. Lewis, 2012). Bringing this notion back to our bodies, we could say that our nervous systems don't have the capacity to discern whom it is safe to empathize with; our nervous systems rely on *us* to maintain appropriate boundaries while we empathize.

In the Internal Work section for Chapter 2, I described losing my ability to learn during a diversity workshop when two White participants challenged the content of the workshop using race- and gender-stereotypical behaviors—mansplaining and helplessness. In that moment, I wasn't able to consciously consider that neither the mansplaining nor the helplessness behaviors had any immediate, tangible, dangerous effect on my bodily integrity. There was nothing lethal about the behavior of the two participants that required the protection of a flight, fight, or freeze response. Their speech was nothing but sound waves of perfectly safe decibels hitting my eardrums. My body, however, needed to trust me not to drag it (again) into doing all the mental labor to come up with the right facts and figures to convince someone else of the validity of my experience, or all the emotional labor to make someone emotionally comfortable while they were being challenged to see how racism might manifest within and around them. Jumping into fixing mode would have meant giving into my fight impulses based on my nervous system's perception of danger, and in that moment, this would have felt exhausting rather than empowering. In that moment, it would have helped to remember that I was in fact physically safe, which would have given me access to my empathy muscles, through which I could wonder about the emotions expressed by these two participants, notice where my own White tendencies were reflected in their behaviors, and learn from the presenter's skillful engagement in the conversation.

Empathizing while maintaining or establishing appropriate boundaries is not dangerous. In fact, the opposite tends to be true. When we are in a more relaxed, empathetic space, the nervous system can detect more accurately whom we can trust and therefore when and how to assert even stronger boundaries. As it turns out, empathy is a much more effective information gatherer than fear. From this perspective, we could say that empathizing actually makes us safer. But that can be the case only if we can regulate our stress responses. This allows us to be grounded enough to assess the actual risks and choose the course of action from there.

It's Up to Us

For us to be successful in our efforts to co-create a better world for everyone, we must consider the human, physiological context that frames our antiracism. On one hand, we have our innate reactivity as the path of least resistance. On the other hand, the health of our bodies and communities depends on having the capacity to emotionally regulate ourselves enough to act on our empathic concern. While the path of reactivity is effortless, cultivating empathy takes intention and repetition. From this vantage point, the goal is not for our antiracist practice to become comfortable, for us to feel and act flawlessly when we confront racism, or to preserve our sense of safety while disrupting white supremacy. How could any of this even be possible? The goal is to train for the discomfort, to get used to the bumps, to fall and recover, to mitigate our panic at the thought of diminished safety as we question white supremacy, and to develop authentic connections with People of Color and Native people, as well as other White people. We must train our nervous systems to keep our capacity for empathy open enough to learn from, care for, invite in, and join arms with others. This is what it takes to be antiracist.

Strengthening Your Antiracist Practice

Keep Yourself on Top of the Hill: How to Regulate Your Emotional Empathy

We perform at our best when we experience moderate levels of emotional engagement. If we are too disengaged, we'll do very little—at most, we'll think about it. If we are overwhelmed, we function poorly (e.g., gaslighting People of Color, shaming fellow White allies) or freeze.

How do we keep ourselves engaged but not overwhelmed? When I sense myself emotionally disengaging in unhelpful ways, one sure way to raise my emotional empathy is to visually put myself in the other person's shoes. This allows my body to resonate more deeply and directly with the experience of another individual. However, sometimes I can do that too well, so I have to work to consciously pull back a bit, especially if I notice myself becoming hopeless, helpless, or otherwise overwhelmed. To pull back, I use a few different strategies, depending on what's available to me in that moment:

1. I try to consider that particular experience from a wider historical or spiritual perspective.

2. If I can tell that my body got stuck in a fight, flight, or freeze response, I make time to refuel in nature by taking a walk or sitting outside.

3. As a general rule, I consistently encourage myself to feel, name, and share my feelings with trusted people in my life.

These strategies don't always work immediately or forever, but overall they have been immensely helpful in my ability to back away from the intensity of my emotions and come back to an internal state from which I can more clearly and effectively act.

How to Strengthen Your Empathic Concern: Loving-Kindness Meditation

The Loving-Kindness Meditation is one of the simplest yet most powerful ways to foster your empathic concern. This specific kind of empathy directly fuels your clarity and confidence in operationalizing your antiracist intentions. This practice consists of repeating short statements through which you wish yourself and various other people well. These short good wishes are individually chosen, can vary depending on the circumstances, and can even shift from day to day. Consistency of practice, not of phrases, is what matters.

Here are a few examples of good wishes:

- May I feel safe.

- May I know love.

- May I be at peace.

- May I be healthy.

The key to this practice is to repeat these phrases with no expectation or implied request that the recipient (including yourself) would achieve any of those states. These good wishes are freely given, with no strings attached. This practice is all about expanding the big-heartedness of the sender, not about changing the receiver.

Traditionally, the practice involves mentally sending two to four such wishes sequentially to five kinds of people:

- Yourself

- A loved one

- A neutral person (someone you don't feel much about one way or another)

- A difficult person (starting with a relatively low-stakes one)

- All living beings

At times, the practice (which, again, originates in Buddhism) is culturally adapted for Westerners by inverting the first two steps, since it's often easier for those of us brought up in the West to begin rousing our empathic concern by sending good wishes to a loved one first, rather than to ourselves. However, remember that you are not expected to feel anything

(Continued)

(Continued)

in particular while repeating these phrases. As Salzberg said in the workshop I described earlier, love is a practice or a verb, not a feeling or a noun, so your task is simply to express these wishes, not to force yourself to feel them.

You could practice a single step, like I did (e.g., sending wishes to yourself), or simply repeat the wishes you created once through for all five kinds of people, or anything in between. You could dedicate some quiet time to the practice or simply do it in conjunction with any other rote daily activity, such as brushing your teeth, taking a shower, washing dishes, or commuting to work.

How long should you practice it for? You decide. You can start with doing it for a few days or a week, and then decide from there at what pace you want to carry it forward. The idea is to practice it long enough for you to experience a degree of goodwill, concern, and care, even toward people you might be in conflict with. Identify which contexts you would like to bring more of this skill to, and let that be your guide and inspiration for the practice.

Notes

1. In Chapter 10, we will address how crucial it is for us to learn how to grieve the horrors of racism and how to actually do that.

2. This concept was developed in the early 20th century by psychologists Robert M. Yerkes and John Dillingham Dodson, hence the name.

3. The Center for Compassion and Altruism Research and Education at the Stanford University School of Medicine has done much research on the social, emotional, and physiological impact of this practice (for more information, see http://ccare .stanford.edu).

4. I will describe more about what that looks like in the Internal Work section for Chapter 7.

5. I don't love this term for a number of reasons: first, because of its obvious roots in ableism. It also camouflages the fact that many of us, based on our identities, are heavily socialized into the belief that it's rude or inappropriate to set boundaries. We aren't bad at setting boundaries because we're idiots. It's because many people from marginalized groups are taught to please people with more power, and they face strong negative consequences when they don't do so.

Can White Antiracist People Feel Proud of Being White?

> *Without inner change, there can be no outer change; without collective change, no change matters.*
>
> —Reverend angel Kyodo williams (n.d.)

In the racial identity development framework for Black people and People of Color,[1] the mark of a strong positive racial identity includes pride in oneself and one's group. At one of my recent talks on "What White Children Need to Know About Race," a White parent asked me, "Why is that not the case for White people? Why is pride not part of a strong, positive racial identity for White kids?"

This same confounding question is central to the podcast *Scene on Radio: Seeing White*, which is an excellent resource for understanding the history of Whiteness. In Episode 7, host John Biewen says:

> At the end of that episode about slavery and race in Colonial America, I was kind of marveling, not for the first time, at the realization that race, and whiteness, were not created by nature and simply observed by people. They were man-made, built, for reasons that had entirely to do with power and greed. (Kumanyika & Biewen, 2017)

His collaborator, Chenjerai Kumanyika, replies:

> I gotta say, it's kinda good news and bad news on that note. The good news is, really, when you think about this thing called whiteness, there's not anything genetic that you share with folks that's different from what we all share with each other. So there's a message in here about our connectedness. But the bad news is that, in a way, the effort to get people to come together under the banner of whiteness has sort of always been about power and exploitation. So, I don't know what that means about trying to salvage the idea of, like, good whiteness. You know? That's something that you gotta

wrestle with. . . . Like, when was whiteness good? It's kind of like, when was America great? [Laughs.] . . . It seems like the whole project was related to exploitation. So, if you identify that way . . . yeah. I don't envy you, in terms of having to try to think about what that means. You know? (Kumanyika & Biewen, 2017)

I was riding my bike while listening to this episode, and I had to stop. I was so overwhelmed by the depth of the challenge that Chenjerai was laying out that all my energy for biking suddenly vaporized. I sat on the grass and pondered. There has to be some goodness in Whiteness, doesn't there? Can a White person be good, even though they're White? To return to the parent's quandary, can we teach White children to be proud of who they are, including as White people? In this chapter, I use racial identity development theory to wrestle with this question.

To begin, keep in mind that the racial identity development framework is not a framework for how a person feels about their entire self-image. It's a framework for understanding *how a person feels about their racialized identity*, or their race. Nobody chooses their race. But as long as we live in a racialized society, we still have to actively engage with the meaning and impact that our race has in our lives.

Racial identity development, as defined by Dr. Beverly Daniel Tatum (2017), psychologist, author, and former president of Spelman College, is the "process of defining for oneself the personal significance and social meaning of belonging to a particular racial group" (p. 16). This means that as we grow up in a heavily racialized society, in which every person is put into racial boxes (whether we want to be or not), we undergo an identity process during which we reckon with what it means to find ourselves in our particular box.

The precise moment when we begin this reckoning happens at different ages for everyone. Many People of Color and Native people are shocked that I didn't really start my own process of racial identity development until I was 18 because they learn it early—often before starting kindergarten. My friend Mathu Subramanian (2014) said she was in preschool: "[Another four-year-old] told me firmly I could not play with them because I was a 'darky'" (p. xii). Although Mathu didn't understand exactly why she was being excluded, she says that moment sticks with her because it was when she first realized that skin color has meaning— and that understanding that meaning would be vital in her life.

People of Color learn from a young age that skin color matters. Arguably, they begin a process of racial identity development before they should have to, before anyone is developmentally ready to contend with the weight of the social dysfunction that is racism. But they do so because some part of our society (a classmate, a neighbor, a teacher, a security guard, a police officer—or a movie, a TV show, a commercial, a blurb on the news) lays racism at their feet in a way that they cannot ignore. Many People of Color people develop strategies for protecting themselves against racism before they even consciously recognize they are doing so.

Most White people don't have to contend with racism at an early age. Many White people of my generation and a middle- or upper-middle-class background grew up in segregated communities, naively believing that racism was a thing of the past. We did not know People of Color and Native people well enough to see how they were already navigating racism while we went about our merry colorblind ways. White people tend to learn about racism in school or at work, and usually—as it was for me—because it is required. And when we do, the approach to teaching about racism is not a framework that helps us recognize and give a name to our own experiences. It's more of an unveiling, a surprise that throws us off guard. It leads us to ask, "How could I have not seen this? How could this possibly be true, and I had no idea it was going on all around me?"

This is not to say that White people are not learning racial messages from a young age. Arguably, those first 18 years of my life, I was being schooled in white supremacy and my place within it. But I didn't know anything about racism as a construct—I wasn't able to see it and call it such—which then normalized the racial caste structure I was living within. So it's not that I wasn't learning racism or Whiteness. I was actually well trained (albeit unknowingly) in racism and in the color-blindness required to uphold it. However, I was not learning to look at it critically, name it, and disrupt it. The surprise that I felt when I first started learning about racism was actually predictable, because I had been actively taught to see the opposite—a fair society in which everyone had an equal shot, where if you worked hard, you got ahead.

As White people learn to see a racial hierarchy that historically has put White people at the top, we begin to see how we have had advantages in our own lives that would not have been possible had we not been White. We start to see a system that benefited our ancestors and that begins to explain certain things about our own lives: that small inheritance, perhaps, or that lack of debt, or grandparents who lived into their 90s, or the small family cabin with so many fond memories. For White people who grow up poor or working-class, the advantages of Whiteness may seem more elusive. But for every person who is White, it is worth wondering how our lives would be different had we not been White. How might our ancestors' lives have been different had they not been White? It is worth asking how we've been taught to see ourselves as different from (and better than) People of Color and Native people, which then makes it hard to stand together and demand policies that would benefit all of us. For many of us, many of the things we know, love, and hold dear were facilitated by our Whiteness. This realization creates a personal crisis of identity that can be painful, as it conflicts sharply with our belief in meritocracy and puts into question our values around fairness, sharing, doing no harm, and being good people.

The next section will describe a framework for the different identity stages White people go through as we learn about racism, which both include and go beyond guilt.

White (Antiracist) Racial Identity Development

These feelings that White people experience as we learn what it means to be White fall into common and predictable stages of racial identity development. There are multiple frameworks for White racial identity development, each with its own advantages and disadvantages. Here, I outline the framework developed by Dr. Janet Helms (2020), a Black psychologist at Boston College, with one small addition of a stage called "pre-contact" (see Figure 5.1). I use Helms's framework because I really see my own development in the stages as she has laid them out. I also find her writing on how White people with different racial identities interact to be incredibly valuable as I learn how to invite other White people to move along an antiracist path.

Helms's framework is based on the work of Dr. William Cross (1978, 1991). In the 1970s, Cross created a model of Nigresence, the first

Figure 5.1   The Stages of White Racial Identity Development

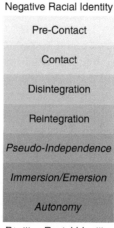

Negative Racial Identity

Pre-Contact

Contact

Disintegration

Reintegration

Pseudo-Independence

Immersion/Emersion

Autonomy

Positive Racial Identity

Source: **Based on the White racial identity development model by Helms (2020).**

framework for racial identity development designed to give names to the common stages of identity development that Black people go through as they learn to contend with anti-Black racism in the context of U.S. society. Building on his work, Helms set out to design a model of White racial identity development, which she did by interviewing hundreds of White people about what they experience as they learn about racism.

Today, there are at least 12 racial identity development frameworks for different "racial groups." I put that term in quotes because "racial groups" are a social construct. Nonetheless, the research on racial identity theory demonstrates that even if a part of our identity is socially constructed, it still has a huge impact on how we think of ourselves and therefore on how we behave and relate.

Most of the racial identity frameworks are laid out in a way that suggests a progression from a negative racial identity to a positive racial identity. Negative racial identity doesn't necessarily mean that a person thinks badly of themselves. *Negative* is used by the authors of these frameworks to suggest an *absent* identity, a lack of consciousness about how race and racism affect one's life. Imagine a negative in photography, in which the image and color are inverted. Similarly, a positive racial identity doesn't mean that you love being White; it means you have an affirmed, proactive, race-conscious identity as a White person trying to be antiracist in a racist society.

Helms's framework is laid out in stages, which she later relabeled as *statuses*[2] to emphasize that the framework is not linear, as it might first appear. I like to think of it in the same vein as Elisabeth Kübler-Ross's stages of grief (Kübler-Ross & Kessler, 2005). The stages are nonlinear and particular to the individual. Like the stages of grief, the stages of racial identity development can happen over the course of a few minutes or a few years. Unlike human developmental stages, some people go through every single stage, while others go through only one or two. There's no single way to go through the stages, and there's no right timeline for it. Just as the process of moving through the stages of grief is catalyzed by a loss, the process of moving through racial identity development is catalyzed by a person's first conscious contact with racism, either real or vicarious. Every time we come into contact with a new incident of racism, we are likely to move through the stages of racial identity development anew, perhaps faster this time because we have built the capacity to experience all the different stages and move through them with more ease. But just as grief is not diminished by past loss, learning about or experiencing racism doesn't necessarily get easier with time. And just because a person has a positive (aka antiracist) racial identity, it doesn't mean that they won't have to go through the stages again and again each time they experience or witness racism.

The First Four Stages of Racial Identity Development: A Negative Racial Identity

Pre-Contact Stage:[3] When You Don't Know What You Don't Know

The first four stages of racial identity development encompass what Helms calls a *negative racial identity*. The first stage that Helms describes is called *contact*. But I include here an additional stage I call *pre-contact*, because I lived 18 years of my life before experiencing contact. This is the time before a person experiences or has exposure to racism. It is common for White people in this stage to insist on color-blindness, to say that racism doesn't exist, and to believe in the myth of meritocracy. People in this stage tend to have an ahistorical sense that all people have been treated equally, which leads them to believe that People of Color and Native people who don't have the same wealth or standing as White people must not have worked hard or must be deficient in some way. A fierce belief in the existence of a fair system means that White people with a negative racial identity must rely on racist explanations involving biological difference (and inferiority) to explain economic and educational disparities between racial groups.

How to Move Forward

What moved me from pre-contact into contact was a required course in college. I was grateful that it was required because I actually wanted to take it, but I was hesitant because I didn't feel like I "belonged" there. But there is no right way to enter the contact stage. Other common contact moments include hearing about racism experienced by a Person of Color or a Native person, going to a conference, reading a book, listening to a podcast, or watching a movie about race or racism. These are all common ways people begin their racial identity journey and move into the next stage of contact.

Remember that if you are in the pre-contact stage, many of the ideas about racism you'll be exposed to through dialogue with others will likely sound contradictory to fundamental beliefs you have about U.S. society. Given that, try to listen to what people say—especially to the stories of People of Color and Native people—*as if they were true*. The stories of racism may not make sense to you immediately. But *if you truly want to hear and learn*, do not argue against them; rather, reflect on or journal about the "what if's" and "buts" that come up for you as you listen. Or seek out a White ally who has been learning about racism longer than you have, and let them know you are trying to learn more.

The reason I suggest finding a White ally to support you in this stage is that when White people are still early in our journeys, we often ask

People of Color and Native people to defend or prove their experiences of racism. At this point, there is far too much history and experience that we still do not know for us to fully understand their experiences of racism, and one conversation will not be sufficient to fill in the blanks. Asking them to make those connections for us is likely to hurt them more than the mitigation of our ignorance could help. We would be asking People of Color and Native people to talk about some of their deepest pain with someone who is not yet equipped to honor it.

This is not to say that there is a rule against asking People of Color and Native people for support. If you are in a mutual relationship with a Person of Color or Native person who trusts you and wants to be with you for part of this journey, talk to them about it, let them know you value their trust, and make sure they know that they can tell you if it becomes too much for them to have you rely on them in this way. But if the People of Color and Native people you go to for education and support are coworkers, people who work for you, people you know casually in another context, the person who happens to live next door, and so on, be wary of your instinct to recruit them into educating you or exposing their pain for the sake of your learning.

Contact Stage: First Contact With Racism

After pre-contact, which can last quite a long time, a person experiences *contact* with racism. This contact can be either experiential or vicarious. The first-year seminar on African American Literature that I described in the introduction was a *contact* moment for me. It was the first time I heard someone talk about racism as anything other than "old-fashioned" racism, which is overt, intentional, and violent. It was the first time I heard Black peers my age talking about the racism they had experienced personally.

Those conversations propelled me to have many other *contact* moments—moments when I began to see racism in a way I hadn't seen it before. Other early contact moments for me included when I learned what my friend Gertrude had been through growing up in Apartheid South Africa, when Amadou Diallo was shot by police 41 times in the Bronx my senior year in college, when I first realized that almost all-White communities (like the one I'd grown up in) don't happen by accident, and when I started to see historical, political, and economic connections between all these phenomena.

How to Move Forward

When you find yourself in contact, know that you are at the beginning of a cycle of racial identity development. I still find myself in contact when I learn about an incident or pattern of racism that I have not previously been exposed to, such as when I heard about the death of Breonna Taylor, who was killed while lying in her bed when police stormed her apartment in a botched raid (Oppel et al., 2021). Revelations like that give specificity to racism; suddenly I could see the life-threatening ways in which Black people are routinely harassed by police in their own homes with a new graphic awareness. Even though I technically know a lot about racism—and know to expect it—I still feel confused and surprised by the murders of unarmed Black people by the police. Even though I have come to understand how modern-day police have their historical roots in slave patrols, and even though I have read *The New Jim Crow*,[4] I don't have the visceral distrust that, say, my Nuyorican colleague Carlos has of police, having been harassed and harmed by them all his life. My body reacts with relief when I see police because of years of socialization in which they were friendly to me and conveyed the message that they were there to protect me. Carlos's body reacts with fear because of the way he's experienced police who are out to intimidate, to falsely accuse, to monitor, and to humiliate young People of Color and Native people. Every time I go through contact, I'm propelled forward in my racial identity journey, toward the next stage: disintegration.

Disintegration Stage: Childhood Worldview Starts to Disintegrate

The contact stage leads to *disintegration*. Once a person begins to see racism, they begin to question much of the mythology and the false narratives they learned growing up. In this stage, for example, people begin questioning their belief in meritocracy—a belief that is hard to maintain when you realize how much racism and inherited wealth (or debt) shapes the potential outcomes in a person's life or family. Or you begin to see evidence of your own implicit bias, which leads you to question your self-image as a person who is colorblind and who does not see race. This stage is called *disintegration* because one's worldview begins to *disintegrate*. You are beginning the process of deconstructing a worldview based in white supremacy—and reconstructing a worldview based on the possibility of equity. You can feel, as I did, as if you have a foot in two different realities—the one that you grew up in and the one that you're learning about. You can begin to feel distant from family and friends who still believe that U.S. society is fair and that we should all be colorblind. *Disintegration* can be disorienting and confusing, which leads to feelings of vulnerability, uncertainty, a lack of confidence, self-doubt, disconnection, sadness, anger, and guilt.

How to Move Forward

When you are in the stage of disintegration, consider the foundational beliefs you have been taught, as well as how an understanding of systemic racism might challenge them. If you are trying to learn more about racism, you may have to break with some of the foundational learnings taught to you by family members or teachers, and this can be challenging, especially if it causes relational tension with people you love.

To move through the disintegration stage, you want to be able to sit with the heat of those uncomfortable feelings without shutting down and refusing to continue to listen and learn. Journal about your feelings. Find a White ally who is further along on their journey and let them know you could use some support. Ask if they could check in with you every week or two.

Again, a close Friend of Color or Native friend might support you in this stage as well; it is certainly not only White people who can do this. But I encourage you to consider a White ally because sometimes White people in disintegration seek out a Person of Color or Native person because we yearn for forgiveness or reassurance that might help us get out from under the heavy feelings of guilt that are common in this stage. This scenario stunts our own growth and is a burden to our friend.

No Person of Color or Native person can forgive a White person for all racism or colonialism, and we shouldn't ask them to. A White ally would not attempt to forgive or excuse you; instead, they will commiserate with you and accompany you as you navigate the impact of disintegrating a worldview that you took for granted for so long. White people in disintegration often assume that other White people cannot support us in matters of race. On the contrary, when we lean on White allies, we make it possible to show up to our Friends and Colleagues of Color and our Native friends and colleagues with a greater willingness to listen and collaborate, rather than a need for exoneration.

Reintegration Stage: Trying to Put Your Worldview Back Together the Way It Was

Feelings aren't wrong or bad—they're just feelings. And having them doesn't make us weak or defective. But human beings most definitely don't like and try very hard not to feel most of the feelings that come up during disintegration. As Eleonora explains, our nervous systems often identify these negative feelings as threats and seek ways to move us away from the stimulus that provokes them. That is why disintegration often leads to *reintegration*. During this stage, we *reintegrate* our self-concept with our former worldview and close ourselves off to learning more about racism. Without the self-awareness and skills to manage our discomfort, reintegration is almost inevitable. Learning about racism becomes so uncomfortable that we decide—usually unconsciously—to turn our vulnerable feelings of guilt and sadness into more externally directed, self-protective, combative feelings of hostility, anger, and self-righteousness.

In this stage, White people are just realizing that many People of Color and Native people and even many White people see them as White, and we begin to feel self-conscious about that. We become tentative about speaking up about race or about talking at all in multiracial spaces, and we fear that our input as White people is not wanted. We believe we will never be seen as "right" on the subject of race, because we are White. Given that we are just beginning to learn about racism, we may be accurate in our perception that what we are saying is eliciting resistance or annoyance in others. More often than not, a person in reintegration blames People of Color and Native people (individuals) for racism (systemic problems) and believes that if things are not going well for People of Color and Native people, it must be their own, individual fault.

When we are in reintegration, we are unpleasant to be around. I can still remember one night when I went to see my parents, excited about all I was learning about why colorblindness was harmful. I thought it provided some important answers to the questions my dad had been asking about race. But when I began to explain what I had learned, he became angry. He said, "Why would you even talk at a conference like that if you were White? *They* are always going to attack us. *We* will never get to be right, because we are White." The anger in his usually mellow tone was palpable, and I was so flustered that I started to cry. I called my sister later that night to say, "Listen to what's happening with Dad—I don't know what's going on. I thought we were making so much progress!"

She listened and then said, "Yeah. I think Dad is reintegrating." She was referencing the Helms framework that I had once found so useful—a framework that I barely remembered.

"What does that mean?" I asked. "What do you do for that?"

We talked it through and decided that what my dad needed most was support. If movement into the reintegration stage is catalyzed by an unwillingness or an inability to be vulnerable enough to experience all those negative feelings, perhaps he would be able to move through it with more emotional support.

The irony of this plan of action, which I have generally found to be a strategic way to respond to most White people in reintegration, is that when a person is in this stage, the last thing I (or anyone) wants to do is support them. It's painful and uncomfortable for me to align myself with people who are reintegrating because I don't want others to associate me with them or think that I endorse their views. Sometimes people in reintegration are outright hurtful to me or say hurtful things about People of Color and Native people—both of which are scary. Eleonora would say that the fight, flight, or freeze reaction that propelled a person into reintegration to begin with triggers my own fight, flight, or freeze reactions. As I attempt to flee my own discomfort, I begin to ask myself, "Why does it have to be my job to say something?"

But the whole point of this book is that, in fact, it is the job of White allies to reach out to other White people in *all* stages of racial identity development so that People of Color and Native people don't have to.[5] If White people who are reintegrating are particularly hostile toward or avoidant of People of Color and Native people, it may not even be safe or possible for a Person of Color or Native person to be the one to reach out. That is why this is a fundamental task of White people who are trying to be allies.

One could argue that most White people in the United States are in the reintegration stage of racial identity development. So many people know just enough about racism to know that knowing about racism makes them feel bad. Because they don't understand how their physiology tries to protect them from feeling bad, they take their own danger signals very seriously and literally. We then witness their fight, flight, or freeze strategies, which successfully close the door to an antiracist path before they can even experience how liberating it is. And the sad part is that it's quite often another White person who locks the door behind them, because rather than offer support for the stress and sadness inherent in this part of an antiracist journey, we distance ourselves.

I use my dad as an example here, but I have found myself in reintegration plenty of times since my sister reminded me of what that is. Any time I hear myself thinking, "Why do I even try? I'm never going to get this right, because I'm White," I have to remind myself, "I'm *reintegrating*."

Identifying that stage in myself is useful because it helps me figure out what I need. Rather than take the full weight of my frustration and anger out on the people around me, I can recognize my own fight, flight, or freeze reactions, hand myself some degree of compassion for simply being human, and then ask myself what I need. That usually leads me to call a White ally and complain or cry, as a way to process the event or grieve a possible moral injury (see the Internal Work section for Chapter 7 for more on the concept of moral injury). When the person I reach out to knows and appreciates my antiracist intention, they can help me root myself back in that intention. A White ally can help me see and be accountable for the harm I've caused while maintaining perspective, not only about the harm's relative proportion to my overall impact but also about everything else that makes me who I am.

Moving ourselves and other White people out of reintegration allows us/them to move toward a positive racial identity, rather than stewing and stagnating in the dead end of reintegration. Reintegration is the stage where resentment and blame toward People of Color and Native people begin to grow. A person in this stage is so unpracticed at receiving constructive feedback on their viewpoints about race that they quickly shut down in the face of criticism. A person in reintegration is likely to feel angry, even enraged, in conversations about race and to express hostility toward People of Color and Native people, as well as toward White people who are trying to be antiracist. It is not a stage that ends here but one that lays the groundwork for a receptivity to overtly white supremacist ideas and violence. That is why it is so important for us to help people move beyond it.

How to Move Forward

Take some deep breaths and remind yourself that no one is bad or wrong just because they're White. And at the same time, remind yourself that being White and having a White lens might mean that there are certain things you couldn't see before. If you recognize that you are in the reintegration stage, remind yourself that the world is not either/or. You're not *either* right *or* wrong, good *or* bad. Sometimes you will be right, and sometimes you will be wrong. Often it will be a mix. Interrupt the binary thinking that suggests you are a hopeless, ignorant racist because you got one thing wrong.[6] Find people who will be patient with your questions and confusion. Remember that learning about racism is hard because society gives us so many reasons to believe that racial inequality is the result of the personal failures of People of Color and Native people. When you are also tempted to do that, ask, "How is this particular person or situation the result of group treatment now and in the recent past?" Try looking past individuals toward the system that shapes us all. Commit to talking to one person you trust, going to one event, or reading a chapter in a book that will help you keep learning more. When People of Color and Native people or White people who are trying to be antiracist annoy you, remind yourself that we are all imperfect. Remind yourself that they also get to show up and offer their gifts, with all their imperfections, just like you. Journal about how you react to that ongoing learning. Journal about all you get right, as well as what you still need to learn. Remind yourself of your deep values and your unique skills. Consider how your values and skills could be assets to you as you keep traveling an antiracist path, especially when it's hard.

Moving Toward a Positive Antiracist Racial Identity

Pseudo-Independence Stage: Feeling All the Competence With None of the Humility

The next three stages of identity development begin to move a person toward a positive racial identity. If we can make it beyond a negative racial identity, we enter *pseudo-independence*. In this stage, we understand enough about racism to know that it is wrong and to want to do something about it. But we begin to take action while our self-concept is still firmly planted in the White rungs of the racial caste system. We may want to help People of Color and Native people, but we believe that racial liberation will result when they act more like White people, rather than when we change the system.

Because we often rush past our own self-examination, at this stage we still operate from an unconscious sense of racial dominance, which makes us believe that we know the best, most effective ways to end racism—even more than People of Color and Native people (refer back to the second myth of white supremacy: "We can and should be perfect—or at least appear perfect"). In this stage, we also tend to *think* about racism, rather than *feel* about it (reflecting the fourth myth: "It's better to think, rather than feel, about racism")—because it's easier to intellectualize than to connect emotionally to the pain of racism. Pseudo-independence, then, can become a performative stage, where White people feel deeply invested in making sure that other people *see* our attempts at antiracist allyship. The performance—and the energy required to maintain it—unfortunately distracts us from being able to show up, be imperfect, take feedback, and work in solidarity with People of Color and Native people.

Most White people (including Eleonora and me) who are trying to be antiracist tend to sit in the pseudo-independent stage most of our days. It is a never-ending, iterative process to recognize the inevitable ways in which we act from an automatic instinct to normalize and reinforce a racial hierarchy. We are still in the matrix while trying to dismantle it. There is really no way to bypass that reality, except through ongoing practice, as well as seeking and taking feedback.

When other White people enter the reintegration stage, White people in pseudo-independence tend to shame them or distance ourselves from them because we are too self-conscious about how antiracist we appear. We don't want to be associated with people who are so obviously not aware. You can see, then, how being in pseudo-independence actually makes it harder to intervene with the vast majority of White people, so many of whom are in reintegration. We are too worried about our own self-images to be able to offer the support they need to move forward in their racial identity journey. That is why it is so necessary to keep learning the signs of pseudo-independence and to keep building the capacity to move beyond it. When we are in pseudo-independence, we are still operating from the mindset that one antiracist White person (me!) is enough.

As I mentioned previously, one key indication that a person is in the pseudo-independence stage is that we still *think* about racism more than we *feel* about it. That is why I have described *learning to feel* as a big part of my own personal work. It might seem ridiculous to say that I need to "learn to feel." But as Eleonora has pointed out, it's not because I've been a bad student that I don't resonate with the pain of People of Color and Native people as much as I do with White people; it's because I've been too good a student. If I am not well practiced at feeling empathy toward People of Color and Native people, it's because I've learned all too well how to numb myself to their pain. The racial caste system cannot stay in place if I begin to empathize with the pain of People of Color and Native people. Enslavement and Jim Crow worked only because White people could look directly into the eyes of Black people and somehow write off, ignore, or even celebrate their pain. The children of Native people could not have been confined in abusive boarding schools if White people had recognized the love that Native people had for their children as akin to the love they had for their own. Without pausing to feel, we let our bodies pull us back into the emotional and physical safety that comes with intellectualizing.

Thinking about racism feels safer, and it gives us the impression that we are doing something. But thinking about racism doesn't give us a consistent, sustainable, effective compass for what to actually do about racism. *Feeling* about racism is not something only for the naive or something we should do once and get over with as quickly as possible. It's how we develop a gut that can intuitively move us to action. As Eleonora described in the Internal Work section for Chapter 4, it's the very lens we need to deeply understand how racism works and how we can use our individual skills, talents, and spheres of influence to dismantle it.

How to Move Forward

When you are in this stage, listen deeply to People of Color and Native people, particularly when they are responding to something you said or did. You are likely to feel deeply defensive of yourself because you identify as woke—or at least awake—and as having the right answers. This is where you will have to work the hardest at identifying your defensive response. I know I'm defensive when I start to say or think, "Do you know how many books I've read on this topic?!" I'm insecure about my intelligence, so I use my knowledge as a shield against any feedback that threatens my sense of knowing. This is how I reject or contest challenging feedback—either out loud or in my head. Find your defensive shield so that you can consciously lower it after you've unconsciously raised it. See all feedback as a gift; invite it, sit with it, and integrate it into your life.

Immersion/Emersion Stage: Deepening Your Understanding of What It Means to Be White

Following pseudo-independence is a stage called *immersion/emersion*. It is so named because it describes a stage in which White people try to immerse themselves in what it means to be White and often emerge with a new, antiracist White racial identity. White people in this stage are taking workshops, reading books, joining White antiracist learning spaces, and finding White antiracist role models, so that they can begin to redefine what it means to be White. Sometimes White people in this stage will actually try to immerse themselves in Communities of Color and Native communities, almost as if they could cast off all the oppressiveness of Whiteness simply by adopting new cultural styles and hanging out with people who are not White. They may truly want authentic relationships with People of Color and Native people but sometimes reject White people because they want to distance themselves from Whiteness (refer back to the third myth of white supremacy: "We need to 'win' by competing with one another"). This behavior seems to be a reaction to the continued discomfort of realizing how complicit we have been and still are with an unfair system. We are able to keep learning, but we can do so only if we feel we have acceptance from Communities of Color and Native communities. In a way, we seek absolution from People of Color and Native people.

I was in this stage in college when I lived with my friend Gertrude and her family while studying abroad in Cape Town, South Africa. The Sgwentu family are Black South Africans who lived in a "grey area," which was an area of South Africa where people of several non-White racial backgrounds (Black people, Coloured people, and Indian people[7]) lived. It was uncommon for a White person to live there—much less a White person who lived with a Black family. I found myself identifying so deeply with Gertrude's family[8]—and perhaps wanting to distinguish myself from the White South Africans who wished to deny the full impact of Apartheid—that I began thinking of myself as belonging to their family and community. One day I looked in the mirror, and I saw my White skin so clearly—starkly, even. I wanted so badly not to be White that I was almost surprised by my own White skin, so pale and so different from the faces I saw around me. But in that moment, I could see how hypocritical I was being. I wanted to be Black and South African—but with U.S. dollars and education. I was not only White but White and American, which meant that I could stand outside the legacy of Apartheid as a harsh judge of White South Africans, but as a White American, I had even more global power than they had. And I had a racist legacy of my own that I inherited, which I had never fully acknowledged.

Some of the most prominent cases of White people in this stage of development include Rachel Dolezal and Jessica Krug, who pretended to be People of Color in all aspects of their lives, fighting racism, but under the ruse that they were People of Color. Dolezal was the president of her local NAACP and an instructor of African studies at Eastern Washington University. Dolezal wore her hair locked or in Black curls, said that her father was Black, and claimed to be mixed. Krug was a professor of ethnic studies at Georgetown University who pretended to be Black and Latinx from the Bronx, with a fabricated history about a drug-addicted mother and other stereotypical narratives. In reality, Dolezal was White from rural Montana (K. Johnson et al., 2015). Krug was White from suburban Kansas City (Flaherty, 2020).

Add to this list Andrea Smith, a scholar of Native studies who claimed to be Cherokee, studying with funds reserved for Native scholars, publishing well-regarded work in the field of Native studies, and doing so all with an identity that was fabricated (Viren, 2021). It seems as if each of these White women could not conceive of working against racism from within a White body. As one Native scholar wrote of Smith, "had she written as an ally, honesty would be woven into the thread. Other scholars have written as allies and their work has been honest and valued" (P. J. King, 2018, para. 4). These cases present extreme examples of racial or ethnic theft, which is not a typical expression of immersion/emersion.

At the same time, it's not uncommon for White people who have thought deeply about racism to feel more affinity with People of Color and Native people and to align themselves socially and relationally with People of Color and Native people while excluding or staying away from White people. This is not necessarily wrong—building relationships across racial groups is at the heart of antiracism. But when this relationship-building comes as a result of image management, accessing resources and opportunities reserved for People of Color and Native people, or a desire not to be White, it means that White people are not actively and strategically using their racial privilege to confront a racist system. It also has the potential to violate affinity spaces for People of Color and Native people. While building relationships with People of Color and Native people is crucial to building a healthy multiracial community, relying on People of Color and Native people to validate one's antiracism or to excuse one's White identity is not a healthy form of relationship-building. The springboard to solidarity cannot be based on evasion of one's own White identity but must include an honest and informed reckoning with it. The more emotional-regulation skills you have, the more you will be able to grow through all the experiences and relationships you engage with in this stage. The more you can open yourself to *feeling*, the more you will learn.

How to Move Forward

Remember that we cannot *not* be White. And also remember that racism is a White person's problem. So if you want to do something about it—and if you want Whiteness to mean something other than "oppressive"—you are well positioned to help make that so. This means that you are also well positioned to talk with White people who are not as far along in their journey as you are. Use your learning—and the mistakes you have made along the way—to help other White people learn. Develop genuine collaborative and mentoring relationships with them. It's not enough for us to be antiracist and be friends with People of Color and Native people. We need to lean in and help direct more White people to travel this path, because we need millions.

Autonomy Stage:
The "Beloved Community" Stage

According to Helms, the last identifiable stage is that of *autonomy*. In this stage, a person has a conscious antiracist White identity, where they don't feel guilty or embarrassed for being White, but they also don't try to pretend that they aren't White. In this stage, White people take responsibility for Whiteness and for the specific ways in which it has benefited them—and use their racial privilege to work against racism. In this stage, White people work well in multiracial teams and follow the leadership of People of Color and Native people while also taking appropriate antiracist initiative in their personal and professional lives. White people in autonomy are deeply rooted in their antiracist purpose, which then makes it possible for them to take in feedback when they are missing the mark, rather than making them feel that they have to protect their self-image by defending their intention.

When I first read Helms's framework, I found it liberating to read that there were multiple theoretical identity stages for a White person. I was at a stage in my life when I felt guilty about everything race-related. As I have written, I was stuck in the cyclical misperception that guilt was the apex of my development. Realizing there were more stages meant that I still had a long way to go, but it also meant that I had a positive racial identity to look forward to. It meant I didn't have to feel guilty and bad all the time—that was just a predictable, and therefore understandable, stage. Knowing that a positive racial identity would make it possible to be a part of a healthy multiracial community made the journey more attractive and exciting.

How to Move Forward

There are moments—sometimes days—when I feel like I'm in the autonomy stage. But those are few and far between. When you find yourself in autonomy moments, savor them, remember them, use them as motivation to keep working your way back to this stage, and note what helped you get there in your own relationships, process, and development. In this stage, you will be better able to meet White people wherever they are in their own development and help them move forward. Remember that meeting another White person where they are and helping them move forward on an antiracist path isn't about being magnanimous; it actually gives us the opportunity to use and practice skills we need to continue to grow and learn in our own journeys.

Racial Identity Is a Key Ingredient in Relationships

One powerful aspect of Helms's model is that it works in concert with the racial identity frameworks for different groups of People of Color.[9] Helms developed the idea that in a therapeutic relationship, we want counselors to have a more developed racial identity than their clients. Helms calls this a *progressive relationship*. Here's an example: if a counselor–client relationship is a progressive one, the counselor has a stronger racial identity than the client. This means they have thought about race, racism, and their own racial identity enough that they will be able to meet the client wherever they are in their own racial identity journey. Whatever the client is feeling as a result of the racial identity stage they are in, the counselor will know how to support them. This is what was happening with my sister and my dad. My sister was far enough along in her racial identity development to be able to identify that my dad was in reintegration and to coach me through how to support him. The very act of supporting him, in turn, helped me progress in my own identity development.

Helms (1990) warns that most counselor–client relationships are *regressive*. These are relationships in which the client has a stronger, more well-developed racial identity than the counselor. This is particularly true for People of Color who work with White therapists (most therapists in the United States are White[10]). In this case, the counselor might feel surprised, offended, confused, or hurt by the emotions expressed by the client. They will not be able to meet the client wherever they are in their racial identity because the client is further ahead. Arguably, this is true for many classrooms as well. Given that most teachers in the United States are White (80 percent, according to the National Center for Education Statistics, 2020), and given that racial competency is not a requirement for certification in most programs for teaching, it is not uncommon for students or therapy clients to have a regressive relationship with their teachers or counselors. In these cases, student and client voices and experiences are silenced, and they rarely get the support they need. Sometimes they are even punished for their views on race by a teacher or invalidated by a counselor, both of whom have power over them and are unaware of what they do not know.[11]

White people who want to support other White people in developing a strong, positive racial identity will be much more helpful and effective if they have a progressive relationship with the other person. Whether that person is your uncle, your child, students you teach, colleagues at work, or even your boss, having a strong positive racial identity yourself will help you meet that person wherever they are and help them move to the next step. Having a progressive relationship is not about being better than the other White person; this is not a competitive framework. If both of you have a strong, positive racial identity, you will be able to go farther and faster together, meeting each other where you both are, supporting and challenging one another to go further. Understanding this framework can help you gauge what stage that person might be in during a given interaction—and thus what kind of intervention might be useful in their learning.

So Why Isn't Pride Part of a Positive White Racial Identity?

Let's return to the question a parent asked me, which I shared at the beginning of this chapter: Why isn't pride part of a positive White racial identity? To answer this question, we need to review the parameters of the framework we just learned. For White people, having a negative racial identity means that we are ignorant of the impact of race and that we think race and racism have no influence on a person's life. We internalize negative stereotypes of People of Color and Native people and assume those misperceptions are true. Psychologists say that a negative racial identity is necessarily a delusional identity (Marshall, 2002) because we hold biases and stereotypes about People of Color and Native people, believing that they are reflections of reality. This is what I described in my own life in the introduction. I believed Black people and communities were dangerous because I didn't realize how much that understanding of Blackness was based on inaccurate stereotypes, as well as a false sense of safety in predominantly White communities. Nor did I see how little of it was based in real-life interactions with Black people.

When we are in that negative racial identity stage, we have not yet fully learned how much those biases and stereotypes are false, so we let them shape our understanding of society, the people we meet, and even ourselves. When White people have a negative racial identity, we believe—speciously and usually unconsciously—that we are part of a superior group. It's a negative racial identity because it's not based in reality. It's a self-concept based in delusion, in a fictional social construct. It's based on a racial hierarchy that has been thoroughly debunked yet is actively promoted by white supremacists while being tacitly accepted by most of mainstream society.

As people move through the stages of identity development, they experience common emotions, exhibit reactions, and develop a new self-concept that comes from better understanding how race works in their lives—and in the lives of others. In that process, they reject racial hierarchies, they reject racism, and they reject a system that ascribes stereotypes or foregone conclusions about one's identity.

As White people move toward a strong, positive racial identity, we begin to unlearn a false racial hierarchy. We are no longer deluded into thinking that we are the best. We are just as good as everyone else. The ability to heal our delusions and see reality accurately is its own reward; feeling pride in that belief becomes irrelevant. A positive racial identity is a nondelusional one, a healed one. That is why pride in being White is not part of a positive antiracist White racial identity.

This doesn't have to feel bad. In fact, it's good. But it doesn't feel like pride. And, in fact, by the time White people develop a strong positive racial identity, pride is not something we seek to feel. It's not something we think we deserve to feel. And that's not because we are not good people or because we haven't ever done anything to feel proud of. Indeed, there are many things about ourselves and our lives that we can and should feel proud of. But being White is not one of them. We have now learned that the racial hierarchy in which we were raised is entirely fictional and that we have been falsely led to believe that there's something better about us because we are White. That's hard to feel proud of.

This is different for People of Color and Native people because unlearning the delusions of racism can truly lead to a feeling of pride in oneself and one's group that is not usually promoted by mainstream society. If a Black child has a negative racial identity, and they see that princesses in movies don't look like them, or that models in magazines tend to have lighter skin, smaller bone structure, and straighter and lighter hair, they might assume that Eurocentric norms are accurate measures of beauty, and they are likely to internalize the sense that something is wrong with them for not meeting those standards. A positive racial identity helps that same child recognize and identify Eurocentric beauty norms as being limited, biased, and impossible for many in our society to achieve regardless of racial background. A positive racial identity rejects those norms and asks why we don't have a system that values Afrocentric features. A positive racial identity pushes past a Eurocentric history curriculum to ask, "What about African, Asian, and Native civilizations that thrived long before colonization and slavery?" A positive racial identity is a protective mechanism that can help children refuse to be measured by a system that will inevitably find them lacking because it requires being White[12] for success, beauty, and normativity (Lee, 2005). A positive racial identity for People of Color and Native people intrinsically leads to pride that is not possible in the negative racial identity stage in which they conform to White cultural and linguistic styles and norms, with the unconscious assumption that "White is right." Unlearning the idea that "my group is wrong because White is better" leads to pride in the positive aspects of one's own group. That is where pride comes in.

What I find complicated about this is that it's hard to teach a child that they shouldn't be proud of who they are. I am currently raising two White children. I do not want to convey the message that either of them should be ashamed of themselves for being White. I don't want my son to think that there is something wrong with him because he is White and male—or that White boys and men are inherently bad. But I also do not tell him that he should be proud of being White. What's important for kids to learn is that the concept of race is itself a fiction and that it is designed to make unfair things happen. We resist that unfairness and work to build a world where everyone can be their full selves.

Is It Okay to Be White?

Some White people hear me talk about the problem of Whiteness and roll their eyes. They ask themselves, "Is it even okay to be White anymore?" I suspect that members of the alt-right are familiar with the same feeling I used to have, when I came away from any class, workshop, or conversation about race feeling guilty about being White. This was not the intention or design of the conversations; it was just where I happened to be in my own racial identity development. The alt-right knows this stage well, and they are quick to exploit it. Shortly after the election of Donald Trump, signs started showing up on college campuses around the country reading IT'S OKAY TO BE WHITE (see the image for an example). Familiar with the way antiracism makes White people feel

Source: An example of a hate slogan cataloged by the ADL (Anti-Defamation League), https://www.adl.org/education/references/hate-symbols/its-okay-to-be-white

like there's something wrong with them for being White, the alt-right was playing to the fears and insecurities of White people—especially young White men—by reassuring them that there's nothing wrong with them. "It's okay to be White," they proclaimed.

This need for an affirmational identity is connected to a fairly basic human instinct for belonging. Eleonora speaks about it in the context of our fundamental need to belong to a community. It is why movements like Black Pride, Black Lives Matter, and Native Lives Matter exist in the first place. A big part of antiracism involves affirming the people who have been rendered inferior or insufficient by systemic racism and asserting that the system that rendered them as such is wrong. The affirmation asserts that *they* are not wrong; *the system* is wrong. It is about asserting first for them—and then for all—that they matter. White people who tend to believe that everyone is treated equally—or at least that the system is fair and thus that if you're not getting equal results, it's your own fault—feel undermined by this kind of pride. If Black lives matter, then that must mean non-Black lives don't matter. This, in turn, leads them to assert that White lives matter, too. A color-blind belief in equality, mixed with a lack of knowledge about systemic racism, renders people confused about why group-level affirmation would be necessary. "All lives matter," people sputter. Asserting one group's humanity then becomes a zero-sum game where groups compete to say whose lives matter, in spite of the fact that there has never been systemic evidence to suggest that White lives don't.

Now it has gone even further as white supremacist groups tell us, "It's (still) okay to be White." This is the question I struggle with here: Is it? Is it okay to be White? I don't want to agree with the alt-right on this one. At the same time, I have never thought that being antiracist means it's not okay to be White.

I asked my colleague Caroline Blackwell (personal communication, November 30, 2017), Vice President for Equity and Justice for the National Association of Independent Schools (NAIS), who has spent most of her adult life helping adults and young people learn about race, whether she thought it was okay to be White. I said sheepishly, practically in a whisper, "I mean, I know it's a rallying cry of the alt-right, yet at the same time, I think it's important for White people to understand that we can identify with our Whiteness, so that we can begin to take responsibility and do something about it. Especially for young people. But can we tell our kids that it's okay to be White?"

After pausing for a while, she responded, "I don't think that's the right question. It's not about whether it's okay to be White or not. It's about what you want Whiteness to mean. Historically, Whiteness has been associated with oppression. It continues to mean benefiting from a system that was set up to advantage White people at every turn. It currently means treating People of Color and Native people as less than. It's not about whether it's right or wrong to be White, because you did not create Whiteness or construct it to be this way. It's about saying, 'Now that you know you are White, what do you want Whiteness to mean for you and for others?' Developing racial competence helps White people see what Whiteness has historically meant, as well as how they can begin to change those meanings for a better future."

Charting a New Way to Be White

Dr. Beverly Daniel Tatum (2017) wrote that there has to be a way for White people to identify as White so that they can begin to take responsibility for their part in racism. She specified that when it comes to racial identity, White people seem to have the option to identify only as ignorant, colorblind, or racist. Those mainstream tropes about White identity result in most White people not seeing themselves reflected in Whiteness. One of my mentors, Antje Mattheus, said something similar: "white supremacists have hijacked White identity. Because many White people did not want to have anything to do with white supremacists, they distanced themselves from White identity altogether." I saw this early when I taught my child—in an attempt to be antiracist—that we are White people. We sent her off to kindergarten, where she definitely talked about being White. And I wondered, "Who does that? What kind of White people teach their children to consciously acknowledge their White identity? Will her teacher think we are white supremacists?"

The problem with not acknowledging our White identity is that it once again places White people outside the racial dynamics of the United States. In that configuration—one in which People of Color and Native people are affected by racism that is caused by systems that have nothing to do with White people—racism can be a problem only for People of Color and Native people. And as long as White people are not overtly racist—as long as my family doesn't use the n-word—then I can safely assume that it has nothing to do with me. This is why so many White people grow up thinking that racism is a problem that belongs to someone else and that being White means you live outside racial dynamics in a neutral, relatively race-less and racism-less world. I taught my children that they are White because I want them to (eventually) take responsibility for dismantling the racial hierarchy that they and I have inherited.

This is why Tatum says we need a fourth path for White people. We need White people to understand that Whiteness is about them and that racism is their problem. We need an antiracist path for White identity, so that White people can identify as White people who are trying to be antiracist. Highlighting a White antiracist identity pathway for White people means that White people can turn away from a system that teaches us to be colorblind or ignorant and affirm for one another that each of us was raised inside a system that was designed for us not to know about it. Racism thrives on our not knowing. Our colorblindness and ignorance are not accidental. The option of an antiracist identity is a turn toward intentionally knowing, in defiance of a system that would rather we don't. Identifying as antiracist—or as a person who is trying to be antiracist—doesn't mean we automatically know all we need to know to be racially competent, but it puts us on a new path in that direction.

This is also why Tatum says that White people need antiracist role models. White children need to see ways of being White that make them proud—not for being White, per se, but for making Whiteness mean something different altogether. As my colleague Caroline said, it's not about whether it's okay to be White or whether we should feel proud of being White. It's about having a choice about what being White will mean. When we look at the history of Whiteness, it has meant a false superiority that justified violence and oppression. But in the case of some White people throughout history, it has also meant antiracist action, boldness, and participation in multiracial community. What we can take pride in is the very process of learning how to take an antiracist stance, within a system that incentivizes us to do otherwise.

As White people, we can be proud of what we've done as individuals—perhaps how we've treated people or how we've challenged oppression. We can also be proud of White people throughout history who worked to shift the racial hierarchy. But when we know enough about racism and Whiteness to have a strong, positive racial identity, we realize that Whiteness itself is not something we can feel proud of until we transform it into something new. I tell my children that they can be secret agents for antiracism. They can transform Whiteness because they are White people—and that is a sacred task that requires acknowledging our own White identities to begin it.

Notes

1.   By and large, there are not frameworks of racial identity development for Native people. Dr. Perry Horse (2001) describes a paradigm of American Indian Consciousness but says the following about racial identity models:

Those who are searching for a single racial identity model that fits all American Indians are cautioned that such a model would assume coherent and commonly held ideas of race and ethnicity among American Indians. Such may not be the case, given the wide diversity among Indian peoples. (p. 91)

2. We use the term *stages* because it is less clinical and easier to envision, but we maintain that the stages are not linear.

3. Helms does not include pre-contact in her framework—it is a stage I borrow from William Cross's (1978, 1991) model of Nigrescence, which includes an initial stage called *pre-encounter*. I feel I have to include a pre-contact stage in the story of my own development because I don't know how to describe the years of my life before contact otherwise.

4. In *The New Jim Crow*, Michelle Alexander (2020) argues that modern policing does the work of controlling Black people that overt Jim Crow laws can no longer legally be used to do.

5. This is really the crux of my argument in this book—that White people need to reach beyond the White people who make it easy to be antiracist. But I also want to acknowledge that there is a point, particularly with difficult or abusive family members, where it's also not safe or effective for White people to keep reaching out to the people who hurt them. Generally I think we're too willing to cut people out of our lives when we could engage them about race. We do this because we do not accurately gauge harm when it comes to race, and we don't have the skills to engage across difference. But if you have family members who are abusive to you, they are unlikely to listen to your opinion on race no matter how you approach them. In that case, prioritize your safety and work with people who could hear you if given the right combination of support and challenge.

6. Psychologist Claude Steele (2010) calls this *stereotype threat*. Eleonora will address the emotional pitfalls of stereotype threat and how to recover from them in the Internal Work section following this chapter.

7. These are the main racial categories used by the Apartheid government in South Africa. They are still informally used today (Thompson, 1995).

8. To be fair, my deep identification with Gertrude's family never changed. We still talk weekly, and our families and lives have been inextricably intertwined since we met. But what's changed is that I stopped unconsciously trying to become Black or to deny my Whiteness. I'm simply part of an international, cross-class, multiracial, intergenerational family that is deeply important to me. And the work I do on my own racial bias and my own class bias helps our relationship be even stronger and more life-giving. It is one of the things I am most grateful for in my life.

9. Native psychologists who have written about racial identity development with regard to Native people have suggested that because Native identity is not a racial identity, and because Native people do not experience racism in the same way that People of Color do, frameworks of racial identity do not neatly or adequately describe Native people's experiences (Horse, 2001).

10. As of 2015, 86 percent of psychologists in the United States were White (Lin et al., 2018).

11. In Black psychology, not knowing what one doesn't know and holding power over another is called *peculiar arrogance* (Asante, 1987).

12. Whiteness often is not only a prerequisite for traditional success but also idealized in an essentialized form that most people can't meet. This is another way in which racism hurts White people, too.

INTERNAL WORK

Don't Get Stuck in Stereotype Threat

. . . .

Racial identity development is not something we simply think about; it's something we become. It's also not something we go through once and leave behind us—like first grade or puberty. As Ali describes in Chapter 5, we tend to cycle through the stages of racial identity development each time we expand our racial awareness and direct our antiracist actions toward new and wider contexts. Being able to recognize which stage we might be experiencing at any given moment is immensely helpful in navigating the situation with a degree of grace and effectiveness. This is where our White allies can offer invaluable support to us in helping us reflect on why we might be reacting a given way and then brainstorm how best to proceed.[1] However, the fact that we revisit these stages multiple times means that we will inevitably experience something called stereotype threat.[2]

Stereotype threat refers to the fear we have of confirming a stereotype about our group. This term is often used to understand the impact that group-level prejudice has on People of Color or other marginalized groups. But as White people learn to see themselves as members of a group called White people, we experience stereotype threat, too. What would you say is the term we most fear being called as White people? For most White people, it's *racist*. Ironically, the more we find racism distasteful and the more we are committed to being antiracist, the more susceptible we are to this particular stereotype threat—the fear of being seen as racist. Part of the problem, of course, is that we think of being racist as a terminal diagnosis, an incurable disease, a character trait. These are all terms that imply that the problem has its source within the individual, rather than in the social fabric that socializes us in deeply racist ways. If we actually looked at ourselves from this wider angle, we would see that committing to an antiracist path is committing to a lifelong process of re-socializing ourselves and inoculating ourselves from the racism we learned from birth and are relearning every day. That can't possibly be a flawless, linear process, as much as we would like it to be so.[3]

But that's not what we are told as White people—and often not what we tell one another. There is much in our culture that teaches us to believe we are either a good person or a bad person. And our solution for bad people is to punish them and shut them out. We see this punitive system playing out everywhere—in our justice system, in schools, and even among activists who are quick to write off people who make mistakes or don't know the right terminology. Every step we take along the way can feel like a new opportunity to prove to both ourselves and others that we are antiracist—and each step also presents a risk that we will prove that we're actually racist. This perspective reflects what psychologist Carol Dweck (2006) calls a fixed mindset. We manifest a fixed mindset when we believe that our essential qualities—for example, goodness, intelligence, athletic ability, math skills, even racial competence—are fixed at birth and immutable. We then view our performance on various tasks simply as confirmation or disconfirmation of these innate traits. A fixed mindset, therefore, makes saying or doing something racist feel like an irredeemable verdict. It sends us into a downward spiral, which makes us desperately grasp at proof of our own goodness.

In contrast, we exhibit a growth mindset when we believe that we have the capacity to learn and grow in our skills, including our ability to act ever more in line with our antiracist values. When we have a growth mindset, we see the outcome of our performance in any given situation not as a verdict but as a step toward achieving greater competence. A growth mindset allows us to receive and learn from feedback.[4] When we base our antiracist actions on a fixed mindset, we look for quick, simple, sure answers that are certain to be perceived as "right." When we operate through a growth mindset, we are willing to tackle the real challenges in front of us, and we open ourselves to learning from the outcome of our efforts.

When the stereotype threat of being seen as racist is triggered (notice I said *when*, not *if*), it is processed by our nervous system like any other threat. As studies have shown, when we experience stereotype threat, our anxiety rises, and all our cognitive and emotional resources are diverted from the topic at hand to manage that anxiety (Steele, 2010). As our stress responses engage to defeat the perceived threat, our higher-order thinking shuts down, and we can no longer effectively intervene in, nor learn from, the situation. Instead, our fight reactions take the lead, and we fixate on proving to ourselves and others that we are not racist. When so much of our energy is spent doing that, we move further from our original intention not to cause harm, and we divert our attention completely away from the information that would help us actually unlearn racism.

While it's almost inevitable that we will feel the sting of stereotype threat, we are not doomed to get stuck in it. Thankfully, there are a number of simple and effective strategies to manage and counteract it. Here, I describe two of them. The first will help you deescalate your stereotype threat reaction in the moment. The second is a preventive strategy that will lessen the actual frequency and intensity with which you experience stereotype threat.

Strengthening Your Antiracist Practice

How to Disentangle From Stereotype Threat

Learn to Deescalate a Stereotype Threat Reaction

The active ingredient in stereotype threat is its narrowing of our sense of self to a single characteristic—in this context, our White identity. Seeing ourselves just as White—and seeing Whiteness just as meaning ignorant or incompetent—means that we forget all our other skill sets and aspects of identity. All it takes to make a single aspect of ourselves block out all our other qualities is a setting or wording that primes us for it.[5] Antiracist contexts and conversations do that intrinsically for White people, as they highlight the oppressive nature of the very concept of Whiteness. Once we are triggered, our task is to quickly re-anchor ourselves in a much wider awareness of who we are, inclusive of more aspects of our identity and values. Yes, we are White, and as such, we carry unearned privileges and racial biases. *And* we are also introspective, kind, open-minded, hardworking, flexible, and so on—we have qualities that are essential to antiracism.

So when you feel the grip of stereotype threat, you can simply take a few minutes, or even just a few breaths, to reorient yourself toward valued aspects of your identity (e.g., teacher, friend, sibling) and your aspirations (e.g., kindness, mutual care, peace). You might say to yourself, "I am a loyal friend; I am a caring neighbor; I enjoy seeing others thrive." In other words, remind yourself that you play a variety of positive roles in people's lives and that you feel a sense of fulfillment and pride for being deeply invested in other people's well-being. Just as it can take a split second to prime us for stereotype threat, we can almost as quickly re-prime ourselves for remembering our whole self. And once our sense of self re-expands to the entirety of who we are, we can remember that we are more than our racist socialization and can be ready to do what it takes to unlearn it.

(Continued)

(Continued)

Learn to Prevent Stereotype Threat

While stereotype threat is triggered by narratives that bring into relevance a single aspect of ourselves above all others, the power of stereotype threat relies on a fixed mindset. In the context of race, for example, a fixed mindset leads us to think of being racist and being antiracist as immutable character traits. So the best strategy to decrease the likelihood that you will experience stereotype threat as a White person trying to be antiracist involves learning about and adopting a growth mindset—which will be helpful in many areas of your life and especially when it comes to antiracism. This book adopts a growth mindset by addressing racial *competence*, while a fixed mindset would lead us to describe antiracist *traits*. A growth mindset is not about learning all the "right" answers but about transforming ourselves into increasingly skilled agents of social change.

You have already started learning about growth mindset just by reading this Internal Work section, and many other resources are freely available online. You can find them easily by typing "how to practice a growth mindset" or "Carol Dweck mindset" or "growth mindset language examples" in any search engine. You might start by listening to Dweck's (2014) TED talk on the topic, then intentionally practice anchoring yourself in a growth mindset as you go about your daily life. For example, you can begin by identifying times when you use language that reflects a fixed mindset (e.g., "I'm not good at dealing with conflict," "Taking a breath when I'm frustrated is too hard," or "I'll never be that knowledgeable about history") and changing what you say to yourself to practice using a growth mindset (e.g., "This might take some time," "I'll learn how to do this," "I'm not good at this *yet*," or "What am I missing?"). Most important, in conversations about race, focus on what you are learning that will already make you do it better next time. Any increased self-awareness around biases or knowledge of historical facts is invaluable in enhancing your racial competence. Practice reframing perceived mistakes as powerful learning moments.

The aim is to re-socialize ourselves to think of antiracist practice as a set of skills we can develop, not a set of traits we either do or do not possess. As White people, we must reclaim the fact that we are fully capable of learning and developing competence about race-related topics, and we must support other White people in doing the same. A fixed mindset shuts the door to racial competence; a growth mindset opens it widely.

Notes

1. Chapter 8 provides great guidance on how White people can support one another's antiracist growth.

2. Psychologist Claude Steele coined this term in the 1990s to describe the detrimental impact of negative stereotypes about intelligence on Black students' test performance. Research has expanded widely from there, much of which is described in his popular book *Whistling Vivaldi: How Stereotypes Affect Us and What We Can Do* (Steele, 2010).

3. Recall the second myth of white supremacy: "We can and should be perfect—or at least appear perfect."

4. Chapter 7 is about how to receive feedback in a way that helps us learn and grow.

5. Remember how powerful priming is; see the Internal Work section for Chapter 3.

CHAPTER 6

Who Is White . . . and Why?

If you can only be tall because someone is on their knees, then you have a serious problem. And my feeling is that White people have a very, very serious problem. And they should start thinking about what they can do about it. Take me out of it.

—Toni Morrison (as cited in Kirkland, 2019, para. 3)

If you are reading this book, chances are good that you identify as White and are committed to walking an antiracist pathway. The chances are also good that you have met White people who resist being labeled as White.

Much of the confusion over the question of who is and isn't White is political. As writers Ibram X. Kendi, Isabel Wilkerson, Paul Kivel, and others point out, Whiteness gets redefined regularly as it becomes politically expedient to those in power. But with the political categorization comes the cultural thinking. Beyond the question of White people who simply don't want to see themselves as having any race, there are others who may express concern about racism but who don't identify as White—and thus resist taking responsibility for racism. This is problematic, of course. Their unwillingness to recognize their advantage within the racial hierarchy can make it hard for them to stand in solidarity with People of Color and Native people—which, in turn, makes it hard for us to collectively address racism.

There are two common factors for this kind of lack of resonance with identifying as White. The first part of this chapter will look at the stories of two men, both in their 60s at the time these stories took place, who struggled to identify as White—one because he was Italian, one because he was Jewish. I will explore the ways in which this confusion makes sense but also how the history of Whiteness can help us gain clarity, so that people who don't fit neatly into a White identity might consider their relationship to it.

The second part of the chapter focuses on a larger theme that arises for White people when we think about being White: it's often difficult to see and account for how we have privilege when we also experience oppression and feel that the world doesn't adequately factor our experiences of marginalization into the conversation on race.

I'm Not White Because White People Have Excluded My Family

Are Jews White? Are Italian Americans White? You may have heard people asking questions like this—and you might even wonder about this with regard to your own identity. Here, I'll explore the reasons why people ask these questions, why the answers are complicated, and why we must attempt to answer them with integrity nonetheless. First, a story.

My partner and I went to graduate school at the same time. I was studying Whiteness and teacher education at a school of education. He was studying to become a rabbi at a rabbinical college. In our first year, his rabbinical college held a retreat for new students, partners, and faculty. At one point, I was paired in conversation with a highly respected professor, one I knew only through his books. He asked me about my graduate work. When I told him I was studying Whiteness, he asked me, "Now, would you consider me White? Because I know some people would, but I have never identified as White in my life. I am Jewish . . . and Jews where I grew up were not allowed to be White."

At that point in my own learning, this kind of conversation left me feeling baffled and even threatened. I felt that not recognizing one's White identity was a way White people defend against the hurt and sadness that might come from recognizing their complicity with Whiteness. Having grown up in a Protestant family, descended from many generations of Settler-Colonists,[1] I was not at all in touch with the cultural or ethnic identities that my ancestors from Scotland, Denmark, England, and Germany held. Understanding my own Whiteness meant being accountable for the group that had been assigned to me and my ancestors in the United States. It meant naming the unnamed and seeing the previously unseen. But for this rabbi, it was less straightforward. His identity was imposed on him by White people (including my own ancestors) in the 1950s as *not White*. When he was a child, his family was not permitted to buy a home in the White part of town. For him to identify as White today, he would have to align himself with a Whiteness that included people who excluded his family early in his life. What could I say to him to help him be accountable for the very real ways in which European-descended Jews (primarily Ashkenazi Jews) have "become White" in the decades since World War II? Was there a way to make this clear while also honoring his particular experience of race and Jewishness over those decades?

A year later, I was teaching a graduate-level class on Whiteness that included an Italian American man in his early 60s. He felt that understanding Whiteness was important to his work with students. But he too said he wasn't White. According to him, he was not White because when he was growing up, he played in the little league that Black and Italian kids in South Philly were assigned to play in. White-kid baseball was off limits to him. He did not identify as Black, but he also felt that he had been kept out of Whiteness by White people, as they were defined then. How could he claim it now?

How Jews and Italians Became White Folks

In both of these cases, the category of being White had shifted underneath the feet of these two men during the course of their lifetimes. As Jewish writer Karen Brodkin (1998) writes in *How Jews Became White Folks and What That Says About Race in America*, she entered elementary school as non-White. But in high school in the 1960s, when the color line was redrawn across New York City, she found herself definitively on the White (i.e., not Black) side. How Whiteness has shifted in the United States differs by place and time, but there were broad trends throughout the nation that were relatively consistent. Post-war trends rendered many European ethnics, including recent immigrants who were Italian, Irish, German, European Jewish, and Scandinavian, as White (Brodkin, 1998). This meant they could buy homes in the predominantly White suburbs, attend schools for White people, and experience widespread social acceptance among White people. For that reason, both of these men might have been widely considered to be White during the years we were in conversation (2010–2011). Yet they did not see themselves as such because as children—during a time of profound identity development—they were told by White people that they were not White.

One thing that has changed since they were children in the 1960s is that Italian-ness and Jewishness have been reconceptualized in the United States as ethnicities. Given that, the phrase in Brodkin's title, *How Jews Became White Folks*, embodies a misnomer. Not all Jews became White folks because, in fact, many Jews are People of Color who are rendered as such not by their Jewishness but by their skin color. Brodkin's book is really about how people who are Ashkenazi Jews, who are descended from European Jews, came to have access to many of the privileges of Whiteness in the United States. But even so, for Ashkenazi Jews, having racial privilege did not change the fact that they were living as a religious minority in a country where "American" identity is still conflated not only with Whiteness but also with Christianity—more on that later in the chapter.

Where Did Whiteness Come From?

To understand why these two men resisted being associated with Whiteness, we need to look at how Whiteness developed as a category over time. Whiteness was first used as a category in the United States during enslavement, as a way of disincentivizing connections between White indentured servants and Black enslaved people. White landholding and slaveholding people realized that they would be outnumbered if the indentured servants formed community, unity, and political power with enslaved people. They grasped the concept of Whiteness—which already existed elsewhere in Europe and in more vague terms—and employed it as a form of prestige that could be given to indentured laborers as a form of social capital, so that they would have something that Black enslaved people did not, something that would differentiate them and be worth fighting for (Painter, 2011).

In 1790, when the United States was a young nation, Congress made a policy that "restricted naturalization to 'white persons'" (Haney López, 2006, p. 1). While not always enforced, the policy provided a useful mechanism for controlling the flow of Whiteness, like turning on and off a tap, so that White people could maintain a majority and retain power. In the early days, it was mostly Anglo-Saxon Protestants who were granted the status of Whiteness. As more European immigrants from a variety of countries entered the United States, the categorization became more ambiguous. Overall, this restriction remained on the books until 1952, when it was removed through the Immigration and Nationality Act. As Isabel Wilkerson (2020) notes:

> While the requirements to qualify as White have changed over the centuries, the fact of a dominant caste has remained constant from its inception—whoever fit the definition of white, at whatever point in history, was granted the legal rights and privileges of the dominant caste. (p. 19)

The Courts Decided Who Was White

Because White identity was tied to naturalization (citizenship) and naturalization was tied to land ownership, between 1878 and 1952, there were 52 racial prerequisite cases in which people went to court to petition the government to recognize them as White. These cases included, among others, people who were Chinese, Japanese, Native American, Syrian, Afghan, and Punjabi. They sought in court an official designation as White, not because they wanted a different racial identity but because they wanted the material and political protections that were afforded to White people, to the exclusion of—and often at the expense of—those who were not White. At the time, these protections included the following:

- Naturalization
- American identity
- The right to marry a naturalized American
- Economic advantage
- Labor union membership and protection
- Access to jobs
- Access to schools
- Prestige
- Protection of the state
- The right to vote
- The right to run for office or act as judges
- Police protection

They were also seeking the right not to be seen or treated as Black. Not being Black was materially desirable because, along with legal restrictions on Black people, the federal and state governments regularly ignored or actively enforced daily discrimination, as well as violent attacks on Black communities, especially those that were independent or economically successful. A number of cases during this era stand out for both violence and governmental indifference. In 1898, for example, about 2,000 armed White residents of Wilmington, North Carolina, forced Black elected officials to surrender their offices. In this coup, more than 300 Black people were estimated to have been killed (Richardson, 2021). In 1921, in the Greenwood area of Tulsa, Oklahoma, known as Black Wall Street, White vigilantes destroyed 35 blocks of Black-owned businesses and homes, killing hundreds of Black people and destroying Black generational wealth (Madigan, 2003; Parshina-Kottas & Singhvi, 2021). In 1924, in Manhattan Beach, California, White people seized all beachfront property from Black owners, destroying a Black tourism destination and evicting the owners from the enclave (Fortin, 2021). For years, White vigilantes in Chicago used violence to keep Black workers out of White-only unions (Wilkerson, 2010). These are just a handful of examples pulled from hundreds throughout U.S. history in which Black Americans who were building a livelihood and contributing to civic life were threatened, assaulted, removed from power, or killed.[2]

After World War II, the umbrella for Whiteness expanded further than it ever had before as the suburbs began to take shape around every major city. European ethnics such as Italians, Irish, Germans, and European-descended Jews, who previously had been kept out of a White real-estate market, suddenly had access to affordable mortgages for homes in suburban communities that were exclusively open to White residents (Lipsitz, 2018). The new White suburbs kept Black people out through restrictive covenants, banks denying mortgages, and the FHA underwriting of loans to people from White areas of cities but not from redlined Black areas (Rothstein, 2018; Wilkerson, 2020). The apocryphal melting pot that so many of us grew up believing in now included most European ethnic groups but still not People of Color, especially Black people.

The extent of the systematic divestment from Black families and communities in the United States is well documented and has happened in hundreds of cities and neighborhoods throughout the nation's history (Rothstein, 2018).[3] European-descended Jewish veterans and Italian American veterans of World War II were not treated with the same exclusion and inferiority as Black veterans.

The existence of the suburbs catalyzed and accelerated the formation of a new and expanded Whiteness. This broadening of the category, in turn, meant that more individuals were invested in White identity and benefited from their placement in that category.[4] This is precisely when my student and my partner's professor would have been children. Depending on where they lived and what their family circumstances were, at some point in their early lives, they likely started to assimilate into Whiteness and the often invisible advantages that came with it. As I discuss further at the end of this chapter, Italian Americans and Ashkenazi Jewish Americans did not experience an assimilation into Whiteness in the same way, because Jews still faced anti-Semitism. But both groups have been beneficiaries of a system that denied equal access and opportunity to Black people.

For immigrants, *not being Black* was a tactical (if not always conscious) move: "becoming White meant defining themselves as furthest from its opposite—Black" (Wilkerson, 2020, p. 50). As Nobel Prize–winning author Toni Morrison has written, "it doesn't matter anymore what shade the newcomer's skin is. A hostile posture toward resident blacks must be struck at the Americanizing door before it will open" (Morrison, 1993, para. 6). This meant that immigrant families from China, Japan, Pakistan, and India, to name a few, had to decide whether to align themselves with (live near, befriend, work with) White Americans or Black Americans. For those who could choose, many immigrant groups chose to align themselves with Whiteness in a way that granted access to resources but still involved cultural and skin-color prejudice. Researcher Stacey Lee (2005) studies Whiteness, Asian immigrants, and Asian American experiences of schooling. She writes,

"Honorary whiteness of Asian Americans was granted at the expense of Blacks (Winant, 2001). It is also significant that as 'honorary Whites,' Asian Americans do not have the actual privileges associated with 'real' Whiteness" (p. 6).

Over the course of U.S. history, the government employed countless laws and policies that functioned to construct Whiteness and differentiate it from Blackness at the federal, state, and local levels. Up until the civil rights era of the 1950s and 1960s, much of the racial differentiation was written into the law. It included things such as the slavery codes that defined who could and could not be enslaved, as well as segregation laws that determined where people could live, go to school, work, be treated for sickness, and even drink water. It included policies and practices such as legally defining racial identity through the hypodescent rule and then putting people's race on their birth certificates, marriage licenses, and death certificates (Wilkerson, 2010). It included antimiscegenation laws, also called *endogamy*, which means "restricting marriage to people within the same caste" (Wilkerson, 2020, p. 109).

Even if we just take the laws prohibiting interracial marriage alone, we can see how they have shaped what Whiteness looks like, as well as our current reality. Isabel Wilkerson writes that interracial marriage was first banned in Virginia in 1691, almost a century before the United States even became a nation. This ban would then be taken up by most states for the next three centuries (Wilkerson, 2020) until its repeal by the Supreme Court in 1967. Wilkerson (2020) invites us to consider how this legalized prohibition affected the creation of multiracial families:

> Endogamy, by closing off legal family connection, blocks the chance for empathy or a sense of shared destiny between the castes. It makes it less likely that someone in the dominant caste will have a personal stake in the happiness, fulfillment, or well-being of anyone deemed beneath them or personally identify with them or their plight. (p. 109)

The point is that Whiteness didn't just happen spontaneously. It was crafted through laws, policies, individual practices, social norms, and culture that developed within a society where such deep segregation existed. It grew up out of the social networks and relationships that formed between people who had material access to resources, education, and employment because they were permitted to live on the metaphorical and literal White side of town. For immigrants to get ahead, signs that they were achieving the American Dream were signs that they were growing closer to Whiteness, by living in White neighborhoods, attending White schools, behaving according to White cultural norms, employing White linguistic styles, and so on.

Inevitably, then, American belonging became a story of assimilation into Whiteness. What European ethnics gave up to become White is a story that often gets told in the United States. It began at Ellis Island on the East Coast and Angel Island on the West Coast, as people were forced to take on new, Americanized names. From there, the price of assimilation continued to inflate as new European immigrants remained in the United States. They gave up foods, cultural styles, languages, sometimes friends and family, religious practices, religious affiliations, gesticulations, and much more to become part of the White American mainstream. What White culture became was not a melting pot of all these different cultures but a bland, sterile, White-washed version of culture in which people lost real connection to ancient traditions, rituals, and language that once connected them to a place or a group. This was the "price of Whiteness" (Lipsitz, 2018). For the Native peoples of this land and for enslaved Africans, a similar type of assimilation was forced. In these cases, culture and language—and the meaning and connections therein—were not lost or given up; they were stolen.[5] The loss of culture and language was not a strategic choice made to improve one's life; it was forced on them through violence, schooling, and even legal means.

The great tragedy of this story is that this history continues to unfold before our eyes. I used to look at the racist history of the United States and judge those who lived through it as bystanders who didn't do enough. And while that judgment stands, I can no longer see myself as separate from them. This racialized history persists every day in the United States, at all levels. As a player within it, I find it very hard to challenge the rules of the game in a way that will make a difference. I see this in my own work with schools, where children are deemed successful when they can approximate Whiteness, speak a certain middle-class English, develop friendly relationships with White middle-class teachers, and demonstrate ways of being that are consistent with White middle-class norms.[6]

All the while, Whiteness itself is not static but continues to change. The fact that Whiteness is constantly shifting is not an accident. Racism has always been used to divide and control. Ibram X. Kendi (2020a) says that this boundary shifting is an intentional mechanism for ensuring that White people continue to be a democratic majority in the United States. As historical and cultural circumstances shift over time, Whiteness adapts with them.

This history of Whiteness lays bare how White people have been manipulated to be invested in Whiteness while simultaneously not seeing it. If we don't see it, we can't be critical of it. If it stays invisible to us, we are more susceptible to its subtle incentives and rewards, without us necessarily consciously doing anything. I, for example, grew up thinking that my family lived in an almost all-White suburb because my parents wanted to live in a strong community with sidewalks and "good schools." It felt comfortable and right. No one ever said anything about wanting to be around only White people or wanting to invest in a White community. Framed that way, it sounds ridiculous.

Once a person becomes conscious of Whiteness, it is almost impossible not to want to distance oneself from it. But that is precisely the moment when we need to take responsibility for it.

But what do we say about all this to a White person who doesn't think they are White?

So . . . Are European-Descended Jews White?

What did I say to my partner's professor, the rabbi who said he was not White? First, I listened to his story, and I honored his experience. I believe I said something along these lines: "You are making me want to learn more. My instinct says it might be useful for you to identify as White, but as we talk, I'm realizing I don't really know why." That first conversation kicked off an inquiry for me that helped me guide many other strongly Jewish-identified people in their own questions about Whiteness. Through the historical research of Eric Goldstein (2008), I learned that in 1943, at the behest of many Jewish organizations, the Immigration and Naturalization Service (INS) instituted a policy under which European Jewish immigrants were no longer written down as "Hebrews" and were marked as "White" instead. *Jewishness* was to be recategorized as an ethnicity rather than a race in an attempt to "distance government classification schemes from those used by the Nazis" (Goldstein, 2008, p. 192).

Unfortunately, according to Goldstein (2008), "by offering a much greater degree of incorporation to Jews and other European groups than to Blacks, the government's wartime policies had the effect of redrawing American racial boundaries rather than erasing them all together" (p. 192). In other words, the government tried to get away from categorizing Jews as a race because that's what the Nazis did. By doing so, the government demonstrated that they understood racial categorization to be manipulable (i.e., not biological). But at that time, they didn't choose to eliminate the racial categories that formed the caste system in the United States. Rather than decon-struct race as a legitimate category of human classification, the government simply declared Jewishness an ethnicity, paving the way for Ashkenazi Jews to merge into a conditional Whiteness—one that protected them from racial inferiority and violence but not from anti-Semitism. Today, anti-Semitism[7] is especially visible—from the violent Unite the Right Rally in Charlottesville, Virginia, in 2017 where White Nationalists shouted, "Jews will not replace us," to the Tree of Life Synagogue shooting that took the life of 11 Jews in Pittsburgh, Pennsylvania, as they were celebrating a baby naming on Shabbat.

What we are seeing today is that European-descended Jews continue to occupy a space within Whiteness that does not protect them from anti-Semitism. But several activists suggest that fighting anti-Semitism can support antiracism (Rosenblum, 2019; Ward, 2017). There are several reasons for this. First, anti-Semitism is used to distract attention from those in power and redirect the attention toward Jews, because it blames Jews for what the people in power do. Discrediting anti-Semitism makes it clearer who actually holds the power and is responsible. It sharpens our analysis. Second, many Jews are People of Color. Fighting anti-Semitism is a way of confronting the compounding oppressions of racism and anti-Semitism that affect them. Finally, we need as many White people as possible to be on an antiracist path. We need Ashkenazi Jews to be part of this struggle to dismantle the racial caste system and redefine Whiteness. European-descended Jews should not have to ignore their Jewishness to work against racism. But that means an antiracist struggle must stand up against ideologies that diminish their humanity—such as anti-Semitism—just as it challenges racist ideologies that do the same to People of Color and Native people. It also means that we cannot allow far-right narratives of anti-Semitism (refer back to endnote 7) to fracture multiracial progressive coalitions that need White Jews, Jews of Color, Palestinians, Muslims, White non-Jews, non-Jews of Color, and Native people to see how their oppressions are interrelated so that they can maintain a strong, diverse majority.

Given All This, How Can European-Descended Jews Identify?

Another rabbi I work with leads a big congregation in the South known for being both multiracial and welcoming to the LGBTQ+ community. The rabbi said that as a queer person who wears a kippah (also known as a yarmulke), he would never be accepted by many White people in the South as a White person. Historically—and still today—Whiteness is often conflated with Christian identity and straight identity,[8] particularly in the South. He doesn't necessarily want to be accepted as a White person, but at the same time, he wants to be accountable to the fact that he is treated differently by society than the Jews of Color in his congregation. So he self-defines today as a "Jew who receives White privilege." And when this is confusing, he chooses to identify as White so as not to appropriate experiences of People of Color. To me, this is an example of wrestling with Whiteness with integrity. It acknowledges how Whiteness operates in one's life while still being true to one's experience of Whiteness in a local time and place. If this rabbi lived and served in New York City, where European-descended Jews have been treated as White since the 1960s, and where Jewish and LGBTQ+ experiences and cultures are more recognized and honored by the mainstream, he might simply identify as White, since that social construction would be more straightforward. But with race, time and context do matter.

For people who receive White privilege but do not identify as White, it can be a powerful act of allyship—in conversations about race and racism—to self-identify as people who benefit from Whiteness and want to do something about it. In affinity spaces[9] in schools and workplaces, for example, participants might state that they don't identify as White but that they want to learn more about how Whiteness affects them—and how they can help change it. A person can identify as someone who receives White privilege and can do the work of unlearning White racial socialization, without identifying simply only as White.

Finally, while time and context matter, how a person self-identifies is only ever a part of the equation. Just because a person doesn't identify as White does not mean that they are not seen and treated as such by our society. This is particularly hard for White people to grasp because being White is an experience that is easy to take for granted. Most White people are accustomed to being seen as an individual first. It seems impossible to believe that we are simultaneously being seen as group members even before we are seen as individuals. But this is something People of Color and Native people experience from a young age—they are usually seen as group members before they are seen as individuals.

Race is not just how we think of ourselves—it always matters how other people identify us. That's why race is a social construction; it's how we get positioned and understood within society by others. W. E. B. Du Bois (1903/2020) says that race gives a person a "double-consciousness." It both gives us our identity and takes it away; it is both how we perceive ourselves from the inside and how others perceive and treat us from the outside. Race gives us our identity when we connect to our racial group or feel shaped by it. It gives us our identity when we derive belonging or connection from it. But race also takes away our identity because it gets assigned to us, whether we like it or not. When people see us and make a predetermined judgment about us based on what they see, they are also primed to see our group-level identity and whatever stereotypes or assumptions they have about our group before they see us as individuals. This is a way in which race takes away our identity. This is one of the reasons it can be so hard to identify as White and recognize group membership with a group and a position one might not fully relate to. It is a problem that people from every racial background struggle with. And as we begin to see how we get lumped into the White group in ways that eclipse our individuality, we begin to get a visceral sense of the double-edged nature of race with which most People of Color live.

Mainstreams and Margins

It's not uncommon for me to be invited to a school where the faculty is working to create an antiracist climate, and where a few White teachers are unable to get on board. In one case, the principal called me and said, "Our entire faculty has frozen over because we tried to talk about White privilege." One teacher had said, "Why do I need to talk about my White privilege when no one around here is talking about the homophobia that I experience on a daily basis as a queer teacher?" Another White teacher who grew up working-class had said, "I don't have privilege—I grew up with no money. I'm not White the way these other people are White." These protests were endlessly frustrating to the People of Color and Native people on the faculty who looked on, thinking, "Yeah, but imagine being both gay *and* Arab," or "Try growing up poor *and* Black." A frustration emerges when people seem unable to acknowledge the privilege, advantage, and protection afforded by their White identity, even as they have other, less protected aspects of their identities.

Diversity educator Rev. Dr. Jamie Washington explains this phenomenon this way: "we tend to live in the pain of our marginalized identities while we act out of the arrogance of our mainstream identities" (personal communication, 2008). In other words, most people tend to be hyperaware of those aspects of their identities that are marginalized—or oppressed. These are the identities that we need to protect—the ones that put us at most risk for exclusion, invalidation, or violence. If we are not aware of these identities and how other people perceive them, we risk more pain and exposure. Remember that our bodies are designed to seek safety, and they do a very good job at detecting what is and is not safe. This is why those identities are so precious and present for us most of the time.

On the other hand, our mainstream—or privileged—identities are often invisible to us. They prop us up and give us a certain amount of advantage and social power. But because they are mainstream, we are often completely unaware of them. Our physiology doesn't have any dire reason to keep them front and center at all times. Being cisgender, for example, is a gender identity that most people do not ever question because it is so widely expected that people will identify as either a man or a woman. Locker rooms, bathrooms, sports teams, and official forms are all designed with the assumption of cisgender identity. If you are cisgender, you likely don't think much about having social power that comes from being cisgender. Contrast that with being transgender, which is an identity that requires conscious awareness. If you are trans, you are very aware of the many walls you inevitably bump into in a society that was not designed with your identity in mind.

Similarly, while most People of Color and Native people are hyper-aware of the fact that they live in a society where White identity is a mainstream identity with the most social power, most White people take their White identity for granted as normal or unremarkable. Yet, to paraphrase Washington, we act from the arrogance of our mainstream identities, unconscious of the platform, voice, amplification, and recognition given to us by the social power of being White. While it's frustrating when White people won't own their racial privilege because they are so focused on their own marginalization, it shouldn't be surprising. In fact, the very existence of a power structure makes this the case.

In the case of the school I mentioned previously, I worked with a Black colleague to run three eight-hour sessions in which the faculty worked to mend their conflicts and thaw the freeze. Part of how we helped them face this conflict was by challenging all members of the group to acknowledge their mainstream privileges. When other members of the group are able to acknowledge their cisgender privilege, their heterosexual privilege, their male privilege, their class privilege, their able-bodied privilege, their Christian privilege, and so on, it enables White people with marginalized identities to feel fully seen enough to acknowledge their White privilege. This is not just strategically helpful in how it enables White people to open up to their responsibility in facing racism; it also builds a stronger community in which people are better able to support one another fully in the intersections of their identities. This is not all we did. But if we hadn't done this, we would not have been able to subsequently do the other antiracism learning with that group.

When we are accountable for our mainstream privileges, we affirm the existence of an inequitable system that benefits and finds favor with us while disapproving of and disadvantaging those who are marginalized. In other words, when White people are accountable for our privilege as White people, we are acknowledging that racism exists, that it hurts People of Color and Native people, that it benefits us, and that we are part of the racial dynamic it creates. The alternative is to frame racism as a problem that belongs to People of Color and Native people, to frame sexism as women's problem, and to frame homophobia as an LGBTQ+ problem. Yes, these problems affect these groups. But they benefit White people, men, and straight people. They cannot be solved without people from those mainstream groups seeing how they are implicated in the very systems that cause that oppression and doing something about it.

Conclusion

For White people and people who receive White privilege today, White-ness is inevitably a part of our identity, whether we claim it or not. It was assigned to us by history, politics, and society's racial caste system. Only by getting clear about the role it plays in our day-to-day lives and choices can we gain power over it and begin to make it something other than oppressive.

As you continue to read this book, it will support your antiracism to consider whether you identify as a White person and whether other people (especially people you don't know, such as police officers, shop clerks, hospital staff, bankers, real-estate agents, and teachers) see you as White. It's essential for all of us to think about the times when we have resisted identification as White. Why didn't White feel like the right racial designation? For some of us, our parents or grandparents were not considered White. Yet what kinds of resources and opportu-nities did you have access to or not have access to because of how oth-ers saw you? Once White people can see the varied ways we have been implicated by Whiteness without our conscious consent, we also begin to see the agency and purchase that we have over Whiteness so that we can begin to transform it.

Notes

1. *Settler-Colonist* refers to a person who is part of a larger project designed to displace or exterminate the Native people of a land, so that they can form a society in its place. I don't have a record of my ancestors having interaction with Native people, but by virtue of their presence on the unceded lands of Native people, they are Settler-Colonists, and so am I.

2. To read more about this history, see *The Warmth of Other Suns: The Epic Story of America's Great Migration* by Isabel Wilkerson (2010), *The Color of Law: A Forgotten History of How Our Government Segregated America* by Richard Rothstein (2018), and the daily emails put out by the Equal Justice Initiative.

3. A devastating fictional portrayal of the countless barriers put up in front of Black people at every historical turn can be found in Colson Whitehead's (2016) *The Underground Railroad*. While not a true story, this novel helps readers feel the visceral weight

of the racial hierarchy bearing down on Black characters, and it can provide great motivation to do something about it in our own day.

4. To learn more about the formation of Whiteness, I highly recommend these books: *How Jews Became White Folks and What That Says About Race in America* by Karen Brodkin (1998) and *The Possessive Investment in Whiteness: How White People Profit From Identity Politics* by George Lipsitz (2018).

5. Thank you to Dr. Eddie Moore Jr. for helping me see the difference in this framing.

6. Stacey Lee (2005) writes about this phenomenon with detailed clarity in the book *Up Against Whiteness: Race, School, and Immigrant Youth.*

7. If we are going to counter anti-Semitism as part of an antiracist strategy, it's important to draw lines around what anti-Semitism is. While Donald Trump was in the White House, he promoted a preexisting far-right narrative of anti-Semitism that suggests any critique of Israel is necessarily anti-Semitic. Kenneth Stern (2019), the American Jewish Committee's anti-Semitism expert and lead drafter of the working definition of anti-Semitism, argues that this is a distortion. The working definition of anti-Semitism is filed under Title VI of the Civil Rights Act and affords protections to Jews, Sikhs, and Muslims from "intimidation, harassment, and discrimination."

The narrative Trump was promoting had started in 2010, when far-right organizations such as the Zionist Organization of America used Title VI to challenge any speech that is critical of Israel, calling it anti-Semitic. Stern, himself a Zionist, says that this undermines the purpose of the provision and renders it practically inapplicable. For comparison's sake, he says, "There's no definition of anti-black racism that has the force of law when evaluating a Title VI case. If you were to craft one, would you include opposition to affirmative action? Opposing removal of Confederate statues?" (Stern, 2019, para. 6). Title VI, which was created to protect religious minorities from discrimination, is now being used to censor speech that is critical of a nation-state. No nation-state can be protected from critique without violating fundamental free-speech principles that we protect in a democratic society. If people in your community conflate critiques of Israel with anti-Semitism, they are silencing critique in a manner aligned with authoritarian politics. They may be doing so out of fear that their experience of anti-Semitism might remain unseen, or they may be repeating the tropes promoted by the far right. But either way, it is not a helpful conflation as we consider how to battle anti-Semitism in our schools and organizations. For a current definition of anti-Semitism that does not conflate critique of the nation-state with the experience of individual Jews, see the Jerusalem Declaration on Anti-Semitism (https://jerusalemdeclaration.org).

8. Whiteness is also often conflated with heterosexuality, cisgender identity, and maleness. That is not to say that White women and LGBTQ+ people don't receive racial privilege. But ultimately, they take their places in a racial caste system that puts straight, cisgender White men at the very top.

9. Affinity groups are antiracist learning tools used to differentiate instruction within race conversations. Because people from different groups often need different things (White people often need more background about racism and their role in it, for example, whereas People of Color and Native people need more support, connection, and strategies for how to love oneself and one another while navigating racism), affinity groups are used to provide those different spaces. The separate groups usually come back together afterward. The theory is that groups will be stronger and more effective if everyone within the group is getting their learning needs met. It's a way of integrating intragroup learning into the intergroup dialogue that typifies antiracism education. See Chapter 9 for more information on White antiracist learning spaces, sometimes called *affinity spaces*.

But It's Not Fair!

A country's history is not just an aggregation of facts, and it is not just in the past. How we tell and understand our history creates perspectives that prime us for very specific ways to perceive one another, the world around us, and how we belong in it. As we consider how priming affects our ability to detect racism and act in antiracist ways, it's especially important to pause and consider the concept of fairness, how our collective history frames it, and how our physiology interacts with that framing.

When it comes to what we consider to be fair, we are not simply biased by white supremacist beliefs about our supposed specialness, exceptionalism, and deservedness as White people. Fairness is also something we have an innate, biological preference for—and therefore something we will strenuously defend. This might come as a surprise, given how unfair racism is. And it certainly came as a surprise to behavioral economists, who thought human beings' primary motivation was always going to be greed. As it turns out, our motivation for fairness is just as strong as our motivation for getting our needs met. Human beings like things to be fair, even when that means losing something or giving something up.

There is good and bad news here.

Without knowledge of historical and systemic racism, our sense of what is or is not fair is imbalanced. That means that if we think we should have something and are primed through white supremacy to conceptualize People of Color and Native people as unfairly taking that something away from us, we will likely oppose programs designed to counter racism. In other words, we likely will opt to support racism, even when it is in fact detrimental to most of us (McGhee, 2021).

Picture a cartoon depicting three men: a well-dressed White man with a tray full of cookies, a less well-dressed White man with three cookies on a tray, and a Black man with a single cookie on his tray. The wealthy White man points to the Black man while looking at the less wealthy White man and says, "Be careful, he wants to steal your cookies!" The punchline is such an accurate depiction of how racist tropes get used in support of economic exploitation. The cartoon is also a perfect depiction of how our innate preference for fairness can be manipulated to promote racism. And it's quite easy to make us feel cheated by antiracist practice when the very premise of racism is that we are special and deserve what's not, in fact, ours. This means that as long as we haven't eliminated racism (which is unlikely to happen within our lifetimes), it's not a question of if but only when, how intensely, and how often our bodies will initiate a fight, flight, or freeze response to antiracism, as it intrinsically and directly challenges our perception of what is rightly ours.

We must not underestimate the power of this conflict around fairness. Even knowing exactly how my nervous system works, every time I add a social justice organization to my list of donations, I always struggle with how much to donate—and find myself reaching out to allies to make that decision. I don't have a particular hang-up around money, and I'm not usually someone who gets confused about the antiracist actions I have integrated into my daily life. My confusion comes from the fact that there is a part of me that absolutely feels that the money I have is mine for the keeping, even though I am fully aware and consciously believe that much of it is not earned but rather the result of privileges spanning generations, of which I am the financial beneficiary. But white supremacist priming around specialness and deservedness (not to mention othering of the "less deserving") still lives within me. So I find myself unclear as to how much money to give to rectify unfairness and promote more just policies in my communities and the world.

But there is also good news in our innate bias toward fairness. When we come to understand how deeply white supremacy is embedded in our society and in our own lives, we will begin to develop a yearning to counter it in the name of fairness. The antidote to the outcry of unfairness in antiracist policies is then twofold. First, we need to commit to learning and rehearsing new, antiracist, *actually fairer* narratives—around legacy and reparations, interdependence, and interconnectedness—and reading what Ali shared in Chapter 6 is a great place to start. Second, we need to practice sharing what is not entirely ours to begin with, to whichever extent and in whichever way we are able to do so. This can involve donating money, time, or things you own or sharing intangible resources, such as social capital. What matters is practicing actions that match our burgeoning understanding of history and its racist legacy, as well as our growing realization of our fundamental interconnectedness.

Love Can Be Divisive

If our innate preference for fairness was a surprising hindrance to our antiracist aspirations, our capacity for love might be an even more surprising one. Indeed, love can lead us to commit terrible cruelties, and that is because we are designed to overprotect those we love. The same hormone (oxytocin) that facilitates our ability to bond with and trust one another makes us overprotective of our group—whoever we consider to be "us." In fact, Brian Hare and Vanessa Woods (authors of *The Survival of the Friendliest*, 2020) renamed oxytocin (sometimes called the "hug hormone") the "momma bear hormone." Just think of any time someone even attempted to harm your child, your partner, or your parent. I'll bet that even just for a few seconds, your whole body got activated and you might have been ready to do just about anything to protect your loved one.

Because human beings are immensely adaptable, we can create "us/them" divides along *any* lines—from eye color, to country of birth, to sports team. All these lines are culturally constructed; few if any are biologically encoded. But our love or allegiance for our in-group leads us to dehumanize those in the out-group. This happens because our ability to empathize with others is physiologically diminished the moment we classify them as "not us." This, in turn, makes it a lot easier to harm them, and all the more so if we believe that doing so will protect us or our loved ones. This instinct is so strong that just sensing that someone else sees us as "the other" leads us to dehumanize them. We see this dynamic at play in national political discourse all the time, both in the United States and abroad. So the moment we separate people into different competing categories, or place groups into hierarchies, we ignite our potential for injustice, discrimination, hatred, and violence.

What to do? Very simply, we must recognize the ways in which we are constantly divided and pitted against one another along racial lines. We must realize that these divisions are not a reflection of some natural order but something we actively fabricate and that often creates lethal side effects. Once we see the ways in which we frame fellow human beings as the other, we can practice strategies to undo that habit and enlarge the circle of "us" so that we may reinstate our ability to empathize and connect. At the end of this section, I describe a simple yet powerful practice that helps us do that. In the Internal Work section for Chapter 4, I described another effective practice called Loving-Kindness Meditation, which is also helpful in this context.

At times, Ali and I debate what folks on an antiracist path need most: the ability to introspect and emotionally regulate or the ability to learn knowledge and theory about racism and white supremacy. While I tend to argue for the former and Ali for the latter, in reality we agree that we need both—which is the whole point of this book. Without knowledge and theory, we are at the mercy of white supremacy's narratives that initiate fight, flight, or freeze reactions and make us dehumanize one another. Without the ability to introspect and emotionally regulate, we won't be able to actually hear such knowledge and theory and truly learn from it, nor translate it into tangible actions. Theoretically, emotional regulation allows us to tap into our innate capacity to be attuned to and learn from our lived experiences, as well as to connect with and love one another. In practice, our socialization into white supremacy is too strong of a primer to allow us not to repetitively fall into fight, flight, or freeze states and reactively see what we believe (rather than believe what we see). And what we already believe is full of biases that move us away from empathy and connection with others. So we need both abilities: we must access knowledge and also engage in introspection.

Ali's chapters are gold mines for new narratives and new knowledge. They give us new glasses for seeing the world we live in. But reading them for content without applying them in our daily lives will not change our hearts, nor will it lead us to identify opportunities for disrupting racism in real time. We must wear these new glasses all the time and actively retrain ourselves to have an accurate sense of reality. If we don't actually wear these new glasses and consciously notice the new data they reveal in our daily lives, we'll continue to stumble in the blur of white supremacy and by default remain complicit.

Strengthening Your Antiracist Practice

Practice Fairness: Sharing Is Caring

Because racism intrinsically implies that White people are in some way exceptional and deserving of special privileges, and because we have developed our physiological sense of safety within that belief system, our bodies might perceive antiracist practice as unfair—even when we intellectually understand that it is not. To rebalance that inaccurate sense of unfairness, it's helpful to practice giving in a structured, consistent way. We might decide to redistribute resources financially, depending on means, or in other ways. That might mean grappling with how much money to donate to which organizations, whom you might let pass ahead of you in a line, when you might step aside on a sidewalk, or how many items you buy in a grocery store before a storm. To be clear, these are not actions that will end racism. Small though they may be, any practice that makes

(Continued)

(Continued)

you pause before assuming preferential access to resources is an opportunity to practice envisioning a world where there is enough for all and to recalibrate your sense of fairness.

Enlarge the Circle of "Us": The "Just Like Me" Practice

This practice (together with the Loving-Kindness Meditation described in the Internal Work section for Chapter 4) is a great tool to begin undoing the ways in which white supremacy separates us, so that we can remain in empathetic connection with one another. White supremacy doesn't just separate White people from People of Color and Native people; it also separates White people from one another by encouraging competition—even among activists. In fact, a primary goal of this book is to equip White people to work with each other and form coalitions. So it's important to apply this exercise to White people as well as to People of Color and Native people. Thinking specifically about a White person will help you support and be supported by other White people on an antiracist journey. This could be another White person with whom you deeply disagree on issues of politics. It could be a White person with whom you are aligned politically but who just annoys you. Thinking about a Person of Color or Native person will help you notice your tendency to see those who have been artificially classified as different or as "the other" and will help you begin to undo that priming.

Here is how this practice works: As you go about your day, notice or think about people you might feel some degree of disconnection, disagreement, or animosity toward. Once you notice your internal reaction to them, pause and reflect on the ways in which you are actually similar to them by actively rehearsing these in your mind. For example, you might say to yourself, "Just like me, they love their child," "Just like me, they get impatient sometimes," "Just like me, they want to belong," "Just like me, they strive to be useful," or "Just like me, they feel aches and pains in their bodies." You might even use something you feel in that moment and imagine that they too feel that same way sometimes (e.g., "Just like me, they are in a rush," "Just like I feel different from them, they feel different from me"). In other words, practice undoing the othering tendency you have developed toward the person you are thinking about and rehumanize them by appreciating the ways in which you share longings, aspirations, sorrows, challenges, and joys. To be sure, this is not the same as thinking of others in colorblind ways, as this strategy is not based on denying that white privilege and racism exist. Rather, this strategy is grounded in an awareness of the very real impact of white privilege and racism, and it invites us to practice challenging white supremacist assumptions that we are fundamentally separate groups in competition with one another. When we challenge these assumptions in the micro-moments of our lives, we shift the very ground that larger systemic inequities are built on.

PART 3

WHO WILL WE BE AS THE RACIAL HIERARCHY FALLS?

CHAPTER #7

Taking Feedback and Using It Wisely

[So] you begin to train in holding the vulnerability—the rawness and vulnerability in your heart—knowing first of all it is the beginning of something really fresh and new in your life, turning you in a whole different direction. And second, it is making you braver and stronger and more there for other people, and it will bring out your best human abilities.

—Pema Chödrön (2015, p. 87)

The first thing is to be honest with yourself. You can never have an impact on society if you have not changed your-self. . . . Great peacemakers are all people of integrity, of honesty, but humility.

—Nelson Mandela (as cited in Winfrey, 2000)

Part III of this book is about dismantling the racial hierarchy by intervening with other White people, building loving and accountable structures that will help White people grow as antiracists, and taking action toward building a more equitable society. In this chapter, we start again with ourselves. We start with seeking feedback and accepting it as a gift. If we are going to collectively unlearn white supremacy, we need to be able to hear how it works through us. We need to be able to accept feedback from People of Color and Native people and from other White people. This is how we begin to know what we don't know. Before we learn how to deliver feedback to other White people, we need to develop the skills to take it in ourselves. Learning how to give feedback requires that we know how tender and vulnerable a person needs to be in order to receive it.

As we think about traveling an antiracist path, not just for our lifetimes but for our children's children's children's lifetimes, we will need a lot of White people to walk this path. Every intervention is an opportunity to invite people to the path or keep them traveling along it. Too many White people think antiracist action means attending a rally across the country or changing careers, when actually the antiracist action we need to take is right where we are—where we live, where we work, where our kids go to school. And for us to be able to take antiracist action in our lives, our first antiracist action must happen within ourselves.

Prioritize the Goal, Not the Moment of Discomfort

Every summer, we take our kids to a family camp that is for both deaf and hearing families. The camp hires multiple interpreters to interpret the words of the director and counselors but also to help facilitate conversation and connection between the people who speak sign language and those who don't. I'm always amazed and impressed at how two interpreters together correct one another. If someone is interpreting for the group and they get it wrong, another interpreter will chime in to correct them, and the first one will immediately correct themselves. There are no apologies, no criticism delivered between slices of praise. It's direct and immediate feedback that is taken and incorporated just as directly and immediately.

Watching them, I hypothesized that maybe they can integrate feedback so seamlessly because so many things are happening at once and because there's an urgency to the communication; maybe there's simply not enough time to get bogged down in defensive behavior. When I asked about it, an interpreter told me that communicating accurately is the highest and unquestioned priority for an interpreter. She said nobody would even think to be defensive or resistant to that kind of feedback because they first and foremost want to know if they might have misheard or miscommunicated meaning.

When it comes to race, could we ever value a common goal this deeply that we would so eagerly take in feedback and incorporate it without defensiveness or resistance? When we offer one another correction so that the language we use can be more accurate, more affirming, and more inclusive, all too often we bristle, self-justify, and resist change. I know this because I've done it hundreds of times. We resist because our own sense of goodness—and therefore our fear of whether we are going to still be accepted by the group—comes immediately into question. Stereotype threat reigns, rather than the unquestioned priority of not causing harm. We have the very real challenge of yearning to and needing to be a good person, while living in a system that makes us complicit in causing harm, even without meaning to. We were raised to believe that racism is not systemic but rather the product of bad apples. Getting feedback that we did or said something racist, then, seems to confirm our fears: that we are one of those bad apples. It's an impossible setup that inevitably leads to defensiveness. What if we too just took the correction, incorporated it, and moved on? What if we all felt the urgency of the need to communicate accurately and affirmingly so that we can shift the racist ideas that shape our schools, workplaces, minds, and relationships? What if we made racial equity the highest priority?

Racial Humility

Racial competence,[1] as we define it, means that a person has the knowledge, skills, and self-awareness to recognize and intervene in racism, both inside themselves and within their sphere of influence (Mattheus & Marino, 2011; Sue & Sue, 2019).[2] In other words, racial competence is a skills-based competency that anybody can learn. But competence is no longer the highest level of proficiency. Today, scholars are saying that on the far end of the spectrum of racial competency, beyond competence, there is an even more important stance: *racial or cultural humility* (Tervalon & Murray-García, 1998). This is where we end up when we begin realizing how much we don't know. The more we learn, the more we realize we don't know. When we truly build our competence, we ultimately become humble about how much there is to know, how easy it is to make a mistake, and how open we need to be to taking feedback on our journey. Racial humility is the antidote to fragility. It makes it possible for us to keep learning and keep taking in feedback. We stop taking feedback when we think we know all there is to know.

Strategies for Taking Feedback

There are straightforward strategies for taking in feedback in a way that helps a person maintain relationships and learn. I will list these briefly and then share in greater depth how Eleonora and I think about feedback, as well as examples of what happens when a person takes in feedback.

Here are some tried-and-true strategies for taking feedback (Mattheus & Marino, 2011):

- Breathe deeply.
- Listen.
- Watch out for the tendency to become defensive or enter flight, fight, or freeze mode.
- Demonstrate nonverbally that you are taking in what is being said.
- Acknowledge valid points.

- Acknowledge the other person's point of view.

- Take time to understand the feedback on your own or with an ally.

- Set a time to get back to the person offering the feedback, so that you can sort through it together.

- Don't try to make the feedback giver wrong by finding people who will support your point of view.

- Make agreements about what you will do differently in response to the feedback.

- Say thank you for the feedback, as if it were a gift.

When I receive feedback, I treat it like a gift. Sometimes it's a gift I don't want and didn't necessarily know I needed. Sometimes it's a gift I ask for but still dislike. But I never reject the gift as I unwrap it in front of the giver. I usually say, "Thank you," and commit in that moment to learning more. Sometimes I will apologize if it's called for—and if it doesn't foreclose a fuller conversation. Later, on my own, I start taking notes, and I call someone to help me process it.

You can't take feedback on your own. None of us can. When I have tried to take in feedback without processing it with someone, it has festered in the back of my mind, feeding me negative messages that I'm not trustworthy or not good or not sufficiently antiracist. I'm distracted in a way that affects my authenticity. Then, because I want to get back to an emotional equilibrium, I begin to judge and resent the person who gave me the feedback. We have to stop thinking that we can go it alone, particularly when it comes to the vulnerability of getting feedback. This is a team effort.

When I process feedback, I often start by writing down the feedback and how I'm feeling. But then I have to call an ally (someone who is willing to hold me accountable to my antiracist intentions) who can help me process the incident or understand it better. Processing feelings involves three steps: *name it, feel it, share it*. That is what I do in my writing and with my ally.

I almost always end up agreeing with the person who gives me feedback—or at the very least learning something new. But again, when I first receive the feedback, it's so discordant with what I'm trying to do and who I'm trying to be that my body does not want to take it in. Usually if I let some time pass and let the feedback sink in, I am able to grieve the sadness of having caused harm and get back in touch with my overall sense of goodness. This then lowers my defenses and makes it possible for me to hear the feedback. This is particularly important because feedback activates our stereotype threat, which narrows our assessment of ourselves as *either* a racist *or* a good person, making us forget that there is so much more to us and our identities. Taking the time to get back in touch with our own values and goodness is the best antidote to the perils of stereotype threat, which causes this either/or dead end, making it impossible to take in feedback.

Ultimately, feedback really is a gift. While receiving feedback can make me feel bad, it's almost never delivered with that intent. People offer feedback because they feel hurt and want me to stop hurting them. People offer feedback because they take me seriously when I say that I don't want to cause harm and that I don't want to perpetuate racism. Giving feedback makes the giver vulnerable, especially when the giver is a Person of Color or a Native person. Getting defensive increases the harm, particularly because it often gets delivered at the precise moment of that person's vulnerability.

Feedback Example

In spring 2021, the president of a school board, a White man in a community that was more than 50 percent Black, delivered a commencement speech to the graduating seniors. Halfway through the speech, he quoted a story about Frederick Douglass that profoundly minimized the experience of enslavement. Many members of his community, including school leaders, were deeply hurt by this minimization and wished that they could stop him from speaking even as he stood at the podium. This hurt occurred in the middle of the COVID-19 pandemic, at the end of a difficult school year in which racial awareness in the United States—as well as racial unawareness—was visibly heightened.

This particular school board president was known to me because of work that I have done professionally with the district, the administration, and the teachers. I knew that he was not new to racial issues. He had lived in and raised his children in the same racially diverse community for more than 20 years. He had read multiple books on racism. He was one of the most visibly supportive school board members of students' efforts to create police-free schools. He understood the need for more Black teachers. He was and is, in short, the kind of school board member who will help his community achieve greater racial equity. But in this instance, he made a mistake. Or, as he would say, it was more than a mistake. As a community leader, he caused profound hurt and dismay.

I actually found out about the speech through the rumor mill. White people in the community were critiquing him, asking how he could do such a thing, why he didn't have his speech checked, and why he didn't know better. I remember saying to one colleague, "I don't think we should assume that we could have done better. That could easily have been you or me." The man accepted a leadership position in a community that is grappling in deep and systemic ways with racism. He knows a lot. He feels it deeply. Yet he doesn't know everything. He too has faults and oversights.

Troubled by the responses I heard and imagining that he might be getting the cold shoulder from more than a few White residents even as he was opening himself up to the sadness and anger of many Black residents, I decided to reach out. Here is what I wrote:

> *Dear Josh,*
>
> *I'm sending you love tonight! I caught wind of a graduation speech, an omission, and an apology. I didn't get the full details. But as a White person trying to show up for a multiracial community and sometimes doing so imperfectly, I connected with your predicament. I really don't know the details of what happened, but I love that you had the chutzpah to own it and apologize. I'm happy to talk anytime if you want someone to confidentially process with. But in the meantime, just know you're not alone. And I'm grateful for all you do for your community.*
>
> *Love and hugs to you and your family,*
>
> *Ali*

In this email, I was simply trying to make sure that Josh wasn't isolated in the blowback he was getting from all sides. He was getting true, honest, heartbreaking feedback from Black families, and he was showing up to listen. He was not defending himself. He was not excusing himself. He was just listening. But he was also getting judgment from White people throughout his community who were embarrassed by him, who acted as if they would have known better, who leaned away from him presumably so that they would not be tarnished by his mistake. I didn't want him to cancel himself prematurely by resigning from the board as a way of escaping the discomfort of the moment.

Josh called me almost immediately after receiving the email. I was very happy to hear that he was in conversation with one of his White community members who had reached out to support him for similar reasons. None of us were interested in excusing him or offering forgiveness that was not ours to give. Without even planning it, we showed up to give him the company and emotional support that he might need to keep listening to the hurt he caused, to keep hearing the racial hurt buried in his district well beyond his comments on graduation day, and to keep taking in the feedback without going into the reintegration stage. People often go into reintegration when they feel overwhelmed and panicky in the face of racial stress that they are not equipped to handle. In reintegration, a person closes up, regresses to a dominant racial ideology, blames People of Color and Native people for being too sensitive, and expresses both hostility and anger. I knew that he needed support not to go there.

In this case, I needn't have worried. If anything, the pendulum had swung the other way. He was so full of guilt that he thought he deserved to be punished. He had been in touch with a Black diversity educator for the district, who encouraged him to set up listening sessions with the families who had been hurt by his speech. He was in full receptivity mode. He had no desire to defend himself or minimize the concerns of the community. And when other school board members prepared a letter to the community in which they critiqued him, presumably because they felt a need to publicly distance themselves from his mistakes, he thought it was what he deserved. But his wife advised, "If they publish that letter, you will have no choice but to resign."

Josh didn't want to resign. I realized then that this was why I had wanted to be available. Josh was not in danger of reintegrating. He had all the skills for taking in the feedback as a gift. He knew to breathe, stay calm, listen deeply, and commit to learning and change. But he was in danger of flight. In his case, it was political—he feared that staying could be worse for the community. He felt that the board was passively trying to communicate through this letter that he should leave. What choice did he have to stay on as a member of the board so deeply disgraced?

I didn't believe that the board was suggesting he should resign. I asked if anyone had encouraged him to resign, and he said no. "In all honesty," I said, "people in your community do not hide what they think. And no one has asked you to resign. People are hurt. They want you to understand that. They want you to listen to them. They want the leadership of the school board to understand racial dynamics of the community at a deep level. They want things like this not to happen. But they have not said you should leave. By conducting these listening sessions and committing to change based on what you hear, you are becoming more and more the person they want and need you to be. You have already been so deeply formed by this conflict that you will not make this mistake again. You have been so changed by the listening sessions that you now see some of the racial faults of the community even better than before. And more important, you are more beholden to the Black community for sharing so much of their truth with you that you are in their debt."

We know now that the rest of the board did not want Josh to resign. Though they were hurt and saddened, they were looking for the best way to hold Josh accountable, hear from the community, address the fallout, and support healing all at the same time. In a multiracial society like ours, with a fractured, inequitable past like the one we have had, these moments of rupture are going to happen. The board members understood that the only way to the other side is through.

If Josh had resigned prematurely, he would have been canceling himself, which is a form of flight. And I have seen other White teachers and administrators do this. They resign rather than sit in the fire of the conflict and take the heat (Mindell, 2014). They are accused of racism, or they are caught up in a racist system, or their very real racism is pointed out—so they leave. I get that impulse, because I also don't want to stay where I am not wanted. And I certainly don't want to have to defend myself against allegations that feel deeply untrue to who I am. But feedback is not necessarily a sign that a person is not wanted. It is a sign that we or the systems within which we operate are creating racially disparate results. It's a sign that change is necessary. But if we leave, the conflict is often for naught. Rather than leading to change, the feedback leaves with the person who resigns. We get replaced by someone else, statistically likely to be a White person who is even less aware than we are, who will go forward and make similar—if not the same—mistakes.

I believe that when we take in feedback—and when we change and make change based on that feedback—we make ourselves more desirable contributors to a multiracial community. In the heat of this conflict, Josh was becoming the very person his community needed him to be. And of course, I wish it did not take this kind of disruption and hurt for him to become that person, but if we could already be the people that a racially just world needs us to be without doing our work, there would be no need for this conversation to begin with.

Josh realized that he didn't want to resign and that the board didn't want him to resign, which meant he had to work with them to redraft the public letter, even as his board colleagues were still tender and even though everyone was still in pain. He had to get past his sense that he deserved to be punished so that collectively the board could draft a letter that addressed the rupture he caused, while also engaging in repair, leaving the door open for him to continue to be on the board. Josh did decide to stay but thought he should resign as president as a public gesture to signify that the feedback had landed. I supported that decision but advised that if he stepped away as president, the Black woman who was vice president of the board would be thrust into the position of president a year sooner than she had prepared for. If he were to resign as president without consulting her, he would unilaterally place the burden of leadership on her as a way to get out from under his own mistakes. In this case, she graciously agreed to step into the role so that he could step down.

In the weeks and months to come, Josh saw some of the impact of his choices. In particular, he noticed how many White people came to him and tried to let him off the hook—White people who knew him, trusted him, liked him, and felt that he had been treated unfairly. It now fell to Josh to support White people who were in reintegration because of their vicarious experience of watching him navigate so much racial stress. Many White people were inclined to discredit the feedback or those who gave it because they believed so deeply in his goodness. They could not square the idea that he could be a good and selfless person—probably the most racially aware person many of them knew—with the notion that he could still do something racist that he needed to apologize for. He realized that if he had left the school board, he would have deepened the racial divisions in the community, because there were so many White people who would have defended him and insisted he had been wronged. He told me that he has a refrain he finds himself repeating with each conversation that goes something like this: "What I want you to come out of this thinking is: I didn't get canceled. I'm still actively engaged. I learned from this. What people were saying was correct. I shouldn't have said that. Don't see me as the victim."

When this whole conflict started, Josh was searching for what he had to do to appropriately respond to it. Holding listening sessions was absolutely the right step. What's critical is that he didn't rush that process; he sat in the fire and let his sincere empathetic attunement to the feedback provide the learning he needed in order to know what he needed to do next. He let the process change him until he saw something new. His new visceral understanding became his compass for action.

A few months after this conflict, Josh—a relatively nonreligious person—was asked to talk about his experience during a religious holiday focused on forgiveness and atonement. In front of his whole congregation, he recounted the story and all he had learned from it with deep humility and earnestness. In doing so, he took a story that could be a source of shame belonging to gossip circles and social media, haunting him in the back of his mind, and he shaped it into a narrative of learning and growth that belonged to him. In doing so, he also opened new doors for others, shifting a narrative that closed people down into a generative one that helped people access the lessons within it. He allowed the story to shape his growing identity as an antiracist and as a racially humble community leader. By integrating the story into his identity in this way, he can continue to carry it with him and to learn from it, while carrying much less shame or the desire to distance himself from it. He has changed it into something he can hold close and be informed by, rather than something he must fight, flee, or freeze with.

Feedback Needs Guardrails

Here's another scenario. A small college I work with has a growing number of antiracist students who are way ahead of the faculty and administration in terms of their racial awareness. They are Students of Color and White students. They see racism and racist practices everywhere . . . and they're not wrong. They are impatient with the slow pace of change. Their critiques are often delivered with both judgment and annoyance. Their requests are often framed as demands, sometimes in multipoint letters addressed to the administration and posted widely on social media. They disregard what some professors teach because those professors do not have an antiracist lens. They are harsh and unforgiving. Teaching is becoming a struggle. Many professors want to leave. Enrollment is actually going down because other prospective students have learned that the college has a toxic culture where if you don't know how to be antiracist and use all the right words, you will be miserable.

This type of scenario is quite prevalent right now—at this college and others. The colleges try to honor what students ask for, but exhausted by the demands, administrators don't know how to fix the various levels of tension. People are worn out—and not just the people who have less skill and experience managing racial stress. Some professors and administrators have quit their jobs. And not just White people—People of Color and Native people are getting worn out by these experiences, too, especially when White students call them out for not doing enough, or when White students make every interaction about fighting *on behalf of* People of Color and Native people, which in turn throws People of Color and Native people into constant battle, eliminating spaces at the school that could be refuges for rest or an exploration of other topics.

All too often, colleges and schools will take action in such situations by handing power over to the students. They put students on advisory committees and ask them what needs to happen. They give students power because they believe the students know what needs to happen. But in most cases, the students are not necessarily asking to run the institution. They're asking for respect, honesty, clarity, inclusive community, belonging for all students, and high expectations for community members. They know what they need and what they don't have. But they don't necessarily know how to get it because they are not administrators, and they are not teachers; they are students. They are letting administrators and faculty know what they need and what they deserve because they are deeply hurt, even traumatized by racism—not just the racism of the institution but also the racism of society at large. And they do not feel safe. They are reaching out to the institution in imperfect and sometimes difficult ways in hopes of getting what they need.

So what do they need? As Eleonora has written elsewhere, students experiencing unpredictable trauma (such as a global pandemic coupled with institutional racism) require "'flexible predictability' accomplished by creating unambiguous structures that are not so rigid to be experienced as controlling, coercive, or rejecting. [They] need clarity and predictability to feel safe and flexibility to feel a sense of control" (Bartoli, 2020, para. 15).

Just like Josh needed to be transformed by feedback to know how to proceed, the students at this college need their teachers and administrators to have skills and knowledge that they do not have yet; they need them to be open to the process of transformation. But if the teachers and administrators place the solution in the hands of administratively unskilled students, it allows the administrators to bypass their own learning through deep listening, which would allow them to use their skills and positions to make the systemic change. If they let the students hammer them this way, they will reactively close up, precluding the necessary transformation, and they still will not be what the students need them to be.

Guardrails for delivering feedback will support students in achieving the change they seek. The rigidity and nastiness currently pervading so much of the feedback that high school and college students offer their peers, teachers, and professors is a trauma response; it's a fight response. It's critical that they express themselves. But teachers and administrators can support them by asking them to consider this question: "What is your purpose?" If the feedback you give paralyzes the person you're giving it to, the whole growth process freezes. Students want change, but instead they are contributing to a stasis—a paralysis. Students need support to see that this is not how systemic change happens. Change happens when we win people over.

The following are Eleonora's recommendations for guardrails, based on her experience as an administrator and trauma counselor. She suggests that leaders must be

- clear and realistic about what the school can offer and its limitations;
- explicit about the expectations and roles of various constituents, including performance expectations where applicable;

- inviting of and responsive to feedback from all parties (while still remaining responsible for the integration, operationalization, and implementation of suggestions, i.e., while still acting as competent leaders);

- transparent about the values the school aspires to, remaining honest and realistic about the degree to which the aspiring is still a work in progress (i.e., avoiding overpromising);

- diligent in providing regular feedback and avenues for reciprocal communication among all parties;

- able to predict and name stressors, as well as potential reactions to them; and

- able to provide a degree of choice, as applicable (being mindful that too many choices can be experienced as a source of uncertainty rather than empowerment). (Bartoli, 2020, para. 17–23)

When we turn the process of institutional transformation over to students who are deeply distressed by racism and don't have the influence or skills to undo it directly, we exacerbate their lack of safety. We take people who are already traumatized—who are asking for safety and protection—and we give them the impression that they are in charge of fixing the issues that endanger them. Rather than feeling safer, they begin to feel less heard and taken care of. Guardrails convey to the students that somebody with more influence and more experience hears them and is still in charge—that somebody besides them is holding the larger process and that their feedback is not in vain.

Better Mechanisms for Feedback

Part of taking feedback means asking for it. It means issuing anonymous surveys for people you supervise or programs you run. It means reaching out to people in your life who have a strong racial analysis and asking them specifically to hold you accountable. We also need to help students in schools have more mechanisms for offering feedback. During the Black@ Instagram movement, when many Black students, teachers, and alums shared their stories of racial trauma in schools, many non-Black teachers and administrators took in those stories as a form of feedback and worked to create change based on it. But other schools refused to treat the Black@ movement as a form of feedback because it was anonymous, online, and public. And while feedback is always more effectively delivered in person, in private, and with a name attached, the expectation that Students of Color and Native students and their families could do that consistently is unrealistic. It is incredibly difficult to give feedback to one's child's school without being labeled as difficult. Many Parents of Color and Native parents already have to speak up multiple times to ensure that their child has a minimum level of racial and identity safety at school (Steele & Cohn-Vargas, 2013). Countless smaller events go unreported as parents and students choose their battles. All of it—the big, the small, and the cumulative impact—is what came out of the Black@ movement.

What this means is that schools, colleges, and universities need to create easier, more accessible, anonymous, private ways for students and families to give feedback in a way that is comfortable and safe for them. They need to find ways to publicize the feedback they are receiving, as well as how they are responding.[3] Many schools have anonymous systems for reporting bullying. Such a system increases the institution's self-knowledge and decreases the amount of internal angst and even negative gossip that occurs when people have no outlet for their concerns.

Prepare to Give Feedback by Noticing How You Receive It

The next chapter is about how to give feedback in a way that will help people feel open to what you say, rather than shut down. To prepare to give feedback, think about what helps you take feedback in . . . and what doesn't. To get us started, I will share a story of feedback that shut me down.

I once asked a White colleague to teach me about a concept related to racism that I didn't know much about. In the process of answering my question, she shamed me for not already knowing the answer. She got activated, she ranted, and she offered no resources. She told me that racism is maintained for the benefit of all White people, so I am benefiting from it, whether I understand it or not. By the end of the conversation, I was aware—on a physiological level—that I would not go back to her with more questions in the future. I even felt queasy when I passed her office after that, as if my body remembered that she was not someone I wanted to see. Perhaps I would have been able to receive her feedback had I not been so inexperienced and unskilled, but it was what it was. I could take in only what I could take in. This experience closed me down. And while I feel annoyance at that colleague and sadness at the missed opportunity in my own learning, I also know that I have very likely played the same role in the memories of other colleagues or students who felt shamed and shut down by me. Early in my time as a graduate student while teaching classes on race and racism, I know that my responses were often shaped more by my own insecurity and panic than by students' learning needs. I was eager to prove my antiracism, even at the expense of another White person's learning.

While a White ally shaming another White person as a teaching strategy often comes from the White ally's own stress response, there seems to be an assumption that if you are antiracist "enough," you should be able to learn, no matter the form in which feedback is delivered. And in fact, I do believe White people need to build the skill and support systems that will enable them to take feedback from People of Color and Native people in whatever form it's offered. But physiologically we are not designed to take in feedback grounded in shame. When the shaming comes from another White person's stress response or desire to look good, it's not in fact an intentional teaching strategy. The shaming or belittling is a *defensive* strategy on the part of the person offering the feedback. Self-defense then becomes the underlying aim of the conversation, rather than facilitating someone else's antiracist learning for the long haul. In other words, the form feedback takes matters because its impact matters. And the greener people are on the antiracist path, the less likely they are to be able to make use of feedback. If they are new to an antiracist conversation, this may be one of the first times they realize they have violated their own moral code[4] or experienced the anxiety of stereotype threat in relation to race. They may want the feedback but not yet have the skills for taking it in and acting on it.

As you begin to think about what you can do to intervene with other White people, it is extremely helpful to use what opens *you* up to feedback—and what closes you down. Not every White person will react as you do, but knowing what opens you up and what closes you down will help you form a gut sense of what works for you, which can then be a guide.

Because I really didn't feel like I understood the answer to my question after this shaming conversation, I asked the same question to another White friend I knew to be deeply immersed in the particular struggle I was asking about. She opened herself up completely, without judgment. "What do you want to know?" she asked. We had a two-hour conversation in which I was able to ask all my "stupid" questions. She lent me two books that helped me learn more. She introduced me to people directly connected to the struggle, from whom I then spent time learning over the next year. She checked in with me a few months later. We still talk about it when we are together, now 12 years later. Her support has helped me walk further along an antiracist path.

Notes

1. We use the term *racial competence* to refer directly to the competence needed to recognize and intervene in racism, borrowing from the more commonly used term *cultural competence*.

2. I have created this definition of racial competence using the Sue and Sue (2019) model of multicultural competence and the Mattheus and Marino (2011) model for White antiracist intervention, which states that White people need to be able to recognize and intervene in racism, both within themselves and in their sphere of influence. While Sue and Sue recently added "action" to their definition of multicultural competence, I leave it off here because it is embedded in the addition of the Mattheus and Marino model.

3. When Eleonora was the director of the Master's in Counseling Program at Arcadia, she created a public permanent record that was released every two years containing all the feedback they had received and how they responded to it.

4. See the Internal Work section on moral injury following this chapter.

INTERNAL WORK

On Moral Injury and Racial Competence

. . . .

If getting feedback on the limited effectiveness (or ineffectiveness) of our antiracist efforts is a gift, why does it feel awful to take it in? As we have already talked about, being socialized to fear the topic of race is one of the reasons why conversations about race quickly raise our anxiety. We also perceive racial talk as threatening because of the likelihood that a greater awareness of the role of race in our lives will reveal that we have violated our own moral code, meaning that we have committed what is called a *moral injury*.[1] The realization that we have committed a moral injury, by definition, leads to guilt and shame—and our bodies most definitely register guilt and shame as a threat.

We can feel the pinch of a moral injury in minor situations, like snapping at a friend, *even though* we value patience. We feel it in more significant situations, such as failing to speak up when we hear a racist comment, *even though* we value equity and social justice. And then we feel it in the most egregious moral violations, such as acting as a bystander in a bullying situation, *even though* we value fairness or protecting others. Somewhat paradoxically, moral injuries occur *because* we care about others and about being good people. Research on human evolution shows that human beings strive for social belonging and are invested in maintaining mutually caring connections; we can't achieve either of those if we don't live by a moral code. If this hadn't become part of our nature, we simply would not have survived as a species (Christakis, 2019; Hare & Woods, 2020).

As White people attempt to develop an awareness of racism, we inevitably realize how we have acted in hurtful, racist ways, and we begin to see how likely it is for us to continue to do so in the process of developing racial competence. If you are reading this book, it's safe to assume that your moral code includes treating others with respect, fairness, and kindness—and that it does not include acting in racist ways. This means that the very path to developing an antiracist consciousness is likely riddled with the shame and disappointment of having breached your own values, as well as the awareness that you are probably going to do it again.

The shame we feel is not a problem in and of itself. It is actually normative and evolutionarily useful. Shame was encoded in the human nervous system as a way to make sure we remember vividly what we do that harms our communities (to which our own chances of survival are tied), so that we don't do it again. However, wallowing in shame is a dead end: it does not propel us to heal, grow from our missteps, and act in ways more aligned with our moral codes. So a key skill in becoming more racially competent is our ability to process moral injuries and the ensuing shame in helpful ways. There are clear steps we can use to do that (see Strengthening Your Antiracist Practice at the end of this section)—which, as you'll see, bring us right back to the importance of receiving feedback.

Now, just as we talked about in the Internal Work section on stereotype threat following Chapter 5, our punitive culture, combined with a fixed mindset, gives us little room or support to process moral injuries or shame. Rather, these two forces make us supremely susceptible to experiencing stereotype threat (related to being seen as a racist) right at the moment when we become aware of having committed a moral injury. As a result, all too often we don't grow from our mistakes. At best, we stop at feeling shame; at worst, we reactively gaslight the person we have injured by finding a way to make it their fault—which relieves us of our feelings of shame and responsibility. But if we are able to emotionally regulate enough to receive the feedback and engage deeply with it, we can learn from our experiences and identify ways to repair our wrongdoings. All this is exponentially easier to do if you have a supportive community of antiracist allies, as Ali described in detail in her chapter. Developing such a community of allies is a skill in and of itself. The next two chapters will show you how to identify and nurture antiracist connections among other White people.

Strengthening Your Antiracist Practice

How to Recover From Moral Injuries

Recovering from moral injuries, including processing the shame we might feel when we violate our own values, is key for us to be able to learn from our missteps while we develop racial competence. This process involves four steps:

1. Take stock of what you did wrong (aka take in the feedback), without letting your fight, flight, or freeze responses shut you down. This first step requires the

capacity to emotionally regulate. (See the exercise in the Internal Work section for Chapter 1 on how to build the capacity for emotional regulation.)

2. Grieve the choices you have made that brought about the situation, whether you intended them or not.

3. Learn from the experience, identifying what you could have done instead and how you might proceed in the future. (See Chapter 9 for how to develop intentional space for doing this in collaboration with other White allies.)

4. Make amends however possible. This not only allows for the chance to repair important relationships and facilitate others' healing; it's also key to developing our own sense of agency and self-efficacy on our antiracist journeys.

   a. Sometimes you can directly repair what you have done—such as circling back to a conversation where you didn't intervene as needed, explicitly apologizing for a microaggression, or working on a policy change in your place of employment.

   b. When direct repair is not possible (for example, if you are no longer connected to the people or context involved), you can still consider ways in which you can pay it forward somehow. That might involve committing to educate yourself and others on a given topic, recognizing the way in which the issue continues to manifest in your current social circle and working toward change there, or donating to organizations that do work related to the misstep you made.

The more you practice working through moral injuries and making amends, the quicker, more confident, and more empowered you will become at using feedback to increase your racial competence.

Note

1. Here, I use the concept of moral injury as described by psychologist Brett Litz et al. (2009), based on psychiatrist Jonathan Shay's pioneering work on military trauma.

CHAPTER #8

Talking to Other White People About Race

At its best, activism is a form of healing. Activism is not just about what we do; it is also about who we are and how we show up in the world. It is about learning and expressing regard, compassion, and love—for ourselves and for our fellow human beings.

—Resmaa Menakem (2017, p. 244)

How do I talk to other White people about race, particularly when they say or do something offensive? How do I bring it up, especially if they don't mean to be hurtful? How do I talk to my neighbor when he mocks my Black Lives Matter T-shirt as I walk around the block? How do I talk to the older White person on the block who says, "The neighborhood sure isn't what it used to be," clearly implying that it's no longer predominantly White? What do I say to the White woman who is deeply invested in antiracism but keeps calling Black women "girls"? Or how do I respond to the White woman who, when I say during a superintendent search committee meeting that I want a superintendent who understands the need to hire Black teachers, says, "I don't think it's necessary that teachers be Black. I just think they need to be strong, loving teachers. Our college admissions rate is way too low. We need teachers who are going to bring that up."

The previous chapters have laid the groundwork for these conversations—outlining the framework for why it is so important for White people to talk with other White people about racism, explaining the process of White racial socialization and how we build our own racial identity, highlighting the history of Whiteness and its ongoing impact in the United States so that we have a clear historical context, and exploring the process of taking challenging feedback so that we are able to stay on an antiracist pathway and help drive essential change.

This chapter offers you more strategies for meeting other White people where they are while not letting them stay there. It's about intervening in racism while inviting those who make racist comments or otherwise hold up white supremacy to move onto—or further along—an antiracist path.

Scenario 1

White neighbor in his 70s (upon seeing my Black Lives Matter shirt): Nice shirt. I thought all lives matter. *[He smiles.]*

[I'm not sure what this neighbor means. Is he trying to be witty? Does he disagree that Black lives matter? Does he think that I don't believe his life matters? I don't stop to talk, but I respond in passing, with a smile.]

Me: They do! I agree. That's why I'm wearing this shirt.

Scenario 2

White handyman (after 15 minutes of friendly conversation):	Can you believe these TV commercials these days? It's like somebody really has an agenda. Every other commercial has these mixed-race families in them. I mean, I am all for integration, but what the hell? It's like they're shoving it down our throats.
Me:	So you like the message, but you don't like having it in your face?
Handyman:	Yeah, it's just like someone thinks this is how we should all think, so they just shove it down our throats.
Me:	You know, I can relate to that. I hate being manipulated by TV.
Handyman:	I hate it! I feel like they don't let anyone think for themselves anymore.
Me:	You're so right. I feel the same way. But those commercials don't bother me. I'm just happy that there are families out there who love one another. Sometimes it feels like there's not enough love in the world today.

[The handyman considers, then changes the subject.]

Scenario 3

As we talk about some of the new neighbors moving in, many of whom are People of Color, my White neighbor says: Yep, the neighborhood just isn't what it used to be.

[I'm not exactly sure what he means, but because we had just been talking about some of the new families moving in, and because this is fairly common coded language for neighborhood racial demographic change, I respond to what I think he's saying, rooted in my values.]

Me: That's exactly why we moved here! We were looking for a healthy multiracial community to be a part of, and it seems like this community is moving in that direction.

[In this particular circumstance, after this short exchange, I make an effort to introduce this neighbor to some of our Neighbors of Color and to let him know some of the positive things that are happening in our neighborhood because of the new neighbors who are moving in. I don't do this in an explicit way (i.e., I don't say, "I want to give you antiracist training"). I just start introducing people to him in an informal way when people are out walking. He seems to need help seeing past his own comfort with and preference for an all-White neighborhood.

This isn't a short-term project—it stays on my mind throughout our interactions over the next five years. I'm not particularly close with this neighbor. But I will never forget what he said. And when I organize block parties in my neighborhood, it's partly because of this statement, which no one else has said to me but presumably others might feel.]

Intervening

For White people who want to be antiracist, intervening with White people is our work. Along with developing our own self-reflective practice, supporting and challenging other White people is a primary task of the White antiracist ally. This is because White people tend to be in all-White spaces where things are said (both intentionally and unintentionally) that will not be addressed unless we say something. It's because White people will hear an intervention differently from other White people than from a Person of Color or Native person (although not always more receptively). It's because, by and large, the collective White group is what stands in the way of racial justice. White people often hold power positions that make the very policies that harm People of Color and Native people. White people are often bystanders to the self-interested actions of other White people. If White people can change—both individually and collectively—we can change white supremacy.

Talking to White people about race is not just about getting people to see that their language is often offensive or that they are racist for bemoaning the bygone days of an all-White neighborhood. It's about getting them to think about how certain comments and expressions they use uphold a racial hierarchy that, while harming People of Color and Native people, will also damage them, their personal relationships, and even their quality of life. If my older neighbor is cranky about the People of Color and Native people moving in, I need to intervene because he is likely to inflict his discomfort or harm on them. At the same time, I want to help the neighbor see the value of being in a multiracial community while possibly addressing where his crankiness really comes from (Bartoli & Pyati, 2009).

The problem for most of us is that we get stuck when it comes time to speak up and say something in the face of racist behavior. Eleonora previously described what happens to us physiologically when we try to speak up: we have a fight, flight, or freeze response to escape the intensity of our own feelings. In practice, this means that in the heat of the moment, we feel we have only two options: conflict or silence. Since we are committed to being antiracist, we might feel compelled to engage in conflict. But if it ends up escalating or blowing up in our faces—as it will likely do when we are propelled by a fight response—we might decide to retreat back into silence the next time. Many of us don't know how to regulate our stress response and access a wider range of options within ourselves that would allow us to manage the pressure and stay engaged.

The strategies I will describe in this chapter are for White people intervening with other White people. Eleonora and I would not presume to tell People of Color or Native people how they should intervene with White people. There's some excellent research and teaching on how People of Color and Native people can respond to racism, particularly the research of Dr. Howard Stevenson. Stevenson's (2014) work focuses on how People of Color can respond to racism in a way that preserves their dignity while not getting themselves hurt, fired, or expelled. When People of Color and Native people respond to racism, self-preservation should be higher on the list of priorities than keeping White people on an antiracist path. But for most White people, self-preservation does not have to be our first priority because racism does not threaten us the same way it does People of Color and Native people. So when we intervene, we can prioritize both intervening in the racism and helping other White people find, join, and stay on an antiracist path.

Helping another White person travel an antiracist path means orienting any intervention in a way that helps the other person take their next steps, staying engaged in the short term. They are more likely to become defensive if they think that we are trying to make ourselves feel better or look better by calling out their racism. That is why the option of directly calling out often fails.

In the previous chapter, I asked you to consider which strategies for giving feedback have been effective for you as a receiver of feedback. Here, I share additional strategies you can use for supporting other White people to engage an antiracist practice:

- Calling people in

- Being clear where you stand

- Using the support–challenge–contextualize strategy

- Tracking/observing

- Joining and empathizing

- Educating

- Interrupting destructive behavior

- Remembering that family doesn't go away

- Offering feedback for the right reasons

Calling People In

Your most important tool for delivering feedback is your own emotional state. Are you offering the person you're talking to a strategy for growth and knowledge, or are you trying to make sure you look a certain way in the eyes of onlookers?

Sometimes people feel so driven by the common truism "White silence is White violence" that we intervene loudly and publicly so that everyone knows we are not committing the violence of silence. In other words, we invest our energy in fending off our own stereotype threat, rather than in increasing someone else's understanding. That means we often intervene in a way that distances the person we are focused on and undermines our goal of chipping away at racism. Your own emotional state will have a big impact on the outcome of the interaction. This is why having all the "right" language and merely learning what to say rarely yields change in and of itself. In fact, White people's deep investment in saying the right thing or having the right answer is the most common manifestation of an activated stereotype threat. What will allow us to actually scaffold other White people on their antiracist journey is our ability to detect how we ourselves are also still complicit with the system and then to work through our own shame and manage our own reactivity. This way, when we intervene, we can focus on what the person in front of us needs—rather than trying to soothe ourselves by taking out our frustration on them.

Loretta Ross, a Black professor and activist who teaches about white supremacy at Smith College, frames interventions as "calling in" rather than "calling out" (as cited in Bennett, 2020) to invite this shift in consciousness. Think about what this language connotes: *Calling out* suggests that we spotlight people for saying something wrong or that we put them out of the circle of belonging for their bad behavior. Calling out involves shaming or exclusion, which shuts down one's ability to take in feedback, learn, and remain in the conversation by staying in relationship. Ross says we instead need to *call people in*, to help them challenge language and ideas that uphold a racial hierarchy. Eleonora and I don't suggest calling in simply because calling out is not *nice*. If it worked to end racism, we would encourage you to do it all day long. The reason we recommend against calling out is because it's not usually effective.

Calling out is also a product of our punitive culture, which arises from a fixed mindset about racism.[1] By suggesting that the only way to solve the problem of racism is by vilifying individuals, this fixed mindset assumes we can't change. This not only leaves little room for individual growth but also takes the spotlight away from the systemic nature of racism. Very few people individually seek out racist beliefs. But because we are deeply embedded in them, we absorb them over the course of our lives. As Eleonora and I emphasized earlier, we do not believe this means that People of Color and Native people should not call out White people. And even Ross has said that sometimes calling out is the only tool available to us, particularly with regard to people who are committed to *not* listening, such as avowed white supremacists. But many of the White people we engage with would likely choose the antiracist path if they could see the white supremacy matrix more clearly. They just need someone to offer the facts and show them the trailhead. Calling them in can serve to help them find their way.

The first thing to consider when calling in—or when tempted to call out—is to ask yourself, "Why am I doing this?" If you are an educator, it's not uncommon to think, "I'm doing this because I cannot allow that racist or disaffirming language to be spoken in this meeting or my classroom." You might feel an urgency to interrupt potentially offensive speech so that People of Color or Native people who are witnessing the comment won't have to do it themselves or so that they won't be hurt by it. But when you pause to consider it, you might find that you are also doing it because you are afraid of appearing like you're colluding with that person or looking like you didn't know that what they said was incorrect or offensive. To the extent that your intervention derives its energy from your desire to preserve your own self-image, you are more likely to intervene reactively, fueled by fight energy. This has the potential to increase the drama and unnecessarily spotlight the other person, rather than the comment itself. This type of interaction is more about shaming than creating a learning opportunity.

To the extent that you are using the intervention to win *your own* anti-racism points, chances are that the person you are intervening with will feel that and zero-in on an interpersonal conflict dynamic with you, with the goal of protecting *their own* self-image. In a group setting, if you confront someone in a way that magnifies their defenses, not only will the interaction push them away; it will likely cause group harm as well. The aim of collectively unlearning racism often gets lost, while the whole group—including People of Color and Native people who have to witness it—becomes hurt or demoralized by the defensiveness and resistance.

Alternatively, you can intervene in a way that both honors good intentions *and* points the attention back to the system that has created the narrative in question. Then you can clearly and directly explain the problem with what was said. In that case, not only the person making the comment but everyone else in the room is more likely to learn more accurate information, as well as how they can work together effectively to dismantle racism.

The shift from calling out to calling in requires us to ask ourselves, "How can I frame my comments so that this person standing in front of me will actually hear them and take them in? How can I plant even just a seed of curiosity about antiracism and 'pause' this person's habitual, well-trained, and well-rehearsed racist thinking?" This is how the calculus changes. Take in the audience—how many people are witnessing this intervention? The greater the number of people present, the more potentially embarrassing it could be, making it all the more difficult for that person to take in the feedback. Is the person in the middle of saying something that makes them vulnerable (like sharing something personal) or doing something that might raise their anxiety (like leading the meeting or delivering a report)? Are they the leader of the organization? Do they have the least power in the room? All these factors might affect the intensity of stereotype threat and therefore their ability to take in the feedback.

To be sure, sometimes we just have to call racism out for everyone to see. Publicly addressing an individual's disaffirming language or racist misconceptions can be important for setting the record straight, for making sure that other people in the group know it was addressed, or for establishing norms for the group conversation. At the same time, keep in mind the long-term goal. The long-term goal might solely be about getting that person to take the feedback and make a change. But it also might involve changing language norms in the larger group. Or it might include changing how the group thinks about the existing racial dynamics in the community, in which case the feedback has a wider purpose and does not apply exclusively to one comment from one individual. In my experience, if I can say something brief in the large group with grace and without engendering too much shame and then follow up one on one with the individual after the meeting or class, I'm more likely to have that person hear me and learn from the experience. I can also follow up with the group by bringing up language norms proactively at our next meeting.

If I can tell a person is going to feel compelled to make defensive statements in the group—and let's face it, most of us feel compelled to do so when we are called out *or* in—then talking one on one with the person afterward will be a good way to handle things, so that People of Color and Native people won't have to listen to the resistance and be further injured. The person in question can always be given time—after they have processed their own reaction and understood the feedback—to apologize to the group or to share what they've learned. Very rarely are any of us skilled enough to do it all at once: receive feedback in the moment, take it in, apologize for it, and move on effortlessly.

Being called in feels like an invitation. It feels like a culture I want to be a part of. It's not a sign that I'm going to be blamed and excluded; instead, it indicates that my particular contribution is valued, even if it is imperfect. It creates both community and high expectations. It is part of what building a healthy multiracial community should feel like. Being called in means that the people doing so want me, and they want me to actually learn.

Being Clear Where You Stand

If you are a participant in a group meeting in which racism shows up, you can state affirmatively what you believe while honoring that you may have a different set of information than other people. For example, in a recent community meeting for the search process for a new superintendent, I voiced the need to have a superintendent who understands the value and importance of hiring Black teachers and leaders at every level in the district. Directly following my comment, a White woman said, "I don't think it's necessary that teachers be Black. I just think they need to be strong, loving teachers. Our college admissions rate is way too low. We need teachers who are going to bring that up." After a few more comments, I raised my hand again and said, "I appreciate what everyone has said. And I hope it might be helpful for me to add some clarity to my comments. There's so much good research on the value of having Black teachers, not only because they provide mirrors for our Black students but because they are able to cultivate and envision excellence for Black students that White teachers cannot always see. I have a Black colleague who said that she didn't realize she could do chemistry until she had a Black chemistry teacher. Suddenly all the science doors felt open to her because she could see someone who looked like her doing chemistry, after seeing only non-Black people in science fields all her life. Her Black teacher also connected her to opportunities that no one before her had been able to do. I think having more Black teachers will help us raise the college admissions rate, which is something we all want to see. But I realize that my comment probably sounds like it's coming from left field if this research is new to you. I think we want so many of the same outcomes, and we have different experiences that inform how we will get there. If it's helpful, I'm happy to share more research with the group about the importance of having Black educators in the classroom."

In this case, I wanted to explain my thinking further while honoring that not everyone was familiar with the research that gave me so much conviction in my response. When the White woman contradicted me with a colorblind statement, I felt a bump. Ten years ago, the same tiny bump would have felt like daggers. Even just making my initial suggestion would have made me tremble all over—not only because it felt possibly conflict-inducing but also because I wouldn't have been sure a White person should bring it up, I might have been uncomfortable pushing the group norm so far past colorblindness, and I might not have been as rooted in my knowledge. But I felt clear and comfortable in my statement. I understood the reasons behind the White woman's comment, and because it didn't trigger me or feel like daggers, I could respond in a way that felt generous and hopefully informative while committed. My only regret as I went to sleep that night is that I wish I had addressed her as "my thoughtful neighbor" or in some other way that demonstrated I honored her place in our community even while I respectfully disagreed with her perspective on this matter.

Using the Support–Challenge–Contextualize Strategy

The fundamental strategy for a White person intervening with another White person is called *support–confront*. This strategy comes from the workshop *White People Confronting Racism* by Antje Mattheus and Lorraine Marino (2011). Eleonora and I have adapted it slightly to into what we call the *support–challenge–contextualize* strategy. We want to deemphasize the language of confrontation and help people consider the importance of challenging one another in the context of a supportive interaction.

Here's how it works: support the person while challenging the behavior. Just as we say about children who act out—it's not the child who's bad; it's the behavior. When my six-year-old tells a lie, for example, I don't call him a liar. I tell him that he is a good person and that good people

The support–challenge–contextualize strategy looks like this:

1. *Support the person.* Support their intention, cite your knowledge of their commitment to antiracism or fairness, and honor something good that they contribute to your context.

2. *Challenge the behavior.* Describe the behavior without judgment and name why it could be hurtful.

3. *Contextualize the comment or behavior by recognizing the fact that the person takes in racist messaging every day.* Help the person see that racism is all around them. Validate where and how they might have learned what they learned so that they can see how it fits into a larger system that provides the racist rationale for their comments. This piece of the intervention is essential; otherwise, it becomes an individual problem again. We want to move beyond the notion that "you are the problem." When we address only individual-level mistakes, we don't give the person eyes to see the white supremacist structure within which we are all embedded or to see exactly how we are made complicit in it.

Here's how a conversation using this three-pronged strategy might go:

Support: I really appreciate you. I see you showing up to these community conversations and working so hard to learn about racism.

Challenge: Because you clearly have such a deep desire to learn, I thought you would want to know that saying "I don't care whether you're Black, White, Purple, or Green" can be invalidating because people don't come in colors like purple or green. It ends up making it sound like racism is just about superficial color differences rather than different ways we've been treated by the system.

Contextualize: And isn't it amazing how strongly we get that message that color is just skin deep? On the one hand, it's true—we are all human beings with different colors of skin. But that language undermines our different experiences of race and racism. I feel like that sentence used to make sense to me, and I used to say it, too. I get how much you say it as a desire to let people know you see their humanity. But I also sense that you would want to be told how much it minimizes racism because I know that's not what you're about.

Obviously, all these steps do not have to happen at once. Each should happen through a conversation, with room to let the other person respond.

tell the truth. I remind him that he values integrity and that he maintains his integrity by being dependable, by telling the truth. If a person does or says something racist—especially if it's unintentional—I don't call the person racist, but I point out the racism in the behavior or the statement.

When the support–challenge–contextualize strategy doesn't work to help people understand what was problematic about what they said, it's usually because people only support and forget to challenge. Alternatively, sometimes people only challenge and forget to offer support. It's important to remember all three steps and to use them together.

Support does not come naturally when someone's comment activates our own stereotype threat. So we must practice shifting our internal focus from managing our own anxiety to empathizing with the person we are speaking with. Eleonora has helped me see that the reason I'm able to do this is because I don't speed through the support process, grinding my teeth. I anchor myself internally to genuinely recognize the goodness of the person in front of me. One of my workshop participants recently said, "I feel like we can take feedback from you because it's so clear that you genuinely like us." And she's right. I do like my workshop participants, especially when they take risks and make mistakes, especially when they are brave enough to disagree. When Eleonora anchors herself in preparation for delivering feedback, she does it by empathizing with the sorrow of not knowing the right answer and the internal struggle that creates for her. She taps into her love for them as people, her gratitude for their intentions, and her own desire to convey the empowering feeling of learning something new and useful. In other words, she leans in relationally, even more than focusing on the content she's trying to deliver, so that she can facilitate a welcoming (rather than rejecting) emotional climate.

Tracking/Observing

Tracking means to notice without judgment. This includes saying, for instance, "I noticed you used the n-word without abbreviating it. I don't have judgment about that, but I'm curious: Is that a norm around here?" This comment will likely invite further conversation about your own views on saying the n-word without abbreviation. It also calls attention to the moment so that others who want to address the use of the word have a space to say something. For the record, I believe that White people should never say the n-word without abbreviating it. But again, for the sake of engagement, if I'm leading a workshop with people who do so, I do not leap to judgment. I do assume that it is a reflection of their skill level, their background knowledge, and their local norms. I choose to engage them in conversation and help them get curious about their local norms (why and how they exist). When I engage this way, without starting with judgment, they are more receptive to what I have to say than if I just started lecturing them. When I share my opinions, I do so with a sensitivity to the vulnerability created for them by my initial question.

To some people, this understated reaction might seem naive or permissive—or even like a downright collusion with racism. But too often, people do not intervene because they do not have a subtle but direct way to address the harm that is occurring. I have been told about large meetings of highly educated professionals where someone says the n-word without abbreviating it, and nobody responds. These meetings end with hurt, disappointment, and general mistrust as people process what happened *after the meeting*. Tracking without judgment is not just a strategy for generating receptivity from the group you are addressing. Its nonjudgmental style increases the chances that it will get used as a tool because it is practically a neutral statement. You don't have to say, "That is wrong," or "Racism is occurring here." You don't have to be exactly sure of what you will say and how you will convince people of your argument. You simply say, "I noticed this. . . . I don't have judgment about it, but I am curious . . . is this something you/we do in this group?" It gives others the chance to weigh in as well. You have done the hard work of interrupting the flow of the discussion and opening the floor to the question so that others who are feeling something can then speak more openly to the whole group. This allows the groups to address it *in the group* rather than in fractured ways after the fact.

Tracking can also be internal. You can notice your own internal responses to the conversation and observe them without judgment. This nonjudgmental awareness facilitates an internal groundedness that will support you as you decide how to participate in the rest of the discussion. Alternatively, you could track your own physiological reactions to the conversation by saying aloud, "I noticed that when you said that, my stomach clenched. I'm not sure what that means, but I didn't want to let the moment pass without mentioning it. Could we go back to that moment and talk about it?" Tracking aloud allows all members of the conversation to have a conversation *about* the conversation because one of the members noticed a potentially problematic dynamic among them or within themselves.

Joining and Empathizing

To engage in conversation with people, it helps to have a point of connection. To that end, we encourage you to join with the person who does or says something racist by saying, "I used to use that language, too," or "I just learned more affirming language a few years ago, and I'm so glad someone bothered to tell me. Would it be helpful to share that with you?"

You don't have to make things up—the chances are good that you have not always been 100 percent knowledgeable about all things antiracist. If you truly cannot relate to what they said, share another time when you made a mistake and were relieved to get feedback. Assume that people want to get better—and not by being shamed but by being informed. If you are telling someone that they did something offensive—or if you are helping them process something offensive that they did—joining can mean sharing a time when you did something offensive. This takes vulnerability and courage to model your own process this way, and it is often received with great openness and gratitude. Rather than feeling like a terrible irredeemable racist, the offending person usually begins to feel connection, becomes willing to learn from their mistake, and sees a way forward from the embarrassment they are likely feeling.

Educating

When people don't understand racism, it is often because they have not learned the history of racist policies and practices in the United States and perhaps because they have not been exposed to many stories of People of Color and Native people. Educating involves connecting them to resources that will help them learn. The more you can connect a resource to the questions they are asking—or perhaps the field that they are in—the more applicable and relevant it will feel to them. Recommend movies, books, workshops, and podcasts that have been impactful to you; invite them to read something together with you; offer to discuss things with them; or suggest that they consider you as a resource—and if you don't know the answer, you can find out together. Don't overwhelm them with possibilities, but do share things that have really spoken to you.

Interrupting Destructive Behavior

Destructive behavior is violent in language or in action, and it needs to be interrupted. You can interrupt behavior by approaching the person who is being targeted by the destruction, asking if they're okay, or even just making small talk to get them away from the destructive behavior. If the behavior is destructive language, you can say, "Can we pause for a moment?" or otherwise cut off the conversation.

Once I had a White graduate student who repeatedly played devil's advocate by challenging the idea that race is a social construction or suggesting that the racial hierarchy was valid. "I'm not saying I believe it," he would say, "I just wonder if it could be true. Maybe we *are* biologically distinct groups? Maybe there *is* some legitimate reason for the racial hierarchy?"

I could not tell if he was serious and really didn't understand the problem with biological racism or if he was teasing. I held up two hands and introduced him to a spectrum of racism. In a serious and direct tone, I said, "Here's a spectrum of beliefs about race. On one side are the white supremacists who believe that race is biological and that White people are biologically superior to all People of Color and Native people. At the other end of the spectrum are the social constructionists. They do not believe in inherent biological differences between racial groups, because they know race is a social construction. Most academics, historians, scientists, and psychologists are on this end of the spectrum because there is just no evidence for the other side. So I know that you are just playing devil's advocate, and I know you are not willing to commit to one particular side right now, but I want you to know exactly what you are playing at. Even as you play devil's advocate, you come close to asserting the validity of biological racial difference. People on that side—the side that believes racial difference is biological—believe that Black people are inherently inferior to all other people. That is what they believe. They believe White people are superior to all other people. You should not continue to play with devil's advocacy if this is a view you do not wish to be putting forward. It is a view that dehumanizes People of Color and Native people, including your future clients."

This response came after many weeks of patiently supporting and challenging him. I was frank and direct, and I presented spectrum extremes because his constant devil's advocacy was wearing down his classmates—and me. He seemed to be playing with white supremacy to tease or to torment, because he was ignorant or because he believed it. I concluded by telling him I'd be happy to talk with him more after class and saying, "I don't want to tell you what to think, but I do want you to know the impact of the statements you are making because they are not innocuous." As one school leader put it in 2016, a student's right to free speech ends where another student's right to full humanity begins. If your comments suggest that whole groups of people are not full human beings or are inferior human beings, those comments are not acceptable in a classroom space because they violate your classmates' right to learn.

People who are training to be counselors and teachers will do harm to clients and students if they adhere to and defend the racial hierarchy. In this student's case, because of ongoing statements like these, he was eventually asked to leave the program. When repeated attempts at calling in and using the support–confront–contextualize strategy fail, establishing boundaries that minimize the chance of a person doing harm until they are ready to learn again might be necessary.

Remembering That Family Doesn't Go Away

Recently people have been telling me that they want to talk to their families about racism, but they are no longer in relationship. One said, "COVID broke my family . . . so I don't think I'm going to have a chance to intervene." Another said, "During COVID, I was a complete asshole to my sister, so now I feel like I can't say anything to her about her racism because we're not in relationship."

The thing about family is that they just keep showing up. And even if COVID broke you, there's a good chance that at a future family event (a wedding, a funeral, a birthday party, etc.), you will be together again. And again. And again. With the exception of the most estranged families, family has a way of continuing to come into one's life. Consider addressing interpersonal issues with family even if you have not connected with them in a while, so that you are on sturdier ground when race comes up. Because it will. If your family members are not active white supremacists, chances are that they are caught in the mainstream racial narrative that Eleonora and I would still be stuck in were it not for some fortunate early interventions in our own learning. If family members are posting nasty memes, don't respond on Facebook. Call them. Make a time to see them. Connect. Ask them about the things they have said in the context of a relationship. Cutting yourself off from racist family is not a sign of antiracism. If your family is going to listen to anyone, it is more likely to be you. Your angry uncle might not care what you have to say, but he might care what your cousin says—and you might have some sway with your cousin. Start to get strategic about helping people in your family learn. And not just because it's the right thing to do—but because racism is bad for them, too.

Offering Feedback for the Right Reasons

If you have a personal conflict with someone, do not give them antiracist feedback as a way of getting back at them. Do not muddle your antiracist feedback with a desire to hurt them or even a need to address interpersonal conflict. This will not be effective, no matter how tempting it may be. Get right with them first regarding the interpersonal issue, then offer the feedback. Or if you think getting right with them is an impossibility, get right with yourself before letting them know the feedback in a way that is direct and unrelated to other interpersonal conflict between you.

Delivering Feedback as the Facilitator of the Group

Intervening in Comments Made Publicly

Each time someone says something rooted in racism in one of my workshops, I have the opportunity to help the group think with more nuance about the larger racial dynamic that surrounds them. I don't usually like to give feedback in a large group because the size of the audience can magnify the shame it evokes (and subsequently the defensive resistance). But sometimes the situation requires public recognition. I was recently with a large group of teachers when a White woman (Jennifer) tried to build on what a Black woman had said. She couldn't remember the Black woman's name, so she asked me, "What was that *girl's* name?" I asked, "Did you mean Maya?" She said, "Yes, Maya."

After Jennifer finished her statement, I returned to her and said, "Would you mind if I offer you some feedback within this Zoom workshop? I know you are so open to learning and so committed to an antiracist practice that I thought you would want to hear it. When you were asking about Maya, you called her a girl, which is a term I've heard you use previously to refer to all women. But I thought you would want to know that it can be insulting when used toward a Black woman, because of the ways in which the term has been used deliberately to disempower them—while it can sometimes be used as an endearing term among White women."

In front of the whole group of more than 80 people, Jennifer thanked me effusively for the feedback, apologized for using the word *girl*, expressed surprise that she had used that language, and again said how grateful she was to have the chance to acknowledge it and apologize. In this case, Maya chose to respond as well because I had essentially spoken on her behalf. Maya said, "I wasn't going to say anything in front of all these people, but, yes, that did hurt, and I'm grateful that you said something—and I'm grateful that Jennifer is so willing to hear it. It makes me feel so much better about the work we're doing here, and I feel like we're actually growing and learning together."

In this case, Jennifer's intent to be antiracist became even more visible in the way she took feedback. Her clear desire to learn from her mistakes and to apologize for unintended hurt was evidence of her intention. She didn't have to say, "I'm not racist," or "I didn't mean to harm," because her intention was evident in her response. For Maya—and for so many who witnessed the interaction (myself included)—it felt like there was congruity between our antiracist objectives and our interpersonal interactions in the workshop. If nobody had said anything to Jennifer when she called Maya a girl, people in the group might have felt, "Sure, we're here to confront racism, but we can't even do it with one another." Instead, we all witnessed the generative possibility of live feedback, which led to a deeper and more connected group, better equipped to support one another and face racism together—not in spite of but because of that exchange.

The interaction was short, but it was probably the most powerful moment of the entire six-month workshop series. I checked in with Maya afterward to see if there was anything else she needed and to see if she had further feedback for how I handled the situation. I also checked in with Jennifer afterward, to lend her support and gratitude for the openness with which she heard the feedback.

Offering Affirming Language

Another model of delivering feedback comes from Dr. Eli Green of the Transgender Training Institute (TTI; Green & Maurer, 2015). Green prefaces his workshops by saying that he doesn't always know the up-to-the-minute most affirming language to use when talking about gender identity. He admits, "I literally wrote the book on gender identity, yet by the time that book went to press, there were new words in use that I hadn't written about" (personal communication, 2015). Green says there's no way for any of us to keep pace with all the new and rapidly evolving ways to understand and express gender identity, which is why we have to be able to learn from one another if we're using a term that has a more affirming alternative. If there is a more affirming way to say something, he will offer it immediately and directly, providing explanation only if it seems confusing or if someone asks for it. What that means is that over the course of his three-day workshop, most participants get corrected at least once, and everybody sees their classmates taking correction. It also means that all participants see what it looks like to offer correction in a direct and nonjudgmental way. Green might say, "Try using _____," or "If you're talking about someone who transitioned to be a man, the term is *trans man*." Because feedback is part of the norm and because Eli is so nonjudgmental, workshop participants nod, change their language, and make a note of his instruction. Nobody holds up their hands in self-defense and says, "But I'm not transphobic!"

Since taking the TTI course, I have begun offering the same promise in my workshops: "If there is a more affirming way to say something you are saying, I will offer it. If you already knew the perfect way to frame your question, you might not be asking the question to begin with. I want you to be able to ask questions and participate with the language that you have. And if there is more affirming language that you could be using, you can rely on me to share it. That is my commitment to you as a facilitator. And I hope that if there is more affirming language that I could be using, you will tell me as well."

By saying this upfront, I am hopeful that participants will feel more willing to take risks and participate by using a growth mindset. Too often, people participate in a race workshop only if they think that they are going to get it right. Those who have doubts or feel out of step with the current language—those who most need the skills and the practice—often hang back and stay quiet, unsure how to step in. This is not a recipe for growth, skill-building, practice, or change.

Integrating Multiple Strategies

Making a commitment to share affirming language at the beginning of workshops also holds me accountable. A few years ago, I was doing a workshop for more than 100 K–12 administrators at a statewide conference in Colorado. One of the principals said to me, "I'd like to know how I can better support my illegal immigrant students." Immediately I thought to myself, "The first thing you could do is call them *students who are undocumented immigrants* rather than *illegal*." But I didn't say this because I didn't want to shame her in front of her colleagues from around the state. I figured that I could find her after the workshop and give her that feedback one on one. In this case, I regretted that decision. She left as soon as the workshop was over, and I did not have the chance to talk with her. Of all the advice I gave to her for supporting her undocumented students, none was as helpful as it would have been to assist her with changing her language and the language used in her community. Because I was flustered and clearly avoiding the elephant in the room, I don't think my suggestions were particularly useful. Also, in this case, it is likely that many of her colleagues used the same language and needed to learn more affirming alternatives as well.

How could I have responded differently? I could have used the support–challenge–contextualize strategy. *Support:* I could have thanked her for her question, her desire to support her students, and her willingness to learn. *Contextualize:* I could have suggested that the language of calling people "illegal" is common in the United States and then talked about how that language is intentionally used to dehumanize people so that their inhumane treatment can be justified. *Challenge:* I could have turned it into an exercise that did not blame her but that situated all of us in the middle of a social dynamic in which there are active forces attempting to frame the conversation in a way that dehumanizes undocumented immigrants, precisely because their dehumanization is part of a political agenda that minimizes their needs while depicting them as criminals. I could have role-played with her how she might have that conversation with people on her school board or in her community. I could have done all this in a way that was not shaming but provided a lesson for everyone, acknowledging that we are all actively trained to think through the "illegal" lens and that a powerful step is to begin unlearning this.

Since I did not do this in that particular moment, I now tell this story when I'm introducing Eli Green's TTI strategy for offering more affirming language. I tell the story of that principal and the language of *undocumented* versus *illegal* repeatedly, hoping that even if that one principal did not get the message that day—because I did not offer it—thousands of others will.

Taking the Temperature of the Group

When I'm facilitating a group and someone says something that could be interpreted as racist—particularly if it's, say, in the context of a meeting with a faculty of 120 people, and I'm just meeting the group for the first time—sometimes I will wait until one or two other people talk before I address the comment. I might say, "Thanks so much for sharing. We'll come back to that in a minute. Does anyone else want to add anything?" If someone else intervenes before I do, their intervention will give me a better sense of where the comment is coming from. I assume the people in the group know one another better than I do. When I'm not sure what the intention is behind the comment, the group response can help point the way.

In some cases, people pile on, supporting the comment or amplifying it, in which case I learn that this belief or this use of an offensive word is more deeply rooted in their local culture. In that case, when I intervene as a facilitator, I can be intervening with the whole group, rather than the one person who was brave enough to raise their hand and talk first. Again, how I decide to intervene is based on my ultimate goal: for the group to have a successful conversation about race, to take risks, to raise their hands and talk even though they don't know how to do so perfectly, and to learn the things they don't know that they don't know. This means that while I have to offer them feedback on the offensive things they do and say (as that's part of the learning), I need to be thoughtful in how I go about it, because they will not be able to learn it all at once. And they won't learn it at all if they shut down. I need to help them get from Step 1 to Step 2, or from Step 14 to Step 15, not from Step 1 to Step 34. As the facilitator, this might be a two-part process. First, I have to make sure that I myself am in an open, empathetic space, rather than a reactive one where my wish to credential myself to the group might take the lead. Hearing more voices and asking potential follow-up questions gives me the time and space to reground myself. Then, the clarity of my purpose (i.e., the desire to invite people in, rather than call them out) and the strategies I have to accomplish it give me both the confidence and the resilience to remain in the conversation.

I generally think of interventions as being at the group level rather than the individual level. It is theoretically possible that this is one random person in the group who just does not know how to talk about race and feels no compunction in saying offensive things. But it is more likely that they are speaking in ways that are acceptable in their group—or in a subgroup of their group. Their comments are usually reflective of the systemic training we all receive, even though some of us might have had more practice recognizing and unlearning it (or at least not saying offensive things aloud). So when I'm intervening with someone, if I'm able to offer clarity and humility, without accusing or attaching more meaning to their comment than is warranted, onlookers are more likely to take the correction for themselves as well. This is preferable to creating a dynamic where onlookers feel they have to choose sides *for* or *against* the offending colleague (or me). If I can do so in the context of a larger perspective in which I openly hold myself accountable for also being socialized in a white supremacist society and therefore having my own biases, people in the entire group are more likely to feel called in and be more open to what I have to say.

Stalling

When someone says something racist, I can immediately feel my blood pressure rise, and I sometimes need to buy time to reground myself if I want to have a chance to use my skill. So I tell myself first and foremost, "Stall!" This might seem like a cop-out, but in fact, stalling techniques are commonly used in counseling and conflict-resolution contexts. In a group context, the first stalling technique is to go with the resistance by saying something like this: "Yes, that is absolutely what we are taught, isn't it? There is a lot to say about that. How about if for now we . . . and we can talk through it more a little later, as it might all become clearer once we cover a few more things?"

The second strategy is similar but sets the expectation for a private, rather than public, follow-up: "Yes, that is absolutely what we are taught, isn't it? You seem to have some very good and genuine questions about that. You hit the nail right on the head. How about you and I chat a little bit more about that at the end of this meeting?"

A third stalling strategy is to take a few breaths to think how best to address what just happened while paraphrasing what you heard and giving it a benevolent slant: "It sounds like you are wondering about. . . . It's indeed puzzling when we are taught *xyz*, and here I am now describing *abc*. . . . I think we are actually going to cover some of what you are asking about, but let's check in after class if that's still unclear, because that's a really good question." The key is to publicly note the learning need, to affirm that the learning need makes sense, to open up space for addressing it further, and to situate the problem with "what we've been taught" at the systemic level rather than the gross learning deficiencies of that particular individual.

While these are all examples of interventions at a group level, you can use the same strategies in your individual conversations with another White person. If you have time to talk more in that moment, you could add, "I would be glad to share what I have learned, and I would love to hear what you think." If you get the person's consent, you can then proceed with sharing what you know. If you don't have time to address the issues then and there, you can offer to do so at a later time. It's very likely that the person will have follow-up questions reflecting other racist beliefs, which means that having another opportunity to connect will let you address these one at a time.

As you continue to work with the person, you can reuse the same strategies, each time being mindful not to rush toward fixing and explaining. First, take the time to join and establish a relational connection. In all cases, remember that you are not there to rectify an isolated wrong; you are inviting the other White person into a movement and a process that will last their lifetime. You want them to understand the problem with what they did or said, but you also want them to acquire lenses and learn skills that will support them on their longer journey. Your role is to plant as many seeds as the ground allows and to help it remain fertile.

Why Protect White People's Feelings?

Why should we honor and consider another White person's feelings? Isn't this work about getting rid of racism? Isn't this about the feelings of People of Color and Native people? If I know that what you said is wrong, shouldn't I point it out . . . no matter what?

This is the sentiment that guides so many White people when we respond to the racist expressions of other White people. But to what end? To call out racism in that one isolated scenario, regardless of how it alienates the White person from self-reflecting about their racism from then on? To show that you can learn and perform antiracism? To be the placeholder for White antiracism in your institution?

Not only is there more than enough room for more than one antiracist White person; we need millions. We should honor and consider that White person's feelings, not to maximize their comfort but because we want them to stay engaged for the long term; we want them to take in the feedback and use it to help others learn. And we should honor and consider their feelings because today they said something offensive, and right now you might be the one to support them through their learning— but tomorrow it might be you or me in their shoes, and we will need their support to grow. If I model shaming, they learn to shame. If I shame them, I shame myself, and I make it harder and harder for myself to make mistakes, to have a growth mindset, and to take risks. As Eleonora keeps reminding us, shaming ourselves or one another will make us rehearse our ancient and powerful defensive strategies, not help us learn.

I have heard from many leaders on elite college campuses that students are terrified about saying or doing something offensive. These are not meek, inexperienced students that they are talking about; some of the most radical activists are practically paralyzed by fear because they have set such a high bar for what it means to be antiracist that they are afraid even they won't be able to meet it. When we support our students, colleagues, and friends with a growth mindset—with the expectation that all of us will be imperfect—we actually create the circumstances needed for courage and action. If we live in fear of how other progressives will find us wanting (because let's be clear, not one of us is perfect), we will be scared into being bystanders. There is no better way to let racism flourish unchecked.

I am not better than the White person sitting next to me, even if I've been walking an antiracist path for 24 years and they never have. At the end of the day, we are both White people living within a racial caste system that has put White people first for 500 years. Most of the racism that resides in other White people resides in me as well. Part of the harshness with which White people treat one another comes from our own discomfort with seeing ourselves in one another. I can disavow white supremacy all I want, but that doesn't mean that it goes away or that I have extracted myself from it. At the end of the day, I still benefit from the racial hierarchy as much as the next White person for as long as that hierarchy exists.

When we talk about anti*racism*, we are not talking about being anti-*the-White-person-who-is-racist-or-says-racist-things*. We are talking about orienting ourselves in opposition to a system of racism. How I intervene with other White people does not win me or lose me anti-racism points. It does not heal me from my moral injuries, and it only temporarily lets me avoid the anxiety of stereotype threat as a White person who fears I will be seen as racist. The question is not this: How many White people did you call out on their racism today? Instead, the question is this: As a result of your actions, will more White people choose to orient themselves in opposition to a system of racism? Will more White people want to work against racism in themselves and in their spheres of influence? Do they understand the hurtfulness of what they said, and do they feel compelled to engage in repair as a result of that understanding? Did you contribute to healing and transforming racism, or did you simply point a finger? Are the White people around you more aware of the systemic nature of their so-called "*individual* racism"?

Conclusion

In the beginning of this book, I noted many of the messages I received about race when I was growing up. Not only did I receive messages of colorblindness; I explicitly did not see models of what it looks like to intervene in racism. When our neighbor made jokes about African American names, I was told not to retell such jokes—but only after my neighbor had left. I didn't see what it looked like to say to someone's face, "Hey, that's not funny," or "I don't think jokes about people's names are funny," or "Jokes about Black people—names or otherwise—really aren't funny," or "I think jokes like that make us think less of Black people. Can we talk about something else?" or even "You are so nice; why are your jokes so mean?"

I didn't see what this would look like. Most White people did not. So when the time comes for antiracist action, we often have very little practice or modeling. This means that giving and receiving feedback publicly can really be a double gift. While we begin the conversation that helps people learn, we also model what that intervention looks like for others.

In the next chapter, we will introduce the idea of White antiracist learning spaces, where you can practice the skills involved in intervening with other White people. Once you have practiced these skills— just like practicing riding a bike—it makes the actual task much less intimidating.

Note

1. See the Internal Work section for Chapter 5.

Healing Is Essential to Antiracist Practice

So here you are, nearing the end of this book, by now equipped with the knowledge of how racism has come to be part of your own daily reality. You have learned about some of the history that has shaped us as White people. You have begun considering your family lineage and racial socialization. You are learning how to recognize your own racial identity development and practicing how to keep yourself grounded while entering racially stressful conversations. You are forging new connections with other White allies and expanding your antiracist social support network. Still, there will be times when all this won't be enough.

Acknowledging and witnessing injustice is painful. Realizing the ways in which we are complicit with unjust structures is painful. Our passions for justice are often fueled by our own experiences of oppression, which means the hurt can sometimes be personal and very raw. Whenever any of this pain taps into tender parts of ourselves, deeper healing work is needed. Over the years, I discovered that my own direct experience of healing was necessary to achieve not just competence as a psychotherapist but racial competence as well. When we are unable to recognize and manage our own pain, it is almost impossible to remain present with and open to what we see. When we retreat into a defensive stance, at best our effectiveness is diminished, and at worst we become harmful. So my own healing work has been nothing short of essential in my antiracist journey. And while the bulk of my own counseling was concentrated in my early-career years, remaining present to the pain I witness requires my ongoing attention and care.

You might recall the experience I described previously of attending a workshop where I was so overwhelmed by rage that I could no longer stay present and engage with the learning. Why were the behaviors of the two specific participants I talked about so activating for me? Once I took the time to revisit my experience of the workshop with the support of other White allies, I realized the ways in which these highly gendered behaviors were reminiscent of painful experiences in my own life—when I was physically unsafe and felt helpless. During the workshop, my own wounds quickly translated into the urge to shame other White people and disempower a Person of Color, the presenter—actions that would have not only diminished everyone's learning but also caused a great deal of damage. While on the outside, my doing nothing might have seemed like a rather effortless action step, on the inside, it was an intentional skill possible only because of much mindfulness training.

I can't overemphasize the fact that learning about racism and engaging in antiracist practice will activate every fiber of your being. And with that, even parts that you thought you had put to rest will show up. Sometimes I am not aware of what I still carry inside until something in my clinical or antiracist practice bumps into it. A few years back, I was walking the hallways of my academic department when a colleague stopped me to process a meeting she just had with a student. Something had happened on campus that caused intense conflict between staff members, with the student getting caught in the cross fire as the leader of a campus organization. The root issue turned out to be anti-Semitism. As I learned more about the incident, I offered my colleague help. Our intention was to assist the student in finding ways to navigate the situation that were empowering to them, while also placing the onus of the resolution back onto the faculty and staff involved. What began as a one-on-one impromptu conversation with a colleague in the hallway quickly escalated into a flurry of intense interactions with several students and colleagues across campus. Within a week or so, I found myself thoroughly overwhelmed. I noticed that I had started waking up every morning feeling the weight of the world on my shoulders. I was quickly sinking into hopelessness.

While I tend toward anxiety, I don't frequently feel depressed. I also know that while anxiety is a fight reaction, depression is a way for our bodies to signal to us to back off—a reaction to the feeling that we don't measure up to the challenge in front of us, so we should give up sometime before we even start. I realized that my feeling helpless fell outside my usual style and was out of proportion for the situation at hand. So I reached out to my therapist and scheduled a session. It didn't take long to make the connection that the layering of emotional empathy I felt toward the various people I was meeting with had latched onto some early experience related to witnessing a close family member in pain. Building on prior counseling and a well-established therapeutic relationship, I was able to work through the memory in a few sessions. As I did, I came back to my advocacy with much greater resilience, perspective, and ease. I was still fully engaged and empathetic—by no means numb or detached—but I was no longer derailed by a rawness that belonged to the past, not the present, and that was specific to me, not the other people involved.

Over the years of doing my own counseling work, I have become familiar with several of the key events in my past that end up being triggered by antiracist practice. Through that, I have developed shortcuts to navigate my own tender spots when they reemerge. For example, when I go into overreactive fight mode, I pull back a little by telling myself, "No one is waiting for you to save them." When I want to flee a situation because I'm feeling incompetent, I tell myself, "You are valued and needed here." And when I freeze because I feel hopeless, I tell myself, "It's okay; you can do it. Join with others; lean into others' love and into your love for others." Because I have healed enough around each of the experiences that created these soft spots, these affirmations are often enough to recenter me. And when they are not, I don't shy away from accessing more counseling.

This is my main point: it's not a question of whether you might be triggered by antiracist practice. It's only a question of when, how often, and how intensely. And there is absolutely nothing wrong with you that this is the case. It's just the nature of being human and part of the process of opening ourselves up to the profound injustice that surrounds us. So make sure to care for yourself in these moments. Access the support you need. For me, that support has come through a combination of my own counseling and authentic, loving relationships with other antiracist allies. For you, it may take those or other forms. Whatever you end up choosing at any given time, remember that we heal in relationship, with one another's support. So don't go it alone.

As you can see, healing is not selfish work. In fact, it is only by taking care of our own wounds that we gain the power to heal the world around us. When we don't, we are bound to carry forward the intergenerational patterns of thought and behavior that have closed our ancestors' hearts and led them to do or ignore terrible things. What we don't heal, we are bound to repeat. What we don't change within ourselves, we transmit to the next generation. As you dive deeply into yourself, you can't help but create new, needed ways of being in—and responding to—the world around you. This is where inner work and outer work meet most profoundly.

Strengthening Your Antiracist Practice

How Do You Know That You Need Help?

When we remain reactive, exhausted, and disconnected, when we let life's hardships shut our minds and close our hearts, we become more useful to the white supremacist project. As we have learned, our fight, flight, and freeze

(Continued)

(Continued)

impulses are our default; they are powerful, and they are often rewarded, even glorified, because they maintain the status quo. This means that we might tend to feel that we don't need or deserve to pause and take care of our wounds. We might believe that our safety and strength reside in our quick, impulsive responses; in our commitment to work to exhaustion; and in fulfilling the ideals shaped by "rugged individualism." Given this, my suggestion is to err toward the side of accessing support—often. The good news is that all the practices suggested in this book will give you powerful self-knowledge and make you much clearer about when you simply need a good night's sleep and when you need to reach out to others. You'll notice more and more, as I did, when your distress seems out of proportion to the task at hand, when it takes an unusual form, or when it becomes challenging enough to keep holding it in your body that the quality of your work—not to mention your life—is notably diminished. As you build your ability to discern when you need help, practice reaching out and experiment with what works for you.

What Does Help Look Like?

You are the only person who can know exactly what help you need, want, and can access. There is only one rule: don't go it alone. I'm a psychotherapist; counseling makes sense to me, and I have access to it. That might not be answer for you, but it's critical that you find intentional spaces to process deeply and begin healing the wounds that might make you close down as you sit with others' pain. We are not meant to navigate our lives by ourselves; we are designed to heal in connection with one another. We need one another, both psychologically and physiologically. So create community, lean into your allies, and give and take support in your unique ways. Antiracist practice brings us in touch with the very core of ourselves and calls us to hold all that comes up with and for one another. Doing that will bring healing both individually and collectively.

Creating and Sustaining White Antiracist Learning Spaces

CHAPTER #9

> *In the longest-term vision I can see, when we, made of the same miraculous material and temporary limitations as the systems we are born into, inevitably disagree, or cause harm, we will respond not with rejection, exile, or public shaming but with clear naming of harm; education around intention, impact, and pattern breaking; satisfying apologies and consequences; new agreements and trustworthy boundaries; and lifelong healing resources for all involved.*
>
> —adrienne maree brown (2020, p. 11)

An increasingly common way for White people to systematically build their racial competency is for them to get together with other White people and *do their own work*. You may have heard a Person of Color or Native person ask for this, saying, "I am tired of teaching White people about racism. I just need White people to *do their own work*." It's the idea that White people have a certain amount of basic skill-building to do before we can be effective antiracist actors—or even effective friends and colleagues to People of Color and Native people. It's the idea that my lack of knowledge, experience, competence, and humility with navigating racial stress should not be the responsibility (or the liability) of People of Color and Native people in my life. They shouldn't have to teach me about racism; I need to find a way to learn. A White antiracist learning space is a place where this can happen. This is exactly the kind of group Eleonora and I were a part of what when we first met.

If you are like most people, you have lots of questions about this. This chapter will look at the following:

- Frequently asked questions about establishing a White antiracist group

- My own experiences with White antiracist learning spaces

- How to structure a White antiracist learning space so that it's not just another book club

- What to do in a White antiracist learning space

- How to counter the myths of white supremacy when they come up in your group

- Common pitfalls of White antiracist learning spaces

Frequently Asked Questions

The idea behind using an all-White group for some aspects of antiracist learning is that White people have particular learning needs when it comes to antiracism. White antiracist learning spaces make it possible to address those particular needs. This is similar to dividing students into separate classes because a student learning arithmetic needs different instruction from a student learning calculus, even though they're both learning math.

How Can White People Learn About Racism Without People of Color and Native People?

It's true that White people can't learn about racism without hearing the voices and stories of People of Color and Native people. But that doesn't mean that the People of Color and Native people in our lives must sit and share their stories with us over and over again until we get it. We might not even be able to hear what they are telling us if we haven't done enough of our own learning and internal work. If we are early in our racial identity development process, we might question their interpretations of events they describe as racist. We might say (as I have), "Maybe you misunderstood," "Maybe they didn't mean to be racist," or "Maybe you are being oversensitive." Such responses invalidate People of Color and Native people and make it hard to continue sharing. If our friends and colleagues are responsible for teaching us about racism, they are going to burn out quickly. It is for this very reason that many of them already are burned out.

In a White antiracist learning space, you can still learn from the voices of People of Color and Native people without draining friends and colleagues in your immediate sphere. You can use books, movies, podcasts, and blogs by People of Color and Native people who talk about how racism has affected them. There are countless resources designed by People of Color and Native people for the explicit purpose of helping White people learn about racism and white supremacy.

In White antiracist learning spaces, White people support one another in their learning. This means that rather than exclusively listening to the experiences of People of Color and Native people—still a crucial part of cross-racial dialogue—we get to discover and process our relationship to and involvement in a racist system. Collectively and individually, we can learn how racism has shaped us and continues to influence our thinking. This understanding is critical because it facilitates White people clearly seeing our part in the racial puzzle in ways that guide us toward action.

Can't we do this in multiracial groups? Yes, but in the early stages of developing antiracist knowledge and skills, it creates an incredible demand on People of Color and Native people. Too often in multiracial dialogues, White voices are silent. Sometimes White people don't speak up because we don't want to take up too much space in the conversation. Sometimes we don't speak up because we're too surprised by the stories of People of Color and Native people, and we don't know how to respond. Sometimes we don't speak up because we are afraid of saying something that offends others. Sometimes we don't know how to verbalize what we're thinking, or we fear that it will come out wrong. Sometimes we want to talk about our bias but fear we might rub salt in the wounds of the People of Color and Native people who hear us. Sometimes we simply don't know what to say.

For all these reasons and more, White people are often silent in cross-racial dialogue. So while we learn from those conversations, we often take more than we give. And to give more, we need practice. That is where an all-White group comes in.

Isn't That Segregation?

People sometimes resist all-White group structures because they sound like racial segregation: "I thought we were trying to break down racism, not segregate ourselves!"

This is a valid concern and a good question. Anyone asking it, in fact, should be in the group. A White person who believes they see something racist going on and is actually willing to make a stink about it should definitely be in this group. They may not yet understand the purpose of a White antiracist learning space—and with good reason. There is no reason for White people to gather with only White people for any purpose other than antiracist learning. The irony of the complaint is that White people are often segregated in situations where we shouldn't be. Think about your own life. If you are White, how often do you find yourself on a hiring committee, in a board room, in a neighborhood, on a team, at a PTO meeting, or at a celebration that is all-White? White people are all too often in all-White spaces where we should be asking, "Why are there no People of Color and Native people in the room?" or "Why are there only White people at the table?" But we often take the all-White demographics of such spaces for granted while questioning all-White spaces that exist explicitly for talking about race and racism. In reality, the reverse should be true.

When White people have their own learning space, they can move at their own pace and ask questions they might not otherwise ask. White people can take solid steps forward in our own process, rather than faking understanding to keep up in a cross-racial dialogue and missing substantial parts of the conversation. We can begin the work of building racial competency, which means gaining knowledge and developing the self-awareness and skills that enable us to see how the history of racism has affected us and our families, how bias still clouds our vision, and how racial privilege affects the way we view ourselves and others. Building racial competency also means talking about the families and communities we grew up in, where we learned and internalized both racial bias and racial dominance. It means learning to talk about Whiteness specifically, a concept that helps White people see themselves and their own stories as central to the racial story of the United States. It means speaking about hurtful things we have said and done, processing what got us to those moments, and practicing new antiracist ways to approach them.

When we do this work well, we can return to the People of Color and Native people in our lives with greater racial competence and racial humility; we can participate in cross-racial conversation in ways that are generative rather than burdensome or hurtful.

Can't White People Learn About Racism in Mixed Spaces?

Absolutely—White people cannot build racial competence without being in relationship, conversation, and learning with People of Color and Native people. A White antiracist learning space would be ill conceived if White people engaged in such a group and learned how to talk about racism with one another but never engaged with People of Color and Native people.

Ultimately, the goal is not to stay in racially segregated spaces but for members of all groups to build the skills needed to come back together in a racially integrated group in a way that helps everybody be stronger and more connected. When White people have done some of the skill-building needed to be in relationship and allyship with People of Color and Native people, they will be better able to both listen and speak in multiracial spaces. I don't like to call White antiracist learning spaces "safe spaces," because this suggests that if People of Color or Native people were a part of them, their presence would make them unsafe. In actuality, White antiracist learning spaces create safety for People of Color and Native people because they allow White people to do the deep and necessary work of bias exploration in a way that People of Color and Native people don't have to witness or be retraumatized by.

The White antiracist learning space is a pedagogical tool, just like pair work, group work, writing assignments, or the decision to structure a class using lecture or seminar. It is a tool that can be employed when needed and dispensed with when not. It may last many years, or it may happen just once. I know school faculties that have used one-off affinity groups for processing certain difficult racialized events so that all teachers would have a space to work through their different reactions and necessarily different action-step responses. I also know organizations, schools, and businesses that have longstanding White antiracist learning groups to support ongoing learning and growth.

Why Affinity?

Sometimes people feel unnerved by the idea of White people building connections based on racial affinity. The term *affinity group* has been criticized for White antiracist learning groups because it seems strange to have a group of White people gathered together based on an affinity of Whiteness. Remember: that's not what this is. This is not about an affinity for Whiteness or White people. It's about White people supporting one another around a common intention to cultivate an antiracist practice. For this reason, some people call such groups *caucuses* or *White antiracist learning spaces.* Some schools may choose to use the term *affinity* because the White antiracist learning group is listed with the other racial affinity spaces, and it's easier for organizational purposes. What matters is that the intention of creating a space for White people *to learn and practice antiracism* is stated clearly. These are not just places to hang out and be White together.

It's important to remember that we use affinity groups all the time. As my colleague Toni Graves Williamson says, the soccer team is an affinity space for people who love playing soccer (personal communication, April 2020). The choir is an affinity space for people who love to sing. More specifically, we have affinity spaces for children whose parents are divorced, or we may have affinity spaces for students who have lost a loved one. In an affinity space, you don't have to explain yourself to others or deal with their discomfort over your identity because you start with a baseline shared experience. For Students of Color or Native students in predominantly White institutions (PWIs), building relationships without having to explain or defend your experience can be healing and empowering.

My Own Experiences With White Antiracist Learning Spaces

In my own experience, White antiracist learning groups have been some of the most effective spaces for helping me process my own learning (including the lessons I took away from cross-racial dialogue in classes and workshops) and put it all together in a way that was integrated into my life. As we mentioned in the prologue, Eleonora and I had a White antiracist learning group for years with my partner, my sister, and my sister's partner. We connected with each other at a conference where we learned about this type of group and created our own within my immediate family circle. This was a small, casual gathering that met in our apartments—nothing fancy, complicated, or widely advertised.

Later, while in graduate school, I did start an official group called White Students Confronting Racism, which was more institutional by design. We advertised the group throughout the university, received funding as a student group, and held events that were open to everyone but clear about our audience: White people who wanted to work against the racism around us and inside ourselves. Because of its positioning within the institution, this group did more than just help its White members build skills and self-reflect. Through it, I met White people from numerous university departments who were engaging in antiracist practice in their isolated spheres. We would have stayed isolated in our own graduate programs had we not had a group with a visible presence that served to bring us together. Joining and learning with one another made us exponentially more effective in our antiracism. We gave one another feedback on our research and theses and dissertations, even though we were all studying antiracism from different fields. The group also served as a visible presence for the groups run by and for Students of Color and Native students. When racist events happened on campus or those student groups wanted to engage in an education campaign or cohost a book discussion, they knew where to find the White people who were trying to be antiracist and could collaborate, strategize, and cohost.

The third White antiracist learning space I've been involved with is a workshop series called *White People Confronting Racism* (Mattheus & Marino, 2011). This is a multiday workshop offered through Training for Change in West Philadelphia, created in the 1990s by Lorraine Marino and Antje Mattheus (both White women) in collaboration with an advisory council of People of Color. I have mentioned this workshop multiple times throughout this book because I attribute so much of my ability to take action and receive feedback to the activities in this workshop, which are designed specifically for the learning needs of White people. In graduate school, I learned much of the knowledge that I use in my antiracist practice, but most of my facilitation skills and antiracist intervention skills come from this workshop, which I took as a participant and then facilitated[1] for about eight years.

White People Confronting Racism is where I learned—as we've written elsewhere—that White people need allyship from one another. It's common to hear people talk about allyship from White people toward People of Color and Native people, but it's less common to recognize how White people often feel quite isolated in their antiracism from other White people. When White people are engaging in an active antiracist practice, we may work closely with People of Color and Native people, but we also need to respect their need for affinity spaces with their own groups. And we may also work with White people who do not understand or approve of the antiracist stance we take. This can be lonely in a way that makes our work both less sustainable and less effective. We need other White people who are trying to walk an antiracist path to offer company, companionship, feedback, and supportive accountability for the journey. In White antiracist learning spaces, we can cultivate this kind of allyship with other White people.

How to Structure a White Antiracist Learning Space so That It's Not Just Another Book Club

In summer 2020, right after George Floyd was killed, the *Washington Post* published an op-ed by educational activist Tre Johnson titled "When Black People Are in Pain, White People Just Join Book Clubs." Johnson (2020) was asking White people to go beyond knowledge acquisition, and work to acquire self-awareness and skills for taking action for confronting racism, both outside and inside ourselves. How do we ensure that our White antiracist learning spaces are not just another book club? This section details explicit aspects of a White antiracist learning space that differentiate it from a book club:

- Explicit goals
- Clear description
- Practice
- Building self-awareness
- Accountability partners
- Facilitation

And the subsequent section will suggest practical ideas for implementing these aspects within a meeting structure.

Explicit Goals

The group itself should have explicit goals grounded in both antiracist learning and antiracist action. Individuals in the group should also be given time to write their own personal goals and check in on their progress. This creates an accountability structure within the group, to establish the expectation that everybody is working toward concrete actions, to encourage people to be responsible for their own growth and learning, and to help people support one another in their stated objectives.

Clear Description

The group should have a clear name and tagline. One group's tagline was "White people helping White people be better White people." If you're doing this in a public way that gets advertised to the community, consider having an annual open house where anyone can come, meet members of the group, learn more about what you do, and offer input on what they might like you to do. White people really shouldn't be meeting in all-White spaces, unless it's for an antiracist purpose, so this should be explicitly stated everywhere your group is represented publicly.

Practice

Consider these spaces an opportunity for White people to practice the skills of talking about race, engaging with other White people about racial questions and dilemmas, receiving feedback, offering feedback, voicing questions they are afraid might be ignorant or racist, recognizing racism, intervening in racism, and so on. There is no reason to expect yourself to know what to say and how to respond effectively when you see or hear something racist. In fact, if anything, you have been trained *not* to respond. As with every other skill, the skills described throughout this book take practice, and since we have been socialized to feel shame and discomfort around the topic, it requires that we practice within a group that can hold us, care about us, and challenge us.

Building Self-Awareness

My colleague and mentor Dr. Frederick Bryant, a Black man who taught about antiracism all his life, once said, "For White people, self-reflection is a form of action" (personal communication, 2013). We often have no idea how much damage we cause simply by not seeing the racism and internalized dominance that live inside us. What we don't see we leave untouched or end up actively supporting. White people often know that overt racism is wrong, but we rarely see how systemic racism has shaped our own lives and afforded us access to resources, opportunities, safety, connection, and even basic human rights that we might not have if we were not White. Racial competence includes the skill of being able to recognize and intervene in racism both outside us and *inside* us. We can't act in nondominant ways in our interactions with People of Color and Native people if we don't see how our sense of dominance shapes our understanding of ourselves and others. The idea that self-reflection is separate from action is a bit of a false dichotomy. One must be in service of the other. And in fact, successful self-awareness cannot but lead to action.

White antiracist learning spaces have to include this critical self-reflection piece. For example, if the group is reading *The New Jim Crow* by Michelle Alexander (2020), we will learn the history and the dynamics of the criminal justice system that have been responsible for stripping Black people of their rights in covert, systematic ways since the end of the more overt, in-plain-sight version of codified Jim Crow–era racial injustice. But we also need to move beyond that knowledge and ask questions such as these: "How did this history affect me? Where was I when this was happening, and where am I now while it continues? What was going on for my family, and what do I still participate in currently? What biases have I internalized about Black people as a result of their criminalization? What biases do I have about White people and predominantly White spaces? Do I prefer predominantly White spaces and feel more comfortable in them? How have I benefited from this history, and how am I still benefiting from it?"

People of Color and Native People as Accountability Partners

The question of how much White people can engage in antiracism learning and action on our own, without People of Color or Native people, is important to consider. As we've discussed, White people fundamentally cannot engage in antiracism practice if we are not in relationship with People of Color and Native people. This is because as White people, it's hard for us to see racism or to know which aspects of racism are affecting the People of Color and Native people within our local communities and spheres of influence. If we are never in relationship with People of Color and Native people, our attempts to challenge racism become largely theoretical, making it hard to know how racism impacts our communities at the local level.

Beyond that, one way to maintain the integrity of an all-White antiracist space is to ask a Person of Color or a Native person to act as an accountability partner to the group. That person would not attend meetings but would meet with members or leaders of the group to talk about what they're working on and suggest things that the organization (and the White people in it) need to work on. This person should be somebody who has interest and skill in helping White people learn about racism. Too often, People of Color and Native people are put in the position of helping White people learn about racism simply because of their identity, not because they have training or expertise in that area, and not because they are interested in doing so. This person should also be compensated for their role as an accountability partner so that their time, energy, and expertise are honored. This compensation could take the form of money, time (one less class to teach, for example), or reciprocation.

Facilitation

I recommend that White antiracist learning spaces have a facilitator. It doesn't have to be the same facilitator every time; in fact, it's good for people to take turns playing that role. But so many White people have been socialized to be colorblind and not to talk about race that without a formal structure, we are likely to default to conversations about anything but race. If we don't revert to more superficial conversation, we might pivot to other topics connected to oppression, such as gender identity, transphobia, or classism. These other topics are incredibly important but can take the focus off race. If you go off-topic, a facilitator (or any group member) can track it for the group, which means that you notice it without judgment. I suggest this strategy because straying from the topic of race is not always bad. Sometimes the group is having an important conversation that will help them be more effective allies to one another and to People of Color and Native people. A gay group member talking about homophobia within the group or organization can give group members the opportunity to take feedback and practice the skills of being allies along a different line of identity. When the facilitator tracks the divergence, they can ask the group if they want to continue in that vein or redirect. When the group can see how they have strayed, they can collectively and consciously decide how to proceed. Sometimes, especially if other oppressions such as homophobia are undermining the unity and purpose of the group, it will make sense to take time to talk about it together. The skills required for those hard conversations will definitely transfer to antiracist allyship.

Even in the small informal group of five that Eleonora and I were a part of, we found that we needed a facilitator to help us stay focused on race. We found it useful to rotate facilitators and to always have somebody come prepared to lead the discussion, choose a skill-building activity for us to do, and help prompt us to do the self-awareness pieces. The facilitator also helped us think about and practice taking action. The facilitator ensures that the group is not just filling the space with conversation but that individuals in the group have time to check in about goals, do some personal reflection, and practice the skills being discussed.

What Do We Do in a White Antiracist Learning Space?

This section addresses how to establish a strong group dynamic that will support people in doing challenging work, building honest and authentic relationships rooted in antiracism, and continuing to come back.

Conditions for Building a Cohesive, Productive Group

In group dynamics, we talk about *building the container*, or establishing the conditions for a cohesive group so that people feel held and secure enough within the group to do the deep work of examining their own racism. There are several logistical structures for accomplishing this, many of which I have already mentioned previously:

- Have a facilitator.

- Have (and respect) a clear start and end time.

- Establish a clear purpose for the group.

- Share a general agenda for the time together, so that group members know what to anticipate.

- Establish some rituals of interaction, including an opening and closing during which all members of the group have a chance (and are expected) to share, even if it's only one word.

- Have the group sit in a circle with enough chairs for everyone, without extraneous chairs.

- Plan clear break times.

- Give the group time to work in pairs.

- Share food or something to drink, if possible.

Ensure That You Don't Have a Leaky Container

The preceding suggestions are not necessarily the only ways to build a strong container for the group. The process of container-building will vary according to the culture of the organization, the makeup of the group, and the task at hand. But if you've ever tried to be a part of a workshop on a sensitive subject that just didn't seem to be working, you could probably point to indicators that the container was leaky. A leaky container can include the following:

- A lack of clarity about purpose, so that the conversation remains superficial or off-topic and people get distracted wondering if it's worth their time

- A facilitator who surprises the group or does "gotcha" activities, which means group members don't know how to participate and end up just listening, wide-eyed

- Participants walking in and out to use the bathroom or grab food because there are no clear break times or because the group doesn't have a norm of honoring one another with time and attention during designated times of engagement

- A group that runs more than 5 to 10 minutes past the established end time, which leads to these issues:
  - Participants who have to leave feeling guilty and resentful
  - Participants who stay feeling restless but eager not to miss out
  - A group that slowly dissipates, rather than ending cohesively
- Several empty chairs that give the impression that the facilitator didn't know how many people were coming; this can also make the circle bigger than it needs to be, making it harder to hear as well as less intimate
- A participant who dominates the conversation
- People who attend the group but never have a chance to use their voice or contribute to the group
- People sitting scattered around the room, not organized in a way that allows everyone to see and hear one another
- No mechanism for hearing from other group members, leaving individuals to wonder about what everyone else thinks

A leaky container means that people will be less willing to share because they aren't quite sure how, they don't trust the group enough to be vulnerable, or they don't know if that kind of risk-taking will be welcomed or understood. When I am called in to facilitate conflict resolution with a school faculty, the central conflict often connects back to a race conversation that was held in a leaky container, where the dialogue was ripe for misunderstanding, no facilitator was working to slow down the conversation and hear both the intention behind what happened and the impact, and the leakiness or uncertainty of the group dynamic led people to retreat and become more defensive, rather than reach out to teach others proactively, as the conflict demanded.

Container-building is about group process, the meeting structure, and the space you carve out for your group within the institution. You don't have to decide all these components in advance—you will learn some of them as you go. But the earlier suggestion of a name and tagline, for example, is not random; it is part of container-building. When the tagline communicates your purpose to the institution at large, along with contact information for an organizer who can field questions, people will feel more willing to come to the group. When they get there, they will have fewer questions and experience less uncertainty. All of this builds a group where people can get to the work at hand.

Some people will not understand why you are having a group like this—which makes sense, of course. The idea of an all-White group for learning about race and racism is not mainstream yet, although it seems to have become more so after George Floyd's murder as White people try to learn more about racism and do more to end it. Every time someone asks a question about your group is a chance to practice articulating your aims and to get feedback on how it is perceived from the outside. This can even be a skill that you practice discussing in the group. Roleplay with one another how you would respond to this question: "Why do White people need a group for learning about racism?"

Meeting Structures That Support a Strong Container

I recommend that every meeting follow a clear structure to support a strong container. There are lots of ways to do this, but here is an outline of one possible structure (I'll explain the details in the paragraphs that follow):

OPENING
Review discussion norms and the group's purpose.
Share a loose agenda based on some content you have read/viewed ahead of time or will read/view within the meeting.
Do work in pairs.
Allow time to respond to two prompts:
• How does *this content* make you feel?
• How does *this content* affect you as a White person?
Allow time to revisit personal goals. Ask this question:
• What do you see that you didn't see before, and what shift in your personal or professional life does this inspire?
CLOSING

Aside from the opening and closing activities, this design really focuses primarily on three questions that can be engaged with regard to almost any content. Meetings in a White antiracist learning space might include activities, a book discussion, a discussion of current events, or listening to a TED talk, podcast, or song and then talking about it. Some school faculty antiracist learning spaces will spend time each week reading one or two posts from their school's Black@ Instagram posts and brainstorming changes they could implement as a result. Some community groups I've worked with are structured around the 14-part series called *Seeing White* from the podcast *Scene on Radio* by John Biewen and Chenjerai Kumanyika. Some groups are reading *The Racial Healing Handbook* by Anneliese Singh or *Me and White Supremacy* by Layla Saad. Some groups might talk about a recent article that addresses how systemic racism shows up in their field. There's no particular content that has to be engaged in such a group, no definitive text you need to follow. But group meetings should include content to learn from, and the particular content you choose should be related to your learning needs and goals.

The opening and closing moments give group members a chance to have their voices heard as part of the group. In a ritualistic way, these moments also help the group form and take shape. The opening could be vague and not race-related, such as "Share how you are feeling today." Given that these groups will often have just a short time to meet and are convening for the explicit purpose of talking about race, you might consider having quick race-related openings, such as "Share one thing you learned about race this week," "Share one way you felt conscious of having a White lens on your work this week," "Share what motivates you to stay engaged with antiracism," or "Share three words for what the world could look like if there was no racism." What you choose will depend on the group and the moment. The content isn't as important as finding a question that helps the group connect, ease into the space, get their voices heard, break the common norm of colorblindness by talking about race, and invite people to be equal partners and participants in the group. Change the prompts each meeting. If a race-related event is happening at school or in the news, consider structuring the opening around reactions to or questions about the event.

Similarly, the closing can help wrap up the meeting. Prompts such as "Share two words for how you're feeling after that discussion" or "Share one thing you're taking away from our discussion today" can help group members get a sense of the rest of the group and the feelings they are leaving with. When group members see what other group members are learning, it can help them feel like a part of something bigger than themselves and be less judgmental of one another. It can also help them calm their own self-doubt and insecurities that emerge when they don't hear what other people are thinking.

You could also ask, "What is a question you are still chewing on?" "What is something you wanted to share today but didn't have the chance to?" or "Share one appreciation for the group or someone from the group you've worked with over the past few weeks." This last prompt can give the group an opportunity to appreciate one another, something they likely do internally but may not always have the chance to express.

The opening and closing are democratizing structures that help the group belong to the people in it, rather than to the facilitator or organizer. Antiracism work in schools and organizations often defaults to cliques of people who are deeply committed but who also tend to be part of an activist vanguard in ways that many less radical White people feel excluded from and judged by. We want White antiracist learning spaces to belong to the group. We want more White people to feel that they can and should be speaking up and taking action—that it's not the responsibility or even the exclusive province of the few. Facilitated spaces like this help structure that democratic belonging in ways that interrupt the cliquishness and the fixed mindset about who is aware and who is not, who should be allowed to speak and who should not, and who is still learning and who is only teaching.

Similarly, group leaders (whether they are official coordinators or de facto social leaders) should maintain open and honest relationships with group members. If someone says or does something offensive, the leader should talk directly to that person. They should not go to other members of the group who are more experienced to complain about how dense that person is, nor should they report back the offense to Colleagues of Color or Native colleagues. They definitely should not post the offense publicly or text about it with others. They have a leadership imperative to lead in ways that foster group trust and support members in their antiracist goals; outside talk that demeans members of the group will undermine that obligation. Again, that doesn't mean they should ignore racist comments—but the racist comments should be addressed directly with the person who made them by using the skills described in Chapter 8. The fact that the offending person is showing up at the meetings should be enough of a statement that they are poised and willing to learn.

Facilitators Should Lead With Humility and Modeling

Group facilitators should honor their role as facilitators, honor the willingness of the group members to show up, and practice self-critique as a way of modeling what they are asking of participants. Facilitators can briefly answer the prompts publicly before asking the group members to answer them, so that group members can see what it looks like for a White person to be introspective in that way. It can be useful for facilitators to share a deep and vulnerable answer along with a lighter, less serious answer, so that participants feel comfortable sharing a range of possible responses. Remember that being the facilitator doesn't make you more savvy, cooler, or less White than the rest of the group, nor does it require you to be *more* savvy. It just means you've been entrusted with the responsibility of helping your group move forward by meeting the members where they are and helping them take the next step. It means showing up willing to take stock of your mistakes and the things you do not know, putting forward the things you do know, and inviting feedback on what you might not yet see. Facilitators are always part of the group and the process, not above it or outside of it. The point is to facilitate and then learn with the group, not to play the role of expert.

Use Structures That Create the Possibility of Vulnerability and Introspection

The sample agenda I provide also includes time for pair work. I do this for two reasons. First, the fastest way to build safety in groups is to put people in pairs. When a person knows one other group member and is known by them, they feel safer to share and be vulnerable in the whole group. Second, the primary purpose of these groups is for White people to practice talking about race—to challenge our socialization that taught us to avoid engagement in the topic. When people are in pairs, they spend half the time talking. Thus, every member of the group is getting to practice talking about race. This should happen at every single meeting, even if only four people are attending. Especially when the meeting has only a few people, clear structures like this will help the group maintain its purpose rather than fall into the hive mind that happens when a group is small.

The other structure I encourage is to have group members respond to the following prompts, regardless of the content:

1. How does *this content* make you feel?

2. How does *this content* affect you as a White person?

3. What do you see that you didn't see before, and what shift in your personal or professional life does this inspire?

The first question helps group members get out of their heads and begin to feel an emotional connection to the material and to the experiences of People of Color and Native people. As Eleonora shared in the Internal Work section for Chapter 4, fostering this emotional connection is critical to figuring out how to act. The second question helps us focus on the self-awareness aspect of racial competency. And the third question begins steering us toward connecting what we are learning to our own lives—even when we don't yet have an answer for it. All these questions move us beyond knowledge— beyond the book group—to the deeper, emotional, self-reflective work that leads White people toward actually doing something different in our daily lives. To that end, at regular intervals, give the group members time to revisit and update their personal goals. This can be done through individual time to reflect, as well as pair time for support and accountability.

Hold One Another in Mutual Vulnerability and Accountability

One thing that belongs in every White antiracist learning space—and should be repeated on a regular basis—is an activity in which White people relate to one another by sharing White group-level behaviors that they have engaged in themselves.

I use two lists of White group-level behaviors for this exercise. Both are lists of ways in which White people act that assume a privileged or superior position, as compiled from interviews with People of Color and Native people. White people, because of our socialization, engage in common behaviors that are not new to People of Color and Native people. But for many White people, we are so embedded in our own normal that it's hard to see them. If I ask a White woman, for instance, if she's ever been mansplained, she likely knows exactly what that means. Mansplaining is when a man explains sexism (or anything, really) to a woman or tells her how to handle it, as if the woman couldn't possibly know where to start. It can also take a patronizing tone, as if the woman he is talking to is not an intelligent, thinking, sentient being. Women know mansplaining, but it may be harder for a man to recognize it in himself because it likely feels more implicitly obvious within his socialization as a man to behave as if his ideas are more important and more complex than those of a woman.

You may not have heard the term *White group-level behaviors*, but some of these behaviors are more popularly discussed on social media as "whitesplaining" or being a "Karen." *Whitesplaining* is when a White person explains racism to a Person of Color or Native person as if the other person doesn't know what it is, or as if the White person must know better. The idea behind the term *Karen* is that there are common behaviors among some White women that result from the entitlement they feel as White people in a white supremacist society. Dictionary.com (2020) describes *Karen* as

> a pejorative slang term for an obnoxious, angry, entitled, and often racist middle-aged white woman who uses her privilege to get her way or police other people's behaviors. . . . In 2020, *Karen* spread as a label used to call out white women who were captured in viral videos in what are widely seen as racist acts. (para. 1–3)

The exercise I'm about to describe is not about calling each other Karens or even pointing out whitesplaining. It's about realizing that those are two behaviors on a long list of behaviors that any one of us is likely to fall into because of our common socialization as White people. It's about sharing stories of how we have engaged in these behaviors and listening to stories of other White people, to create a supportive container for ourselves and for other White people to see and acknowledge our oppressive behaviors. These are behaviors that feel deeply shameful, that we instinctively deny, and that we shame other White people for doing ("They're making us all look bad!"). But holding a conscious awareness of these behaviors at arm's length doesn't mean we stop doing them. Creating spaces to be able to see that we too participate in such behaviors means that we give ourselves the opportunity to change them. We can't stop them until we see them. We can't see them if we're too mired in shame to admit them.

Here are some common White group-level behaviors, used with permission from Dr. Kathy Obear (personal communication, 2022). She calls them "Common Unproductive, Possibly Biased Behaviors of Some/Many White People That Perpetuate Racist Dynamics and Structural Racism":

Some/many white people tend to (consciously and unconsciously):

1. Interrupt and talk over People of Color[2] in meetings and casual conversations more frequently than white colleagues.

2. Minimize, undervalue, ignore, overlook, and discount the talents, competencies, and contributions of People of Color.

3. Rephrase and reword the comments of People of Color much more frequently than those of white colleagues.

4. Ask People of Color to repeat what they have just said far more often than white colleagues.

5. Question, challenge, and doubt the validity and credibility of what People of Color say far more often than with white colleagues.

6. Require and demand "proof" if People of Color raise concerns about racist dynamics.

7. Question and undermine the authority of leaders of color; resent taking direction from a Person of Color.

8. Not follow the direction of leaders, managers, and facilitators of color.

9. Walk on eggshells and act more hesitant, distant, and formal with People of Color; feel uncomfortable and nervous and not develop the same depth of effective working relationships for fear of saying or doing something racist.

10. When asked to examine the impact of their behavior, get defensive and argue their "good intent" rather than explore the negative racist impact of their action or inaction.

Here are some common White group-level behaviors from the *White People Confronting Racism* manual (used with permission from Marino & Mattheus, 2022):

1. Avoiding areas, places, people, and relationships that are not predominantly white.

2. Consciously or unconsciously excluding persons of color in meetings, membership, input into decisions, processes, etc.

3. Equating one's experience with the experience of a person of color.

4. Interactive white flight; withdrawing from an interaction altogether or changing the topic when a racial interaction becomes uncomfortable.

5. Lack of inquiry or willingness to talk about or learn about race differences.

6. Not being sensitive to the risk involved for people of color to put out ideas, express feelings, etc. in a predominantly white environment.

7. Not listening.

8. Not noticing when and where there are only white people.

9. Overriding the ideas of people of color or not taking them seriously.

10. Reacting on an individual level; wanting to be seen for one's individuality.

Both of these lists appear in full, with the permission of the researchers, in Appendix A and Appendix B. The exercise for processing these lists, which I also learned from Obear, requires group members to read through the list and mark the behaviors they have engaged in. Then, in small groups of four, one person tells a two-minute story of a time when they engaged in one of those behaviors. The other three members of the small group listen and find ways to connect. After the first speaker finishes, another member of the group offers a way in which they connect to that story by sharing a time they did something similar. Then that person shares a story about one of the behaviors they marked on their sheet. The group proceeds like this by connecting to one another's socialization.

Sometimes I have seen people engaged in this exercise try to connect by saying, "I once called someone out for doing that." That's not how this exercise works. Showing how you once knew not to do these behaviors does not contribute to a container in which people can be vulnerable. You need to get vulnerable and connect to the negative behavior where you can and where it is truthful. Otherwise, you just make the person who shared feel worse and close up. As people take risks, other group members will, too. As a result, everyone experiences greater learning and self-awareness.

When I do this exercise, I find that people feel so relieved to hear one another's stories. They also find that they relate to other people's stories in ways that they have forgotten about. They start to see more of their own oppressive behaviors by listening to those shared by others. This is such an important exercise for us to engage in together, so that we can see how each of us—often unwittingly—perpetuates racist behavior. It creates the container we need to really see ourselves clearly, so that we can change.

You might ask, "Isn't that just collusion or connecting based on racism?" No. This is vastly different. Collusion is about *going along* with racism without doing or saying anything, so that you can fit in. This exercise is about giving one another space to see our own racism so that we can *change* it. It's about connecting based on a shared goal of doing better. It's about undoing racism around us and in ourselves. It's about connecting in antiracism.

One of the reasons this activity is so important in a White antiracist learning space is that it helps people actively practice this skill of connecting—not shaming but leaning in and recognizing racism. It also helps us learn how to narrate our own mistakes in a way that can help other White people learn, even outside the group. If we are pointing out something racist they are doing, they are usually much more receptive if we share a time when we did something racist or when we engaged in a White group-level behavior ourselves. Or alternatively, if they have been called out for doing something racist and are flailing in the aftermath as they reckon with this feedback, sharing our own humiliation at doing something similar at another time can help them feel less panicked and alone.

When I share in this way, I find that it immediately defuses some of the other person's shame that could otherwise lead to a fight, flight, or freeze response. It helps the other person see that I don't think I'm better than them. And it helps them feel connected and supported to keep going.

If we are trying to help other White people walk an antiracist path, this is one of the most effective tools for intervening. That is why practicing it in White antiracist learning spaces is so important—and why it can be done repeatedly over time without getting old.

The Use of the Term *Karen*

In the previous section, I introduced the commonly used pejorative term *Karen*. This term can run contrary to a growth mindset for White people trying to learn about race. Don't get me wrong—I love that we have a term for White people who call the police in order to get Black people in trouble. We should have a term that calls attention to that unacceptable behavior. The fact that such behavior sometimes passes for acceptable is a reflection of how deeply our society believes that the police and other law-enforcing institutions exist to protect White women, while harassing, imprisoning, and sometimes killing Black men, Latinx men, and Native men. The fact that there have been cases in which local governments refuse to entertain such calls means that we are capable of learning and doing better. Remember the case of Amy Cooper, a White woman who refused to leash her dog after Chris Cooper (no relation), a Black man who was birdwatching in New York City's Central Park, requested it? He started filming her refusal, and she panicked, called 911, and said that a Black man was threatening her. After the incident, the Manhattan district attorney, Cyrus R. Vance Jr., said of Amy Cooper's inappropriate use of 911, "We are strongly committed to holding perpetrators of this conduct accountable" (Ransom, 2020, para. 6).

In this case, it was easy for White women to distance themselves from Amy Cooper and to see her actions as unconscionable. But I wish we had a better way of talking about this behavior than simply shaming her as a Karen. This is partly because calling her a Karen minimizes the deadliness of her behavior. It becomes a light social violation, rather than a deeply criminal threat. But it also leads us to write her off without asking how the same socialization that led to her entitlement in that scenario might live in us, too.

The term *Karen* has now become widespread, well beyond White women who mobilize the police as a weapon against People of Color and Native people. It's become synonymous with a White woman who is the least bit ignorant about race. I have heard White teens and pre-teens calling other kids Karens. This amounts to name-calling and competition—two of the behaviors that ultimately push White people off an antiracist path. Again, that doesn't mean it's inherently wrong to use the term. But for White people who are trying to help other White people walk an antiracist path, we have to avoid such seductive shortcuts.

How to Counter the Myths of White Supremacy

Remember the myths of white supremacy discussed in Chapter 2, which hinder White people from addressing racism with one another, even when doing so is the express purpose of our gathering? In this section, I will revisit how those myths show up in White antiracist learning spaces (both the formal, organized types of groups discussed in this chapter and the informal interactions that happen between White people on a daily basis).

Myth 1: It's Rude to Talk About Race; We Should All Be Colorblind

Because so many White people are socialized to be colorblind, White antiracist learning spaces have to be structured in a way that makes it possible for White people to practice talking about race—to unlearn the automatic habits of leaving out racial terms or not considering how our White lenses affect the way we see or talk about a situation.

Structure your group and your interactions with other White people in ways that allow them to practice talking about race. If they say something offensive, notice whether they do it in air quotes or whether they stumble over what they're saying, as if looking for a better way to say it. Use these demonstrations of uncertainty as an opportunity to offer them alternative language. Say, "I could tell you weren't quite sure how to say that. Do you mean _____?" I did this recently with a participant who used the term *White trash* to refer to a student who surprised everyone by being a math genius. I said, "I saw you using air quotes, which suggested you weren't quite sure of that term. Do you mean the student was White and was from a working-class, poor background?" The teacher said, "Yes, thank you," and continued with his point, which was about academic tracking.

Position yourself and the group as a resource for White people who have questions that they are afraid to ask, for fear that they will look stupid or racist. Emphasize that this group is not the place for demonstrating performative activism or competition but rather a space for showing humility. Model how everyone is there to learn together, as well as how everyone will need feedback at different points by asking questions and welcoming feedback yourself. That doesn't mean letting one another off the hook; it just means holding yourself accountable, just as you hold one another accountable. You intervene when someone says something offensive, not out of a desire to shame them or make yourself better than them but because they came to learn—and because you need the practice. You intervene to honor their learning goals and support them. And you hope they will intervene with you as well.

Help the group differentiate between racial talk and racist talk, so that they can be assured that engaging in talk about race is not automatically racist. Also help the group understand how to identify racist talk (see Chapter 4), so that they can intervene with themselves, with one another, and with others.

Finally, practice seeing and naming racial dynamics. You can even begin that practice in your group despite the fact that it's all-White. In Chapter 8, we described a tool for this called *tracking*, or noticing without judgment. You can track the group dynamic externally in ways that allow the group to have an analysis of itself by saying, "I noticed that we all got quiet when Sue mentioned police murders, and then the conversation changed topics. I'm not actually sure what it means, but I thought I'd mention it to see what others were feeling and if we want to return to that topic now or maybe in the future." Or you could track what is happening for you internally, by saying, "I am just noticing that as soon as you started talking about a Black co-teacher who was being undermined by a White colleague, my chest started constricting. I think it hits close to home. I want to look more at why I might be feeling that. Did anyone else have a reaction to that?"

Myth 2: We Can and Should Be Perfect—or at Least Appear Perfect

White antiracist learning spaces must create the conditions that make learning possible. This includes encouraging a growth mindset that enables us to learn and get better at being antiracist.

Too often, White people don't want to say anything about racism unless we can be perfect. This expectation is simply unrealistic. It's impossible to achieve perfection within a socially constructed framework that was designed to be confusing. And it's impossible to get better without practice. Perfection itself is an illusion. We are talking about race here, a social construction that dominates our lives. It's bizarre and disorienting to have an idea that is both false and so deeply rooted in our identity and community. Any talk about race is bound to be imperfect because we are talking about a constantly shifting social construct, always expanding its reach and adapting to new contexts. We are not talking about something more static like algebra or the periodic table, where one might expect that right and wrong answers are always provable. It's a much more elusive topic, which is both context-dependent and experiential.

So how do we support one another to accept our imperfection when talking about race? It means recognizing and acknowledging when someone is taking a risk. It means honoring mistake-making as part of the journey. It means acknowledging that every time a person has the opportunity to give or receive feedback, they are building skills they need for antiracism. It means pausing and honoring the moments when someone takes in feedback humbly and receptively. It means encouraging people to try things that are hard and challenging. It means trying something yourself that is hard and challenging.

When people plan to take action, help them role-play, plan, and be strategic. But also remind them that every action we take is a draft. As a draft, it cannot be improved upon and become a second (better) draft unless we create the first draft and get feedback. Once we take action in the world, we will see how it looks outside our heads, and we will be able to view it from other people's perspective, especially those who are directly affected by it. When possible, of course, we should use the White antiracist learning space to practice the conversation we want to have, brainstorm ideas, consider how the action will affect People of Color and Native people, and strategize ways to get input from People of Color and Native people, so that when we offer a draft to the world, it is informed and considered. But that is not always possible, either. Sometimes, we have to take action as best we can in a given moment and learn how we might do better in the future.

Seeing every action as a draft also makes it possible to ask for feedback on it. If you take action only when you're absolutely sure it's the right action, you might feel insulted by getting negative feedback on it: "I finally took this risk and put all this time and energy into this action, and nobody has anything but criticism for me." If you take the attitude that every action is a draft, the feedback is something you will not only welcome but actually solicit, because you genuinely want it for your second and third and fourth drafts. This is how we become ever more effective in our antiracism.

If there are White people in your institution who are causing racial harm, talk with them directly about it. Use the strategy of support–challenge–contextualize (see Chapter 8). Give them support by letting them know that you are imperfect, too, and offer comparable examples of mistakes you have made so that they feel less isolated in their shame, much of which is coming from moral injury (see the Internal Work section for Chapter 7). If you see another White person receiving public feedback in an online posting or an in-person setting, reach out to them to see how you can support them in taking in the feedback, learning from it, and making reparations. Remember, this kind of support is about helping people receive feedback, not reiterating it. By standing with that person (rather than fearing you will be tarnished by association), empathizing, sharing stories of your own mistakes, and strategizing methods of repair, you scaffold their growth and ability to move further along an antiracist path. As an ally, it is your job to believe and uphold the feedback from People of Color and Native people however it is delivered, while also supporting the White person enough to reduce their own panicked defensive reaction and hear it.

Myth 3: We Need to "Win" by Competing With One Another

The way in which White people interact with other White people too often perpetuates the idea that an antiracist path is one full of self-righteous, holier-than-thou hypocrites. When interacting with other White people around racism or leading a group, remember that it's not enough for one White person to be antiracist. We need millions of White people to walk an antiracist path. When I think about the jury in the trial of Derek Chauvin, every single member of that jury needed to see that Chauvin was guilty of killing George Floyd by kneeling on his neck for almost nine minutes. There were six People of Color and six White people on the jury. All it would have taken was one person who did not feel they could find Chauvin guilty, and the jury would not have been able to convict him. It matters that we help the White people around us cultivate belonging in and allegiance to a multiracial community. It matters that White people recognize racism, see it as a White person's problem, and feel agency and compulsion to do something about it.

I have heard White people in antiracist learning spaces say they didn't know they were allowed to laugh in those spaces—or be kind to one another. Again, if these spaces are training grounds for learning how to be contributing members of a healthy multiracial community, who does it serve for us to sit in silence, without laughter or kindness? Who does it serve for us to simply perseverate on the right definition of *microaggression* while making sure we don't say anything offensive? These need to be spaces where we are able to grow, learn, make mistakes, and feel connection. These need to be spaces where we learn the joy of unlearning racism and uncover our own reasons for why antiracism is in our own best interest. These should be spaces where we feel accountable, not because people are mean to us but because they are kind—because they hold themselves accountable and support us in doing the same.

Notice that I use the term *kind*, not *nice*. There is a whole volume titled *The Price of Nice*, edited by Angelina Castagno (2019), about the ways in which many people hide behind niceness or politeness to avoid addressing racism. I began Castagno's book in October 2020, at the height of a four-year period in which overt racism—and outright meanness—were used to divide and weaken the country. I kept asking myself, "Can't we be antiracist *and* nice? I'm so tired of all the meanness." But the research on niceness does not conceptualize *nice* as the opposite of *mean*. Niceness, which allows racism to flourish, is the theoretical opposite of authenticity, responsibility, disruption, honesty, racial literacy, competence, equity, goodness, and even kindness, all of which are required for building a racially just society. These are the qualities we need to be antiracist. And kindness is part of that.

Against my own wishes, I still find myself wanting to lean away from other White people. Often, it's because I don't want to be associated with the racist White person who might make me look bad or because I want to protect my own image as woke or antiracist. Sometimes I lean away from White people who remind me of stages of identity development that I've been through myself. I most often lean away from White people who engage in shaming or call-out culture behavior, or from younger White people who do not approach their antiracist practice with humility. I might also lean away from White people who make me confront whatever skills I'm still lacking that would allow me to engage with them. Because racism feels so big, other White people's ignorance and confusion can easily add to our sense of hopelessness and helplessness. Whatever the reason, the thing about leaning away[3] is that it tends to be more effective at othering and excluding White people, and it does not tend to do anything to change racism.

To counter the myth that we should be in competition with one another, or that we need to be the best antiracist in the room, we should lean *toward* other White people. It means committing to practice being allies, even when the White person in front of us is at the very beginning of their journey and shows up looking very asleep indeed. It means recognizing our common socialization, and while I may have been learning about antiracism longer than another person has, I am, in fact, not a better White person than they are. We are equally embedded in a system that puts us in a position to benefit from the exploitation and vulnerability of People of Color and Native people. No amount of antiracist practice extracts me from that context. As long as a racist caste system and a racial hierarchy are in place, I benefit from them just as much as the next White person does.

Remember that just because the group you are forming is trying to be *antiracist*, this does not automatically make everyone in the group *not racist*, nor does it mean that White people who are not part of the group are necessarily racist. This is a formulation that many people will try to make—or implicitly feel—and it needs to be countered. Continuously work to break down the boundaries that people construct around *tuned in* versus *not tuned in*, or *racist* versus *antiracist*. They contribute to a fixed mindset, which leads to less risk-taking, less questioning, and less change. Continuously affirm that there is a place for your White colleagues in the conversation. I know one White antiracist learning group of high school students that monitors the Twitter feeds of their White classmates for antiracist messaging, such as support for Black Lives Matter. Whenever they see such messages, they'll send a tweet saying, "It looks like you are a White person who cares about antiracism. We need you for our work! Come join us—we meet on Wednesdays at 3:00 pm!" In doing so, they make it clear that they are not exclusionary, that all are invited, and that all are needed. Creating welcoming spaces is a powerful antiracist action in and of itself. For youth, this is especially valuable because they often don't know how to get involved and their action tends to be limited to shares on social media. They need help creating spaces where they can ask questions, learn, grapple with new ideas, and practice talking out loud about race (rather than only sharing preexisting memes online).

As White people learn more about racism, this tendency to compete can also come up in our relationships with People of Color and Native people. I have heard so many stories from People of Color and Native people about White people critiquing the way they practice antiracism, the way they choose to intervene, or even the efficiency of the food drive they have organized. One White colleague of mine asked whether a Black woman who chooses to approach White people with love is letting us off the hook. Another White colleague asked whether it's truly effective for a Black person to express so much anger. I always respond the same way—that it's not my job as an ally to critique how People of Color and Native people choose to engage in racial and social justice. My job is to learn from People of Color and Native people about how racism affects them—no matter how they choose to share it—and to do my own work to be able to take it in and help other White people do the same, so that we might more effectively dismantle racial hierarchies together.

Remember that traveling an antiracist path means that you are joining a path that is long and wide—one that has been trodden by People of Color and Native people for the past 500 years. Just because it is new to you does not mean it is new. Just as my body has learned how to help me feel safe within this system, so too do People of Color and Native people have deeply embedded mechanisms for detecting racism and resisting it.

They have deep bodily knowledge of how much they can say and do while minimizing the risk of getting hurt or excluded or fired. Nothing has made me humbler on my own antiracism journey than watching how People of Color and Native people subtly and strategically engage in antiracist practice. When I think I know the right way to speak up, to intervene, or to make White people listen, I realize how much less practice I have relative to so many People of Color and Native people. I am also constantly re-socialized as a White person into white supremacy. I have so much to learn from people who do not see the world through White lenses.

Walking an antiracist path means leaning into other White people while also following the leadership of People of Color and Native people. It means not assuming that we can do this ourselves or that we know all the answers. It especially means not trying to outshine, outdo, out-ally, or talk over People of Color and Native people. But it also means putting a halt to any competitive instinct that we have with regard to other White people.

Myth 4: It's Better to Think, Rather Than Feel, About Racism

This myth manifests in all-White spaces (and among White people in multiracial spaces) when we think about racism intellectually, logically, and analytically. This not to say that logic and intellect have no place in race conversations. People of Color and Native people have been analyzing racism for as long as it has existed. But because they also live it and experience it viscerally, they often have a deep emotional understanding of racism that informs their gut about what is safe and what is not safe. Howard Stevenson (2014) calls this his "spider senses" (p. 7). As a White person, I do not have a gut that helps me understand what is safe and unsafe for People of Color and Native people. As a woman, I have pretty well-developed "spider senses" that let me know when a man is comfortable with me, respects my contributions, values my humanity, understands how I consider myself an athlete even though I'm not in perfect shape, and believes in my equal worth. I also know when a man is looking at my breasts, trying to avoid looking at my breasts, believes that a 43-year-old mother of two could never be an athlete, is willing to write off my ideas, is not listening to what I say, or otherwise doesn't take me seriously. It's different from an awareness of racism, but it's my window for seeing how one could have a gut sense about something that is even more informative than any intellectual analysis.

As White people, it's important that we get in touch with feelings about racism so that we can begin to develop a gut sense about what we should be doing about racism. When your gut says something is wrong, it literally throws your body into action (see the Internal

Work section for Chapter 4). When I think something is threatening my children, my blood races, my vision focuses, my jaw hardens, and I spring into action. I might then have to take a breath and make sure my action aligns with what might be best for my children. Without that gut feeling, not much happens at all. In White antiracist learning spaces, you can help the group practice *feeling* about racism in various ways.

In a group, practicing feeling can include many different possible activities for engagement:

- Simply name the dynamic of how people tend to think about racism more than we feel about it, and provide opportunities for the group to shift that balance.

- Introduce tools for locating physiological reactions that are connected to feelings, such as those Eleonora has offered throughout this book.

- Use Howard Stevenson's Calculate, Locate, Communicate, Breathe, Exhale (CLCBE) exercise (as cited in University of Pennsylvania, 2020). This exercise invites people to pause and assess their physiological reactions to racially stressful situations, rather than just react.

- Remember that one of the reactions we can have is freezing, which does result in numbness. Note that numbness is not "nothing" but rather a reaction ripe with meaning.

- Work to invite feelings in; picture what you are learning happening to your own child, yourself, your partner, or your parents.

- Notice when othering People of Color and Native people has become so second-nature that the work is to begin seeing that this is not happening to "them" but rather to our own brothers and sisters and siblings. Physiology doesn't change overnight, but just the intention of leaning into our own feelings and the experiences of People of Color and Native people tenderizes us in powerful ways over time.

- As the facilitator (or as a participant), model a connection to your own feelings by expressing how you are feeling or verbally noticing your reaction in your body and the sense you make of it.

- Reassert the value of recognizing, locating, and having feelings with the group. Help people continue to see this as a growth edge. White supremacy thrives because it has managed to numb White people to the pain of People of Color and Native people, particularly Black people. It keeps us from being in relationship and empathetic connection with one another. Antiracism has to include reestablishing that connection, which will necessarily be painful because it means no longer being numb to the pain of racism. But just like slowly weaning off pain medications after surgery, experiencing the pain goes along with feeling joyful and life-giving physical sensation as well. Un-numbing is what makes it possible both to feel about racism and to experience the joy that comes from unlearning it.

Remaining vigilant about leading with feelings rather than thoughts is an ongoing process. You can use the strategy of tracking to notice it with the group—or even inside yourself. Remember that tracking is noticing without judgment. Tracking makes it possible to notice it so that you can change it, not so that you can punish yourself or other White people in the group for being rooted in white supremacist culture. You can dislike that we have been socialized into white supremacy without our consent, but to judge it is to turn it back into an individual problem. It is not. Notice when intellectualization takes over, and remind yourself that you need to keep moving from the mind to the heart.

Now to address a related question: Won't feelings lead to tears? White antiracist learning groups are the perfect places to cry about racism. Too often, we don't cry about racism because we don't want to make People of Color and Native people take care of us, we don't want to recenter Whiteness, and we don't want to show how naive we are that some of this learning about racism is still new for us. But to connect to our feelings and connect to the pain of racism, we need to cry and feel angry and experience some strong emotions. What better place to experience them and express them than a White antiracist learning group?

Myth 5: Race Is Real and Biological; Racial Differences Are Immutable

As you engage in antiracist learning with your group, continuously find ways to remind yourselves that race is a social construction and to see the similarities you may have with People of Color and Native people, regardless of your racial and cultural differences. Remember that antiracism requires a constant balancing of the contradiction that while race is not real, racism is. As you consider your relationships with Colleagues of Color or Native colleagues, you might reflect on what you have in common, what qualities you share, or how you might differ as individuals. You can also reflect on the instances of privilege and racism that each of you experiences individually, as well as how your family and ancestors have been affected.

Common Pitfalls of White Antiracist Learning Spaces

There are a couple of things to watch out for when starting or being a part of a White antiracist space. First, remember that this is not the only way to learn about racism, and it is not necessary to have one in every school or every workplace. It's not always the right way for antiracist education to take place, particularly if it feels threatening or untenable to People of Color and Native people in your school or workplace. This is just one way of helping White people learn.

In some schools, creating affinity groups at the middle-school level has often led to more conflict and confusion than it mitigated. One school I work with taught its racial literacy curriculum in affinity groups, and word about the ignorant things the White students said would get out—out of context—and be even more hurtful to their Peers of Color and Native peers who heard it secondhand. Because of that, this school chose to teach the racial literacy curriculum to all the students together and to use racial affinity spaces to help students process their experiences and feelings about that joint curriculum.

In some research on affinity groups in schools, it's clear that Students of Color and Native students generally find their groups fun, social, and life-giving, while White students tend to learn vocabulary, concepts, and what not to do. I encourage leaders of affinity spaces for White students to remember that ultimately you want to create investment in antiracism; you want to help your White students be more primed to connect with Classmates of Color and Native classmates, not to just get paranoid and *be weird*. This will mean different things in different contexts, but there's something to be said for taking some of the intellectualism out of it and introducing more feelings and more possibilities for connection. Also, help the White group experience joy and support within their group. A group that laughs together is a group that can cry together. Doing deep emotional work requires relationships and trust. Taking time to develop these will help the members of your group have a deeper, more transformative experience in their affinity time.

All that said, be cautious about your group becoming a way for people to access power. I know of a school that started a White male affinity space for learning antisexism and antiracism, and it became the place where all the White men who wanted to have a personal relationship with the head of school would gather. It turned out to be a résumé-building, promotional tool. Be wary of that.

When I was a part of White Students Confronting Racism in graduate school, a few of our Asian American colleagues approached us and asked if they could join the group to work on their own anti-Black racism. They said they knew it was a place for White people to do their internal work, but they needed to do their own internal work, too, and because they were so few in number, it wasn't feasible to have their own space. We considered the reasons our group was all-White. We wanted White people to do the deep work of looking at their own biases honestly and out loud. We wanted White people to tell their own stories and not fear they were taking up too much space. We wanted to create a space of antiracist learning for White people with a wide spectrum of understanding (i.e., we wanted to accommodate beginners). We wanted White people to learn about racism through external resources, rather than rely on the People of Color and Native people in the school to teach them. And we did not want to further injure People of Color and Native people by making them listen to our stories of internalized racism and bias. We talked this over with our Asian American colleagues and agreed that they could join the group if these goals worked for them. In other words, if they would do their internal work, if they would not feel compelled to be the teachers, if they would come to the group knowing everyone in the group was still learning, and if they would let us know if we were reinjuring them with our bias discovery—then it could work. And it did. For several years, White Students Confronting Racism became Students Confronting Racism and White Privilege.

Since White identity itself is a construction, there will always be people who don't fit perfectly into racial designations and for whom the use of affinity spaces based on racial designations will be invalidating and confusing. The best we can do is create space for those feelings, reassert the goals of the space, find a way to adjust the structures so that people don't feel invalidated and confused, and continue to work to honor the varied learning needs of people who are positioned differently within a racial hierarchy.

Conclusion

White-on-White work has been meaningful to me because it created space for me to dig deep into my own work in a way that helped me really learn. I wasn't posturing in these spaces to impress People of Color and Native people. And even though I wish I would never have postured or felt like I needed to do so in front of People of Color and Native people in the first place, I just didn't have enough skills yet not to do so. To get to the point of being both clear and compassionate with myself, my biases, my lack of knowledge, and my mistakes, I needed a space to practice those things. I needed a space to get comfortable with the idea that it is really not about me or how good I look—it's about ending racism.

Notes

1. I was trained to facilitate this workshop by Lorraine Marino, Antje Mattheus, Sarah Halley, and Molly McClure. I cofacilitated primarily with Sarah Halley, who taught me so much of what I know about facilitation.

2. Because these lists are quoted from other researchers, we have not amended them to include Native people. But the behaviors described here are likely to be experienced by Native people as well as People of Color.

3. My colleague Sarah Halley has seen this so often that she has named it "the lean."

To Prepare for Antiracist Action, You Must Train for Courage

· ·

Antiracist action, by definition, unsettles the status quo. As you begin intervening in racism, sometimes family relationships become distant, friendships dissolve, you are pushed out of committees, your papers are not published, your teaching is not appreciated, your competence is questioned, you receive hate mail, your finances suffer, or your life might be threatened. In other words, your community, reputation, job, and safety are often on the line. Not all these consequences are ubiquitous, nor do they occur all at once or all the time. However, successful antiracist action successfully challenges systems founded on white supremacy—to which our safety as White people is tied.

You can't eliminate fear when the threat is real, because your body is accurately perceiving it. You can only expand your ability to tolerate strong emotions so that you can operate effectively while being fearful to an appropriate, realistic extent. While it's not for Ali or me to tell you what you should risk on your antiracist path, our message is simply that you have to prepare for it. And to be sure, the antidote to fear is not self-blame or shame. Shame only makes you more afraid. The antidote to fear is courage.

Courage does not mean the absence of fear. Courage is the ability to remain grounded enough to still take thoughtful, intentional action while experiencing fear. You might even say that you need your fear to know when, where, and to what extent you are disrupting white supremacy—which sometimes does mean saying the unpopular thing, being seen as a know-it-all, or annoying your boss.

Some of the most effective tools for working with fear are exposure techniques. You learned about one of these techniques (graduated exposure) in the Internal Work section for Chapter 1. You practiced it as a way to better detect your flight, fight, and freeze reactions. At the end of this section, I will guide you through another kind of exposure, called Worst-Case Scenario Script (WCSS). It will revolutionize your ability to engage with some of the antiracist actions that you might have wanted to do for a long time but have found too scary to navigate in strategic and effective ways.

Prepare to Fail

Training for courage also requires preparation for failure. For many years, I taught a course on counseling theories and techniques. In that course, I used to assign a book titled *Fail, Fail Again, Fail Better: Wise Advice for Leaning Into the Unknown*, by Pema Chödrön (2015).[1] Throughout my career focused on training professional counselors, I warned my students that they would inevitably do it wrong the first 99 times—and then invited them to dive right in to get those out of the way, so that they could reach the more skillful 100th try. And even then, despite white supremacy's delusion that anyone could be perfect, nobody is in fact perfect, we'll never do it perfectly, and we'll never do it all— whatever these mean to each of us. It's all an ongoing practice. We'll inevitably fall short. But by taking risks and learning from them, we'll get increasingly better at dismantling racism. We must be bold and dive in.

Strengthening Your Antiracist Practice

Becoming Bold: Worst-Case Scenario Script (WCSS)

This is a great tool that will help your body feel safe enough to take action—the key word being *enough*. As I've noted, there is no real safety in challenging white supremacy. But since we have human bodies, we do need to feel safe enough to take action while being afraid. Otherwise, our bodies won't let us follow through. The WCSS makes your fear manageable; dislodges your paralysis, confusion, or worry in a specific situation; brings you greater clarity; and increases your ability to act. As a bonus effect, it builds your resilience to racial anxiety in general. As with any practice, the more you use it, the more you'll be able to do it quickly, in the very moment you begin feeling stuck.

Example of a Worst-Case Scenario Script (WCSS)

Here is an example of a Worst-Case Scenario Script that I created based on a racially stressful interaction:

(Continued)

(Continued)

Event

I am speaking with a Black woman (an acquaintance) about my view of white supremacy and my work with White women. I read skepticism in her eyes, and she voices her deep frustration with White fragility. She experiences White people as largely apathetic and complacent, and she feels that they just get coddled in diversity training.

Worst-Case Immediate Consequences

My anxiety rises, I become foggy in my thinking, and I lose my ability to articulate my thoughts. I sound naive. I reveal myself as a fragile and racially incompetent White person. I am embarrassed and replay the conversation in my mind for hours afterward.

Worst-Case Long-Term Consequences

I feel that I have reached my limit in racial competence, that I am useless in the fight against white supremacy, and that I am revealed as such over and over again—especially in my awkward interactions with People of Color and Native people. I fear that the more I try to be antiracist, the more I accidentally oppress with my words, actions, and omission—because of my ignorance and stupidity. Longtime close Friends of Color and Native friends become disgusted with me and feel deeply betrayed, and White allies withdraw. I live out a mostly injurious, reprehensible, deluded, and shameful life.

Instructions for Writing a Worst-Case Scenario Script (WCSS)

Let's look at how I crafted my WCSS:

1. First, it involved taking notice of a stressful racial interaction and going back to it.

2. Second, I followed these instructions:

    a. I divided it into three sections of just a few sentences each: the event, the immediate consequences I fear, and the worst-case scenario's long-term consequences.

    b. I wrote it in the first-person present tense.

    c. I kept it short, concise, and to the point.

    d. I made sure it reached the ultimate logical conclusion. I made it truly a worst-case scenario while keeping it realistic. What I wrote is an honest reflection of my own personal nightmare outcome.

In this particular Worst-Case Scenario Script, only the actual event and the beginning of the immediate consequences took place. Most of the other immediate consequences I wrote down were merely what I dreaded might happen. However, in some scenarios, the immediate consequences can all be very real. In this specific one, I had already worked enough with the fears described that as I noticed my anxiety rise, I breathed, came back to listening closely to my acquaintance, and intentionally reengaged my empathy. By doing that, I was able to remain in the conversation with minimal anxiety, genuine curiosity, and some degree of clarity. In spite of that, the intensity of my initial stress response was significant enough that I decided to still work with this scenario.

How to Work Through a Worst-Case Scenario Script (WCSS)

So what happens after you write a WCSS? Usually, some parts evaporate just by shining a light on them. When I reread the last sentence of my WCSS, I chuckle to myself. It's quite dramatic, and seeing it on paper makes it lose much of its power. Other parts, however, might feel even worse after you write them. For example, the dreaded reaction of my Friends of Color and Native friends stirred quite a bit of sorrow when I wrote about it. Those are the parts you will need to work with, as I'll describe shortly. Finally, parts of your script might put you in touch with deeper, older hurts. These need healing that might go beyond this exercise. In my case, the pain of hurting others resonates with the pain I witnessed early in life that elicits sadness and grief. Sadness and grief may require a different kind of work, as we talked about in the Internal Work section on healing at the end of Chapter 8.

So what does it mean to work with the Worst-Case Scenario Script until it doesn't cause you virtually any fear or anxiety? Here is what to do after you write the script:

1. Reread the script aloud daily for at least 10 minutes in one stretch without taking breaks (or 5 to 10 times in a row). You should read it from the beginning to the end, going right back to the beginning. You can also record

(Continued)

yourself reading it and listen to that recording again in subsequent days.

2. Feel free to tweak the script as you reread it the first few times, as more details about your fears may become apparent to you. But don't let the editing distract you from the process of rereading it after the first day or two. Be careful about making it too long. Keep it short and to the point.

3. Make sure to really let yourself feel the dread and any other emotion that may come up as you read the script. Don't make the process rote, and don't tune out.

How do you know that you have successfully worked through the Worst-Case Scenario Script? This happens when every aspect of it feels quite boring and doesn't stir virtually any anxiety or apprehension. That can take anywhere from a handful of days to a handful of weeks. You should work with only one WCSS at a time to get the maximum benefit from it. The good news is that the more you sit with a WCSS about racial anxiety, the less anxious you will feel across a variety of racially charged interactions. What scares us tends to revolve around recurrent themes, which become easy to detect across a few Worst-Case Scenario Script exercises. This means that working with even just a handful of scenarios will give you a powerful basis for anchoring much of your antiracist action.

Note

1. The book is based on a graduation speech Pema Chödrön delivered at Naropa University, which was inspired by novelist, poet, and playwright Samuel Beckett's famous phrase "Ever tried. Ever failed. No matter. Try again. Fail again. Fail better."

Taking Action

*by Eleonora Bartoli
and Ali Michael*

CHAPTER

#10

> *Both individually and collectively, people can accept and
> internalize the racial order, resist it, or transform it.*
>
> —Bernardo M. Ferdman and
> Plácida I. Gallegos (2001, p. 32)

A recent housing-voucher program in Evanston, Illinois, gave African American families $20,000 vouchers for down payments on homes. The program caught our eyes because an op-ed in the *Washington Post* (Mullen & Darity, 2021) argued that this program did not reach the goal of reparations, as the architects of the program had intended. The writers argued that true reparations would require engagement at the federal level and would cost an estimated $14 trillion annually. While this argument is clearly backed by research, we were dismayed by the critique, which seemed to say, "Too little, too late." We felt embarrassed for the city council members who made this attempt at reparations and then got called out publicly for using a term (*reparations*) that others seem to hold to a higher expectation. We felt frustrated by a critique of a local initiative that is so much more significant than what most cities or communities are doing. The critique felt unrealistic and harsh. A few weeks later, another op-ed came out, also in the *Washington Post* (Perry & Ray, 2021), arguing that while this program alone was not going to be able to account for all the reparations that needed to happen, it was a step in the right direction.

As we look back on those op-eds, we can see that they both played a useful role. Both contributed necessary dialogue. Interestingly, had the first op-ed not been published, millions of people (including us) might never have read about the local suburban Chicago housing-voucher program in a national newspaper. Had the first op-ed not been published, there would not have been a national-level conversation about what reparations might look like and how deep the national debt to African Americans actually is. Had the second op-ed not been published, we might have been unfairly judgmental of the Evanston program, which, while not enough, is more comprehensive than programs offered by most localities. Between these two op-eds, the national dialogue went from a conversation about the enormity of meeting the standard for true reparations to an acknowledgment that many smaller local efforts could help us get there. All of this brings us closer to knowing what it will take to build a racially equitable society.

We write this at the beginning of the chapter on action because sometimes the action we need to take is huge: reparations, ending mass incarceration, transforming funding formulas in public schools, and so on. And while all these things need to happen to build a just society, many of us often fail to see the very immediate things we can do within a smaller sphere of influence. The people who created the Evanston City Council program did not have control over what it would take to mobilize a national reparations effort, but they certainly did what they could on the local level. In all likelihood, the program was the culmination of years of advocacy by multiple parties, involving much organizing and educating of the Evanston community.

Imagine being on the Evanston City Council, dealing with all the messy business of running a community, structuring a budget that would make it possible to fund a housing-reparations project, and fielding phone calls from constituents who hate the reparations bill and who engage conservative organizations such as Breitbart to smear your name and get its followers to send you hate mail. Then imagine turning around and seeing an op-ed in the national news that criticizes the program. What would be your reaction?

If we're being honest, we would have thoughts like these: "How can you be so ungrateful?" "Don't you see what we're trying to do here?" "Do you know how hard this was?" "Do you know how much racism we have had to combat while fighting for just this one housing program?"

We know these thoughts well, because the same resentful questions have come up for us when our own antiracist actions have been critiqued. Yet as outsiders to this particular story, we can appreciate that the national dialogue that sprung from the critique of the program contributes to the very purpose that the program was designed to address. The critique took the specifics of the actual program and put them before the country, asking us to see both the profound significance of the existence of such a program locally *and* the relative insignificance of the program in the larger scheme of what is fair and needed.

It raises the essential question for all of us: What action needs to be taken to create an antiracist society and world, and what action will each of us take, given our resources and spheres of influence?

What Action Should I Take?

We wish that we could tell you exactly what to do to take antiracist action. There are actually lists available online—30 antiracist actions you can start today, top 10 things an antiracist ally does, and many others. These lists can be incredibly helpful to people who are struggling for a foothold. But the action that we get excited about—the action that our skills, talents, and relationships prime us to take—will not be the same action that energizes you. The action that someone online believes all White people should take is based on the needs they are seeing in their own workplace, school, and community. When we read, "I just wish White people would . . . ," we have to remember that the writer is thinking of a specific White person in their orbit—or perhaps many specific White people. What they wish for is never going to be all that we should—or can—do. While such honest perspectives are valuable for identifying racial dynamics more generally, the actions they recommend are not necessarily the actions that you or we need to take.

Every White person is needed for and is essential to antiracist action in a different way. Here, we invite you to consider your unique skills, talents, relationships, and sphere of influence, so that you can determine the actions you can take to make your sphere of influence more racially equitable.

As we look back at our past 20 years of practice in taking antiracist action, we have committed to these maxims that continue be our guideposts and anchors:

- Everyone is an essential worker for antiracism.
- All antiracist action will be imperfect and incomplete.
- Privilege depth over breadth; pick a setting and an action and stay the course.
- Everyone is needed; everything is useful.
- Critiques will help me see how to do better.
- Knowledge, self-awareness, and action are interdependent.
- Don't go it alone: Who are your companions on your antiracist path?
- When I take action, I do it for myself.

Here is what we mean by each of them.

Everyone Is an Essential Worker for Antiracism

We are all essential workers for antiracism. Yes, we need lawyers, policy makers, and community organizers. But we also need teachers, writers, police officers, tour guides, nurses, accountants, mechanics, investors, librarians, store managers, cooks, and artists. We invite you to consider your own gifts and talents. Each of us is responsible for traveling an antiracist path in the way that's right for us. How will you use your particular skills and sphere of influence in service of social change? Your voice, your presence, and your actions matter. While as White people, we might have a tendency to overestimate our value, when it comes to the influence we have for disrupting racism, we also tend to massively underestimate it. To offer your gifts and talents, you need to believe that you matter.

All Antiracist Action Will Be Imperfect and Incomplete

When we join an antiracist path, we are metaphorically placing ourselves on a path that has been traveled for hundreds of years by People of Color and Native people, whose very being resisted the racist restrictions society placed on them. It has also been traveled by White antiracist people before us. Anyone who knows this path understands that it is a journey, not a sprint. And the more successful we are, the more powerful the resistance we generate. This means that we have to maintain a lofty vision of where we are headed and why, while at the same time recognizing that antiracism is not a solo or short-term endeavor. We like to think of it as a relay—a collaborative engagement that happens across both time and space. We are taking the baton from those who came before and carrying it toward those who come after, honoring all who have held the baton, and helping those who step in ready to take it.

Privilege Depth Over Breadth; Pick a Setting and an Action and Stay the Course

If we are working in our own spheres of influence, with each step we take, we will see additional actions we can and must take to dismantle racism. Some days I (Ali) can't believe that I haven't made time to talk to my school board about its history curriculum or to my local municipality about changing Columbus Day to Indigenous People's Day. I have a mile-long list of things I want to do, and realistically I will never get to all of them. Yet right now, I'm writing this book with Eleonora. And I'm designing programming around Indigenous People's Day for educators. And I do trainings for teachers in my district. I cannot do everything that is needed. But when I use my unique skills and talents to work with educators with the time I have—within my sphere of influence—change happens. And conversely, if I tried to do everything on my list, chances are that I would never get to do any one thing long enough or well enough for it to have an impact. So while I keep my wish list going, and while I support the efforts of people around me, I prioritize going deep with what's mine to do—my writing and my teaching.

Everyone Is Needed; Everything Is Useful

The steps we take matter. Everything is useful, *and* nothing we do will solve racism completely. What we do matters, *and* it will only ever matter to an extent. Our offerings will inevitably be imperfect and incomplete. In short, you are necessary, and you are not everything. Racism is not an individual story. A liberated society will not happen because of the efforts of one person alone. We must focus on adding our sentence to the book of a liberated society. We must trust the collective as we give ourselves wholeheartedly to our individual part. To do this, start each time from exactly where you are—in terms of location, sphere of influence, and skills. When doubts seep in, remember this: everyone is needed, and everything is useful.

Weeks after the stories about the voucher program in Evanston, Illinois, came out, a story was published on *NBC News* (Planas, 2021) reporting that a Black woman from Indiana named Carlette Duffy thought her home was being undervalued by appraisers. So she engaged in an experiment. For her third appraisal, she had a White friend pretend to be her brother showing the house in her absence, so that the appraiser would think she was White. The value of her house on the third appraisal doubled the value of the house that was given in the first two appraisals. The article reported that appraisers in Indiana are overwhelmingly White and male. It said that homeowners in Black neighborhoods nationally lost a collective $156 billion in 2017 because of disparities in appraisals. If you are in the business of appraising houses, this story could be the seed of your action. Have your office read the *NBC* article and discuss it together. Read the Brookings Institution report "The Devaluation of Assets in Black Neighborhoods" (Perry et al., 2018). Create positions for Black appraisers in your firm. Run experiments for yourselves to see if you fall into the same bias trap. Hear testimony from Black homeowners about the impact on them. Create a rubric for appraisal that includes a bias check, examining appraisals given to homes owned by White people, and contrasting them with comparable homes owned by Black people. Talk to your White colleagues about why this matters— not just for Black people, not just for the moral high ground, but for them, too.

Your action will not be our action, and our action will not be yours. But when we engage deeply, exactly where we are, over time, in concert with others, we will make progress that has a profound impact.

Critiques Will Help Me See How to Do Better

Because our action will be imperfect and incomplete, we will never quite reach our aim. And it is very likely that someone will critique what we did and be disappointed by it. Or perhaps even more predictably, we will critique our own intervention and be disappointed by it. This is a setup—and a sure path to cynicism and burnout. Do not fall into the trap of believing that imperfect action is irrelevant or regrettable. Remember that every action you take is a draft that you can improve on. If you had not produced that imperfect draft, you would not be able to get feedback on it so that you could revise it and create a subsequently better draft.

I (Ali) recently gave a talk to a group of school administrators in which I inadvertently addressed the White people almost exclusively. In other words, in a talk on racial equity, I did not address the People of Color present or their concerns. There are several perfectly logical explanations (PLEs) for this: I'm currently writing a book for White people, so my general focus right now is what White people need to know; in preparation for the talk, I interviewed White administrators to find out what they were struggling with—and I did not interview Administrators of Color; and the group itself was predominantly White. But all these PLEs are just excuses that get in the way of self-reflection. When I finished the talk, I knew I was missing something, and I couldn't quite put my finger on what it was.

I solicited feedback from People of Color I knew who hadn't been there. I sent them recordings of the talk, and they confirmed my fear: I had not addressed the People of Color in the room. This led me to have conversations with some White people and People of Color who had been there, to hear the impact on them.

This feedback was demoralizing—even though I predicted it, sought it out, and was unsurprised by it. It made me feel inadequate in my work, frustrated that I cannot locate my oversights even when they are right in front of me, and anxious that I'm abusing my position of authority as an invited speaker. Yet so much good came out of that talk. People told me that they felt more empowered to lead for equity than they had for years. One of the People of Color who confirmed my oversights also said she took six new ideas from my talk that she was going to implement immediately.

My job is to learn from my mistakes, revise the draft, and do better next time. For me, that means inviting further feedback and making amends by listening to the reactions of people who were at the talk. This internal work involves feeling the embarrassment, the sadness, and the mortification of being an invited speaker on race who still has obvious racial oversights, without being overwhelmed by it or discouraged from taking further action. As we said in Chapter 7, my job is to sit with the feedback and allow it to transform me, so that I know better what to do and how to be next time.

All of us must take action as best we can. The more we do that, for better or for worse, the more feedback we will generate! And the more feedback we hear and integrate, the more skilled we get. The process of giving, receiving, and exploring feedback in community not only helps us do better; it helps others know how to do better, too. That is why critique and feedback are especially precious gifts.

Knowledge, Self-Awareness, and Action Are Interdependent

While we need to increase our knowledge and self-awareness to take appropriate action, *action itself* is what will expand our knowledge and self-awareness. All must happen together—not sequentially—as each informs the other. How do we improve our strength? It's certainly helpful to learn movements that are good for the body, but no personal training plan will ever make us stronger if we don't actually lift those weights. How do we become more patient? It's certainly helpful to know when it's more appropriate to be assertive or to breathe deeply, but unless we find ourselves driving behind a local school bus or waiting at the back of a checkout line, we will never get to practice becoming more patient. Again, this means that we will have to take imperfect action to get better at it. This means—if we're lucky—we will receive feedback on our action's imperfections and discover something new about ourselves or the world around us. We must continue to remind ourselves that that is how we grow: take action, receive the feedback humbly, make repairs, and take more action.

Don't Go It Alone: Who Are Your Companions on Your Antiracist Path?

This is not an easy path to travel, especially at the start. As children, we are socialized by white supremacy not to see racism. And when we do see it, white supremacy wants to shut us up. So when we first speak up in antiracist ways, we can face sudden and intense criticism and even lose footing in our community. We also quickly realize how unknowledgeable and unskilled we are in racially stressful contexts. Those first conversations with White people about racism can feel so difficult and ineffective. We're not sure how to respond to those who insist that racism is a problem only for People of Color and Native people. And often when we commit to becoming antiracist—trying to find our role and balance in the conversation—we get the message that we're taking up too much space.

Once again, mainstream U.S. values of independence and competition don't help us here. We positively cannot do this work alone. The good news is that we don't have to. There are boundless resources online, and you probably already know people who are on an antiracist path or are itching to join. Sikh activist, filmmaker, and civil rights lawyer Valarie Kaur (2020) writes in her book *See No Stranger* that you need three companions on your antiracist journey:

1. Someone who sees the best in you

2. Someone who is willing to work with you (i.e., someone you can consult before you take action, someone you can debrief with after you have taken action or have gotten feedback, or someone who actually takes action with you)

3. Someone who fights for you (remember that antiracist action is always risky, so you might need someone to speak up on your behalf)

Kaur calls this collection of companions your "pocket of revolutionary love" (p. 98).

When I Take Action, I Do It for Myself

When we take antiracist action, we do it for ourselves as individuals, based on our empathy and values. Our empathy and values are a form of sustainable and clean fuel that will continue to motivate us and drive us forward in our practice. If we root our antiracist action in ego, performative action, or charity, we will quickly burn out and give up. Seeking recognition for taking antiracist action disconnects us from our fuel, distorts our aim, and is bound to sour our alliances. Operating from charity continues to replicate the savior dynamics that both come from and lead to power imbalances that preclude solidarity and mutuality. Our empathy and values also serve as our compass. We know we are cutting ourselves off from that fuel when we feel our anxiety rise and get the urge to ask others (especially People of Color and Native people) what we should do. The more we let ourselves see and feel in our guts how racism operates around us, the more obvious it becomes what is ours to do and why we do it for ourselves, too.

What's Mine to Do

Pushing through uncertainty can lead to successful outcomes. When my (Ali's) child came home from kindergarten with a pilgrim's hat on Thanksgiving, I decided to take action. I ordered about 10 children's books recommended by the American Indian Library Association, and I took them in to my child's teacher. I offered the books as resources, and I said that I didn't know exactly how to teach about Thanksgiving to kindergartners but that I wanted to make sure she had the resources for teaching not only from the colonizers' perspective. When it was clear that my intervention was not necessarily going to change much, except for a few meaningful read-alouds, I felt stuck. I didn't know what a kindergartener should be learning about Thanksgiving, but I was pretty sure they were not supposed to dress up like "Pilgrims and Indians."

Instead of pretending I knew what to do, I shifted to inquiry. I got together with colleagues to design a day in October called "UnColumbus Day." This was a day for teachers to get together and share lesson plans on how to rethink, reimagine, and retell the mainstream story of Columbus—which, as we know, rarely includes the truth about his violent and genocidal practices toward the Native people of the Americas. We now offer an UnColumbus Day every other year, and I always invite my children's teachers to join in. For the first several symposia, it was free for any teachers from our district. This has led to the production of materials for schools, blog posts, and conversations among teachers that are far-reaching. I have learned much more about what they could (arguably should) be teaching, while also creating a more robust vehicle for helping teachers learn; the intervention is bigger than just addressing my concern as a parent about what my own child is learning. It's about academic integrity, historical accuracy, and solidarity with Native people. The best part of these symposia tends to be the keynote, which usually includes a Native person who talks to us about how the mainstream history that erases their story has affected their personal lives.

While this is not the kind of intervention every dissatisfied parent can take, it's an example of using one's particular social networks, expertise, and skill sets to create an intervention that is bigger than just one parent and child.

How Do I Figure Out What Is Mine to Do?

The first step in selecting concrete antiracist actions is to distinguish what we might consider "lifestyle" actions (no different from brushing your teeth) from what is uniquely yours to do (e.g., being an educator). The first column in Figure 10.1 lists several lifestyle actions. Although we might not always be in a position to perform all of them, they don't require unique talents or spheres of influence. I (Eleonora) could vote once I became a U.S. citizen, and I could begin donating money to various organizations (e.g., the ACLU) once I graduated and started working full-time. I was also able to access healing for myself in different forms over the years, depending on resources and needs. With knowledge, self-awareness, and much practice, I have gotten better at noticing when I commit a microaggression, at speaking up, and at loving more wisely and widely across identities. However often you can perform lifestyle actions, these are intentions and activities you sprinkle throughout your life, for the rest of your life.

Figure 10.1 Menu of Antiracist Actions and Spheres of Influence

Anytime: It's a Lifestyle!	Pick *One:* Your Field	Pick *One:* Your Action
• Vote *always* (especially in local elections) • Donate money or services • Watch where you shop • Educate yourself • Engage with healing practices • Participate in protests • Practice witnessing and listening • Notice and make amends when you commit microaggressions • Access media run by People of Color and Native people • Practice speaking up and asserting boundaries • Practice loving wisely and widely	• Real estate • Mental health • Medicine • Education • Government • Environment • Voting rights • Finances • Service industry • Criminal justice • Mentoring youth • Foreign affairs • Photography • Coaching • Marketing	• Organizing • Creating art • Running for office • Cooking • Contacting a legislator • Volunteering • Writing • Speaking or educating • Hiring • Sitting on boards • Planning curriculum • Singing • Administrating • Publishing • Bodywork or fitness

It's helpful to distinguish these lifestyle actions from what you decide is uniquely yours to do. Remember that you are starting exactly where you are in terms of talents, space, and time. The second column in Figure 10.1 lists some areas you might work in or have a particular passion for. This is not by any means an exhaustive list. The point is to identify an area that deeply matters to you. It doesn't have to be something you are dedicating the rest of your life to, just what genuinely has inspired you to pick up this book or want to do more for racial justice. It might be an area directly related to your job or community, or it might be a growing interest outside those realms.

Finally, using the third column of Figure 10.1 as inspiration, you want to identify what you are good at or want to become good at. Remember that everyone is needed, and everything is needed. Pick something you feel truly called to offer, even if you are not fully clear how big of an impact you can have through it. White supremacy infiltrates all aspects of life, and so must our antiracist work. As you begin working with a specific action, you will discover more reasons why it's useful and more ways to connect it to racial justice.

While I (Eleonora) am an ineffective community organizer and have no legal or policymaking skills to speak of, I value both tremendously. So I decided that the types of organizations I donate money to will be ones that organize and design policies. I integrate supporting them financially into my lifestyle, rather than working directly within them. However, I do have specialized mental health training and a passion for education. So I have used my academic career to train multiculturally competent counselors, and I am using my current consulting work to share trauma-informed concepts and tools in support of individuals and communities trying to stay on an antiracist path. In my case, I decided to put antiracist practice front and center in my career. But that doesn't have to be the case for you to travel an antiracist path. Some of you might be financial advisers, others may work in daycare, and others may work in restaurants or the service industry. Again, there is no area of life where racism doesn't show up, which means there is no area of life that can't use your input. The more meaningful and closer to home the area you choose, the more practice you will have in recognizing how racism manifests in the systems you are most familiar with, and the easier it will be to know how you can make a difference exactly where you are, through what you do.

Campaigning Publicly

What's yours to do may involve speaking up at school board meetings for policies that will increase equity or using your position as a board member to encourage and support your organization in challenging policies and practices, such as hiring mostly White people or neglecting to recognize and serve the particular needs of your Clients of Color and Native clients. As I (Eleonora) described in my introduction, you may restructure your entire academic program over the course of 12 years. You might run for school board, public office, or the administration of your organization. Whatever you do, remember that the skills we have introduced throughout this book are applicable at any level. Knowing how to talk to other White people so that you don't shame them but instead invite them in will be more effective whether you're talking with your neighbor, your superintendent, your police chief, or your governor. Providing people with resources, support, and challenge will help them take informed and convicted action. Training for courage, finding an anchor within yourself, and practicing your actions beforehand will help you regardless of context. This book talks broadly about antiracism because the concept embodies so many possible actions. But remember that when you are advocating for change, you should advocate for specific policies that will have antiracist outcomes. Campaigning generally for antiracism tends to be unnecessarily confusing and polarizing, forcing people to choose sides depending on what they might associate with that term.

Remain in Empathetic Relationship With People of Color and Native People

The physiological work we have talked about throughout this book—the importance of noticing and deescalating our fight, flight, or freeze responses to see and understand racism—is foundational to figuring out how to take action. White people and People of Color and Native people in some sense live in parallel universes. While I (Eleonora) worked in academia, I became aware that my bosses responded quite differently to me than they did to People of Color among the faculty. I rarely witnessed that differential treatment, as I was rarely in the room when it happened, but I heard and felt the consequences of it when I was collaborating with my colleagues. Even when we shared bosses and as we shared the same campus, we might as well have worked in completely different settings with completely different administrations. And the most disorienting part was that there would have been absolutely no way for me to see that had I not worked closely with People of Color on campus and therefore heard about their experiences.

At the same time, it is often precisely hearing the truth about racism experienced by People of Color and Native people that sends us into fight, flight, or freeze mode. This is happening all over the United States right now. The *New York Times* (Epstein, 2021) reports that in Wausau, Wisconsin, the community has been engaged in deep conflict over the term *A Community for All*. Several People of Color in positions of leadership within the community encouraged the community to take a stance against racism in the wake of the murder of George Floyd. But the predominantly White town feels that the very discussion implies that they are being called racist and privileged, which they resent. In a town where most of the White people are working-class farmers and factory workers, they claim systemic racism doesn't exist there. They have clearly normalized white supremacist narratives such as individualism and competition. They have internalized the values that keep those narratives in place and are bumping up against the shame of moral injury, as well as the anxiety of stereotype threat. But while they deny the existence of racism, their fellow citizens who are People of Color and Native people are receiving racialized death threats and racist hate mail for their public actions. This situation has fight, flight, or freeze written all over it. The White townspeople cannot hear the reality of what is happening to the People of Color and Native people who live near them. And while they repeatedly assert that they are not racist, their assertions only contribute to the noise that renders it impossible to hear the actual reports of racism that their neighbors are trying to tell them about.

In this case, People of Color and Native people are being drowned out not just by the protestations of non-racism but also by certain national cable "news" channels, such as Fox News, which have heightened the fears of the White neighbors and convinced them that antiracism means communism or that their land will be taken away and redistributed.

It's easy to look at this situation as a White person and think, "I would never do that. I would listen. I would act." But this situation repeats itself in ways large and small on a daily basis in our society. Fight, flight, or freeze is activated when listening to the reality of People of Color and Native people threatens the story that we tell about ourselves as White people. It threatens our good intention and our integrity. It threatens our vision of the fair world we wish we lived in. When we are able to remain in empathetic connection with People of Color and Native people—when we are able to override the fight, flight, or freeze response—our action becomes clear.

Part of taking antiracist action means that we have to engage with the fears and concerns of White people who resist our actions, which is why it's essential that we know how to talk to and respond to White people, including White people whose fears are being magnified and distorted by news agencies or politicians whose agendas are elevated by division and fear.

Is This Just More Navel-Gazing?

Sometimes we imagine that people will read this book and wonder, "Won't that approach just create a bunch of navel-gazing White people? How will coddling White people bring about change?" As we hope our book has made clear, there is no way to bypass our human bodies. There is no way to circumvent our bodies' propensity to keep us safe. So navel-gazing and action are two sides of the same coin. You can act only to the extent that you successfully hold and heal yourself. You have to do your internal work to take action. There is no other way.

Here is an example of what that looks like in practice:

In summer 2021, I (Ali) worked with two White educators, both of whom had been named on their schools' Black@ Instagram feeds, in which Black students, families, and alums had written about the traumas they endured as Black students in predominantly White institutions. One, who had previously been a dean of students, was devastated by the feedback. He thought he was a conscious, antiracist teacher, and the feedback he received suggested he had actually hurt Black students. He felt it would be best for him to leave his school and to leave teaching altogether. I, along with several other friends and colleagues he had tapped for support, encouraged him to see that his was a flight reaction and to keep listening, to keep accessing support, and to hear what his former students were trying to tell him. By the end of the summer, he had taken in the feedback, engaged in dozens of conversations, and created a clear plan for how he wanted to change his teaching practice going forward. The feedback he received had the potential to make him more like the teacher he thought he had been, the one he wanted to be. And he could model that for others. Staying open and in connection enabled him to change his practice for the better. Through overcoming his flight response and staying in empathetic connection, his actions became clear.

Another teacher was named in her school's Black@ Instagram feed in the same way. She was enraged. She was sure that there was a movement designed to remove her from her position. She assumed that all the feedback was generated exclusively to make her look bad. She gave it no credence and no attention. She cut herself off from the Black students who were offering feedback. Hers was a fight response, but she wasn't able to recognize it as such. She perceived her interpretation of the situation as an accurate assessment of reality. And while this person might still ask in the coming years what she could do to better support her Black students, she may never realize that she cut herself off from that very knowledge when she went into a fight response rather than hearing the feedback from students. And until she does actually hear how her Black students experience school, any action she will take will be pure guesswork, based on her own experience. And that's a problem.

The Black@ movement was incredibly important in the movement for Black lives. Black people were able to speak openly and honestly about the trauma they have endured in their experiences of school. Yet in the year following the start of the Black@ movement, I (Ali) worked with several White teachers who were afraid of being named publicly and who feared that any mistake they might make in talking about race would be posted on social media. When talking to these teachers, I encouraged them to remember to notice and then work not to succumb to their fight, flight, or freeze reactions and to continue to stay open to what students are telling them.

The Black@ movement was also a shift in how feedback gets delivered to teachers and schools. It had to happen the way it did because for too long, Black students and their families have not had ways to give schools feedback that was both anonymous and taken seriously. Now, it's up to schools to create intentional online, anonymous, easy-to-access methods for children and families to register their concerns in a way that ensures they will get heard and acted on. At the same time, preparing teachers to take in the feedback requires that administrators give them permission to embrace a growth mindset and stay open to learning from mistakes. This is what makes it possible for the voices and experiences of Students of Color and Native students to rise freely, without becoming censured, drowned out, ignored, or gaslighted.

How Do We Grieve Together?

A White man who works at a college recently told me (Ali) about a vigil he had attended for the Asian and Asian American victims of racial violence in Atlanta in 2021. Members of the impacted community spoke. As he listened, he felt compelled to speak, to let members of the community know they were not alone, to claim some responsibility as a White person. But he didn't want to take up space, he didn't want to trigger people, and he felt that his comments would elicit offense, because he was White. I was not there, so it's possible that his reading of the situation was correct. Either way, I can relate to this feeling that no matter what I say, it will be wrong . . . because I'm White. And while this sentiment comes from a sensitivity that we need to cultivate to be effective allies, it also has a way of silencing us at the precise moments when our voices are needed.

What would it look like to take up too much space in that situation? Taking up too much space would involve eclipsing or contradicting the voices of the people in mourning. It would mean suggesting that you know exactly what they are feeling. It could mean philosophizing or even legitimizing the reasons for the violence. It could mean centering oneself, whether it be one's allyship, one's grief, one's guilt, one's questions, one's beliefs, or one's responsibility. It might mean intellectualizing by talking about policy changes and gun-law reform, rather than being in the grief. All these actions would likely be an unwelcome use of space at a vigil.

But consider that in attending a vigil, you are essentially at a funeral. You want to honor the family of those who have died. You want them to know they are not alone. You want to shoulder some of the grief and bear witness. And you can do this by listening and actively participating in the rituals performed. You can do this by taking in and really hearing what people are saying. You can do this by sharing your feelings and respect for the community. When a White person, particularly a White man, speaks up to give voice to vulnerable feelings, he is using space in a way that is atypical and usually welcome. Using space in this way is not the same as taking up space, because it is consciously intended to foster grieving and bear witness while being contrary to how many White men have been socialized to show up in public.

If a tragic event moves you to want to take action or do something, make an internal commitment to do so. You don't have to announce your action or even have your action recognized. If you think it would be a relief for people to hear that action is coming from this experience, then share it. But remember that grief is a profoundly human, natural, and healthy reaction to loss. It actually causes harm to attempt to heal or take away people's grief. You don't need to fix anything.

But you can be with those who grieve, and you can grieve with them. Almost inevitably, simply allowing ourselves to be moved by that grief—and to be in empathetic connection to those who are mourning—will not only support others but also compel us to take appropriate action. It is when we intellectualize to avoid grieving—or blow hot air about ourselves to avoid recognizing our responsibility or to seek absolution—that we block ourselves from the empathetic connection we need to determine what is ours to do. That is when we take up space and at the same time cut ourselves off from the very feelings that could guide our next steps.

In the vigil scenario, there was no single correct response. The White man's saying something grounded in his Jewish tradition might have contributed to the collective process of grieving or witnessing. Being present and staying quiet could have been just as valuable. How do you know for sure what will be most useful to the situation? You don't. And while asking that question is a worthy intention to hold, a fixation on there being a right answer or a most useful response means you have begun to focus on the wrong aim. This desire for rightness will most likely activate your stereotype threat, making you anxious and thus less able to empathize—and so much less clear about what to do. First and foremost, you must *feel with* those around you and let your empathy, not your striving or anxiety, be your guide.

I (Ali) can remember in June 2020 when a Black colleague posted to Facebook, "Black Lives Matters signs are in the lawns up and down my street, but not a single one of my neighbors knows my name." Around the same time, another Black friend wrote, "Everyone I work with says 'Black Lives Matter' on Facebook, but no one has called to see how I'm doing." When I first read these posts, to be perfectly honest, I felt put off. I went into fight mode. In my head, I thought, "Do they really think I'm going to call every single Black person I know and see how they're doing?"

After a few moments of fight, I thought back to my friend who said no one had checked on her. I thought of her in her apartment, alone, four months into an isolating pandemic, overwhelmed by an online teaching load, scared and grieving for George Floyd, grieving for family affected by COVID, and scared for friends joining the protests. How could I not call and check in? It was actually such a gift that she made herself vulnerable enough to let people know that she wanted a check-in.

And even though I felt sheepish reaching out to her just after she had publicly announced that her community (myself included) had let her down, I figured something was better than nothing. After connecting with her, I thought of other Black friends and neighbors and colleagues, what COVID might have been like for each of them, how George Floyd's death might have affected them. I held them one by one in my heart and then wrote emails, made phone calls, sent texts, and wrote cards.[1] Days later, I'd remember someone I'd forgotten and write to them. While trying to decide what to write, I reminded myself that people are grieving. When people are grieving, you can't fix what they are going through. You can just be with them as they go through it.

Before I started reaching out to people I knew and loved, I really struggled with the question, "What should I do?" It wasn't until I took time to be in the grief with my Black friends and colleagues that my own action steps became clear. Being in the grief helped me realize the gravity of the situation—and my relative smallness within it. I don't think anyone in the world was wondering, "What will Ali Michael do?" In the big scheme of things, what I did or didn't do wouldn't change police behavior. But reading about the dismay of my colleague on Facebook—and being in emotional connection with her—shifted my gaze from abstract thoughts about policing to the immediate sense that I belong to a place, to a community, to people. What I do matters because I belong to an interdependent community made of mutually caring connections, and my community was grieving. Connecting more personally with that grief helped me recommit to take action. I also heard White people yearning to engage at a deeper level but unsure about how to do that. That was when I began offering monthly coaching sessions for White people who wanted to be a part of White antiracist learning spaces. I contributed the proceeds of these workshops to COVID-relief efforts in Black areas of Philadelphia and South Africa.

Why was the murder of George Floyd so different from so many murders of Black people before him? Why was the reaction from White people so different than it had been before? George Floyd died at a time when the entire country was stilled by the pandemic. There were fewer distractions, fewer ways to get away from it all. For some of us, it was seeing a human being brutally tortured and ultimately murdered, on camera, by individuals sanctioned by our own government. For others, it was resonating with the grief and rage of friends and colleagues. For others yet, it was the energy of the protests sweeping towns and cities globally for months. Something happened to many of us in unprecedented numbers. We felt it: terror, sadness, and outrage. The question then became what do to with those feelings, and for White people, that quickly became complicated. When we see racism clearly, we can't help but know that we are implicated. And that realization makes us question our right to truly feel the horror of what happened or take up space to process it, since it hasn't happened to us. This is such a salient reminder of how wholly we have internalized racial divides. For many Black Americans, it was easy to feel as if George Floyd was a kinsman—a brother, husband, child, uncle, or cousin. If it weren't for racism, everybody could feel that way. Antiracism means finding ways to feel connected to George Floyd and to the injustice of his death. However we end up coming into contact with our grief around racism, we must be able to recognize it as grief and let it work on us. That very intention humanizes us. That very process breaks the delusion that there is an "us" and "them." We must work with our grief while recognizing that we are implicated in what has created it. It doesn't work to do just one or the other. We can't flip-flop between the two; we have to do both.

White culture doesn't give White people much permission to grieve, let alone a roadmap for grief. We don't know how to welcome one another's grief, nor do most of us have rituals and dedicated spaces for processing it. We have even less space when our grief is about racism. But finding these communal spaces is essential because grief is not something we can process on our own. The White man who attended the vigil understood that being present and bearing witness was important to honor the grief in the Asian American community he was connected to. What he struggled with, however, was how much of his own grief he was allowed to feel and where it was appropriate for him to share it and process it. His experience is far from unique among White people. Many of us feel out of place at such vigils and rarely—if ever—have a chance to process our grief about racism with other White people.

The Circle of Grief[2] offers a helpful roadmap. The model uses concentric circles, in which the loss marks the center of the circles, and each concentric circle around that loss represents greater distance from the loss. The idea is to process one's grief in its rawest form with people who are further away from the center of the grief. So, for example, if your friend's husband dies, and you are sad about his death, you are not going to share the rawness of your sadness with your friend. You want to hold her sadness, anger, guilt, frustration—whatever she's experiencing—without shutting down or centering your own feelings. And for that to even be possible, you must have an external space to process the rawness of your own grief, sadness, rage, and frustration. That way, when you are with your friend, you can cry and mourn *with* her but not fall apart or ask her to hold space for *you*.

When it comes to the death of George Floyd, arguably every Black person I (Ali) know was closer to the center of grief than I was, even though they did not know him. Yet I had a lot of questions about his death that I needed to process, not least how to talk about it with my children. I started sharing this dilemma with a neighbor while we were out walking.

But it quickly occurred to me that her children were biracial and that she was closer to the center of grief than I was. So I pivoted and asked how she was doing with all of it—not shutting out my feelings but not centering them, either. I could work through the fullness of my question later with other White allies. Would it have been wrong for me to talk with her about it? Not necessarily; it is relationship- and context-dependent. But this guideline helped me navigate the question in a way that allowed me to focus on her first and keep my own experience in perspective.

This is why it is essential that we create spaces for us as White people to process and grieve racism. This means doing for one another what my White colleague did at the vigil. Offer our presence, witness one another's feelings, not fix, not rush to solutions, not judge one another, and not compete for activism points by privileging a specific way of feeling or reacting over another. The challenge is not that grieving is a complicated process. Grieving is completely natural; it has its own course and process, and it's not something we have to "do." But therein lies the challenge. Can we create collective spaces where grief can just exist—spaces where we can simply be present with it, validate it, and bear witness to it? If we want to truly understand what racism is, we must feel the awfulness of it. And to feel it, we must have the capacity to grieve it.

Is It Okay to Have a Black Lives Matter Lawn Sign?

Sometimes people go back and forth on the lawn sign or the T-shirt, be it BLACK LIVES MATTER or WE SUPPORT OUR ASIAN AMERICAN NEIGHBORS or something else. Is it our job to bring race into the situation, if People of Color and Native people don't want it there? Are we agitating people more by putting up the sign? We want to honor the consideration people might bring to these questions and encourage you to go ahead and wear the shirt or post the sign that lets people know where you stand. In *Radical Dharma: Talking Race, Love, and Liberation*, Rev. angel Kyodo williams and her co-authors invite us to show our love in public (williams et al., 2016). Just as with everything else, consider whether you are wearing the shirt to be performative or to posture—or do you want that message to be out in the world?

There are schools that have created T-shirts with pro-Black messages such as BLACK HISTORY IS WORLD HISTORY, and when their teachers and students wear those shirts, they promote both the message and the school to the world. I (Ali) often wear Black Lives Matter clothes to my almost all-White gym because I want to interrupt the norms of Whiteness in that space. I also wear T-shirts affirming LGBTQ+ rights to interrupt norms around heteronormativity. For my birthday, I asked my children to give me T-shirts with messages on them that they want the world to hear. One child gave me a trans-affirming shirt that says Support Your Sisters, Not Just Your Cis-ters, while the other gave me one that says Save the Sumatran Rhino. I want to model what it looks like to show love in public—and I want them to know that the things they care about are important to me, too.

Ultimately, as you make these decisions for yourself, lead with love and remember the both/and rule. There won't be a monolithic Person of Color or Native person who will either approve or disapprove of your choice of apparel or lawn art. Balance the authentic with the intentional and show your love from that place.

The Rules Are Guidelines, Not Absolutes

In light of what Ali just shared, what about "White women's tears"? There are certain rules in antiracism circles that dictate good behavior: If you're a White woman, don't cry. If you're a White person, don't take up too much space. If you're White, don't design programming for People of Color and Native people that could be construed as charity. Don't mispronounce a person's name. All these rules are meant to help us create a more inclusive, more racially equitable society. They are meant to help us be in community with one another. But too often, because of the way we treat them as unbendable rules rather than guidelines based on undesirable trends, we end up acting like unempathetic automatons who are too busy mentally calculating the rightness or wrongness of a given action to trust—and act from—our guts.

In an effort to follow the rules of antiracism, White people have side-lined our feelings, our empathy, our capacity for connection . . . in short, our authenticity. Yet our capacity to take antiracist action depends on our ongoing ability to stay in touch with our guts, to honor our feelings, to remain in empathetic connection with People of Color and Native people, and to be motivated by relationships.

When we attempt to do the right thing in the absence of considering how our nervous system works, we end up trapped in an impossible task. Feel, but not too much. Be authentic, but only to the extent that it helps you do and say the "right" thing. Many White people don't have clear avenues where we can feel things out as we learn how to enter spaces in antiracist ways. The result is that for the most part, we take the rules we are given to try to feel in just the right way, to just the appropriate extent—which, of course, becomes more performative than authentic. Meanwhile, simply looking empathetic doesn't actually end up offering us the guidance that our authentic feelings would. We swing on a pendulum from feeling too little and asking others to tell us what to do, to feeling too much all at once and asking others to take care of us. It's an exhausting roller-coaster ride for all involved.

The usefulness of the rules mentioned in this chapter comes from the fact that they give us strategies to manage our internal reactions in the moment, thus allowing the conversation to continue without being derailed (e.g., "If I cry now, I will become the focus of this workshop and conversation, so I must hold myself steady"). However, because they are solutions to symptoms, not causes, even when we manage to enlist our nervous system in following them, they don't yield long-term solutions. In and of themselves they don't facilitate long-term growth. They can still be helpful to guide our actions in the moment. Often, we don't even realize we are in a fight, flight, or freeze state until we see ourselves fitting the very behavioral pattens we read about. But after the moment passes, with support, we have to tend to the origins of what led to our fight, flight, or freeze reaction, or there will be no real progress.

The case of White women's tears is particularly salient in this context. Racism is horrifying. It would only make sense to cry and feel sad about it. But the rule against White women's tears came about because all too predictably, in workshops on race, a White woman's feelings can derail the conversation and activate rescuing behaviors in other participants.

White women's ability to get in touch with the enormity of the pain caused by racism almost inevitably connects to their own unprocessed pain as women. This is the case not only because it's impossible for anyone to go through life without a certain amount of disappointment or hardship but also because it's not uncommon for White women to have experienced traumas *because* they are women. So when we hear about racism, many women can quickly emotionally resonate. And if they haven't healed around their own traumas, hearing the impact of racism can overwhelm them, to a point where they are no longer able to make space to hear about the experiences of People of Color and Native people.

This problem is only exacerbated by the fact that White people are taught that racism doesn't concern us, so we tend to be caught by surprise when we truly see it. Most of us don't seamlessly and naturally process our own feelings in a consistent way, and our own hurts might get poked by what we hear. When we finally feel it all, the intensity of it floods us. How we manage the flooding, then, falls back on our socialization. The combination of (1) having been trained to make our own needs and feelings primary, (2) having few if any spaces to process our burgeoning awareness around racism, and (3) the possibility of having been given gender training around helplessness and powerlessness makes us panic and sucks all the oxygen out of the room. In the antiracism workshop I (Eleonora) mentioned in earlier sections of the book, a White woman tearfully shared at length her sorrow of being abandoned as a child, and a White man repeatedly brought up his experiences of social rejection as a young adult. On the outside, to a cynical onlooker (me), these behaviors can seem manipulative and exasperating, as their sharing distracted from the topic of the conversation, which was racism and antiracist action. But on the inside, how could leaning into racism's true effects *not* resonate with those traumas? Antiracist education does not usually include predicting how such learning will likely activate us, but it could. We could learn how to tend to it in respectful, appropriate, timely, and effective ways. This kind of response in White people is predictable, yet we are rarely prepared for it.

The confusing messages around feeling and remaining authentic are pervasive. In many antiracist trainings, I (Eleonora) have been taught in no uncertain terms that as a White person, I cannot possibly know how a Person of Color or Native person feels, since I don't experience racism directly. This is another rule of antiracism I have taken to heart, modeled, and passed along to others over the years—until recently. After the murder of George Floyd, many psychological and counseling organizations began offering trainings on racial injustice and racial trauma. The topic went from fringe to central in the span of weeks. In one of these trainings, clinical psychologist Dr. Gail Parker said:

> One of the mistakes that White people tend to make when they talk about [racism is saying,] "I cannot possibly know what it is like to be you." That's an invalidating remark. If a client came into your office and told you their story, would you say to them, "Well, I can't possibly know what it's like to be you?" No, you would not, not if you are a good therapist. Because you would understand that this shuts down the conversation; it interrupts the relationship, the connection. (Butler et al., 2020)

Counselor Dr. S. Kent Butler joined right in: "That is an invalidation when you say you can't imagine. . . . I've started to tell people yes, you can imagine. You don't want to imagine, because we can all imagine what that's like" (Butler et al., 2020). When I heard that, for the first time, I tuned into the subtle relief I have been experiencing since adopting this "I can't possibly understand" rule. Because while it still rings very true that as a person living in a White body, I am not responded to in ways that would give me a fully accurate experience of what a Person of Color or Native person goes through, I do know what shame, put-downs, invalidation, and terror feel like in my body. It is uncomfortable to intentionally access those feelings as I attempt to more fully empathize with how People of Color and Native people experience racism. Yet I can't get proximal (using the words of Bryan Stevenson, 2015) without doing that.

So we must imagine; we must feel. That means that antiracist action involves, without question, tending to and healing our own pain that inevitably arises in the process. We must expect strong feelings to emerge throughout our antiracist journeys, and we must identify appropriate resources and spaces to work through them. This is also what it means to be antiracist.

Balance *Chutzpah* and Humility

A colleague who is a White male clergyperson at a religious school recently asked me (Ali) how he could take a stand for racial equity and help White students at his school learn, without taking up too much space as a White person. He said he feels like the best way for him to be an effective antiracist is to be humble, but when it comes to modeling antiracist learning and behavior for his White students, he wants to be more external and visible than his introverted, humble approach tends to allow. This is a problem I have struggled with over time. A friend watched me deliver a keynote at a conference several years ago. When it was over, she said to me, "You are so humble. And that is so valuable in a White person who is trying to be antiracist. But they asked you to give the keynote. Clearly, they think you know what you're talking about. I think you need to have more swagger." Swagger? I wasn't sure what that would look like on me, but I understood what she meant. Since then, I've been trying to figure out what it looks like to have both humility and swagger.

One of the things that has helped me think about the both/and dynamic of having both humility and swagger is my own participation on panels. I generally dislike speaking on panels. It often takes a lot of effort and time to travel to the place, to then have just a few minutes to share what I think. And it must be clear to you by now that I have a lot to say! Because I'm usually on panels about race, I'm often the only White person on the panel. In that case, one of the most important contributions I can make to the panel is to make sure People of Color and Native people have the chance to get their voices heard and not take up space by talking over them or undermining their contributions. At the same time, I am usually asked to be on the panel for a reason. And there are always a whole lot of White people in the audience who will likely benefit from what I have to say. It would be useless for me to bow out of the conversation altogether out of deference to the voices of People of Color and Native people. And frankly, it would not be deferential; it would be false.

When I'm on a panel, I speak when I'm called on. I also speak when it's my turn (usually I go last, unless one of the other participants has asked me to speak before them). I do a lot of listening, and I engage nonverbally. When I speak, I try to connect to what the other panelists are saying in a way that will help White audience members see the bridge to their own lives as White people. I try to listen to what the other panelists say, to learn from it, to be challenged by it, and to share honestly in ways that help people take it in. By showing up in community, in collaboration, with what I've got to offer, I bring humility and swagger. When I speak, I speak confidently, thoughtfully, and with a willingness to be wrong or to accept feedback. Eleonora calls this "humble confidence."

This is a tangible illustration of what it looks like to show up with both humility and swagger, or what my rabbi calls humility and *chutzpah*. The other way I do it is by remembering that my goal is not to show up looking good or right. I had to do this repeatedly throughout the process of editing a book with Black colleagues, during which I often did not agree with our collective choices. In that process, I tried to keep showing up with support and deference for my colleagues, while also being honest about my questions and concerns. I didn't want to undermine their expertise, but at the same time, I didn't want to disrespect them by staying quiet and having little to contribute. I let go of trying to be right or trying to act perfect; I opted instead just to keep being real. It's effective to focus on being real rather than good because it's the same technique psychologists use to counteract stereotype threat. I root my presence in my values and my goals, which are about something bigger than me and my ego. It's easier to act boldly when the goal of my action is to make space for all people in my community to be more fully themselves, to be treated as full human beings. How could I not pursue that goal with audacity and energy, or with *chutzpah* and swagger?

Conclusion

When White people become aware of how Whiteness has historically meant oppression, we often drop our agency. We tend to sink into thinking "I'm terrible" and "What right do I have to take up all this space?" We are human beings. We are going to take up space. We don't have to do that from a place of demoralized self-flagellation. We can do that proactively and consciously, with an intention to connect, with justice as our goal. And we can use the space we're granted to create more space for others.

As hard as antiracist practice is, as much loss as it sometimes entails, it also creates authentic, liberated, full-bodied joy. Our constant fear and suspicion of one another and our incessant flight, fight, or freeze reactions take so much emotional space while narrowing our lives in ways we don't even realize. Part of the joy of an antiracist practice comes from alleviating the effort it takes to live with that. We have found that having an antiracist practice has freed us from living with a certain amount of guilt, anxiety, fear, and confusion. It makes it possible to participate in the world from a place of clarity, by seeing the system involved and understanding that there is work for you to do here—but also knowing that it's not only your work. It helps you see that you are not alone in this work or in this practice—that in stepping onto an antiracist path, you join millions of people of all racial backgrounds who came before you and walk alongside you.

The joy of unlearning racism is about being able to show up fully. It comes from being rooted and accountable in your relationships, which leads to a whole new level of care, communication, and community. Each step you take on your antiracist path will open you up to beautiful connections and a fullness of life. These may be subtle at first. The specific antiracist practice here is to notice and savor the moments of genuine relationship. Breathe into them, and use the feeling of rootedness and interdependence that comes from them as fuel down the road when you feel discouraged.

Remember that there's no way to know the answers in advance. This is a practice—a daily, weekly, lifelong practice. Keep showing up. Stay humble. Bring your true self, which is creative and wise, to the table. Trust the process. Move forward confidently and keep working with your fear of being wrong—because you will be wrong at times. Respond to and grow from feedback in the moment. When we get anxious, we say to ourselves, "You don't get to solve racism today, but what you do matters. Just show up and give what you have to offer." Make it possible for others to share what they know. Take in feedback. Learn from mistakes. Don't try to go it alone. Find a traveling buddy, a team, or a group of people with whom you can move along the path, and support them. Accept their company and companionship.

Keep going.

Notes

1. I have seen this type of action in TV shows that revisit the summer of 2020, with COVID and the murder of George Floyd incorporated as life events navigated by the characters. In the second season of *Love Life*, the main character, Marcus, gets superficial texts of faux support from his boss, who otherwise takes him for granted. I became embarrassed when I saw this, feeling like my outreach to friends and colleagues was cliché and overwrought. But any acknowledgment of grief will ring hollow when it is exercised as a mere courtesy or in the context of general disrespect. The point is not to send notes to every Black person you ever met. The point is to acknowledge that many of your Black friends and colleagues are experiencing complicated grief—akin to a death in the family—combined with vicarious trauma. It is trauma that comes with being Black

in a society where anti-Black violence is so often ignored or condoned—and therefore places those people at risk for similar violence. Reach out supportively and thoughtfully—where appropriate—in the context of your particular relationships. And know that just like with any other grief, you won't fix it. You will simply offer your company, acknowledgment, and support as they move through it.

2. The Circle of Grief, or Ring Theory, is a framework designed by psychologists Susan Silk and Barry Goldman (2013) and introduced to me (Ali) as an antiracism tool by my co-instructor in the USC Equity Institutes, Colleen Lewis.

Appendix A

Common Unproductive, Possibly Biased Behaviors of Some/Many White People That Perpetuate Racist Dynamics and Structural Racism

Source: Compiled by and reprinted with permission from Kathy Obear, www.drkathyobear.com.

I am deeply grateful for the input and feedback from white colleagues over the years, especially those who sent edits on early drafts: Beth Yohe, Beth Douthirt Cohen, Regan Mancini, Jayne Williams, Jen Murray, and Elizabeth Traynor.

Directions:

As you review each of the following statements:

a. Check off any dynamics and behaviors you have observed from white people.

b. Circle the number of any that you have personally done at any time in your life.

c. Add any additional common behaviors that perpetuate racist dynamics and organizational racism you have witnessed, experienced, or done.

Some/Many White People Tend to (Consciously and Unconsciously):

1. Interrupt and talk over People of Color in meetings and casual conversations more frequently than white colleagues.

2. Minimize, undervalue, ignore, overlook, and discount the talents, competencies, and contributions of People of Color.

3. Rephrase and reword the comments of People of Color much more frequently than those of white colleagues.

4. Ask People of Color to repeat what they have just said far more often than white colleagues.

5. Question, challenge, and doubt the validity and credibility of what People of Color say far more often than with white colleagues.

6. Require and demand "proof" if People of Color raise concerns about racist dynamics.

7. Question and undermine the authority of leaders of color; resent taking direction from a Person of Color.

8. Not follow the direction of leaders, managers, and facilitators of color.

9. Walk on eggshells and act more hesitant, distant, and formal with People of Color; feel uncomfortable and nervous and do not develop the same depth of effective working relationships for fear of saying or doing something racist.

10. When asked to examine the impact of their behavior, get defensive and argue their "good intent" rather than explore the negative racist impact of their action or inaction.

11. Focus on how much progress has been made, rather than on how much more needs to change.

12. Diminish and downplay the reality of recent racist behaviors and incidents by expressing shock and dismay (e.g., "I can't believe this is still happening in _____ [year]") to avoid further exploration of the negative impact on People of Color.

13. Respond impatiently when People of Color raise concerns and issues of race; move on quickly to another topic.

14. Get defensive when People of Color express their frustrations with current organizational and societal dynamics.

15. Get angry if People of Color don't enthusiastically appreciate when white people are trying to "help them."

16. Engage in "tone policing" of People of Color by pressuring them to "soften their tone," to not be so emotional and angry, to smile and be nice, to be more "professional," etc.

17. Make racist comments during hiring practices ("We have to hire a Person of Color, regardless of their qualifications"; "We need to find more qualified People of Color"; "They won't be a good fit here"; "They won't stay"; "They were too aggressive in their comments"; "They seemed to have an attitude"; "All they talked about was race"; "They don't have the right degree or the right experience for this job"; "I'm not sure about their research focus"; etc.).

18. Try to teach People of Color about racism (i.e., whitesplaining).

19. Play the white savior by trying to "help" People of Color, giving unsolicited advice, and rushing to fix and solve issues on their own "for People of Color."

20. Proclaim, "I'm not racist!" while refusing to acknowledge the patterns of interpersonal, cultural, and institutional racism People of Color experience daily.

21. Rationalize away racist treatment of People of Color as individual racist incidents, a misunderstanding, or the result of something a Person of Color did or failed to do.

22. Refuse to recognize racist dynamics and dismiss the racist experiences of People of Color with comments such as "That happens to me too . . ."; "You're too sensitive . . ."; or "That happened because of _____; it has nothing to do with race!"

23. Look to and demand their colleagues of color be the "diversity expert" and take the lead in raising and addressing racism as their "second (unpaid) job."

24. Seek and/or demand approval, validation, and recognition from People of Color.

25. After a meeting, tell People of Color how awful something was but don't do anything to actually address the microaggression or problematic behavior in the moment or afterward with the person responsible.

26. Refuse to acknowledge or continue to minimize the devastating emotional labor and racial trauma their colleagues of color experience in the organization and in society.

27. Dismiss what People of Color say; accept the same types of comments as valid when stated by a white person.

28. Look to a white person to validate the comments and ideas of a Person of Color.

29. Look to People of Color (especially when it is not within a paid-position description or outlined within the person's job responsibilities and duties) for direction, education, and coaching on how to act and what not to do related to any issue of race or racial equity.

30. Discount, critique, question, and outright ignore the insights, coaching, and direction from People of Color in leadership roles related to racial equity.

31. Say they support racial equity while still perpetuating and/or ignoring racist dynamics, policies, and practices; focus on being perceived as the "good white person" versus addressing racism; act in a performative way.

32. Believe they are already "woke" (effective allies/accomplices) and resist further education and accountability.

33. When asked to examine their white privilege, get defensive and use perfectly logical explanations (PLEs) and justifications for remaining in resistance.

34. Assume the white teacher/coach/facilitator/employee/etc. is in charge or a competent leader; assume People of Color are in service and support roles.

35. Seem surprised when a Person of Color makes a useful comment or offers an insightful idea, calling them "articulate."

36. Not notice, not acknowledge, or outright ignore the daily racist indignities and microaggressions that People of Color experience.

37. Use PLEs to minimize, dismiss, and rationalize any racist microaggressions or other racist dynamics.

38. Dismiss and minimize the frustrations of People of Color and categorize the person raising issues as aggressive, angry, having an "attitude," working their agenda, not a team player, unprofessional, etc.

39. Judge and critique People of Color as overreacting, too emotional, extreme in their reactions, and unprofessional when they are responding to the cumulative impact of racist incidents.

40. Accuse People of Color of "playing the race card" whenever they challenge racist policies and practices; refuse to explore the probability of negative differential impact based on race or how racist attitudes and beliefs are operating in the dynamic.

41. If confronted by a Person of Color, shut down and focus on what to avoid saying or doing in the future, rather than engaging and learning from the interaction.

42. If confronted by a Person of Color, view it as an "attack" and focus on and critique *how* they engaged, not the original problematic comments or behaviors.

43. If confronted by a Person of Color, use tears to distract from the conversation and recenter themselves to avoid accountability.

44. Disengage when they feel any anxiety or discomfort; blame People of Color if they feel uncomfortable.

45. Demand to always feel comfortable and have "safe space" when talking about issues of race; avoid conflict and seek harmony above truthful conversations about race/racism.

46. Profess feelings of deep guilt and shame without taking meaningful action to interrupt racist attitudes, behaviors, policies, and practices.

47. Defend white colleagues who are confronted about the racist impact of their behavior with comments such as "He's a good guy and would never mean that and would never do that"; "She has biracial kids"; "They're married to a Black person"; "He is part Native American!"; or "You must have misunderstood."

48. Work to maintain the status quo and protect the advantages and privileges they receive as a white person.

49. Believe and insist they know what is best for others and, given their power and privileged status, feel they are entitled to make decisions without inclusive input of those impacted or charged with implementing them.

50. Create, maintain, and enforce work environments based on white cultural norms, practices, and values.

51. Insist there is one "right" way, meaning "my way" or the "white way."

52. Claim to not know how to consistently use or outright refuse or fail to consistently use a Race Lens in decision-making and planning to create greater racial equity.

53. Claim to not know how to consistently use or outright refuse to consistently use a Race Lens to analyze and revise current practices, policies, programs, norms, and services to create greater racial equity.

54. Give white colleagues continuous coaching and developmental feedback to help them be successful, often with the thought that "they remind me of myself"; fail to develop effective coaching relationships with People of Color or give useful, timely developmental feedback.

55. Critique the comments and behaviors of People of Color and discipline them far more often, more quickly, and more severely than white colleagues.

56. Give white people the benefit of the doubt if they make a misstep; hold People of Color to a far higher standard of performance.

57. Either make People of Color (and/or their labor) invisible or scrutinize them under a microscope.

58. Avoid giving direct feedback to colleagues of color and instead complain to a person's supervisor and/or gossip with white peers.

59. Make comments that reinforce and perpetuate racist stereotypes about People of Color.

60. When confronted about the racist impact of their comment, respond defensively with comments such as "That wasn't what I said!"; "I was only joking"; or "You misunderstood me!"

61. Positively comment much more often on the skills and achievements of white colleagues and overlook those of People of Color.

62. Only compliment People of Color on their appearance, hair, and articulate speech while praising white colleagues on their performance and demonstrated competence.

63. Attribute the work of individual People of Color to the whole team, yet single out individual white people for public recognition and appreciation for their contributions, even if achieved through teamwork.

64. Take credit for the work of People of Color on their team.

65. Critique and chastise People of Color who do not conform and assimilate to white cultural norms and practices (e.g., call them unprofessional).

66. Accept and feel safer around People of Color who have assimilated and are "closer to white."

67. Mentor, coach, sponsor, and promote People of Color they view as assimilated and "closer to white."

68. Refuse to acknowledge the existence of and cumulative impact of racist microaggressions.

69. Refuse to acknowledge the devastating, life-threatening impact of systemic racism.

70. Blame People of Color for the racist barriers and challenges they experience.

71. Segregate themselves from People of Color and rarely develop authentic relationships across race.

72. Call security or law enforcement to confront People of Color who are just going about their business or their daily lives; "weaponize" security or law enforcement when they feel People of Color don't belong where they are, shouldn't be doing what they are doing, etc.

73. Exaggerate the level of intimacy they have with individual People of Color.

74. Use credentialing to try to prove they are a "good white colleague," such as "My best friend is Black"; "I'm married to a Native American"; "I adopted a child from China"; "I majored in Latin American literature"; "I am bilingual in Spanish"; "My great-grandfather was Cherokee"; "I have researched and written about issues of race and racism all my life"; "I teach about race and racism"; "I am active in local antiracism organizations"; "I marched in Black Lives Matter protests"; "I have biracial children"; etc.

75. Pressure and punish white people who actively work to dismantle racism to conform to and collude with the status quo.

76. Criticize, gossip about, and find fault with white allies and change agents.

77. Compete with other whites to be "the good white": the best ally, the one People of Color let into their circle, etc.

78. If a white person does or says something racist, aggressively confront them and pile on the critical feedback to create distance from them and prove who is a better ally.

79. Avoid confronting other white people on their racist attitudes and behaviors ever and/or in the presence of People of Color.

Directions for Next Steps

a. Review all the racist dynamics **you have observed** and note: What are 3–5 ways you could effectively interrupt and engage these dynamics in the moment? Follow up afterward? Create changes to policies, practices, and norms that could minimize these occurring in future?

b. Choose 5–10 unproductive behaviors **you have done** and note: What could you have done instead that would have aligned with your core values and furthered organizational racial equity goals? When asked to examine the racist impact of your behaviors, how could you have engaged more effectively to hear the feedback and take responsibility for your impact?

Kathy Obear has many incredible resources, including an open-source course called *Navigating Difficult Situations*, which you can find at **drkathyobear.com/events**. To download a PDF of her book *Turn the Tide: Rise Above Toxic, Difficult Situations in the Workplace*, go to **drkathyobear.com/books**.

Appendix B

Examples of White Group-Level Behaviors/Privilege

....

Source: Compiled by and reprinted with permission from Lorraine Marino and Antje Mattheus, authors of the *White People Confronting Racism* manual.

The following are behaviors that people of color commonly experience from white people. These are identified as group-level because they are so commonly exhibited by white people and reflect white culture, privilege, and lack of awareness, even though exhibited by individuals. Lorraine gathered this material from colleagues of color who provided personal input, research summaries, and recurring themes from their professional experiences as trainers.

Avoiding areas, places, people, and relationships that are not predominantly white.

Colluding through silence. Not challenging racism or racial dynamics.

Consciously or unconsciously excluding persons of color in meetings, membership, input into decisions, processes, etc.

Consistently questioning the competence of a person of color— subtly or not so subtly. Over-questioning and making invasive inquiry toward people of color.

Defensive reaction to BIPOC feedback that challenges the self-image of the white person, especially whites who deem themselves as "already woke."

Developing or supporting curricula, cultures, art, music, readings, etc. that primarily reflect white culture.

Disassociating from one's white group identity; for example, when hearing examples of racism, saying, "Oh, I am not like that." Demeaning or putting down other whites who do not "get it." Overidentifying with BIPOC, not owning one's white group identity.

Dismissive, negating behavior through overt comments and reactions—or by not listening, not responding, or joking. Minimizing comments or feelings that are expressed.

Equating one's experience with the experience of a person of color. Thinking "we are all the same" across race, disregarding the power and ranking differences at the societal level. Believing that "we all have personal experiences that are painful, but race is not different than any other personal wounding."

Giving PLEs (perfectly logical explanations) for each individual incident or as a way to explain away any examples of racism a person of color provides. Focusing on individual incidents and not seeing patterns of repeated behavior or situations.

Interactive white flight. Withdrawing from an interaction altogether or changing the topic when a racial interaction becomes uncomfortable; intellectualizing an emotional issue or a BIPOC's emotional sharing. Meeting a heart-expression with the mind.

Lack of inquiry or willingness to talk about or learn about race differences. Tentativeness in raising the issues of race. Seeing the discussion of race as taboo.

Negating BIPOC's reality. For example, a BIPOC is asked to tell her experiences of racism; however, no examples seem valid enough to the white person. So the BIPOC is asked for more and more examples until the interaction minimizes her experience because there is no perfect example; she is worn out trying to "prove" her reality.

Not being sensitive to the risk involved for people of color to put out ideas, express feelings, etc. in a predominantly white environment. Acting as if there is equal risk and equal opportunity for everyone to say what's on their mind.

Not listening. Defending or explaining one's behavior without taking in feedback. Focusing only on one's intention, dismissing the impact and/or expecting the person of color to dismiss the impact.

Not noticing when and where there are only whites—for example, in decision-making processes and situations, input-gathering, leadership groups, etc.

Overriding the ideas of people of color or not taking them seriously. Talking more in groups; dominating; cutting off people of color; giving credit for ideas to whites though they might have come from a person of color.

Oversimplifying BIPOC reactions as their "being too angry," "being too sensitive," "being a victim," etc. without considering their experiences that we cannot see. Not considering one's own lack of awareness about race dynamics.

Reacting on an individual level. Wanting to be seen for one's individuality, even when behaving or getting feedback about a group-level behavior. Not seeing oneself as part of any group but just as "normal." Having discomfort at being identified as part of a white group; lack of awareness of group-level behaviors and their impact on people of color.

Saying "that happened to me, too," when people of color share negative experiences based on race; trying to equalize their experience with one's own.

Seeing racial conflict as arising from an individual personality or unresolved issue of a person of color. (The individual level does factor in how conflicts play out. However, this refers to a quickness in assuming it is about an individual's issues, personality, etc., and not about race.)

Setting norms in groups derived from white culture that people of color are expected to follow.

Taking unilateral action or making programs or campaigns without input from or partnership with people of color. Not seeking the expertise and points of view of BIPOC.

Tendency to direct, take charge, and act independently; for example, directing the course of decisions, determining the schedule of meetings and events, setting agendas, choosing meeting locations, etc. without BIPOC input or awareness or regard for the impact on them. Choosing locations for events and meetings that are primarily white; not considering the comfort level or access for BIPOC.

Tone policing. Asking BIPOC to use a "calmer," "more rational," "less angry," etc. tone of voice. Requiring the white norm of rational speaking as a way to suppress the expression and take focus of the content off what is being said.

Virtue signaling. A white person communicating their experience with race for the purpose of boosting their image as a good white person, versus sharing it as part of a deeper process or relevant inquiry (speaking of their closeness to BIPOC, having a Black military buddy, extensive training, etc.).

Whitesplaining. Either explaining what a BIPOC said, assuming it was not clearly stated, or feeling right to correct BIPOC or explain something to them in a condescending way.

References

Alexander, M. (2020). *The new Jim Crow* (Rev. ed.). The New Press.

Alim, H. S., & Smitherman, G. (2012). *Articulate while Black: Barack Obama, language, and race in the U.S.* Oxford University Press.

Angier, N. (2000, August 22). Do races differ? Not really, genes show. *New York Times*. https://www.nytimes.com/2000/08/22/science/do-races-differ-not-really-genes-show.html

Anonymous. (2019, May 5). What happened after my 13-year-old son joined the alt-right. *Washingtonian*. https://www.washingtonian.com/2019/05/05/what-happened-after-my-13-year-old-son-joined-the-alt-right

Ansell, D. A. (2017). *The death gap: How inequality kills*. University of Chicago Press.

Appiah, K. A., & Gutmann, A. (1998). *Color conscious: The political morality of race*. Princeton University Press.

Asante, M. (1987). *The Afrocentric idea*. Temple University Press.

Baker-Bell, A. (2016). "I can switch my language, but I can't switch my skin": What teachers must understand about linguistic racism. In E. Moore Jr., A. Michael, & M. Penick-Parks (Eds.), *The guide for white women who teach Black boys* (pp. 97–107). Corwin.

Banaji, M. R., & Greenwald, A. G. (2016). *Blindspot: Hidden biases of good people*. Bantam Books.

Bartoli, E. (2020, October). From survival mode to wellness: Healing from social and environmental upheaval. *Independent School*. https://www.nais.org/magazine/independent-school/fall-2020/from-survival-mode-to-wellness-healing-from-social-and-environmental-upheaval

Bartoli, E., Michael, A., Bentley-Edwards, K. L., Stevenson, H. C., Shor, R. E., & McClain, S. E. (2016). Training for colour-blindness: White racial socialisation. *Whiteness and Education, 1*(2), 125–136. https://doi.org/10.1080/23793406.2016.1260634

Bartoli, E., & Pyati, A. (2009). Addressing clients' racism and racial prejudice in individual psychotherapy: Psychotherapeutic considerations. *Psychotherapy Theory, Research, Practice, Training, 46*(2), 145–157.

Bennett, J. (2020, November 19). What if instead of calling people out, we called them in? *New York Times*. https://www.nytimes.com/2020/11/19/style/loretta-ross-smith-college-cancel-culture.html

Biko, S. (2002). *I write what I like: Selected writings*. University of Chicago Press. (Original work published 1978)

Bonilla-Silva, E. (2022). *Racism without racists: Color-blind racism and the persistence of racial inequality in America* (6th ed.). Rowman & Littlefield.

Boykin, A. W., & Toms, F. D. (1985). Black child socialization: A conceptual framework. In H. P. McAdoo & J. L. McAdoo (Eds.), *Black children: Social, educational, and parental environments.* (Vol. 72, pp. 33–51). SAGE.

Brodkin, K. (1998). *How Jews became white folks and what that says about race in America.* Rutgers University Press.

brown, a. m. (2020). *We will not cancel us and other dreams of transformative justice.* AK Press.

Butler, S. K., Parker, G., & Williams, M. T. (2020, June). *Racial injustice and racial trauma: How can therapists respond? (Part 1)* [Online panel discussion]. PESI and Psychotherapy Networker. https://landinghub.pesi.com/en-us/racial-injustice-racial-trauma-videos_email_sqlanding

Castagno, A. E. (Ed.). (2019). *The price of nice: How good intentions maintain educational inequity.* University of Minnesota Press.

Centers for Disease Control and Prevention. (2020, August 18). COVID-19 hospitalization and death by race/ethnicity. https://www.cdc.gov/coronavirus/2019-ncov/covid-data/investigations-discovery/hospitalization-death-by-race-ethnicity.html

Chödrön, P. (2015). *Fail, fail again, fail better: Wise advice for leaning into the unknown.* Sounds True.

Chou, V. (2017, April 17). How science and genetics are reshaping the race debate in the 21st century. *Science in the News.* https://sitn.hms.harvard.edu/flash/2017/science-genetics-reshaping-race-debate-21st-century

Christakis, N. A. (2019). *Blueprint: The evolutionary origins of a good society.* Little, Brown Spark.

Coates, T.-N. (2015). *Between the world and me.* Spiegel & Grau.

Cretton, D. D. (Director). (2019). *Just mercy* [Film]. Warner Bros. Pictures; Endeavor Content; One Community.

Cross, W. E. (1978). The Thomas and Cross models of psychological Nigrescence: A review. *Journal of Black Psychology, 5*(1), 13–31.

Cross, W. E. (1991). *Shades of Black: Diversity in African-American identity.* Temple University Press.

DiAngelo, R. (2018). *White fragility: Why it's so hard for white people to talk about racism.* Public Science.

Dictionary.com. (2020, July 30). Karen. *Slang Dictionary.* https://www.dictionary.com/e/slang/karen

Du Bois, W. E. B. (1995). *The Philadelphia Negro: A social study.* University of Pennsylvania Press. (Original work published 1899)

Du Bois, W. E. B. (2020). *The souls of Black folk.* Seawolf Press. (Original work published 1903)

Dweck, C. S. (2006). *Mindset: The new psychology of success.* Random House.

Dweck, C. S. (2014, November). The power of believing that you can improve [Video]. TED Conferences. https://www.ted.com/talks/carol_dweck_the_power_of_believing_that_you_can_improve

Epstein, R. J. (2021, May 18). A "community for all"? Not so fast, this Wisconsin county says. *New York Times.* https://www.nytimes.com/2021/05/18/us/politics/race-inclusion-wasau-wisconsin.html

Faber, A., & Mazlish, E. (2012). *How to talk so kids will listen and listen so kids will talk.* Scribner Book Company.

Ferdman, B. M., & Gallegos, P. I. (2001). Racial identity development and Latinos in the United States. In C. L. Wijeyesinghe & B. W. Jackson III (Eds.), *New perspectives on racial identity development* (pp. 32–66). New York University Press.

Flaherty, C. (2020, September 4). White lies. *Inside Higher Ed.* https://www.insidehighered.com/news/2020/09/04/prominent-scholar-outs-herself-white-just-she-faced-exposure-claiming-be-black

Fortin, J. (2021, April 18). California beach seized in 1924 from a Black family could be returned. New York Times. https://www.nytimes.com/2021/04/18/us/bruces-beach-manhattan-california.html

Frankenberg, R. (1993). *White women, race matters: The social construction of whiteness.* Routledge.

Garcia, E. (2020, September 12). Schools are still segregated, and black children are paying a price. *Economic Policy Institute.* https://www.epi.org/publication/schools-are-still-segregated-and-black-children-are-paying-a-price

Garza, A. (2020). *The purpose of power: How we come together when we fall apart.* Random House.

Glaude, E. S., Jr. (2020). *Begin again: James Baldwin's America and its urgent lessons for our own.* Crown.

Goldstein, E. L. (2008). *The price of whiteness: Jews, race, and American identity.* Princeton University Press.

Gooding, F. W., Jr. (2017). *You mean, there's RACE in my movie? The complete guide to understanding race in mainstream Hollywood* (2nd ed.). On the Reelz Press.

Goodman, A. H., Heath, D., Lindee, S. M., Silverman, S., Santos, R. V., Taussig, K. S., Rapp, R., Rose, H., Franklin, S., Haraway, D., Royal, C., Heller, C., Kaestle, F., Soodyall, H., Templeton, A. R., Kittles, R., Marks, J., Duster, T., Escobar, A., & Fujimura, J. H. (2003). *Genetic nature/culture: Anthropology and science beyond the two-culture divide.* University of California Press.

Green, E. R., & Maurer, L. (2015). *The teaching transgender toolkit: A facilitator's guide to increasing knowledge, decreasing prejudice & building skills.* Planned Parenthood of the Southern Finger Lakes.

Haney López, I. (2006). *White by law: The legal construction of race.* New York University Press.

Hare, B., & Woods, V. (2020). *Survival of the friendliest: Understanding our origins and rediscovering our common humanity.* Random House.

Helms, J. E. (Ed.). (1990). *Black and White racial identity: Theory, research, and practice.* Greenwood Press.

Helms, J. E. (2020). *A race is a nice thing to have: A guide to being a white person or understanding the white persons in your life* (3rd ed.). Cognella.

hooks, b. (2006). *Outlaw culture: Resisting representations.* Routledge.

Horse, P. G. (2001). Reflections on American Indian identity. In C. L. Wijeyesinghe & B. W. Jackson III (Eds.), *New perspectives on racial identity development* (pp. 91–107). New York University Press.

Hughes, D., & Chen, L. (1999). The nature of parents' race-related communications to children: A developmental perspective. In L. Balter & C. S. Tamis-LeMonda (Eds.), *Child psychology: A handbook of contemporary issues* (pp. 467–490). Psychology Press.

Johnson, K., Pérez-Peña, R., & Eligon, J. (2015, June 17). Rachel Dolezal, in center of storm, is defiant: "I identify as Black." *New York Times.* https://www.nytimes.com/2015/06/17/us/rachel-dolezal-nbc-today-show.html

Johnson, T. (2020, June 11). When black people are in pain, white people just join book clubs. *Washington Post.* https://www.washingtonpost.com/outlook/white-antiracist-allyship-book-clubs/2020/06/11/9edcc766-abf5-11ea-94d2-d7bc43b26bf9_story.html

Kamenetz, A. (2018, November 5). Right-wing hate groups are recruiting video gamers. *NPR.* https://www.npr.org/2018/11/05/660642531/right-wing-hate-groups-are-recruiting-video-gamers

Kaur, V. (2020). *See no stranger: A memoir and manifesto of revolutionary love.* Aster.

Kendi, I. X. (2020a, November 11). *Antiracism in education* [Presentation]. GESU School 23rd Annual Symposium on Transforming Inner City Education, Philadelphia, PA, United States.

Kendi, I. X. (2020b). *Antiracist baby.* Kokila.

Kendi, I. X. (2020c). *How to be an antiracist.* Random House.

King, M. L., Jr. (2010). *Strength to love.* Fortress Press. (Original work published 1963)

King, P. J. (2018, September 12). Cherokee women scholars' and activists' statement on Andrea Smith. *Indian Country Today.* https://indiancountrytoday.com/archive/cherokee-women-scholars-and-activists-statement-on-andrea-smith

Kirkland, J. (2019, August 6). Toni Morrison broke down the truth about white supremacy in a powerful 1993 PBS interview. *Esquire.* https://www.esquire.com/entertainment/books/a28621535/toni-morrison-white-spremacy-charlie-rose-interview-racism

Kottak, C. P. (2002). *Cultural anthropology* (9th ed.). McGraw-Hill.

Kübler-Ross, E., & Kessler, D. (2005). *On grief and grieving: Finding the meaning of grief through the five stages of loss.* Simon and Schuster.

Kumanyika, C., & Biewen, J. (2017, May 5). Chenjerai's challenge (No. 7) [Audio podcast episode]. In *Scene on Radio: Seeing White.* https://www.sceneonradio.org/episode-37-chenjerais-challenge-seeing-white-part-7

Lee, S. J. (2005). *Up against whiteness: Race, school, and immigrant youth.* Teachers College Press.

Leondar-Wright, B. (2005). *Class matters: Cross-class alliance building for middle-class activists.* New Society Publishers.

Lewis, A. E. (2004). "What group?" Studying whites and whiteness in the era of "color-blindness." *Sociological Theory, 22*(4), 623–646. https://doi.org/10.1111%2Fj.0735-2751.2004.00237.x

Lewis, W. (2012, December 30). The Buddhist notion of idiot compassion. *Elephant Journal.* https://www.elephantjournal.com/2012/12/idiot-compassion

Lin, L., Stamm, K., & Christidis, P. (2018). How diverse is the psychology workforce? *Monitor on Psychology, 49*(2), 19. https://www.apa.org/monitor/2018/02/datapoint

Lipsitz, G. (2018). *The possessive investment in whiteness: How white people profit from identity politics.* Temple University Press.

Litz, B. T., Stein, N., Delaney, E., Lebowitz, L., Nash, W. P., Silva, C., & Maguen, S. (2009). Moral injury and moral repair in war veterans: A preliminary model and intervention strategy. *Clinical Psychology Review, 29*(8), 695–706.

Madigan, T. (2003). *The burning: Massacre, destruction, and the Tulsa race riot of 1921.* St. Martin's Griffin.

Marino, L., & Mattheus, A. (2022). *White people confronting racism: A manual* (3rd ed.).

Marshall, P. L. (2002). Racial identity and challenges of educating white youths for cultural diversity. *Multicultural Perspectives, 4*(3), 914. https://doi.org/10.1207/S15327892MCP0403_3

Mattheus, A., & Marino, L. (2011). *White people confronting racism: A manual for a 3-part workshop* (2nd ed.).

McGhee, H. (2021). *The sum of us: What racism costs everyone and how we can prosper together.* One World Ballantine.

McIntosh, K., Moss, E., Nunn, R., & Shambaugh, J. (2020, February 27). *Examining the Black-white wealth gap.* Brookings Institution. https://www.brookings.edu/blog/up-front/2020/02/27/examining-the-black-white-wealth-gap

McLaren, B. D. (2017, August 25). The 'alt-right' has created alt-Christianity. *Time*. https://time.com/4915161/charlottesville-alt-right-alt-christianity

Menakem, R. (2017). *My grandmother's hands: Racialized trauma and the pathway to mending our hearts and bodies*. Central Recovery Press.

Menakem, R. (2021, May 25). When white bodies say, "tell me what to do." *Somatic Learnings Blog*. https://www.resmaa.com/somatic-learnings/when-white-bodies-say-tell-me-what-to-do

Mills, C. W. (1999). *The racial contract*. Cornell University Press.

Mindell, A. (2014). *Sitting in the fire: Large group transformation using conflict and diversity*. Deep Democracy Exchange.

Morrison, T. (1993, December 2). On the backs of Blacks. *Time*. http://content.time.com/time/subcriber/article/0,33009,979736,00.html

Mukhopadhyay, C. C., Henze, R., & Moses, Y. T. (2013). *How real is race? A sourcebook on race, culture, and biology* (2nd ed.). Rowman & Littlefield.

Mullen, A. K., & Darity, W. A. (2021, March 28). Evanston, Ill., approved "reparations." Except it isn't reparations. *Washington Post*. https://www.washingtonpost.com/opinions/2021/03/28/evanston-ill-approved-reparations-housing-program-except-it-isnt-reparations

National Center for Education Statistics. (2020, September). Race and ethnicity of public school teachers and their students. https://nces.ed.gov/pubs2020/2020103/index.asp

National Museum of African American History and Culture. (2017, August 25). The color of blood. https://nmaahc.si.edu/explore/stories/color-blood

Native Governance Center. (2021, May 12). *How to talk about native nations: A guide*. https://nativegov.org/resources/how-to-talk-about-native-nations

NewYork-Presbyterian. (n.d.). It happened here: Charles Drew. *Health Matters*. Retrieved March 10, 2021, from https://healthmatters.nyp.org/it-happened-here-dr-charles-shaw

Okun, T. (2020). White supremacy culture. https://www.whitesupremacyculture.info/uploads/4/3/5/7/43579015/okun_-_white_sup_culture_2020.pdf

Omi, M., & Winant, H. (2015). *Racial formation in the United States* (3rd ed.). Routledge Press.

Oppel, R. A., Jr., Taylor, D. B., & Bogel-Burroughs, N. (2021, April 26). What to know about Breonna Taylor's death. *New York Times*. https://www.nytimes.com/article/breonna-taylor-police.html

Painter, N. I. (2011). *The history of white people*. W. W. Norton & Company.

Parshina-Kottas, Y., & Singhvi, A. (2021, July 2). How we reconstructed the neighborhood destroyed by the Tulsa race massacre. *NYT Open*.

https://open.nytimes.com/how-we-reconstructed-the-neighbor-hood-destroyed-by-the-tulsa-race-massacre-33fcf32dd086

Perry, A. M., & Ray, R. (2021, April 1). Evanston's grants to Black homeowners aren't enough. But they are reparations. *Washington Post*. https://www.washingtonpost.com/outlook/evanston-hous-ing-reparations/2021/04/01/4342833e-9243-11eb-9668-89be11273c09_story.html

Perry, A. M., Rothwell, J., & Harshbarger, D. (2018). *The devaluation of assets in Black neighborhoods: The case of residential property.* Brookings Institution.

Planas, A. (2021, May 17). After she concealed her race, Black Indianapolis owner's home value more than doubled. *NBC News*. https://www.nbcnews.com/news/us-news/after-concealing-her-race-black-indianapolis-owner-s-home-value-n1267710

Pollock, M. (2005). *Colormute: Race talk dilemmas in an American school.* Princeton University Press.

Ransom, J. (2020, July 6). Amy Cooper faces charges after calling police on Black birdwatcher. *New York Times*. https://www.nytimes.com/2020/07/06/nyregion/amy-cooper-false-report-charge.html

Richardson, H. C. (2021, June 1). June 1, 2021. *Letters from an American.* https://heathercoxrichardson.substack.com/p/june-1-2021?s=r

Rosenblum, A. (2019, October 27). Want to fight anti-Semitism, a year after Pittsburgh? Here's one easy way. *Washington Post.* https://www.washingtonpost.com/outlook/2019/10/27/want-fight-anti-semitism-year-after-pittsburgh-heres-one-easy-way

Ross, H. J. (2020). *Everyday bias: Identifying and navigating unconscious judgments in our daily lives.* Rowman & Littlefield.

Rothstein, R. (2018). *The color of law: A forgotten history of how our government segregated America.* Liveright Publishing.

Rothstein, R. (2019). The myth of *de facto* segregation. *Phi Delta Kappan, 100*(5), 35–38. https://doi.org/10.1177/0031721719827543

Sealy-Ruiz, Y. (2021). *Racial literacy: A policy research brief.* National Council of Teachers of English (NCTE). https://ncte.org/wp-content/uploads/2021/04/SquireOfficePolicyBrief_RacialLiteracy_April2021.pdf

Silk, S., & Goldman, B. (2013, April 7). How not to say the wrong thing. *Los Angeles Times.* https://www.latimes.com/opinion/op-ed/la-xpm-2013-apr-07-la-oe-0407-silk-ring-theory-20130407-story.html

Sparks, S. (2020, February 25). Hidden segregation within schools is tracked in new study. *Education Week.* https://www.edweek.org/leadership/hidden-segregation-within-schools-is-tracked-in-new-study/2020/02

Steele, C. M. (2010). *Whistling Vivaldi: How stereotypes affect us and what we can do.* W. W. Norton & Company.

Steele, D. M., & Cohn-Vargas, B. (2013). *Identity safe classrooms, grades K–5: Places to belong and learn.* Corwin.

Stern, K. (2019, December 13). I drafted the definition of antisemitism. Right-wing Jews are weaponizing it. *Guardian.* https://www.theguardian.com/commentisfree/2019/dec/13/antisemitism-executive-order-trump-chilling-effect

Stevenson, B. (2015). *Just mercy: A story of justice and redemption.* One World.

Stevenson, H. (2014). *Promoting racial literacy in schools: Differences that make a difference.* Teachers College Press.

Subramanian, M. (2014). *Bullying: It happened to me.* Rowman & Littlefield.

Sue, D. W. (2004a). *What does it mean to be white? The invisible whiteness of being* [Video]. Microtraining Associates. http://link.bu.edu/portal/What-does-it-mean-to-be-white--the-invisible/tj1Pt1uHTAo

Sue, D. W. (2004b). Whiteness and ethnocentric monoculturalism: Making the "invisible" visible. *American Psychologist, 59*(8), 761–769. https://psycnet.apa.org/doi/10.1037/0003-066X.59.8.761

Sue, D. W., & Sue, D. (2019). *Counseling the culturally diverse: Theory and practice* (8th ed.). Wiley.

Sullivan, J., Wilton, L., & Apfelbaum, E. P. (2021). Adults delay conversations about race because they underestimate children's processing of race. *Journal of Experimental Psychology: General, 150*(2), 395–400. https://doi.org/10.1037/xge0000851

Tanenbaum, M. (2016, April 7). Philly residents live longest in Old City, Society Hill. *Philly Voice.* https://www.phillyvoice.com/philly-residents-live-longest-old-city-society-hill

Tatum, B. (2017). *Why are all the Black kids sitting together in the cafeteria?* (Rev. ed.). Basic Books.

Tervalon, M., & Murray-García, J. (1998). Cultural humility versus cultural competence: A critical distinction in defining physician training outcomes in multicultural education. *Journal of Health Care for the Poor and Underserved, 9*(2), 117–125.

Thandeka. (1999). *Learning to be white: Money, race, and God in America.* Bloomsbury.

Thompson, L. (1995). *A history of South Africa* (Rev. ed.). Yale University Press.

University of Pennsylvania. (2020, June 18). Navigating difficult conversations: Expert advice for talking about race. Inspiring Impact. https://giving.upenn.edu/navigating-difficult-conversations/?utm_source=social&utm_medium=penn&utm_campaign=tw

Veracini, L. (2017). Decolonizing settler colonialism: Kill the settler in him and save the man. *American Indian Culture and Research Journal, 41*(1), 1–18.

Viren, S. (2021, May 25). The Native scholar who wasn't. *New York Times*. https://www.nytimes.com/2021/05/25/magazine/cherokee-native-american-andrea-smith.html

Ward, E. K. (2017, June 29). Skin in the game: How antisemitism animates white nationalism. *The Public Eye*. https://politicalresearch.org/2017/06/29/skin-in-the-game-how-antisemitism-animates-white-nationalism

Whitehead, C. (2016). *The Underground Railroad: A novel*. Doubleday.

Wilkerson, I. (2010). *The warmth of other suns: The epic story of America's great migration*. Random House.

Wilkerson, I. (2020). *Caste: The origins of our discontents*. Allen Lane.

williams, a. K. (n.d.). *Rev. angel Kyodo williams*. Retrieved March 31, 2022, from https://angelkyodowilliams.com

williams, a. K., Owens, L. R., & Syedullah, J. (2016). *Radical Dharma: Talking race, love, and liberation*. North Atlantic Books.

Winfrey, O. (2000). *The Oprah Winfrey show* [TV series]. Harpo Productions.

Zaki, J. (2019). *The war for kindness: Building empathy in a fractured world*. Crown.

Index

Keep Learning   Educating for Equity

Ali Michael, Ph.D.

As you know, I'm White. When schools and organizations hire me, it's a strategic decision they are making to help White people better understand how they can challenge racism in and around themselves. It's because they want to give their groups a model of what it looks for a White person to practice antiracism consistently, if imperfectly. When people hire me to teach, it is because they seek to motivate and engage White people to understand that racism is their problem too.

Some of the workshops and keynote topics I address include:

- Building a Healthy Multiracial Community
- How Race Matters in Schools
- What White Children Need to Know About Race: A Workshop for Parents
- Building Racially Competent Early Childhood Programs
- Exploring and De-Centering Whiteness in Education

- Strategies for Responding to Racist Remarks in the Classroom
- Supporting Positive Racial-Identity Development in White People
- *The Guide for White Women Who Teach Black Boys* (This is usually co-facilitated.)

More information at: **www.alimichael.org**

Eleonora Bartoli, Ph.D.

My consulting services support antiracism practices and practitioners through trauma-informed resilience-building strategies designed for better understanding of the relationship between our bodies, emotional well-being, and antiracist action. My writings and workshops focus on exploring how to maximize our effectiveness in integrating antiracism in our personal and professional lives.

Examples of my workshops and consultation topics include:

- Trauma-Informed Social Justice Action: It Starts With Us
- Embodied Antiracism: Inner Work With a Purpose
- Connecting Intersectional Communities: Using Difference as a Creative Force
- When Good Intentions Fall Short: The Psychology of Antiracism

- "Good trouble": The Power of Disagreeing Well for Systems Change
- Training for Courage: Concrete Tools for Antiracist Practice
- How to Thrive While Disrupting: Radical Work in a Human Body
- Don't Go at It Alone: Healing and Resilience for Social Change

More information at: **https://dreleonorabartoli.com/consulting**

A SAGE Publishing Company

Helping educators make the greatest impact

CORWIN HAS ONE MISSION: to enhance education through intentional professional learning.

We build long-term relationships with our authors, educators, clients, and associations who partner with us to develop and continuously improve the best evidence-based practices that establish and support lifelong learning.